CORPORATE BONDS

BONDS

STRUCTURES & ANALYSIS

Richard S. Wilson
and
Frank J. Fabozzi, CFA

Published by Frank J. Fabozzi Associates

Designer and Managing Editor: Stephen Arbour
Distribution Manager: Scott Chambers Riether

© 1996 BY FRANK J. FABOZZI ASSOCIATES
NEW HOPE, PENNSYLVANIA

This publication is designed to provide accurate and authoritative information in regard to the subject matter covered. It is sold with the understanding that the publisher is not engaged in rendering legal, accounting, investment advisory, or other professional services.

ISBN 1-883249-07-4

Printed in the United States of America.
1 2 3 4 5 6 7 8 9 0

RSW

To the memory of a good brother
and a proud Marine

William Albert Wilson
March 6, 1931 - June 27, 1995

_____

JJF

To my wife Donna Marie

ABOUT THE AUTHORS

Richard S. Wilson has spent more than 35 years in the securities industry as a senior securities analyst, expert witness, and consultant. He was Executive Managing Director of Fitch Investors Service, L.P., and served as its director of research products and services, manager of private placement rating development, and manager of regional marketing, as well as having a major role in the development of its fixed income securities database. Previously, he was First Vice President and manager of fundamental taxable bond research at Merrill Lynch Capital Markets. He has held senior analytical positions with White, Weld & Co. and, Drexel Harriman Ripley, among others. He holds degrees from the Graduate School of Business of Columbia University and the University of Pennsylvania's Wharton School of Finance and Commerce. A founding and life member, past president, and director of the Fixed Income Analysts Society Incorporated, he is also a member of the Bond Club of New York, the New York Society of Security Analysts, and the Association for Investment Management and Research. He has served as a member of the Board of Directors and the Board of Trustees of the Financial Management Association International. Besides writing extensively on corporate bonds and preferred stock topics, he has been a frequent speaker before academic and professional groups

Frank J. Fabozzi is an Adjunct Professor of Finance at Yale University's School of Management and the editor of the *Journal of Portfolio Management*. From 1986 to 1992 he was a full-time professor of finance at MIT's Sloan School of Management. He is on the board of directors of the BlackRock complex of closed-end funds and the board of directors of the family of open-end funds sponsored by The Guardian Life. Dr. Fabozzi is a Chartered Financial Analyst and Certified Public Accountant who has authored and edited many books on investment management. He is an associate editor of the *Journal of Fixed Income*. He holds a a doctorate in economics (1972) from the Graduate Center of the City University of New York. In 1994, he was awarded an honorary doctorate of humane letters from Nova Southeastern University.

TABLE OF CONTENTS

PREFACE

The corporate bond market has always been evolving with underwriters and issuers trying out new ideas and modifying older concepts. This was especially true in the decade of the eighties with the globalization of investment finance, the evolution of the junk bond market, and the development of the swap market. There has been substantial participation in the new corporate bond market by issuers and investors who, 15 years ago, hardly knew what bonds were. We have witnessed a proliferation of new debt instruments and experienced dramatic increases in price volatility. The quantitative aspects of fixed income securities have never been more important.

Corporate Bonds: Structures & Analysis is designed to help investors of all levels to better understand the increasingly complex world of corporate bonds. Reviewing the fundamentals of corporates from the qualitative and the quantitative sides, this book also discusses the dramatic changes that have occurred. Whether a market participant is a trader, investor, analyst or salesperson, increased knowledge of these markets will enhance performance over the long term.

Richard S. Wilson
Frank J. Fabozzi

ACKNOWLEDGMENTS

Richard S. Wilson extends his appreciation to the many friends and colleagues who helped make this book possible through their support, suggestions, and assistance. These include (but are not limited to): Eunice T. Reich-Berman of J.P. Morgan Securities, Inc.; Loretta J. Neuhaus of Bankers Trust Company; Eugenie M. Ferry of Fitch Information Services, Inc.; Gail Martin of Fitch Investors Service, L.P.; and, Paul Bruehl, consultant to Merrill Lynch Capital Markets. Of course, his wife Barbara, daughters Jennifer and Kristina, and son-in-law Bruce Rychlik encouraged him in his efforts.

Frank J. Fabozzi wishes to thank Andrew Kalotay, Martin Czigler, and George Williams of Andrew Kalotay Associates for their assistance in developing the illustrations in Chapters 11 and 12. He also benefitted from discussions with the following individuals: Ravi Dattatreya of Sumitomo Bank Capital Markets; Chris Dialynas of PIMCO; Stephen Esser of Miller, Anderson & Sherrerd; Gifford Fong of Gifford Fong Associates; Joseph Guagliardo Jr. of Gifford Fong Associates; Frank Jones of Guardian Life; Robert Kopprasch of Alliance Capital; Harsh Kumar of Goldman Sachs; Jack Malvey of Lehman Brothers; Mike Marz of First Southwest Company; Sharmin Mossavar-Rahmani of Goldman Sachs Asset Management; Scott Pinkus of Goldman Sachs; Frank Ramirez of Structured Capital Management; Chuck Ramsey of Structured Capital Management; and, Scott Richard of Miller, Anderson & Sherrerd.

LIST OF ADVERTISERS

Andrew Kalotay Associates, Inc.

BARRA

BondNet Trading Systems, Inc.

Capital Access Corporation

DDJ Myers Ltd.

Fitch Investors Service, Inc.

GAT

Information Management Network

REUTERS

Securities Software & Consulting

SECTION I

CHAPTER 1

Overview of U.S. Corporate Bonds

This chapter introduces nonconvertible, publicly-issued corporate bonds. It discusses the size of the market, ownership of the securities, new issue volume, and trading activity. The general terms and features of bond indentures are discussed in Chapter 2. Maturity features, interest rate characteristics, and retirement provisions are reviewed in Chapters 3, 4 and 5, respectively. Chapter 6 looks at convertible bonds, Chapter 7 delves into speculative grade issues, while rating agencies are surveyed in Chapter 8. Throughout this book we use the term bond(s) in the general sense of corporate debt instruments; when required, we use more specific terminology such as notes or debentures.

WHAT IS A CORPORATE BOND?

A *corporate bond* used to be defined as a promise to pay a specified sum of money at a fixed date in the future along with periodic payments of interest. However, the bond instrument has undergone so many alterations over the past two decades that the "plain vanilla" type of issue, so familiar to bond market investors and students only twenty-five years ago, may now be viewed by some as an anachronism. Bonds with gimmicks, often difficult for the investor to understand, for the salesperson to sell, and for the trader to price, became increasingly accepted in the 1980s.[1] In many cases, the interest rate changes weekly; the maturity date is not always fixed, as issuers can redeem the bonds prior to maturity and holders may demand prepayment; and the specified sum or principal payment due at maturity may fluctuate. Nonetheless, a bond is simply a debt instrument denoting the obligation of the issuer to satisfy the holder's claim; it is essentially an IOU, although more complex than the simple promissory note found in booklet form at legal supply stores.

3

Gimmicky bond issues may cause problems for corporations if the Internal Revenue Service (IRS) decides that they have more of the features or characteristics of equity instruments rather than debt. If a security is classified as debt, then the issuer is able to take a tax deduction for the interest payments in the determination of taxable income. If viewed as equity, the tax-deductibility of interest is lost and the payments may be viewed as dividends. The distinction between debt and equity for income tax purposes has not been formally spelled out by the Treasury Department and no one characteristic is overriding in coming to a determination of debt versus equity. Rather, all of the characteristics are looked at and if it is determined that "it looks like a duck, quacks like a duck, and walks like a duck," then "it is a duck" (at least as far as the IRS is concerned).[2]

If the corporate security gives the holder a right to share in the profits of the enterprise while at the same time sharing in the risks, then the security may be viewed as equity. Debt, on the other hand, generally does not share in the profits of the business and holders do not have the risks attendant to equity. The payment of interest is mandatory; it ought to be paid regardless of profits or losses. But there may be instances where the line between debt and equity is blurred. Factors considered in the debt versus equity problem include, but are not limited to, the following:

- a promise to pay a fixed amount on demand or at a certain or ascertainable date, money in return for a consideration, at a specified interest rate;
- the source and adequacy of the interest payments and the ability of the issuer to defer interest payments;
- the debt leverage of the company (or "thin" capitalization);
- conversion into the company's equity;
- relationship or identity between the shareholders' equity interest and their debt holdings;
- the intent of the parties to the financing agreement and the indicia of the agreement;
- the participation, if any, in the management of the enterprise;
- the voting power accorded the investor;

---

[1] "Hybrids that Buoy Eurobonds," *Business Week* (August 3, 1982), p. 78. This interesting article, while about bonds sold in Europe, is relevant for debt sold in the U.S. market. Referring to these gimmicky debts, one investment banker said, "It's a sign of desperation. All these bastardizations are trying to get investors to take a long-term view when they really don't want to. It's an inflation induced madness." Another said: "We're scrambling to create gimmicks to get cash because most corporations don't want to pay today's [high] interest rates. Gimmicks do help; they're a function of trying to gain the investor's attention." Finally another claimed, "If plain vanilla can't be sold, you need to make tutti-frutti." There will be more about gimmicks in the other chapters.

[2] William T. Plumb, Jr., "The Federal Income Tax Significance of Corporate Debt: A Critical Analysis and a Proposal," *Tax Law Review*, Volume 26: 1971. This lengthy article thoroughly discusses the distinction between equity and debt.

- a maturity date or lack thereof, time to maturity, and provisions for redemption at the issuer's option or the holder's option;
- the place of the securities in the company's capitalization in comparison with other creditors, and
- enforcement upon default.

In 1986, Fox Television Stations, Inc. issued preferred stock in exchange for debentures and notes of Metromedia Broadcasting Corporation. As the Fox company counsel was unable to give an opinion as to whether the shares would be treated as equity or debt by the IRS, the Company decided to treat the stock as debt and deduct the dividend payments as interest. Corporate holders taking the opposite view that the payments are dividends would be eligible for the dividends received deduction. There are also other consequences to the issuer and the investor depending on how these securities are viewed by the taxing authorities.[3] A portion of the Fox shares were redeemed in 1987. Referring to the redemption, a company spokesman used the term "debt" instead of "stock" in describing the securities.

The issuer's (borrower's) rights and duties are spelled out in a loan agreement, also known as an *indenture*. The indenture may be fairly simple and straightforward, although, for most laymen it is complex and often runs to many pages — after all, it is a legal contract between two parties, debtor and trustee. The bond, or evidence of the debt obligation, is most often printed on a single sheet of paper summarizing the more important sections of the loan agreement. Technically, this certificate is the agreement between the issuer and the lender.

The term *bond* actually refers to a debt instrument which is customarily secured by collateral, such as land and buildings or financial instruments. The indenture for secured debt contains a section describing the mortgaged or pledged collateral. A *debenture* is an unsecured loan also setting forth the rights and duties of the borrower in an indenture. In years past a note was characterized as a less formal obligation than a debenture or a bond. According to *Commentaries on Indentures:*

> There is no basic or historically established distinction between 'debentures' and 'notes'. There has emerged, however, a clear and useful distinction in modern usage. According to this usage, in the area of long-term debt securities, a security is properly termed a 'note' when it is not issued pursuant to an indenture and there is no indenture trustee. However, it may be, and usually is, issued to one or a few purchasers pursuant to a purchase or loan agreement which, in addition to provisions dealing with the terms of purchase, includes many of the contractual rights found in an indenture. In today's nomenclature the security is properly termed a 'debenture' when it is issued pursuant to an indenture and there is an indenture trustee.[4]

Thus, the popular *medium-term notes* are more properly called *medium-term debentures*, as most have been issued under an indenture.[5] Today, however, the meaning of *notes* is slightly different. To many, a note has more to do with the original maturity of a debt security rather than with the formality of the documentation; thus, notes are short- to intermediate-term maturity paper, while

---

[3] Prospectus of Fox Television Stations, Inc., Increasing Rate Exchangeable Guaranteed Preferred Stock, February 27, 1986. The prospectus states:

> An instrument labeled "preferred stock" by an issuer will not necessarily be characterized as preferred stock for Federal income tax purposes. Many cases and authorities have considered the issue of characterizations, and no single test or factor has been deemed controlling. Rather, the characterization of an instrument as debt or equity depends upon an examination of all of the terms and conditions of the instrument and all of the facts and circumstances surrounding its issuance. Some of the terms that are characteristic of debt instruments include a definite maturity date, an obligation to pay fixed amounts of interest on definite dates regardless of earnings, and a right to share with creditors and in priority to equity holders in the case of the issuer's bankruptcy. Some of the terms tending to indicate that an instrument is equity include the holding of the instrument by stockholders in proportion to their stock holdings, the absence of a fixed maturity date, inadequate or "thin" capitalization of the issuer (i.e., a high debt-to-equity ratio), and a right to receive distributions only out of corporate earnings, which makes such distributions dependent upon the success of the venture for payment.
>
> In the case of Fox Television Preferred Stock, the guaranty by News America and News Corporation of the payment of dividends, interest on accrued and unpaid dividends, redemption price, liquidation preference, and repurchase obligations upon exercise of the Rights, the ability of Fox Television to redeem the Fox Television Preferred Stock immediately after issuance, the acceleration provision entitling the holder to cause the Fox Television Preferred Stock to be redeemed if certain dividends are not timely paid and the fixed maturity date support characterization of the Fox Television Preferred Stock as debt. The facts that the Fox Television Preferred Stock is denominated "preferred stock," and that dividends are payable only when and if declared by the Board of Directors out of funds legally available for payment of dividends, support characterization of such stock as preferred stock. Accordingly, although the treatment of the Fox Television Preferred Stock is uncertain, based on an analysis of all the facts and circumstances Fox Television intends to treat Fox Television Preferred Stock as debt for Federal income tax purposes. Holders of Debt Securities should be aware, however, that the Service [IRS] is likely to challenge this position, and may do so successfully. Although, as noted above, judicial authority in the debt-equity area is unclear and inconsistent, substantial authority exists that would support the characterization of an instrument having the terms of the Fox Television Preferred Stock as equity. Furthermore, to the extent that holders of Debt Securities elect not to exchange such [Metromedia] securities for cash and/or Fox Television Preferred Stock, the argument that the Fox Television Preferred Stock is equity may be strengthened. The fact that such outstanding Debt Securities are likely to constitute debt of Fox Television for Federal income tax purposes may allow the Service to assert that Fox Television is thinly capitalized, thereby increasing the likelihood that the Fox Television Preferred Stock will be treated as equity.

bonds and debentures are longer-term issues. However, there can be short-term bonds and long-term notes. While we disagree with this usage describing a corporate bond's original time to maturity, it is understandable why many have adopted it; it is a fallout from the market for U.S. Treasury issues — *government bonds* are long-term, unsecured obligations, with original maturities of more than ten years while notes have maturities between one and ten years.

The *physical bond* used to be quite an attractive piece of paper, with some certificates of fairly large dimensions. Attached to or printed on the same page were interest coupons which holders would detach and present for collection through normal banking channels. In the age of registered bonds, however, they are more uniform, generally the size of normal letter paper or a stock certificate. Interest payments are made by check to the registered holder as there are no coupons. The form of the bond is specified in the indenture. The front of the certificate has the company's name and other terms such as maturity date, interest rate, certificate number, and principal amount. It also bears the corporate seal and the signature(s) of the appropriate corporate officer(s) and of the trustee attesting to the authenticity of the certificate. Most important, it will have the name of the registered holder. The reverse of the certificate has a summary of the important indenture terms including call and redemption provisions, a printed bond power or a form of assignment and certain other forms, if needed. To reduce the risk of counterfeiting, the New York Stock Exchange has prescribed certain minimum standards for certificates of listed issues. These include requirements that certain portions of the face of the bond must be engraved and include a vignette.

SIZE OF THE CORPORATE BOND MARKET

According to the flow of funds accounts published by the Board of Governors of the Federal Reserve System, total corporate debt in the United States was nearly $2.2 trillion dollars at the end of 1993, including $207 billion of foreign obligations sold here (see Exhibit 1). This foreign debt, similar in form to that of U.S. business corporations, is issued by international treaty organizations such as the International Bank for Reconstruction and Development, foreign nations, their agencies and political subdivisions, and foreign corporations.

---

[4] American Bar Foundation Corporate Debt Financing Project. *Commentaries on Model Debenture Indenture Provisions 1965 Model Debenture Indenture Provisions All Registered Issues 1967 and Certain Negotiable Provisions Which may be Included in a Particular Incorporating Indenture.* Chicago, Illinois: American Bar Foundation, 1971. This work henceforth will be called *Commentaries or Commentaries on Indentures.*

[5] Medium-term notes are more fully described in Chapter 3. Normally issued in maturities ranging from nine months to 15 years, they can be offered continually on a best efforts basis or at specific times when funds are needed by some of the major investment banking firms acting as agents for the issuers.

Exhibit 1: Corporate Bonds Outstanding by Issuer Type, 1978 - 1993 ($ Billions)

Year	Total	Non-financial Corporate Business	Foreign	Commercial Banking	Savings Institutions	Finance Companies	Real Estate Investment Trusts	Asset-backed Securities
1993	$2,180.2	$1,225.7	$207.4	$133.2	$4.0	$199.9	$4.4	$405.8
1992	1,979.5	1,154.2	146.9	127.6	5.5	195.3	3.4	346.3
1991	1,823.1	1,086.9	129.5	113.2	8.6	191.3	3.0	290.7
1990	1,673.5	1,008.2	115.4	108.9	12.7	178.2	3.1	246.9
1989	1,564.3	961.1	94.1	113.7	18.3	162.7	2.9	211.5
1988	1,418.9	887.2	89.2	109.1	21.7	147.0	2.5	162.2
1987	1,259.9	784.1	82.3	104.0	19.8	141.2	2.3	126.2
1986	1,097.4	705.4	74.9	90.5	15.4	131.6	1.5	78.1
1985	878.0	578.2	71.8	74.4	10.5	105.3	0.9	36.9
1984	737.6	495.1	68.0	55.5	5.9	90.5	0.8	21.9
1983	641.8	447.0	64.2	42.0	4.0	81.0	0.7	3.0
1982	595.8	421.0	61.1	32.4	3.7	77.0	0.7	0.0
1981	543.7	390.3	54.5	26.1	3.2	68.9	0.7	0.0
1980	508.4	365.6	49.0	23.2	3.7	65.5	1.4	0.0
1979	472.1	337.9	47.8	21.9	3.4	59.6	1.6	0.0
1978	447.6	320.6	44.1	22.1	2.0	57.2	1.6	0.0

Source: Flow of Funds Accounts, Flows and Outstandings, Z.1, March 9, 1994, Board of Governors of the Federal Reserve System, Washington, DC.

In the fifteen years since the end of 1978, total corporate-type debt increased by $1.7 trillion dollars or at an annual compound rate of 11.1%. Nonfinancial corporate debt (comprised of utility, industrial and service companies) accounting for nearly 72% of the total back in 1978; has now fallen to 56% (see Exhibit 2). Commercial bank bonds increased at a 12.7% pace from $22.1 billion in 1978 to $133 billion in 1993. The fastest growing sector and the second largest category is asset-backed securities accounting for some 18.6% of total outstanding. From a negligible $3 billion at the end of 1983, the asset-backed category has grown at an annual compound rate of 63.3% to some $406 billion for 1993. This type of debt involves the repackaging or securitization of financial assets, mostly mortgages but also automobile loans, credit card and other receivables, and leases, to name just a few. Much of this does not involve the raising of corporate capital through the direct issuance of debt, but the sale of these financial assets to trusts and other bankruptcy remote special purpose corporations which provide debt service from the cash flows of the underlying securitized assets.

Exhibit 2: Corporate Bonds Outstanding by Issuer Type, 1978 - 1993 (Percentage)

Year	Non-financial Corporate Business (%)	Foreign (%)	Commercial Banking (%)	Savings Institutions (%)	Finance Companies (%)	Real Estate Investment Trusts (%)	Asset-backed Securities (%)
1993	56.22	9.51	6.11	0.18	9.17	0.20	18.61
1992	58.32	7.42	6.45	0.28	9.87	0.17	17.49
1991	59.62	7.10	6.21	0.47	10.49	0.16	15.95
1990	60.24	6.90	6.51	0.76	10.65	0.19	14.75
1989	61.44	6.02	7.27	1.17	10.40	0.19	13.52
1988	62.53	6.29	7.69	1.53	10.36	0.18	11.43
1987	62.24	6.53	8.25	1.57	11.21	0.18	10.02
1986	64.28	6.83	8.25	1.40	11.99	0.14	7.12
1985	65.85	8.18	8.47	1.20	11.99	0.10	4.20
1984	67.12	9.22	7.52	0.80	12.27	0.11	2.97
1983	69.65	10.00	6.54	0.62	12.62	0.11	0.47
1982	70.66	10.26	5.44	0.62	12.92	0.12	0.00
1981	71.79	10.02	4.80	0.59	12.67	0.13	0.00
1980	71.91	9.64	4.56	0.73	12.88	0.28	0.00
1979	71.57	10.12	4.64	0.72	12.62	0.34	0.00
1978	71.63	9.85	4.94	0.45	12.78	0.36	0.00

Source: Flow of Funds Accounts, Flows and Outstandings, Z.1, March 9, 1994,
Board of Governors of the Federal Reserve System, Washington, DC.

Corporate Debt Ownership

The life insurance industry is by far the largest holder of corporate bonds in America with slightly more than 33% ownership amounting to some $724 billion at the end of 1993 (Exhibits 3 and 4). Trailing in second position are private pension funds with nearly $298 billion or 13.7%. Close behind with the third largest corporate debt holdings are foreigners owning $273 billion, or 12.6% of the total corporate outstanding. Foreign ownership has grown at a compound annual rate of slightly more than 17% since the end of 1978 when holdings were only $25 billion. Another high-growth sector has been the mutual and closed-end fund category. Holdings at the end of 1993 of $201 billion were more than 23 times greater than the $8.7 billion held by these institutions at year end 1978. This represents an annual compound growth rate of more than 23%. The last decade has witnessed an increased interest in all types of bonds — corporate, municipal and government — by investment companies as individual investors realize some of the advantages offered by diversified investment portfolios under professional management. It has dawned on them that bonds are not simply "buy-and-hold" investments; bond portfolios need to be managed just as much as equity investments.

All of the sectors have increased their absolute corporate debt holdings over the years but in some cases the relative importance of corporates has diminished. One such example is the household sector which held $53 billion (or 11.9% of outstanding) at the end of 1978. This dropped to only $15.5 billion in 1985, amounting to less than 1.8% of the total. Since then, household holdings have zigzagged upwards to $80 billion or just 3.7% at year end 1993. Even over a longer period households have shown more volatility in their year-to-year holdings than the other sectors.

Public pension funds is another sector where corporate debt has become relatively less important over the years. This relative decline may be partly due to the liberalization of the investment policies of many public pension funds, permitting them to have more diversified portfolios. Investment managers have allocated a larger amount of assets to equities and real estate at the expense of corporate bonds. Back in 1978 their $80 billion of corporate debt holdings was nearly 17.9% of the total outstanding; at latest count the $197 billion in their portfolios amounted to only 9% of the total. Put another way, corporate bonds were some 52.6% of state and local government employee retirement plans' total financial assets in 1978 and only 18.5% in 1993. At the same time, equity holdings have exploded from $33 billion to $507 billion, moving from 21.9% of the plans' total financial assets to 47.6%.

Volume of New Corporate Bond Issues

The volume of new corporate bond issues is affected by many factors including the level and trend of economic activity, and the direction of interest rates. Certainly, if corporate managements are looking forward to a period of lackluster business conditions, they will be more cautious about borrowing for expansion. High interest rates also send chills up the spines of financial officers and leads to reduced desire for funds. It is difficult to separate the two since high interest rates put a damper on economic activity.

Exhibit 3: Ownership of Outstanding Corporate Bonds, 1978 - 1993 ($ Billions)

Year	Total	Households	Foreign (US holdings by foreigners)	Commercial Banking	Savings Institutions	Life Insurance	Other Insurance	Private Pension Funds	Public Pension Funds	Mutual and Closed-End Funds	Brokers, Dealers, and Bank Personal Trusts
1993	$2,180.2	$79.9	$273.3	$99.8	$92.4	$723.9	$99.1	$298.0	$196.5	$201.4	$115.5
1992	1,979.5	115.6	251.9	95.9	80.0	653.9	97.9	280.9	180.7	134.9	87.7
1991	1,823.1	117.8	233.4	96.3	72.7	595.1	97.2	275.7	150.3	113.2	71.5
1990	1,673.5	94.9	217.2	88.7	75.6	566.9	89.2	235.5	147.1	102.2	56.2
1989	1,564.3	52.0	211.9	84.1	91.0	511.0	79.3	226.1	158.4	90.4	60.1
1988	1,418.9	35.7	199.3	89.0	105.3	457.5	65.7	203.9	125.7	83.8	52.9
1987	1,259.9	67.2	185.4	78.1	88.2	388.3	55.5	190.1	103.0	60.3	43.7
1986	1,097.4	45.6	166.6	53.3	64.1	321.4	48.0	178.3	124.7	50.8	44.5
1985	878.0	15.5	126.4	31.1	56.8	280.6	33.9	155.1	117.4	22.6	38.5
1984	737.6	25.9	90.5	21.9	53.7	242.8	25.7	123.4	107.7	18.7	27.3
1983	641.8	27.8	74.9	16.2	42.4	219.1	21.6	107.9	95.0	15.6	21.3
1982	595.8	27.1	68.0	11.1	30.7	202.3	25.8	95.2	102.6	13.0	19.7
1981	543.7	36.6	47.9	10.7	24.0	186.1	26.3	83.3	100.8	12.4	15.6
1980	508.4	35.2	36.9	10.8	27.3	178.8	23.6	77.7	92.2	10.9	14.9
1979	472.1	48.6	27.7	9.7	21.4	170.1	23.6	63.7	83.0	9.6	14.9
1978	447.6	53.2	24.7	8.9	23.2	158.5	21.6	53.0	80.0	8.7	15.9

Source: Flow of Funds Accounts, Flows and Outstandings, Z.1, March 9, 1994, Board of Governors of the Federal Reserve System, Washington, DC.

Exhibit 4: Ownership of Outstanding Corporate Bonds, 1978 - 1993 (Percentage)

Year	Households (%)	Foreign (US holdings by foreigners) (%)	Commercial Banking (%)	Savings Institutions (%)	Life Insurance (%)	Other Insurance (%)	Private Pension Funds (%)	Public Pension Funds (%)	Mutual and Closed-End Funds (%)	Brokers, Dealers, and Bank Personal Trusts (%)
1993	3.66	12.55	4.58	4.24	33.20	4.55	13.67	9.01	9.24	5.29
1992	5.84	12.73	4.84	4.04	33.03	4.95	14.19	9.13	6.81	4.43
1991	6.46	12.80	5.28	3.99	32.64	5.33	15.12	8.24	6.21	3.92
1990	5.67	12.98	5.30	4.52	33.88	5.33	14.07	8.79	6.11	3.36
1989	3.32	13.55	5.38	5.82	32.67	5.07	14.45	10.13	5.78	3.84
1988	2.52	14.05	6.27	7.42	32.24	4.63	14.37	8.86	5.91	3.73
1987	5.33	14.72	6.20	7.00	30.82	4.41	15.09	8.18	4.79	3.47
1986	4.16	15.18	4.86	5.84	29.29	4.37	16.25	11.36	4.63	4.06
1985	1.77	14.40	3.54	6.47	31.96	3.86	17.67	13.37	2.57	4.38
1984	3.51	12.27	2.97	7.28	32.92	3.48	16.73	14.60	2.54	3.70
1983	4.33	11.67	2.52	6.61	34.14	3.37	16.81	14.80	2.43	3.32
1982	4.55	11.41	1.86	5.15	33.95	4.33	15.98	17.22	2.18	3.31
1981	6.73	8.81	1.97	4.41	34.23	4.84	15.32	18.54	2.28	2.87
1980	6.92	7.26	2.12	5.37	35.17	4.64	15.28	18.14	2.14	2.93
1979	10.29	5.87	2.05	4.53	36.03	5.00	13.49	17.58	2.03	3.16
1978	11.89	5.52	1.99	5.18	35.41	4.83	11.84	17.87	1.94	3.55

Source: Flow of Funds Accounts, Flows and Outstandings, Z.1, March 9, 1994, Board of Governors of the Federal Reserve System, Washington, DC.

Exhibit 5: Public Financing in the U.S. Taxable Market by Issuer Classification, 1973 - 1993 (Par Value $ Billions)

Year	Total	Public Utility	Industrial and Transportation	Financial	International
1993	$254.75	$58.81	$103.24	$63.46	$29.24
1992	214.01	42.63	101.13	51.07	19.18
1991	151.27	16.30	81.68	42.93	10.36
1990	88.10	10.74	40.76	27.47	9.13
1989	109.64	11.92	56.78	34.74	6.20
1988	98.87	10.80	47.58	36.57	3.92
1987	104.63	17.63	43.65	38.27	5.09
1986	142.56	34.95	64.11	38.48	5.02
1985	80.12	11.13	33.59	29.46	5.95
1984	48.89	6.66	20.76	18.48	3.00
1983	35.70	8.84	10.29	12.69	3.89
1982	44.17	9.56	15.34	13.59	5.68
1981	40.66	11.89	14.05	9.15	5.58
1980	36.70	13.39	13.70	7.34	2.27
1979	24.94	9.02	7.11	5.44	3.39
1978	20.80	7.76	4.02	4.77	4.25
1977	25.93	8.23	5.35	7.24	5.11
1976	30.17	8.27	8.91	6.70	6.30
1975	34.92	11.29	15.07	3.46	5.11
1974	26.66	11.79	8.77	4.45	1.65
1973	13.32	8.36	1.76	2.48	0.73

Source: Derived from authors' database and various issues of *Moody's Bond Survey*.

The last two surges in corporate bond new issues (1984 to 1986 and 1991 to 1993) were accompanied by declining interest rates. As interest rates fell in 1984 to 1986, corporations issued an increasing amount of nonconvertible debt in the public markets through underwritten offerings. In 1986, a record-setting $142.6 billion of fresh corporate new issues came to market, four times the volume of only three years earlier. New issue activity slowed during the next three years as interest rates drifted upwards, although the amounts issued were greater than any year prior to 1986. The 1991 to 1993 period saw volume soar to new peak levels that would have been thought unbelievable by market participants just a few years earlier. In 1993, more than a *quarter of a trillion dollars* of corporate debt hit the taxable bond market. This time interest rates dropped to levels not seen in a couple of decades. Lower interest rates spurred refunding activity as companies replaced older, higher interest debt with new and lower cost paper. In addition and probably restraining the refunding activity to some extent was the three-year bull market in stocks. Good valuations allowed companies to raise large amounts of equity with part of the proceeds used for debt retirement. it was an excellent time for corporations to strengthen their balance sheets and reduce expenses. Exhibit 5, 6, and 7 show the amount of public offerings for 1973 through 1993. Excluded are non-underwritten offerings such as those sold on a best-efforts basis, medium-term notes, debt issued in exchange for stock or other debt, and structured transactions such as asset-based financings which represent a sale of assets and are based on the nature of the asset and the offering's structure rather than the issuer's credit.

Exhibit 6: Public Financing in the U.S. Taxable Market by Issuer Classification, 1973 - 1993 (Percentage Distribution)

Year	Public Utility (%)	Industrial and Transportation (%)	Financial (%)	International (%)
1993	23.09	40.53	24.91	11.47
1992	19.92	47.25	23.86	8.96
1991	10.78	54.00	28.38	6.85
1990	12.19	46.27	31.18	10.36
1989	10.87	51.79	31.69	5.65
1988	10.93	48.13	36.98	3.96
1987	16.85	41.72	36.58	4.86
1986	24.51	44.97	26.99	3.52
1985	13.89	41.92	36.76	7.42
1984	13.61	42.46	37.80	6.14
1983	24.75	28.82	35.54	10.90
1982	21.63	34.74	30.77	12.86
1981	29.23	34.55	22.51	13.71
1980	36.50	37.34	19.99	6.17
1979	36.15	28.49	21.80	13.57
1978	37.30	19.33	22.93	20.43
1977	31.75	20.61	27.93	19.70
1976	27.42	29.52	22.19	20.87
1975	32.32	43.15	9.90	14.63
1974	44.22	32.90	16.69	6.19
1973	62.75	13.20	18.61	5.44

Source: Derived from authors' database and various issues of *Moody's Bond Survey.*

The composition of the new issue market by issuer type has changed considerably since 1973 when public utility issuers accounted for nearly 63% of the total. Industrial and transportation issuers are now the largest participants with 40% of 1993's volume (and over 50% in 1989 and 1991). Financial institutions are also more important, with about a quarter of the market in 1993. But this sector's importance is down from the levels reached in the mid-1980s. International issues sold in the United States, so-called *Yankee bonds*, have been snapped up in recent years as investors try to increase yields they can't often get from domestic issuers. Countries and institutions that just a few years ago would find access to the U.S. markets impossible, had a much easier time in the early 1990s. The lessening of tensions between the east and west, the expansion of international trade, and the globalization of the markets are just a few of the contributing factors to increased foreign offerings in the United States.

Exhibit 7: Public Financing in the U.S. Taxable Bond Market by Moody's Rating Classification, 1973 - 1993 (Par Value $ Billions)

Year	Total	Aaa	% of Total	Aa	% of Total	A	% of Total	Baa	% of Total	Ba and Lower	% of Total
1993	$254.75	$11.14	4.35	$36.72	14.42	$89.47	35.13	$55.84	21.93	$61.54	24.17
1992	214.01	19.18	8.96	29.27	13.68	71.87	33.58	51.05	23.85	42.64	19.92
1991	151.27	11.77	7.78	31.75	20.99	64.31	42.51	25.07	16.57	18.37	12.14
1990	88.10	8.31	9.43	24.34	27.63	34.98	39.70	17.72	20.11	2.75	3.12
1989	109.64	10.13	9.24	18.17	16.57	33.31	30.38	15.78	14.39	32.25	29.41
1988	98.87	11.76	11.89	13.50	13.66	32.49	32.87	14.64	14.81	26.48	26.78
1987	104.63	10.59	10.12	21.86	20.89	30.52	29.17	16.48	15.75	25.19	24.08
1986	142.56	12.25	8.59	37.94	26.62	40.16	28.17	21.87	15.34	30.34	21.28
1985	80.12	9.02	11.25	16.54	20.64	27.95	34.89	9.77	12.20	16.84	21.02
1984	48.89	2.35	4.81	13.73	28.08	15.12	30.92	4.15	8.48	13.55	27.71
1983	35.70	3.92	10.98	11.11	31.12	9.03	25.30	5.13	14.36	6.51	18.24
1982	44.17	6.07	13.75	14.66	33.19	15.34	34.73	4.27	9.68	3.82	8.66
1981	40.66	11.84	29.11	9.98	24.55	12.66	31.15	4.09	10.05	2.09	5.15
1980	36.70	10.11	27.55	10.72	29.22	11.90	32.43	2.54	6.92	1.43	3.88
1979	24.94	10.40	41.70	5.71	22.90	5.78	23.17	1.74	6.99	1.31	5.23
1978	20.80	7.97	38.30	5.65	27.15	4.42	21.23	1.62	7.78	1.15	5.54
1977	25.93	11.05	42.60	5.24	20.21	5.03	19.41	2.09	8.07	2.52	9.71
1976	30.17	9.91	32.84	8.79	29.13	8.04	26.65	3.02	10.02	0.41	1.36
1975	34.92	11.35	32.50	8.93	25.58	12.01	34.40	2.48	7.11	0.15	0.42
1974	26.66	7.42	27.83	8.51	31.92	7.50	28.13	1.93	7.25	1.30	4.88
1973	13.32	4.05	30.39	3.23	24.22	4.05	30.43	0.52	3.90	1.47	11.06

Source: Derived from authors' database and various issues of *Moody's Bond Survey.*

Another way of looking at new issue volume is by quality or rating category (see Exhibit 7). Using the Moody's Investors Service rating designations, there has been a considerable decline in new issues of prime rated (Aaa) credits, falling from a high of 42.6% of 1977's volume to less than 4.4% in 1993. Since 1981 there hasn't been one year where Aaa issues accounted for as much as 14% of new issue taxable bond activity. For that matter, the two highest rating classifications (Aaa and Aa) accounted for more than 50% of the primary volume each year prior to 1982, and at last count the two categories comprised only 18.8% of new issue. The rating sector at the other extreme end of the scale (Ba and lower including nonrated issues) posted tremendous growth in absolute terms for much of this period. From a low of only $145 million in 1975, volume rose to more than $32 billion in 1989, a jump from less than half of one percent to more than 29% of new issue activity. The next year, 1990, saw speculative grade new issues nearly disappear from the scene with issuance of a relatively minute $2.75 billion. But despite all of the gloom and doom circulating throughout much of the financial press and the securities industry at the start of the '90s, the speculative grade market wasn't dead. It recovered as the mythological phoenix with record volume of $42.6 billion set in 1992 only to be easily surpassed with a new peak of more than $61 billion in 1993.

Exhibit 8: Average Size of Issue, 1973 - 1993
Public Financing in the U.S. Taxable Bond Markets
(Par Value $ Millions)

Year	Total Volume	Number of Issues	Average Issue Size
1993	$254,175	1,705	$149.02
1992	214,010	1,188	180.14
1991	151,270	743	203.59
1990	88,100	437	201.60
1989	109,640	592	185.20
1988	98,868	609	162.34
1987	104,634	706	148.21
1986	142,562	987	144.44
1985	80,118	655	122.32
1984	48,890	403	121.32
1983	35,697	379	94.19
1982	44,168	467	94.58
1981	40,655	333	122.09
1980	36,695	378	97.08
1979	24,941	250	99.76
1978	20,799	244	85.24
1977	25,929	328	79.05
1976	30,165	395	76.37
1975	34,918	471	74.14
1974	26,663	350	76.18
1973	13,315	238	55.95

Source: Derived from authors' database and various issues of *Moody's Bond Survey*.

Since the early seventies the size of the average corporate bond issue has more than tripled from slightly under $56 million in 1973 to more than $180 million in 1992, down from 1991's peak of $203 million (see Exhibit 8). Generally, larger issues are easier to buy and sell in the secondary market as they usually have more market makers and greater investor interest. Increased market competition often means smaller spreads between the price which the dealer is willing to pay for the bond (bid) and the price at which he is willing to sell the bond (offer or asked). This liquidity factor is very important to actively managed investment portfolios and should also be a consideration in the investment decision making process of the "buy and hold" and individual investor.

CORPORATE BOND TRADING

Many believe individual investors ought to confine their corporate bond investments to those issues listed on the New York Stock Exchange (or on the smaller American Stock Exchange) and avoid issues trading in the unlisted or over-the-counter (OTC) market. Exchange officials call this the *off-board market*. Professional investors find that the OTC market is the only one for their needs for a very simple reason; listed trading activity is primarily small orders for *retail* or individual investors in lots of as small as $1,000 par value. An institutional portfolio manager wanting to sell a block of $5 million par value of an issue would find that the listed auction market would most likely be unable to handle a transaction of this size in a prompt fashion; the trade has to be done in the negotiated unlisted market. In most cases, the investment firm will act as a dealer and purchase the bonds for its own account and risk as it may not be able to find an institutional purchaser for the block right away. It will hold them hoping that it will quickly find a buyer. The business of the dealers or market makers is not investment in the traditional sense of a bond portfolio but the profitable trading and turnover of their inventory.

Most individuals like to see their bonds listed in the newspaper just as they do with their stocks and mutual fund shares; unlisted corporate bonds are not normally quoted unless, perhaps, they are recent new issues with institutional interest. For example, *Barron's Market Week* has the New York and American Stock Exchange bond listings and a table of the bid and asked prices, weekly change, and yield to maturity for ten active junk bond issues. The exchange tables show the 52-week high and low prices, current yield, sales volume, and the weekly high, low and last prices, and the net change on the week. Some of the daily papers such as *The New York Times* and *The Wall Street Journal* may have a small table with some price and yield data on a short list of recently issued bonds in addition to the regular daily exchange listings. It should be noted that the exchange tables represent actual trades while the other lists are merely quotes at which trades may take place.

Most retail stock brokers can easily obtain the last sale, current quotation, and size of the bid and offering of listed bonds from their quote machines. Unlisted quotations and bids and offers may be less readily obtainable by the salesmen handling small investors. However, there has been a considerable improvement over the past decade with the flow of fixed income information to retail brokers and their clients. Brokers can more easily get investors lists of offerings from the firm's own inventory. While these may not always be the specific issues of the investor's choosing, they should be acceptable substitutes.

But one recent development could shed more light on unlisted odd-lot trading activity leading to improved efficiencies in the way smaller lots are traded and bringing them into the twenty-first century. This is the proprietary system developed and introduced in mid-1995 by BondNet Trading Systems, Inc. Linking together the odd-lot trading desks at more than 40 large and small broker-dealers around the country, it enables them to view the bids and offers from a large number of debt inventories and consummate trades immediately "over the wire." BondNet should help provide more liquidity and better marketability for the often ignored retail bond investor.

This does not mean that the listed market will always provide investors with higher bid and lower offering prices than the unlisted market. The two markets can behave independently of one another. The listed market and its quotes can easily be impacted by small trades. The quotes provided on an exchange-listed bond represent the highest price one is willing to pay for a certain number of bonds of a particular issue (bid) and the lowest price at which someone wants to sell a certain number of bonds (offer). A quote from a dealer on a bond traded off the board may only reflect what the dealer feels the bond is worth and not an actual bid or offer. It is not uncommon to see the price of a bond fall several points on a sale of a few thousand dollars principal amount only to have it regain that loss on a succeeding purchase. This may occur because the broker has not carefully placed the order. More than likely, the order was to sell (buy) *at the market* without regard to the size of the current bid or offering.[6] It is often better to place limits on orders, especially for those less actively traded issues. Also, inactive issues are just that — they do not trade every day. Listing does not assure an active market. In some cases the several point rise or fall may be due to changes in the interest rate levels since the last listed bonds may have traded weeks or months ago. The current transaction represents today's interest levels, not those of the past.

Many investors place limit orders when trading in stocks which have very active and liquid markets but ignore limit orders for thinly traded bonds. As Ben Weberman said in *Forbes Magazine*, "The listed market is so small and thin, it is easy to manipulate."[7] This may sound a little extreme, but there is more than a grain of truth to it. However, despite some of the drawbacks, the listed bond market provides many investors with the needed peace of mind as the transaction prices are published for all to see.

---

[6] Lawrence Chamberlain in *The Principles of Bond Investment* (New York, NY: Henry Holt and Company, 1911, pp. 67 and 68) had this to say about the unreliability of some listed quotations.

> "Although exchange quotations, especially at New York, are a very convenient reference for purposes of appraisal, hypothecation, and sale, they are not always to be trusted, especially as the basis of value for large amounts of bonds. Suppose that an institution held $500,000 of a certain railway loan which was 93¼ bid 95⅝ asked. The inexperienced inference might be that these bonds would sell for 94 or thereabouts. It might well be, however, that $100,000 bonds were offered at 95⅝ and only three bonds were bid 93¼ and that only a handful were wanted between 93⅛ and 91½. As a true basis for valuation or sale how does listing help these bonds?"

[7] Of course, manipulation is not just a activity restricted to the exchanges. The unlisted market has had its share of criticism over the years regarding bond market manipulation. For additional insight into listed bond trading, see David Henry, "Patience Rewarded," *Forbes* (May 19, 1986), p. 82. See also, Ben Weberman, "Comparison Shopping," *Forbes* (October 6, 1986), p. 203. Lawrence Chamberlain (op. cit., p. 68) gave a couple of examples of exchange manipulation.

> Manipulation of one sort or another occasionally has its bearing on quotations. Some years ago Lake Street Elevated 5s were 87 bid on the Chicago Exchange. On the appearance of two bonds for sale at that price the quotation vanished in thin air and no demand materialized until the bonds were offered down 10 or 12 points. A sale was finally effected off the board, presumably in order not to hurt the feelings of banks that may have been loaning 75 cents to the dollar on them.
>
> The two great issues of the American Telephone and Telegraph Company are listed on both the Boston and New York Exchanges. In the spring of 1908 millions of them were still in the hands of the underwriters. For a while it was then possible to purchase them on the Street for about three-quarters of a point less than on the board. One who is familiar with the flotation of listed railroad issues knows that they too are not always left to seek their natural investment level."

Nowadays, investors are better protected than nearly a century ago. The exchanges and other securities regulators have continual surveillance measures designed to reduce manipulation to a minimum. However, as in all economic activity, let the buyer beware. Better yet, become an informed investor.

The Automated Bond System® (ABS) handles most of the nonconvertible bond trades of the New York Stock Exchange. Convertible bonds are executed on the bond floor of the Exchange and the trades are reported through the ABS. The ABS allows member firms to send their listed bond transactions directly to the Exchange for electronic execution. Orders can be easily entered, changed, or cancelled at a moment's notice through terminals located in the members' offices. Members can get current quotes and information as to what other bids and offers are available for a particular bond. Orders can be entered at levels above or below the current market for the convenience of investors. It is estimated that at the end of 1993 there were more than 60 member firms with some 250 terminals linked with the Exchange's Automated Bond System®.

There are no minimum requirements for the listing of bonds on the New York Stock Exchange.[8] However, the public distribution and aggregate size must be broad enough and large enough to warrant a listing. Appropriate distribution might mean a minimum of 250 to 300 bondholders, or an issue size of about $25 million. If the aggregate market or principal value falls to less than $1 million, the Exchange may delist the bonds. Also, if the company defaults and files for bankruptcy, the bonds may be delisted, but not in all cases. In recent years such companies as Manville, Global Marine, Storage Technology, to name but a few, kept their bonds listed on the New York Stock Exchange. In our opinion, this *is* the time when many holders need the listed market with its quotes and prices available to all. The Exchange is to be commended for retaining the listings. There often are fewer and different market participants in bankrupt issues than in conventional bonds, making for a less liquid market, especially over-the-counter. The spread or difference between the bid and asked prices may be wider, trading activity may diminish in some cases, and price volatility may increase. The regular flow of information coming from the corporation may be less than prior to the bankruptcy despite mandated court filings. But now there are more Wall Street analysts following bankrupt and distressed companies providing the market with better opinions as to the course of the restructuring or the bankruptcy proceedings. Notwithstanding the generally more available and better research, the individual investor still needs the additional market support or liquidity provided by the listed market.

Since early 1992, the New York Stock Exchange stopped charging fees for listing the debt of NYSE equity issuers and affiliated companies, and for debt of issuers exempt from registration under the Securities and Exchange Act of 1934. All other debt issues are charged fees ranging from $50 per million par value for new issues to $25 per million for issues outstanding one year or more. In the past the Exchange charged a one-time fee for listing bonds and there were annual fees from 1981 through 1984. Several companies including New York Telephone, Southern Bell Telephone and Southwestern Bell Telephone refused to make these annual payments. In

---

[8] One thinks that only corporate and foreign government bonds are listed on the New York Stock Exchange. However, that changed in March, 1994, when the state of California announced that it would list $3.3 billion in outstanding bonds on the Exchange. Some other state and municipal issuers also said they would seek listing of other issues. Only time will tell whether or not the municipal bond market traders accept this new marketplace.

1985 the Exchange delisted 58 issues of the three telephone companies after negotiations failed to move the squabblers from their respective positions. Subsequently, Southwestern Bell Telephone Co. listed 12 of its debenture issues on the American Stock Exchange. New York Telephone relisted its bonds on the NYSE in 1993. *The Wall Street Journal* reported: "Since the vast majority of the holders affected by the dispute are institutions, the companies said they don't believe trading in the bonds will be affected."[9] While that may be true, several years later the *Journal* reported the treasurer of a major tobacco and food company as saying: "You're not legally obligated to list your bonds, but you are morally obligated to. Institutional investors can take care of themselves but you owe a lot more to the individual investors."[10]

In 1991, bond volume set a record for the New York Stock Exchange with nearly $12.7 billion (including convertibles and a small amount of foreign issues) traded; this is a daily average of slightly more than $50 million (see Exhibit 9). Listed secondary trading activity then declined for the next two years, falling to $9.7 billion in 1993 and a daily average of $38.5 million. Some attribute this decline to a number of factors including the flow of money out of individual bond issues and into the roaring stock markets due to the decline in interest rates, debt redemptions reducing the number of listed issues, and a reluctance on the part of many investment banking firms to recommend bond listing to their corporate clients, among others. The lowest average daily volume of $1.8 million was posted in 1913. The lowest daily volume on record since 1900 was only $500,000 on August 13, 1900 while the highest single day's activity was on September 6, 1939, when $83.1 million traded. Investors may have thought that the U.S. exchanges would close for a period as much of Europe was declaring war on one another. They remembered August 1914 when the lamps were "going out all over Europe" and the U. S. exchanges closed for several months.

Bond activity on the New York Stock Exchange is minuscule when compared to the unlisted bond market. Figures tallied by The Securities Industry Association (SIA) show that average daily corporate bond trading volume in 1993 was more than $25.6 billion. The SIA figures are not exactly comparable to the Exchange's since the SIA's numbers include new bond underwritings, trades in noncorporate issues, nonregular instruments such as commercial paper, federal agency debt, medium-term notes, and the like. Even taking these other trading instruments into account, listed transaction volume is small in the trading world. But that is not to say that Exchange trading in unimportant. A recent study by Exchange officials examined listed and unlisted trading activity over a five-day period in 147 active bond issues. The report said: "Contrary to common perceptions, exchange-listed trading is not immaterial for the issues listed on the NYSE. Considering both customer-side [direct trading between institutions and broker/dealers] and street-side activity [exchange trading and off-exchange trading between and among brokers and dealers], NYSE trading volume accounted for 11.7% of dollar volume and 72.2% of transactions. As for street-side only, NYSE trading accounted for 31.3% of dollar volume and 90.0% of transactions."[11]

---

[9] Ann Monroe, "Big Board Suspends Trading in Bonds of 3 Phone Firms," *The Wall Street Journal* (July 10, 1985).

[10] Leslie Scism, "Big Board Fights to Revive Bond Market," *The Wall Street Journal* (May 27, 1993).

Exhibit 9: Selected Details for New York Stock Exchange Bond Trading, 1980 - 1993 (Par value $ Millions)

Year	Total Annual Volume	Daily Average	Number of Trades	Number of Bonds per Trade	Number of Issuers	Number of Issues	Par Value	Market Value
1993	$9,743.0	$38.5	439,478	22.17	574	2,103	$2,341,953	$2,528,437
1992	11,629.0	45.8	550,526	21.12	636	2,354	2,008,635	2,044,122
1991	12,698.1	50.2	611,794	20.76	705	2,727	2,219,495	2,227,010
1990	10,892.7	43.1	516,328	21.30	743	2,912	1,689,454	1,610,175
1989	8,836.3	35.1	492,920	16.90	794	2,961	1,435,118	1,412,407
1988	7,702.1	30.4	522,173	14.00	846	3,106	1,610,310	1,561,031
1987	9,727.1	38.4	659,231	14.76	885	3,346	1,650,263	1,621,263
1986	10,464.1	41.4	774,890	13.50	951	3,611	1,379,545	1,457,603
1985	9,046.5	35.9	726,279	12.46	1,010	3,856	1,327,375	1,339,298
1984	6,982.3	27.6	620,547	11.25	1,024	3,751	1,083,674	1,021,791
1983	7,572.3	29.9	712,877	10.62	1,034	3,600	965,252	898,064
1982	7,155.4	28.3	686,186	10.43	1,031	3,233	792,529	766,103
1981	5,733.1	22.7	636,572	9.01	1,049	3,110	681,237	573,893
1980	5,190.3	20.5	594,449	8.73	1,045	3,057	601,527	507,770

Source: *New York Stock Exchange Fact Book*, 1988, 1989, 1992, and authors' database.

It is safe to guess that a decade or two ago the average unlisted trading volume was considerably less than in recent years. The increase has been due to a number of factors including more participants in a much larger market, and the shorter-term view taken by portfolio managers which encourages turnover. Bonds are no longer bought and held to maturity (if they ever were) for they can readily be traded as they get under- and over-valued relative to one another. Bond investment constantly requires assessing the relative value of one issue with another in a market that is not always "efficient." The increasing internationalization of the debt markets and new trading techniques including the use of options and futures in portfolio hedging strategies are other factors contributing to the greater trading volume nowadays.

In recent years, the New York Stock Exchange has had a steady decline in the number of issuers with listed bonds. The number of listed bonds is down by more than 1,700 from 1985's peak although the par value is at record levels. Exchange officials are working hard at encouraging others to list. But it is not an easy task. The over-the-counter market is much bigger and works rather well. We have not come across any studies showing that listing reduces an issuer's interest costs or flotation expenses. With the exception of some odd-lot trading activity, it is questionable that marketability is even improved. Thus, while individuals may find the exchange market more suitable for their needs due to increased confidence in the New York Stock Exchange, it offers the issuer little except possibly some added prestige. After all, the market of choice for professional investors in municipal and U.S. Treasury bonds is the unlisted market.

---

[11] Don G. Dueweke, Michael J. Hyland and Fred Siesel, "Measuring the New York Stock Exchange's Share of Corporate Trading Volume," *ExtraCredit* (September/October 1992).

CHAPTER 2

Bond Indentures

This chapter reviews the indenture, the legal document issued in connection with debt issues.[1] Webster's *New Universal Unabridged Dictionary* defines indenture thusly: "in law, a deed or written agreement between two or more parties: indentures were originally in duplicate, laid together and indented or cut in a waving line, so that the two papers or parchments corresponded to each other."

INDENTURES

The buyer of a bond in a secondary market transaction becomes a party to the contract even though he wasn't, so to speak, present at its creation. Yet many investors are not too familiar with the terms and features of the obligations they purchase. They know the coupon rate and maturity but they often are unaware of many of the issue's other terms, especially those that can affect the value of their investment. In most cases — and as long as the company stays out of trouble — much of this additional information may be unnecessary and thus considered superfluous by some. But this knowledge can become valuable during times of financial stress when the company is involved in merger or takeover activity. It is especially important when interest rates drop as the issue may be vulnerable to premature or unexpected redemption. Knowledge is power, and the informed bond investor has a better chance of avoiding costly mistakes.

Let us briefly look at what indentures contain (some indenture provisions and articles will be discussed more fully in succeeding chapters). For corporate debt securities to be publicly sold they must (with some permitted exceptions) be issued in conformity with the Trust Indenture Act of 1939 (TIA). The TIA requires that debt issues subject to regulation by the Securities and Exchange Commission (SEC) have a trustee. Also, the trustee's duties and powers must be spelled out in the indenture. Some corporate debt issues are issued under a blanket or open-ended indenture; for others a new

---

[1] See Robert I. Landau, *Corporate Trust Administration and Management*, 3d ed. (New York, NY: Columbia University Press, 1985). This is a good reference on corporate trust indenture trends and practices.

indenture must be written each time a new series of debt is sold. A blanket indenture is often used by electric utility companies and other issuers of general mortgage bonds, but it is also found in unsecured debt, especially since the shelf registration procedure became widely accepted in the early eighties. The initial or basic indenture may have been entered into 30 or more years ago but as each new series of debt is created, a supplemental indenture is written. For instance, the original indenture for Baltimore Gas and Electric Company is dated February 1, 1919, but it has been supplemented and amended many times since then due to new financings.[2]

A more recent example of an open-ended industrial debenture issue is found in the Eastman Kodak Company debt prospectus dated March 23, 1988 and supplemented October 21, 1988, which says that "the Indenture does not limit the aggregate principal amount of debentures, notes or other evidences of indebtedness ("Debt Securities") which may be issued thereunder and provides that Debt Securities may be issued from time to time in one or more series." The indenture of Fruehauf Finance Company, according to its prospectus dated December 11, 1985, gives the Company the ability to "reopen" a previous issue of securities and to issue additional securities having terms and provisions identical to any such previous issues of debt. PepsiCo, Inc.'s indenture dated December 2, 1993 between the company and The Chase Manhattan Bank (National Association) is closed-end but with another wrinkle. Debt securities issued under this indenture are limited to a maximum of $2,500,000,000. However, the maximum amount can be increased at any time if authorized by PepsiCo's board of directors. An example of an indenture limiting the amount of debt is Harris Corporation's, dated December 1, 1988, which authorizes debt in the amount of $150 million of 10⅜% Debentures due December 1, 2018.

The model indenture described in *Commentaries* has 15 articles and a preamble, or preliminary statement, called parties and recitals. The model mortgage bond indenture form has 16 articles and a preliminary statement.[3] Of course, the number of articles depends on the terms of the debt being issued. The consolidated mortgage bonds of Illinois Central Gulf Railroad Company, as supplemented, has 23 articles. The preliminary statements note that the bonds or debentures have been authorized by the corporation's board of directors and that it has the authority to execute the indenture. The introductory statements contain granting clauses describing the mortgage property, which is necessary for secured debt.

---

[2] See Thompson King, *Consolidated of Baltimore 1816-1950* (Baltimore, MD: privately published by Consolidated Gas Electric Light and Power Company of Baltimore, now Baltimore Gas and Electric Company, 1950). It says,
On April 30, 1919, the Board of Directors approved a new bond indenture, so designed that it would in time become the first mortgage upon all the company's properties. Provision was made so that considerable future growth could be financed under the new indenture, for it provided that as much as $100,000,000 of the bonds could be outstanding at any one time. Little did the directors realize how much the Company was to grow; in less than 30 years it became necessary to remove the $100,000,000 limitation.
[3] American Bar Foundation, *Mortgage Bond Indenture Form 1981* (Chicago, IL: American Bar Foundation, 1981)

Definitions, Form of Securities and Denominations

The first article of an indenture usually includes the definitions of special words and phrases used in the indenture and certain provisions of a general nature or application covering acts of bondholders, notices to the trustee, the company and debtholder, and governing law, among other things. The second article covers the form of the bond or debenture. It spells out what is to appear on the actual security certificate. The third article is called "The Bonds" or "The Debentures," as the case may be. Here the securities' title or series is stated as well as the form (coupon, registered) and denominations. Today, practically all domestically issued corporate bonds are in registered form — i.e., the ownership is registered with the transfer agent (normally the trustee) and a check for the interest payment is sent to the registered holder. In late 1986, a form of registered corporate bond called book-entry appeared. The book-entry form had been used by the Federal government and its agencies for some time, but Ford Motor Credit Company was the first nongovernmental entity to do so when it issued $200 million of 7⅛% Notes due October 15, 1989, under a prospectus dated October 7, 1986. With this type of registration, only one global registered note is issued; it is deposited with, and held by, the Depository Trust Company (DTC) in New York City and registered in the DTC's nominee name. The global note may only be transferred in whole to another nominee of DTC or to a successor of DTC. Buyers of the notes really acquire ownership of beneficial interest in them, records of which are kept by the participating firms (banks, brokers, dealers, clearing corporations) and the depository.

The Depository Trust Company is a limited-purpose trust company established to hold securities and to facilitate the clearance and settlement of its participants' securities transactions through the electronic book-entry changes in the accounts of the participants. Because of restrictions on the transfer of the global note, some investors might not be able to own book-entry form securities. These would be those who, by state law or other regulations, must have physical delivery in definitive form of the underlying securities that they own. As the book-entry method becomes more acceptable, these rules and regulations will probably be modified. It should be noted that as the Depository's nominee is the sole owner of the global note, owners of beneficial interests will not be considered owners or holders thereof under the indenture. The prospectus states that "neither Ford Credit, the Trustee [The Chase Manhattan Bank]... has any direct responsibility or liability for the payment of principal or interest on the Notes to owners of beneficial interests in the Global Note." But it goes on to say "Payments by Participants and indirect participants to owners of beneficial interests in the Global Note will be governed by standing instructions and customary practices, as is now the case with securities held for the accounts of customers in bearer form or registered in "street name," and will be the responsibility of the participants and indirect participants." Since Ford Credit's first book-entry issue, other issuers have followed suit. Book-entry is used by all issuers of auction market and remarketed preferred stock.

The usual denomination of registered corporate debt is $1,000 (par value) and multiples thereof, although, in some cases, a minimum of $5,000 or $10,000 (and even $100,000 or more) may be required. In cases where the interest is payable in the same security (payment-in-kind or "PIKs"), rights offerings, debt issued in exchanges or on emergence from bankruptcy, the indenture may provide for denominations of less than $1,000, such as $100 or $500 pieces. These smaller denominated issues are called "baby bonds." There have even been a few issues where the minimum denomination or par value was as low as $20 each. As the normal unit of trading is in multiples of $1,000, prices may vary for trades in units other than the conventional $1,000. The third article also discusses the authentication, delivery, dating and the registration, transfer and exchange of the bonds as well as mutilated, destroyed, lost and stolen bonds. Finally, it sets forth the record dates for interest and the interest payment dates.

Remedies

There are several other articles common to both types of debt although one may be, for example, article 12 in one indenture and article 8 in the other. Article 9 in the model mortgage indenture (article 5 in the model debenture indenture) concerns remedies — the steps available to bondholders in case the company defaults bond holders. The trustee is responsible for enforcing the available remedies; while it is only the debtholders' representative, it is ultimately responsible to the majority of the bondholders. In this article events of default are defined and may include the following (i) failure to pay interest on the date due or within the grace period (usually 30 days); (ii) failure to make a principal payment on the due date; (iii) failure to make a sinking fund payment when due; (iv) failure to perform any other covenants and the continuation of that failure for a certain period after notice has been given by the trustee to the debtor company, and (v) certain other events of bankruptcy, insolvency or reorganization which may include defaults of other debt obligations of the company.

If an event of default is continuing, either the trustee or the holders of 25% of the principal amount of the outstanding issue may declare all of the bonds of the particular series immediately due and payable along with unpaid and interest due up to the date of acceleration. This may pressure the obligor to cure the defaults (if it is able to do so) and thus rescind the acceleration or to seek waivers of the defaults while it is trying to find a solution. But such acceleration might force the debtor to seek protection of the bankruptcy courts; it might have been better to work with the debtor and help it on the path to recovery. The article also provides limits to lawsuits which individual bondholders may bring against the company with a default under the indenture provisions. However, no provision may impair the bondholders' absolute and unconditional right to the timely payment of principal, premium (if any) and interest on the bond, and the right to bring legal action to enforce such payment.

The Trustee

While the rights and duties of the trustee are mentioned in various articles throughout the indenture, articles 6 and 10 in the model indentures contain certain specifics regarding the trustee and its activities including resignation or removal. Investors should clearly understand that the trustee is paid by the debt-issuing company and can only do what the indenture provides. The article may begin with wording such as: "... the Trustee undertakes to perform such duties and only such duties as are specifically set forth in this Indenture, and no implied covenants or obligations shall be read into this Indenture against the Trustee...." Further, "... the Trustee shall exercise such of the rights and powers vested in it by this Indenture, and shall use the same degree of care and skill in their exercise, as a prudent man would exercise or use under the circumstances in the conduct of his own affairs," or, "No provision of this Indenture shall be construed to relieve the Trustee from liability for its own negligent action, its own negligent failure to act, or its own wilful misconduct...." Of course, certain exceptions are listed.

One of the duties of the indenture trustee as enumerated in this article is the notification to bondholders of a default under the indenture (except in certain cases such as a cured default or provided that the board of directors or "responsible officers" of the trustee, etc., in good faith determine that withholding of the notice is in "their best interests"). Also, the trustee is under no obligation to exercise the rights or powers under the indenture at the request of bondholders unless it has been offered reasonable security or indemnity. This seems reasonable in this age of frivolous lawsuits, but it could possibly be used by the trustee as a reason not to proceed with an action which it ought to do. The trustee is not bound to make investigations into the facts surrounding documents delivered to it, but it may do so if it sees fit.

Another section of the article requires the issuer to pay the trustee reasonable fees for its services, provide reimbursement for reasonable expenses, and to indemnify it for certain losses which might arise from administering the trust. A subsection states that in case of a conflict of interest, the trustee will either eliminate the conflict or resign within 90 days of the date of determining that a conflict of interests exists. Not an uncommon occurrence, one often will see in the financial press legal advertisements of the resignation of a trustee and the appointment of a successor trustee. As there must always be a trustee, no resignation is effective until a new trustee has been secured. Such potential conflicts often occur where the trustee bank is also a creditor of the issuing company. The prospectus for the $600 million May Department Stores offering on June 8, 1988 says that "the Company maintains deposit accounts with and engages in banking transactions in the ordinary course of business with each [of the trustees]." One bank is a trustee of various employee benefit plans and both trustees have credit agreements with May. In 1984 Citibank, N.A., resigned as trustee for the first mortgage bonds of Long Island Lighting Company citing a potential conflict of interest between its obligations to bondholders as trustee and as a creditor to LILCO. It can't very well serve the bondholders' interests and its own creditor interests at the same time.[4] There is also provision for the removal of a trustee, with or without cause, upon the action of a majority of the debtholders.

The prospectus (dated September 14, 1988) for K N Energy's 10¾% Sinking Fund Debentures due September 1, 2008 says that the indenture contains "certain limitations on the right of the Trustee, should it become a creditor of the Company, to obtain payment of claims in certain cases, or to realize for its own account on certain property received in respect of any such claim as security or otherwise. The Trustee will be permitted to engage in certain other transactions; however, if it acquires any conflicting interest... it must eliminate such conflict or resign."

Reports

The next article (7 and 11 in the model debenture and mortgage indentures, respectively), dealing with debtholders' lists and reports by the trustee and company, is rather short but has caused many investors concern. Under this article, the company is required to furnish the trustee with semi-annual lists of bondholders and their addresses and preserve this information until a new list is available. This is to enable the requisite number of bondholders to communicate with other bondholders about their rights under the indenture. The trustee must submit to the bondholders certain brief reports or statements concerning its continued eligibility as a trustee, any advances made by the trustee to the corporation, any other indebtedness owed by the company to the trustee, and any property or funds of the company held by the trustee. An interesting question is how many bondholders have actually received these reports or have even seen them? More than likely, very few; perhaps the many nominees such as stockbrokers and banks have failed to send them to the beneficial owners because of the added (and possibly unreimbursed) costs.

The bone of contention between bondholders and issuers concerns corporate financial reporting Indentures of public debt issues sold in the United States require an issuing company to file with the trustee copies of annual reports and other reports which it must normally file with the Securities and Exchange Commission. But there is no requirement (unless specifically mentioned) that a company send these reports to debtholders. These reports can be inspected at the SEC or the offices of the trustee, not always convenient for a creditor. Investors desiring such information are often up against the wall, especially when the issuer of public debt securities is privately owned. Companies with fewer than 300 security holders do not have to file regular reports with the SEC Holders of some debt issues of special purpose financing corporations sold by American issuers in the Eurodollar market have discovered this when trying to evaluate their holdings several years after the prospectuses were issued. Many years ago bondholders may have been content with little or no information, that is not so today. Bondholders have a right, although it is not spelled out, to be treated fairly. All holders and other interested parties should be able to ob-

---

[4] On September 28, 1984, a notice appeared in *The Wall Street Journal* addressed to the holders of BankAmerica Corporation's Money Multiplier Notes Due in 1987, 1990, 1991 and 1992. The indenture trustee, The Bank of California, had issued this notice citing a conflict of interest under the indenture due to its merger with Mitsubishi Bank. Apparently, two years earlier a subsidiary of Mitsubishi Bank has acted as underwriter for an overseas offering of BankAmerica notes that were now causing the conflict under the indenture and the Trust Indenture Act. The last paragraph of the notice is interesting:

> The Bank does not intend to resign from its position as Trustee, as we feel that this development in no way impairs our ability to perform the duties and obligations required by the Indenture. We at the bank will continue our efforts to provide the best possible service to you and will be happy to answer your questions...

tain from any public debt issuer or its trustee audited annual reports and quarterly statements, at the very least If a corporation does not want to divulge this information, then it should not come to the public markets. One of the costs of entry to the public markets should be that of full, prompt and proper financial disclosure.

A rating agency cannot rate an issuer's debt if it is not provided with adequate information and a corporation cannot be forced to provide information if it is not legally bound to do so. At the beginning of 1989, the rating agency of McCarthy, Crisanti and Maffei, Inc. (now Duff and Phelps Credit Rating Co.) withdrew its coverage of the bonds of SCI Television, Inc. This certainly doesn't benefit the holder but what good is an opinion based on faulty or no knowledge of the latest operations of the debtor? At that time Moody's gave SCI Television debt ratings of B2 and B3 while S&P gave B- and CCC+ ratings. MCM stated that "Although the company issued bonds publicly in October 1987, it has not filed financial statements with the SEC since December 1987. SCI TV will not make financial reports available to us unlike some other companies which are also not subject to filing requirements, such as Heritage Communications and Continental Cablevision. These companies have indicated that they are providing us with information in order to enhance liquidity for bondholders."

Page 81 of SCI's prospectus dated October 21, 1987 says: "The Company intends to distribute to the holders of the Securities annual reports containing audited consolidated financial statements and an opinion thereon by the Company's independent certified public accountants and quarterly reports containing unaudited consolidated information for the first three quarters of each fiscal year." One would think that SCI's investment bankers would want a client to provide such information in order to have a better market for the bonds.

In contrast to SCI, Adelphia Communications in its December 19, 1988 bond offering said, "The Company has agreed to provide the Trustee and the Holders, and to file with the Commission, copies of quarterly and annual reports and other information, documents and reports substantially equivalent to those specified in Sections 13 and 15(d) of the Exchange Act as long as the Notes are outstanding (whether or not the Company would otherwise be subject to such reporting requirements.)"

However, annual and quarterly reports are normally written for shareholders and may not fully disclose all of the information a prudent bondholder needs. For example, just a simple look at the debt part of the capital structure may often reveal the inadequacy of the financial disclosure. Often the outstanding amount of a particular bond issue may not be clear from the financial statements. A common description such as "4⅝%-10⅜% sinking fund debentures due 1993-2010... $387.5" does not clearly state the outstanding amount of the 4⅝s and each of the other issues.

In the early 1980s one of the authors wrote to the Ford Motor Credit Company and Dart & Kraft, Inc. requesting information about the amounts outstanding for individual issues as the annual reports and Forms 10K were unsatisfactory. Dart & Kraft's Director of Corporate Finance responded on April 25, 1984: "Regarding your request... for principal amounts of Dart & Kraft's publicly issued debt, we presently do not disclose that information other than the amounts disclosed in our 1983 Annual Report." The Treasurer's Office of Ford Motor Credit replied on April 30, 1984: "I regret to inform you that it is now our policy to not disclose detailed information on principal amounts outstanding on specific debt issues."

Shades of the robber barons of the 1890s! An article in *The New York Times* said: "It is ironic that most public companies today, despite the importance of debt financing and the increasingly dynamic nature of the bond market, still regard holders of their debt as second-class citizens when it comes to giving them information."[5] This was written in 1975 but it still pertinent today.

Consolidation, Merger, Conveyance and Lease

Common to indentures of secured and unsecured debt are model articles 12 and 8 dealing with consolidation and merger, or the conveyance, transfer or lease of assets. There might be some indentures which expressly forbid the debtor company to merge or consolidate with another corporation, but most indentures for public debt issues allow corporate mergers, consolidations and the sale of substantially all of the corporation's assets if certain conditions are satisfied. Transfer or sale of less than substantially all of the corporation's property are usually not subject to control by this article. One such condition is that the company be the surviving party to the merger/consolidation or, if not, that the other party be organized and existing under federal or state law. The new or surviving corporation must assume the terms of the indenture including the timely payment of principal, interest and premium (if any) on the subject debt securities, and the successor company is substituted for the predecessor company in the indenture. Of course, if secured, the terms of the transaction (unless waived by bondholders) must provide for the preservation of the security lien and the trustee's rights and powers. The merger, consolidation, or asset sale cannot take place if it would cause an event of default under the indenture's various covenants. Some indentures might place other restrictions on these transactions, including tangible net worth tests of the surviving corporation.

Supplemental Indentures and Covenants

As times change so may corporate law and practices. An indenture that was satisfactory when entered into many years ago may not be so today. Thus, article 13 in the mortgage indenture and article 9 in the debenture indenture provide for supplemental indentures and the amendments to the original indenture. The most common supplemental indenture is one issued under a blanket indenture for new and additional series or issues of debt securities. The supplemental indenture sets forth the terms and conditions for the issuance of the new securities, including authorized amounts of the new issue, interest rate, maturity, and redemption provisions. It may also include restrictive provisions not found in the basic or blanket indenture but, more often than not, at least nowadays, may contain much less restrictive provisions. Of course, the more restrictive provisions of preceding and still out-

---

[5] Harold Wolfson, "Tell It to the Bondholder, Too." *The New York Times*, May 18, 1975.

standing debt issues remain in force until the debt is extinguished or until the original indenture is changed or amended.

Certain provisions may be made without bondholders' consent. These include the addition of provisions for the debtholders' benefit or the surrender of company rights to correct inconsistencies and errors in the original indenture and to bring the original indenture into conformity with new and applicable laws concerning corporate trust indentures. Other provisions may require the assent of a two-thirds (or greater) majority of the debt outstanding; changes of a substantive or essential nature require a 100% vote. The latter category includes changes in the maturity, interest rate, redemption premium, place of payment, currency in which the debt is payable, or any provision which would impair the right to start legal suit for the enforcement of any defaulted payment. Some of the changes sought may include the extension of the maturity, reduction of the interest rate, or the payment of interest in common stock at the company's option. In some cases, the company may seek amendments to the indenture and offer to exchange new securities for old. If the old indenture received the required number of votes, the indenture would be changed and would govern any old securities that were not exchanged for new ones. The new securities issued in the exchange would have a new indenture.

In order for Peoples Express, Inc. (PEI) to merge into Texas Air Corporation in late 1986, the debtholders of People Express Airlines, Inc., a subsidiary of PEI, were required to exchange their old securities for new ones with longer maturities and lower interest rates and to consent to amendments to the old indenture (66⅔% vote of the outstanding principal amount of each issue was required). The amendments included the elimination of provisions restricting the payment of dividends by the Company and the acquisition of shares of common stock. Bondholders who did not tender and who did not vote for the indenture amendments nevertheless would be bound by the new supplemental indenture concerning dividends and stock repurchases even though they kept their original securities.

The debtor seeking indenture amendments often will give consideration to the debtholders in the form of increased interest payments or a one time fee. Companies' solicitations will, of course, often carry the boiler plate statements such as "Management of the Company believes that the proposed changes are in the best interests of the Company and the holders of each issue are being asked to consent to the proposed indenture changes." Many of these proposed changes weaken some of the existing covenants. For example, in 1985 Houston Natural Gas (HNG) asked some of its debenture holders to eliminate the interest coverage test which required available earnings to be at least 2.5 times annual interest charges on consolidated senior funded debt before it could issue new senior funded debt. The proxy statement said, "YING wishes to change its debt incurrence tests to reflect current practice as it applies to corporate obligors of HNG's caliber and to improve HNG's financing flexibility in order to permit HNG to be able to respond to rapid changes in the business and financial environment in which it operates." With no change HNG would have been permitted to issue about $240 million of additional debt on October 31, 1984, assuming a 12% interest rate. With the restrictions eliminated, it would have been able to issue $1,773 million of additional debt under a less restrictive capitalization test. As the proxy statement said, "to the extent that as a result of the proposed amendment HNG increases its leverage through the issuance of additional Senior Funded Debt beyond its ability to reasonably service such debt, the holders of the Debentures would be adversely affected thereby."

In 1977 and 1978 a number of electric utility companies sought changes in their indentures issued between 1928 and 1945. The reasons given were basically about the same, namely, their desire to modernize the indentures by eliminating obsolete and unnecessary restrictions and to increase their financial flexibility. The changes allowed the companies to issue additional debt in greater amounts or at an earlier date than previously. Many dramatic changes occurred in the economy since the indentures were written, and the high capital costs and rising fuel expenses caused by the runaway inflation of the seventies wrought havoc in the utility industry. Of course, weakening of debt restrictions may cause little problem in the short run; indeed, most of the time these changes will not of themselves cause a downgrade in the company's debt rating. But it is at the time of crisis that investors probably wish that less restrictive covenants were not granted so freely. Investors should carefully review any proposed indenture changes. The less restraint on corporate managements in their financing activities might mean more problems for the debtholders.

Covenants

Articles 14 of the mortgage indenture and article 10 of the debenture indenture are concerned with certain limitations and restrictions on the borrower's activities. Some covenants are common to all indentures, such as (1) to pay interest, principal and premium, if any, on a timely basis; (2) to maintain an office or agency where the securities may be transferred or exchanged and where notices may be served upon the company with respect to the securities and the indenture; (3) to pay all taxes and other claims when due unless contested in good faith; (4) to maintain all properties used and useful in the borrower's business in good condition and working order; (5) to maintain adequate insurance on its properties (some indentures may not have insurance provisions since proper insurance is routine business practice); (6) to submit periodic certificates to the trustee stating whether the debtor is in compliance with the loan agreement; and (7) to maintain its corporate existence. These are often called *affirmative* covenants since they call upon the debtor to make promises to do certain things.

Negative covenants are those which require the borrower not to take certain actions. These are usually negotiated between the borrower and the lender or their agents. Setting the right balance between the two parties can be a rather difficult undertaking at times. In public debt transactions the investing institutions normally leave the negotiating to the investment bankers, although they will often be asked their opinion on certain terms and features. Unfortunately, most public bond buyers are unaware of these articles at the time of purchase and may never learn of them throughout the life of the debt. Borrowers want the least restrictive loan agreement available, while lenders should want the most restrictive, consistent with sound business practices. But lenders should not try to restrain borrowers from accepted business activities and conduct. A company might be willing to include additional restrictions (up to a point) if it can get a lower interest rate on the loan. As we have seen, when companies seek to weaken restrictions in their favor, they are often willing to pay more interest or give other consideration.

What do some of these negative covenants cover? Obviously, there is an infinite variety of restrictions that can be placed on borrowers, depending on the type of debt issue, the economics of the industry and the nature of the business, and the lenders' desires. Some of the more common restrictive covenants include various limitations on the company's ability to incur debt, since unrestricted borrowing can lead a company and its debtholders to ruin. Thus, debt restrictions may include limits on the absolute dollar amount of debt that may be outstanding or may require ratio test — for example, debt may be limited to no more than 60% of total capitalization or that it cannot exceed a certain percentage of net tangible assets. An example is Jim Walter Corporation's indenture for its 9½% Debentures due April 1, 2016. This indenture restricts senior indebtedness to no more than the sum of 80% of net installment notes receivable and 50% of the adjusted consolidated net tangible assets. The indenture for The May Department Stores Company 7.95% Debentures due 2002 prohibits the company from issuing senior funded debt unless consolidated net tangible assets are at least 200% of such debt. More recent May Company indentures have dropped this provision.

There may be an interest or fixed charge coverage test of which there are two types. One, a maintenance test, requires the borrower's ratio of earnings available for interest or fixed charges to be at least a certain minimum figure on each required reporting date (such as quarterly or annually) for a certain preceding period. The other type, a debt incurrence test, only comes into play when the company wishes to do additional borrowing. In order to take on additional debt, the required interest or fixed charge coverage figure adjusted for the new debt must be at a certain minimum level for the required period prior to the financing. Incurrence tests are generally considered less stringent than maintenance provisions. There could also be cash flow tests or requirements and working capital maintenance provisions. The prospectus for Federated Department Stores, Inc.'s debentures dated November 4, 1988, has a large section devoted to debt limitations. One of the provisions allows net new debt issuance if the consolidated coverage ratio of earnings before interest, taxes and depreciation to interest expense (all as defined) is at least 1.35 to 1 through November 1, 1989, 1.45 to 1 through November 1, 1990, 1.50 to 1 through November 1, 1991, and at least 1.60 to 1 thereafter.

Some indentures may prohibit subsidiaries from borrowing from all other companies except the parent. Indentures often classify subsidiaries as restricted or unrestricted. Restricted subsidiaries are those considered to be consolidated for financial test purposes; unrestricted subsidiaries (often foreign and certain special-purpose companies) are those excluded from the covenants governing the parent. Often, subsidiaries are classified as unrestricted in order to allow them to finance themselves through outside sources of funds.

Limitations on dividend payments and stock repurchases may be included in indentures. Often, cash dividend payments will be limited to a certain percentage of net income earned after a specific date (often the issuance date of the debt and called the "peg date") plus a fixed amount. Sometimes the dividend formula might allow the inclusion of the net proceeds from the sale of common stock sold after the peg date. In other cases, the dividend restriction might be so worded as to prohibit the declaration and payment of cash dividends if tangible net worth (or other measures, such as consolidated quick assets) declines below a certain amount. There are usually no restrictions on the payment of stock dividends. In addition to dividend restrictions, there are often restrictions on a company's repurchase of its common stock if such purchase might cause a violation or deficiency in the dividend determination formulae. Some holding company indentures might limit the right of the company to pay dividends in the common stock of its subsidiaries. For example, Citicorp, the holding company parent of Citibank, N.A., is restricted, under certain circumstances, from paying dividends in shares of Citibank. The prospectus dated August 20, 1986, states:

> Citibank covenants... as long as any of the notes which mature more than ten years after their issuance are outstanding, it will not declare or pay any dividends, or make any distribution to its stockholders ratably, payable in shares of stock of Citibank, if after giving effect thereto, the Adjusted Stockholders' Equity of Citicorp would be less than 200% of Senior Long-Term Indebtedness; provided, however, that Citicorp may declare and pay such dividends and make any other distributions without regard to the foregoing provisions so long as the aggregate amount... of the value... of the shares of Stock... does not exceed 20% of the Adjusted Stockholders' Equity of Citicorp....

Another part of the covenant article may place restrictions on the disposition and the sale and leaseback of certain property. In some cases, the proceeds of asset sales totaling more than a certain amount must be used to repay debt. This is seldom found in indentures for unsecured debt but at times some investors may have wished they had such a protective clause. At other times, a provision of this type might allow a company to retire high coupon debt in a lower interest rate environment, thus causing bondholders a loss of value. It might be better to have such a provision where the company would have the right to reinvest the proceeds of asset sales in new plant and equipment rather than retiring debt, or to at least give the debtholder the option of tendering his bonds. The April 15, 1986, indenture of CSX Corporation does not prohibit the sale by the Company or any subsidiary of any stock or indebtedness of any restricted subsidiary. The main restricted subsidiaries of this transportation and energy company are The Chesapeake and Ohio Railway Company, The Baltimore and Ohio Railroad Company, CSX Transportation, Inc., Texas Gas Resources Corporation, American Commercial Lines, Inc. and Texas Gas Transmission

Company. one hopes that management has the bondholders' welfare in mind in case they decided to dispose of a substantial operation that may provide some degree of security for the eventual repayment of the debt. A sale/leaseback transaction involves the sale of the property and the simultaneous leasing back of the same property for a fixed number of years. Restrictions on these transactions might be limited to certain property owned, or to an amount of property which can be included in such a transaction, or to the use of the proceeds therefrom.

Some indentures restrict the investments that a corporation may make in other companies, through either the purchase of stock or loans and advances. As *Commentaries* states:

> By restricting the amount of cash or property which the borrower may invest in other enterprises, it is expected that the available assets of the borrower will be applied and devoted primarily to the basic business and purposes of the enterprise. If the borrower does not need the money in that enterprise, it may then be encouraged to use it for accelerated debt repayment. Such a covenant is not commonly used but when used it is more often found in directly placed issues than in public issues.[6]

The May Department Stores Credit Company has a provision in the indenture for its 9% Debentures due 1989 stating that,

> The Company will not... invest a substantial part of its assets in securities other than Deferred Payment Accounts, certain governmental securities maturing not more than eighteen months after the date of purchase, prime commercial paper and securities of a Subsidiary of the Company or May engaged in a business similar to that of the Company. The Company may also acquire debt securities of May in certain circumstances.

Finally, there may be an absence of restrictive covenants. The shelf registration prospectus of TransAmerica Finance Corporation dated March 30, 1994, forthrightly says:

> The indentures do not contain any provision which will restrict the Company in any way from paying dividends or making other distribution on its capital stock or purchasing or redeeming any of its capital stock, or from incurring, assuming or becoming liable upon Senior Indebtedness or Subordinated Indebtedness or any other type of debt or other obligations. The indentures do not contain any financial ratios or specified levels of net worth or liquidity to which the Company must adhere. In addition, the Subordinated Indenture

---

[6] *Commentaries*, p. 458

does not restrict the Company from creating liens on its property for any purpose. In addition, the Indentures do not contain any provisions which would require the Company to repurchase or redeem or otherwise modify the terms of any of its Debt Securities upon a change of control or other events involving the Company which may adversely effect the creditworthiness of the Debt Securities.

Let the Buyer Beware! If corporate managements and boards of directors viewed themselves as fiduciaries for all of the investors in the company, from stockholders to bondholders, indentures with many restrictive covenants might be unnecessary. But in most instances, that is not the case; they strive to increase shareholder wealth (or their own), not the wealth of the total firm, and often at the expense of the senior security investor. In this age of corporate raiders and managements' apparent lack of concern or fiduciary duty towards debt investors, perhaps some consideration ought to be given to the resurrection of good, old-fashioned restrictive provisions. That is, at least until the courts and state legislatures have acted to protect bondholders. One observer of bondholders' rights summarizes,

> Contrary to popular belief, indentures do not have numerous detailed covenants that regulate the bondholder-stockholder conflict. Indeed, an indenture may have no restrictive covenants at all. Such covenants are costly. Other constraints on stockholder gain at bondholder expense are ineffective. Since fiduciary duties are a substitute for costly contracts, directors should have fiduciary duties to bondholders as well as to stockholders. The exclusive focus of corporate law on stockholders is too narrow for modern corporate finance. Bondholders and stockholders are all security holders in the enterprise and equally deserving of board protection.[7]

---

[7] Morey W. McDaniel, "Bondholders and Corporate Governance" *The Business Lawyer*, vol. 42, no. 2, (February 1986), pp. 413-460. See also Morey W. McDaniel, "Bondholders and Stockholders." *The Journal of Corporation Law*, vol. 13, no. 2, (Winter 1988), pp. 205-315. These articles review the position of bondholders in today's world of leveraged buyouts, corporate reorganizations and decapitalizations. Another interesting article is "Fiduciary Duties of Directors: How Far Do They Go?" *Wake Forest Law Review*, vol. 23 (1988), pp. 163-180. Two Delaware court decisions in 1988 reaffirmed that corporate managements and directors do not owe bondholders any fiduciary duty. In *Shenandoah Life Insurance Company v. Valero Energy Corporation*, the Chancery Court said that "no breach of fiduciary duty occurred because neither an issuing corporation, nor its directors, owed fiduciary duties to holders of corporate debt." — (as reported in *Delaware Corporation Law Update*, vol. 4, no. 6, (October 1988), pp. 1, 8-11. The Delaware Supreme Court found in *Simons v. Cogan* (No. 429, 1987, DelSupCt, 10/19/88, Lexis 328) that "the issuer of certain convertible debentures owed no fiduciary duty to a debenture holder..." Further, "a debenture is a credit instrument which does not devolve upon its holder an equity interest in the issuing corporation. It is apparent that unless there are special circumstances which affect the rights of the debenture holders as creditors of the corporation, e.g., fraud, insolvency, or a violation of a statute, the rights of the debenture holders are confined to the terms of the indenture agreement pursuant to which the debentures were issued."

Covenants Change Over Time

Debt covenants can change over the years as companies issue debt under new and more modern indentures. For example, Kansas-Nebraska Natural Gas Company, Inc., now KN Energy, Inc., has issued debt during the past twenty years under three indentures with the same indenture trustee. In each of the indentures there were differences between the various provisions. Exhibit 1 summarizes some of the more important covenants as disclosed in the prospectuses for the particular issues. The 1976 and 1982 issues have provisions limiting dividend payments and share repurchases; the 1988 issue does not. The two earlier issues have a debt issuance test whereby debt cannot exceed 60% of pro forma capitalization; the 1988 issue does not have such a test. The 1976 issue has an interest coverage test for debt issuance which is not in the 1982 and the 1988 indentures.

SECURED DEBT

Since we have been introduced to corporate bonds in general, let us get to some specifics. The starting point will be bonds that are secured by some form of collateral, the first of the four Cs of credit: the *collateral*, which is pledged to ensure repayment of the debt; the *character* of the borrower, which ensures that the obligation will be paid on a timely basis; the *capacity* of the borrower, which ensures that it will have the means of repaying the debt; and *covenants* which define the legal contract setting forth the relationship between the borrower and the creditor.

Utility Mortgage Bonds

The largest issuers of debt secured by property, i.e. mortgage debt, are the electric utility companies. Of the major electric companies which periodically issue debt, there is but one — The United Illuminating Company in Connecticut — which issues only unsecured debt; all of the others have mortgage debt as the primary debt vehicle in their capital structures.[8] Other utilities, such as telephone companies and gas pipeline and distribution firms, have also used mortgage debt as sources of capital but generally to a lesser extent than electrics.

Most electric utility bond indentures do not limit the total amount of bonds that may be issued. This is called an *open-ended mortgage*, a contribution to American corporate finance attributed to Samuel Insull, the pioneer of the electric utility business who once served as the secretary to Thomas Alva Edison.[9] The mortgage generally is a first lien on the company's real estate, fixed property, and franchises, subject to certain exceptions or permitted encumbrances owned at the time of the ex-

---

[8] It should be noted, however, that a subsidiary of United, Bridgeport Electric Company, has an issue of first mortgage bonds outstanding.

[9] Forrest McDonald, *Insull* (Chicago, IL: University of Chicago Press, 1962). See also Peter Furhman, "Do It Big, Sammy," *Forbes*, (July 13, 1987), p. 278.

ecution of the indenture or its supplement. The after-acquired property clause also subjects to the mortgage property acquired by the company after the filing of the original or supplemental indenture. For example, the prospectus for Sierra Pacific Power Company's 10 ⅛% First Mortgage Bonds due 2018 says that the "New Bonds will be secured... by a first lien on substantially all properties and franchises owned by the Company at October 31, 1940 [the indenture is dated December 1, 1940] and on property and franchises subsequently acquired which in each case are used or useful in the business of furnishing electricity, water or gas, or in any business incidental thereto or operated in connection therewith, except properties released pursuant to the Mortgage...." Property which is excepted from the lien of the mortgage may include nuclear fuel (it is often financed separately through other secured loans); cash, securities and other similar items and current assets; automobiles, trucks, tractors and other vehicles; inventories and fuel supplies; office furniture and leaseholds; property and merchandise held for resale in the normal course of business; receivables, contracts, leases and operating agreements, and timber, minerals, mineral rights and royalties. In Sierra Pacific Power's case, "there are specifically excepted from the lien of the Mortgage certain current assets, securities and other personal property; timber; oil and other minerals; certain other property owned at October 31, 1940; and all property subsequently acquired, not used or useful to the Company in its utility business."

Permitted encumbrances might include liens for taxes and governmental assessments, judgments, easements and leases, certain prior liens, minor defects, irregularities and deficiencies in titles of properties and rights-of-way which do not materially impair the use of the property. For example, the mortgage for Indiana & Michigan Electric Company as supplemented in 1987 for the issuance of 9⅛% First Mortgage Bonds due 1997, is "(a) a first lien on substantially all of the fixed physical property and franchises of the Company... and (b) a lien, subject to the lien of IMPCo's mortgage, on the fixed physical property acquired in connection with the merger of IMPCo into the Company...." These and other bonds issued after July 1, 1986, were subject to some $24 million of judgment liens, the enforcement of which had been stayed. These judgment liens, according to the prospectus dated June 23, 1987, may have a priority senior to the first mortgage lien of the bonds. Citizens Utilities Company 7⅞% First Mortgage and Collateral Trust Bonds due 1996 are secured by a direct first lien on substantially all of the public utility properties located in Arizona, Colorado, Idaho and Vermont, and a direct second lien on property located in Hawaii (there was a small prior mortgage on the Hawaiian properties).

Historically, bonded debt — at least for the electric utility industry — was viewed as permanent capital and, as such, was not expected to be repaid, only rolled over or refunded. This is the current view taken of the federal government's debt. Prior to the mid-1970s, most of the new utility issues were long-term with maturities of thirty years or so. Sinking funds were either nonexistent or, if insignificant, could usually be satisfied with additions to property and not with actual debt retirement. It made little sense to repay permanent debt if one only had to borrow the amount that was just repaid. Therefore, other protective measures were incorporated in the indenture to satisfy the lender that the mortgaged property was being cared for.

Exhibit 1: Comparison of Three Debentures as Outlined in the Prospectuses of Kansas-Nebraska Natural Gas Company, Inc. and K N Energy, Inc.

Indenture Trustee: Continental Illinois National Bank and Trust Company of Chicago

	$20,000,000; 9% Debentures; January 1, 1996	$25,000,000; 13% Debentures; October 1, 2002	$35,000,000; 10¾% Debentures; September 1, 2008
Indenture date	February 1, 1948	October 1, 1982	September 1, 1988
Supplement date	January 1, 1976		
Prospectus date	January 27, 1976	October 20, 1982	September 14, 1988
Payment of dividends and acquisitions of stock	Company may not declare or pay any dividend or make any distribution on its common stock or purchase or redeem any shares of its capital stock of any class (exceptions include sinking fund on $5.65 Class A Preferred) except out of (x) surplus and income earned and accrued after 12/31/74 and (y) $10,000,000. No subsidiary is permitted to purchase any shares of capital stock of K-N. Neither K-N nor any subsidiary may purchase, redeem or acquire any capital stock or take any action by way of dividends or distribution resulting in the decrease in the par or stated value of its capital stock or surplus if the consolidated funded indebtedness of K-N shall exceed 60% of total consolidated capitalization.	Company may not pay or declare nor make any distribution on any capital stock, nor may K-N or any subsidiary make any payment to acquire shares (exceptions for fixed dividends and purchase fund payments) if such payments subsequent to 12/31/81, including the above exceptions, would exceed the sum of (a) consolidated net earnings subsequent to 12/31/81, (b) $25,000,000, (c) proceeds from the sale of stock after 12/31/81, and (d) debt converted into capital after 12/31/81.	No Provision
Debt issuance capitalization test	Neither K-N nor any subsidiary may create, incur, assume or guarantee, any additional funded debt, unless the consolidated funded debt including the additional debt shall not exceed 60% of the total consolidated capitalization.	Neither K-N nor any subsidiary may incur, directly or indirectly, any funded debt if consolidated funded debt, giving effect to the proposed additional debt and the receipt and application of proceeds thereof, would be more than 60% of pro forma consolidated capitalization.	No Provision.
Interest coverage test	In addition, in order to issue such debt, consolidated net income for 12 consecutive months out of 15 immediately preceding months must be at least 2½ times total interest charges on pro forma funded debt (3 times coverage required as long as any debentures issued prior to 1975 remain outstanding).	No Provision.	No Provision.

Exhibit 1: Comparison of Three Debentures as Outlined in the Prospectuses of Kansas-Nebraska Natural Gas Company, Inc. and K-N Energy, Inc. (Concluded)

	$20,000,000 9% Debentures January 1, 1996	$25,000,000 13% Debentures October 1, 2002	$35,000,000 10¾% Debentures September 1, 2008
Consolidation, merger and sale of assets	No Provision.	Company may consolidate with, or merge into or transfer all or substantially all of its assets to, one corporation if (i) the corporation assumes K-N's obligations under the indenture, (ii) after the transaction the consolidated capitalized debt is not greater than 60% of the consolidated capitalization of the resulting corporation, (iii) no default will occur as a result of the transaction, (iv) the surviving company is organized under the law of the United States or one of the states.	Company may, without the consent of any holders of debt securities, consolidate with or merge into or transfer all or substantially all of its assets to one or more other entities, provided (i) the surviving company is organized under the law of the United States or one of the states and assumes all of the Company's obligations on the debt securities under the indenture, and (ii) no default will occur as the result of this transaction.
Prohibition of advances	Kansas-Nebraska may not make or have outstanding any advances or extensions of credit, except to a Subsidiary, otherwise than in the ordinary course of business.	No Provision.	No Provision.
Events of default	Failure to pay interest or any sinking fund installment for 30 days;	Default for 30 days in payment of interest;	Failure to pay interest when due, which failure continues for 30 days;
	Failure to pay principal (and premium, if any) when due;	Default in payment when due of principal of, or premium, if any;	Failure to pay principal of or premium, if any, when due;
			Failure to deposit any sinking fund payment, when due;
	Failure to perform any other covenant for 60 days after notice;	Failure by K-N for 90 days after notice to it to comply with any of its other agreements;	Failure to observe and perform any other covenant in the Indenture which continues for 90 days after written notice;
	Default under an agreement or instrument under which there is issued funded debt in excess of $1,000,000 with the result that such debt shall have been declared due and payable, or failure by the Company to pay or refund any debt in excess of $1,000,000 within 30 days after maturity or extended maturity;		Default under any mortgage, indenture or instrument under which funded debt is issued in a principal amount exceeding $2,000,000 with the result that such debt shall have been declared due and payable, or failure by the Company to pay or refund any debt in excess of $2,000,000 within 60 days after the maturity has not been cured or waived;
	Certain events in bankruptcy, insolvency or reorganization.	Certain events in bankruptcy, insolvency or reorganization.	Certain events in bankruptcy, insolvency or reorganization.

Source: Company prospectuses.

To provide for proper maintenance of the property and replacement of worn-out plant, maintenance fund, maintenance and replacement fund, or renewal and replacement fund provisions were placed in indentures. These clauses stipulate that the issuer spend a certain amount of money for these purposes. Depending on the company, the required sums may be around 15% of operating revenues, as defined in other cases, the figure is based on a percentage of the depreciable property or amount of bonds outstanding. These requirements usually can be satisfied by certifying that the specified amount of expenditures has been made for maintenance and repairs to the property or by gross property additions. They can also be satisfied by depositing cash or outstanding mortgage bonds with the trustee; the deposited cash can be used for property additions, repairs and maintenance or in some cases — to the concern of holders of high-coupon debt — the redemption of bonds. More will be said on this topic in Chapter 5.

Another provision for bondholder security is the release and substitution of property clause. If the company releases property from the mortgage lien (such as through a sale of a plant or other property that may have become obsolete or no longer necessary for use in the business, or through the state's power of eminent domain), it must substitute other property or cash and securities to be held by the trustee, usually in an amount equal to the released property's fair value. It may use the proceeds or cash held by the trustee to retire outstanding bonded debt. Certainly, a bondholder would not let go of the mortgaged property without substitution of satisfactory new collateral or adjustment in the amount of the debt, as he should want to maintain the value of the security behind the bond. In some cases the company may waive the right to issue additional bonds. System Energy Resources, Inc.'s prospectus for its 14% First Mortgage Bonds due November 15, 1994, says: "Property may be released upon the bases of (i) the deposit of cash or, to a limited extent, purchase money mortgages, (ii) property additions, after adjustments in certain cases to offset retirements and after making adjustments for qualified prior lien bonds outstanding against property additions, and (iii) waiver of the right to issue First Mortgage Bonds, without applying any earnings tests."

Although the typical electric utility mortgage does not limit the total amount of bonds that may be issued, there are certain issuance tests or bases that usually have to be satisfied before the company can sell more bonds. New bonds are often restricted to no more than 60 to 66⅔% of the value of net bondable property. This generally is the lower of the fair value or cost of property additions, after adjustments and deductions for property that had previously been used for the authentication and issuance of previous bond issues, retirements of bondable property or the release of property, and any outstanding prior liens. Bonds may also be issued in exchange or substitution for outstanding bonds, previously retired bonds, and bonds otherwise acquired. Bonds may also be issued in an amount equal to the of cash deposited with the trustee. Sierra Pacific Power Company's $70 million of 10⅛% First Mortgage Bonds due 2018 were issued against the early retirement of $60 million 15⅜% First Mortgage Bonds due 1991. The remaining $10 million 10⅛s were issued on the basis of unfunded additional property additions at 60%.

A further earnings test found often in utility indentures requires interest charges be covered by pretax income available for interest charges of at least two times. The Connecticut Light and Power Company prospectus for its 6⅛% First and Refunding Mortgage Bonds, Series B due February 1, 2004, states:

> ... the Company may not issue additional bonds under the B Provisions unless its net earnings, as defined and as computed without deducting income taxes, for 12 consecutive calendar months during the period of 15 consecutive calendar months immediately preceding the first day of the month in which the application to the Trustee for authentication of additional bonds is made were at least twice the annual interest charges on all the Company's outstanding bonds, including the proposed additional bonds, and any outstanding prior lien obligations.

The earnings coverage figure for the twelve months ended September 30, 1993 based on the bonds and prior lien obligations outstanding was 4.2 times.

Mortgage bonds go by many different names. The most common of the senior lien issues are *First Mortgage Bonds* as used by The Cincinnati Gas & Electric Company, Long Island Lighting Company, and Sierra Pacific Power Company, among others. Baltimore Gas & Electric Company has the title of First Refunding Mortgage Bonds *(First and Refunding Mortgage Bonds* for Connecticut Light and Power Company) while Canal Electric Company, a wholesale electric generator, uses First and General Mortgage Bonds. The Baltimore issue, subject to a first mortgage lien (with certain exceptions), is also secured by a pledge of 100,000 shares each of Class A stock and Class B stock of Safe Harbor Water Power Corporation, an operator of a hydroelectric plant in Pennsylvania. The Baltimore bonds are also secured by the common stock of other directly owned subsidiaries but not stock of second level subsidiaries, i.e., subsidiaries of subsidiaries. The Canal Electric lien is broad-based, covering all of its property adjacent to the Cape Cod Canal, after-acquired property and pledged contracts relating to a couple of its generating units. Texas Utilities Electric Company issues *First Mortgage and Collateral Trust Bonds.* These are secured by Class "A" Bonds held by the trustee, which are first mortgage bonds issued by former subsidiaries (now divisions), and a first mortgage lien on certain other property of the Company. Texas Utilities has also issued Secured Medium-Term Notes as a series of the First Mortgage and Collateral Trust Bonds under the December 1, 1983, Mortgage and Deed of Trust.

There are instances (excluding prior lien bonds as mentioned above) when a company might have two or more layers of mortgage debt outstanding with different priorities. This situation usually occurs because the companies cannot issue additional first mortgage debt (or the equivalent) under the existing indentures. Often this secondary debt level is called *General and Refunding Mortgage Bonds* (G&R). In reality, this is mostly second mortgage debt. Long Island Lighting Company first issued G&R bonds in June 1975.

Let us take a look at the mortgage debt issues of Public Service Company of New Hampshire (PNH). Besides first mortgage bonds and general and refunding mortgage bonds with varying degrees of security, it also had third mortgage bonds as well as publicly issued unsecured debt. All in all, there were four levels of claims against the company and its properties. PNH, the largest electric utility in the state, supplies power to about 75% of the population of New Hampshire. Along with a number of other neighboring utilities, it embarked on the construction of an ambitious nuclear project located at Seabrook, New Hampshire. As did many other nuclear facilities under construction during the late 1970s and early 1980s, it encountered rapidly increasing construction costs, skyrocketing financial costs, and regulatory delays due to consumer and other opposition to nuclear facilities. (In 1976, a prospectus estimated that Seabrook Unit #1 would be in service in 1981; by the end of 1988 it still had not yet been placed on stream.) The end result was a strain on the finances of the Company, especially internally generated cash flow, resulting in a lack of financial flexibility. The Company finally omitted common and preferred stock dividends in May 1984 and, on January 28, 1988, filed a petition for reorganization under Chapter 11 the Bankruptcy Reform Act of 1978. The Company came out of bankruptcy in 1991.

Due to provisions contained in the Company's First Mortgage Bond indenture restricting the issuance of additional senior mortgage debt, PNH entered into a General and Refunding Mortgage Bond Indenture in August 1978. The terms of this indenture are somewhat similar to the First Mortgage with the exception of the removal of the restrictions on the issuance of additional debt and a modification relating to the use of the allowance for funds used during construction in the earnings test. The G&R bonds have a lien on substantially all of the property and franchises owned by the company (as do the first mortgage bonds), "... *subject*, however, to the payment of the Trustee's charges, to the lien of the First Mortgage, to the lien on after-acquired property existing at the time of acquisition or created in connection with the purchase thereof... and to Permitted Liens."[10]

The G&R indentures (as supplemented) also provide that the bonds are additionally secured by a pledge of the maximum amount of first mortgage bonds which may be issuable at the time of the issuance of the G&R debt. Thus, the G&R constitutes a second mortgage on the property of the Company and, in some cases, backed up by a first mortgage. At the end of 1987 PNH had six G&R issues outstanding of which four had the additional security of first mortgage bonds as shown in Exhibit 2. The prospectus states that the principal benefit to the holders of G&R bonds that have first mortgage bonds pledged as additional security would be in reorganization or insolvency when the allocation to the holders of these G&R bonds might be increased by the reason of their participation in the First Mortgage through the pledged bonds. Upon the retirement of all non-pledged First Bonds (2006 or earlier) the G&R bonds would become the equivalent of first mortgage debt as the original First Mortgage would have been discharged or satisfied.

---

[10] Prospectus for $30,000,000 Public Service Company of New Hampshire General and Refunding Mortgage Bonds, Series C 14½% due 2000, dated January 22, 1980

Exhibit 2: Selected Data on General & Refunding Mortgage Bonds, Public Service Company of New Hampshire at December 31, 1990 ($ Thousands)

G & R Bond Issue Issue (%)	Year	G & R Amount Outstanding ($)	Pledged First Mortgage Bonds ($)	Percent of G & R Collateralized by FMB
"A" 10.125	1993	32,700	9,658	29.54
"B" 12.000	1999	60,000	9,126	15.21
"C" 14.500	2000	30,000	None	0
"D" 17.000	1990	23,000	None	0
"E" 18.000	1989	50,000	24,135	48.27
"H" Variable	1991	112,500	10,080	8.96

Source: Prospectus for Series A and B First Mortgage Bonds, May 9, 1991.

The next level of debt in PNH's capitalization represented a third mortgage through the issuance in early 1986 of $225 million of 13¾% Deferred Interest Third Mortgage Bonds Series A due 1996. The Company resorted to this level due to the G&R earnings test, which permitted the issuance of only about $26 million of G&R debt at December 31, 1985. The prospectus states: "The... Bonds,... are secured by a mortgage on substantially all of the Company's New Hampshire properties. The Third Mortgage is junior and subordinate to the liens of the First Mortgage and the G&R Indenture..." While the Third Mortgage does not have an earnings test, additional bonds under the indenture may only be issued if the total of the outstanding First, G&R and Third Mortgage Bonds does not exceed 90% of the book value of the Company's New Hampshire properties subject to the Third Mortgage. The final stratum of debt is unsecured, consisting of promissory notes and debentures. PNH was a rare bird among electric utility companies (or even among non-railroad companies) due to its capital structure. Most companies might not have more than two — or at the most three different types of debt on the books.

After the bankruptcy filing, holders of the mortgage bonds brought suit in court to have the Company resume interest payments on the secured debt. The Court granted the motions of the First Mortgage and General and Refunding bond holders and interest was resumed, and defaulted interest paid, in June 1988. The Court found that the value of the bond collateral exceeded the amount of the debt and thus post-petition interest on this debt is an allowed claim. Further, current and projected cash flow were adequate to allow payment of interest, and the payment of such interest would avoid future litigation expense which might arise from continued nonpayment of the interest. As the property was in use and decreasing in value due to depreciation and wear and tear, the holders were entitled to receive adequate compensation; in this case interest payments.

In allowing the interest payments, the Court order said: "Accrual of unpaid interest on senior secured debt erodes the position of junior secured debt and, therefore, current payment of interest on the Debt will provide a measure of protection of interests in the Bond collateral which are junior in priority to the liens securing the Debt because such payment will reduce the amount of the secured claim of the holders of the Debt for interest regarding any period during which such interest is currently paid." Resumption of interest payments or adequate protection was denied the Third Mortgage Bonds. Apparently, they were found to be not fully secured as the Seabrook nuclear generating unit's status was not clear at that time. Seabrook only has value if permitted to generate electricity. However, the Third Mortgage Bonds' claim for accrued and unpaid interest was satisfied when the company emerged from bankruptcy.

As stated earlier, electric companies utilize mortgage debt more than other utilities. However, other utilities, such as telephone and gas companies, also have mortgage debt. Among the telephone companies with mortgage bonds are some of the subsidiaries and affiliates of the GTE Corporation system. Illinois Bell Telephone Company and New York Telephone Company issued first mortgage debt until the early 1970s, when the mortgage was closed and they started issuing unsecured debenture debt. Prior to the Bell System's breakup, the mortgage bonds and debentures of the Bell subsidiaries carried the same rating. For example, the bonds and debentures of New York Telephone and Illinois Bell were rated triple-A by Moody's and Standard & Poor's. After the divestiture, however, Moody's applied different ratings to the secured and unsecured debt, while S&P had the same rating whether the debt was first mortgage or debenture. In early 1994, Illinois Bell's mortgage debt was rated Aaa/AAA and the debentures Aa1/AAA. Similarly, New York Telephone's secured debt was rated A1 and A, while the unsecured carried A2 and A designations.

Gas pipeline companies also use mortgage debt. Here, again, the issuance tests are similar to those for the electric issues, as are the mortgage liens. However, the pipeline companies may have an additional clause subjecting certain gas purchase and sale contracts to the mortgage lien.

OTHER MORTGAGE DEBT

Non-utility companies do not offer much mortgage debt nowadays; the preferred form of debt financing is unsecured. In the past, railroad operating companies were frequent issuers of mortgage debt. In many cases, a wide variety of secured debt might be found in a company's capitalization. One issue may have a first lien on a certain portion of the right of way and a second mortgage on another portion of the trackage, as well as a lien on the railroad's equipment, subject to the prior lien of existing equipment obligations. For example, Burlington Northern Railroad Company's 10% Consolidated Mortgage Bonds, Series J, due November 1, 1997, has direct and indirect liens on various parts of the railway's property as follows:

> (1) a second lien on the railroad properties subject to the first lien of the Great Northern General Gold Bond Mortgage (including approximately 4,086 miles of main line and 2,814 miles of branch line); (2) an indirect first lien on such Great Northern Railroad

properties through the pledge under the Consolidated Mortgage of $350,135,000 principal amount of Great Northern General Mortgage Bonds; (3) a third lien on railroad properties subject to prior liens on the Northern Pacific Prior Lien Mortgage and Northern Pacific General Lien Mortgage (including approximately 2,398 miles of main line and 1,360 miles of branch line); (4) a third lien on the railroad properties subject to a first lien of the former Chicago, Burlington and Quincy Railroad Company (CB&Q) First and Refunding Mortgage and to the second lien of the Great Northern General Mortgage (including approximately 4,963 miles of main line and 1,543 miles of branch line); (5) an indirect first lien on such CB&Q properties through the pledge under the Consolidated Mortgage of $70,000,000 principal amount of CB&Q First and Refunding Mortgage Bonds; and (6) a first lien on approximately 8 miles of Great Northern branch line, approximately 169 miles of Northern Pacific main line and approximately 718 miles of Northern Pacific branch line, and approximately 19 miles of branch line of Colorado and Southern Railway Company.

There are certain railroad properties which are not subject to the lien of the above Consolidated Mortgage. Other exclusions include (1) lands not used or acquired for use in the railroad transportation service, (2) any lands adjacent to the lines of the railroad, used or acquired by the Company for industrial purposes and not for use in the railroad transportation service, (3) all timber and all oil, gas, coal and other minerals, (4) all air rights which may be used without unreasonable interference or adverse effect on the use for railroad purposes of surface land, and (5) all certificates of convenience and necessity for motor and water carrier operations and equipment used in connection therewith. The mortgage lien does not attach to property or improvements which are not appurtenant to any property subject to the lien thereof.

Another example is Chesapeake and Ohio Railway Company's Refunding and Improvement Mortgage Bonds, 3½% Series due May 1, 1996, which has a direct lien on 2,406.59 miles of track (819.32 miles as a first lien, 1,354.88 miles as a second lien, and 232.39 miles as a third lien), on the company's interest in 9 miles operated under leasehold agreements, and 411 miles operated under trackage rights, on C&O's owned equipment, and on its leasehold interest in equipment, subject to prior mortgage liens and outstanding equipment trust obligations. Railroad mortgages are often much more complex and confusing to bond investors than other types of mortgage debt.

In the broad classification of industrial companies, only a few have first mortgage bonds outstanding. The steel industry's Inland Steel Company, National Steel Corporation, Youngstown Sheet and Tube Company and Jones & Laughlin Steel Corporation had mortgage debt. The latter two were part of the bankrupt LTV Steel complex. While electric utility mortgage bonds generally have a lien on practically all of the company's property, steel company mortgage debt has more limited liens. The prospectuses for Inland and National Steel describe the particular steel properties subject to the mortgage lien and make special mention that "various other properties of the

Company... are not now subject to the lien of the Mortgage."[11] The mortgages of Youngstown and Jones & Laughlin retained the respective liens on their respective properties after their own merger and the subsequent merger with Republic Steel. Mortgages may also contain maintenance and repair provisions, earnings tests for the issuance of additional debt, release and substitution of property clauses, and limited after-acquired property provisions. In some cases, shares of subsidiaries might also be pledged as part of the lien.

Some mortgage bonds are secured by a lien on a specific property rather than on most of a company's property as in the case of an electric utility. For example, Humana Inc. sold a number of small issues of first mortgage bonds secured by liens on specific hospital properties. The 16½s of 1997 are secured by a first lien on a 267-bed hospital in Orlando, Florida, while the 16¼s of 1996 have lien on a 219-bed hospital in St. Petersburg, Florida. Although technically mortgage bonds, the basic security is centered on Humana's continued profitable operations. Because the security is specific rather than general, investors are apt to view these bonds as less worthy or of a somewhat lower ranking than fully secured or general lien issues. As the prospectuses say, the bonds are general obligations of Humana Inc. and also secured by the first mortgage. Standard & Poor's has mentioned that "It is difficult to assure that debtholders secured by specific collateral such as a hotel or hospital will, following a bankruptcy and liquidation of assets, realize values which make them whole."[12] The ultimate realization under these adverse circumstances greatly depends on the value of the property obtained in liquidation or assigned as part of the reorganization process. In many cases, by the time a company must resort to bankruptcy action, the properties are not worth what they once were. Any deficiency between what is owed and the value of the property then becomes a general unsecured claim against the debtor.

OTHER SECURED DEBT

Debt can be secured by many different assets. Forstmann & Company, Inc. issued $60 million 11¾% Secured Senior Extendible Notes due April 1, 1998, secured by a first priority lien on substantially all of its real property, machinery and equipment, and by a second priority lien on its inventory, accounts receivables and intangibles; the first priority lien on these latter assets is held by General Electric Credit Corporation (GECC) for its revolving credit loan. The revolving credit at August 3, 1986, amounted to nearly $44 million and may go to as much as $72 million. The prospectus points out:

> There can be no assurance that the fixed assets of the Company are currently, or in the future will be adequate collateral for the Notes. While the Fair Market Value of the Company's fixed assets (assum-

---

[11] Prospectus for $125,000,000 Inland Steel Company First Mortgage 7.90% Bonds, Series R due January 15, 2007, dated January 12, 1977.

[12] "Rating 'Secured' Industrial Debt." Standard & Poor's *Credit Week*, August 16, 1982, p. 944.

ing a continuation of current operations) has been appraised by American Appraisal Associates, Inc., an independent appraising firm, at $89,616,000 and the Company believes the replacement value of those assets to be more than $150,000,000, the Orderly Liquidation Value of those assets (assuming a piecemeal disposition over a reasonable period of time) has been appraised at $38,481,000. In addition, there can be no assurance that the Company's current assets will, after satisfaction of the claims of GECC, provide any collateral for the Notes.[13]

In the view of Forstman's management, "it is highly unlikely that the assets of the Company would be sold in a liquidation situation because of the greater marketability of the Company if sold as a going concern."

Collateral trust debentures, bonds and notes are secured by financial assets such as cash, receivables, other notes, debentures or bonds, and not by real property. Louisville and Nashville Railroad Company's 11% Collateral Trust Bonds due July 15, 1985, were secured by a pledge of L&N's 11% First and Refunding Mortgage Bonds, Series P, due April 1, 2003, in an amount equal to 120% of the collateralized bonds. The mortgage bonds were a direct first lien on 3,949 miles of road, a direct second lien on 1,373 miles, and a third lien on 512 miles. In 1969 the Canadian company, Hudson's Bay Oil and Gas Company Limited, sold an issue of 7.85% Collateral Trust Bonds due 1994 in the United States. These bonds were secured by an equivalent amount of U.S. dollar payable First Mortgage Sinking Fund Bonds (covering the Company's Canadian properties) with the same maturity, interest rate and payment dates and redemption and sinking fund provisions as the collateral bonds. The pledged securities, being nearly similar in every way to the collateralized bonds are called "shadow bonds" by some, and "mirror bonds" by others. Thus, the collateral bond indenture constitutes a first lien on the pledged bonds and an indirect lien ranking pari passu (equally) with the holders of the Company's other First Mortgage Bonds on the Company's property as described in the Deed of Trust and Mortgage dated May 1, 1955, and supplemented.

Collateral trust notes and debentures have been issued by companies engaged in vehicle leasing, such as RLC Corporation, Leaseway Transportation Corporation, and Ryder System, Inc. The proceeds from these offerings were advanced to various subsidiaries in exchange for their unsecured promissory notes which, in turn, were pledged with the trustees as security for the parent company debt. These pledged notes may later become secured by liens or other claims on vehicles. Protective covenants for these collateralized issues may include limitations on the equipment debt of subsidiaries, on the consolidated debt of the issuer and its subsidiaries, on dividend payments by the issuer and the subsidiaries, and on the creation of liens and purchase money mortgages, among other things.

---

[13] Prospectus for 60,000 Units Forstmann & Company, Inc., dated September 26, 1986.

Debt can be secured by the pledge of assets such as a partnership notes (DCS Capital Corporation 12.20% Series A Notes due 1994 or Pembroke Capital Company Inc. 14% Notes due 1991). DCS Capital Corporation is owned by DCS Capital Partnership, whose general partners are The Dow Chemical Company, Union Carbide Corporation and Shell Canada Limited. The partnership note is secured by a cash deficiency agreement and performance guarantees with the three partners on a several basis, initially in the following proportions: Dow 52%; Union Carbide 27%; and Shell, 21%. These agreements and guarantees are not assigned directly to the holders of the Series A Notes, but the trustee has the right to enforce them if the notes are not paid when due. The Pembroke issue is secured by a partnership note of Pembroke Cracking Company, a partnership of Texaco Limited and Gulf Oil (Great Britain) Limited, wholly owned subsidiaries of American corporations. If the Pembroke Capital Note is not paid on a timely basis, the general partners are severally obligated to make, or caused to be made, payments sufficient to pay the principal and interest on the notes if their respective subsidiaries fail to do so.

Since 1985, *LOBs* (for *Lease Obligation Bonds*), *SLOBs* (for *Secured Lease Obligation Bonds*) and *SFBs* (for *Secured Facility Bonds*) have been issued as a result of sale and leaseback transactions of electric utility companies. Some utilities have sold interests in generating plants and transmission facilities to third parties, which, in turn, leased the assets back to the utilities. A utility enters into these transactions essentially for tax purposes as it may have limited near-term use for depreciation allowances. It essentially substitutes lease rental payments for depreciation and capital recovery requirements associated with ownership. The third party lessor in these leveraged lease transactions obtains the funds to purchase the assets from the sale of these SLOBs, LOBs, and SFBs. The source of repayment for these bonds is from the rentals paid by the utility to the lessor in amounts sufficient to provide for the payment of principal and interest on the bonds. Additional security may be pledged lessor notes which, in the case of SLOBs, are secured by a lien on and a security interest in the ownership interest in the leased property. LOBs do not have any security interest in the leased property although, under certain circumstances, the lease indenture trustee may acquire a lien and security interest on the property. SFBs are secured by a lien and security interest in the leased assets and the lessor's rights under the lease.

Private Export Funding Corporation (PEFCO) issues secured notes with the pledged security being an equivalent principal amount of obligations backed by the full faith and credit of the United States of America, such as guaranteed importer notes, or cash. The interest on PEFCO's secured notes is unconditionally guaranteed by the Export-Import Bank of the United States, a U.S. government agency. Thus PEFCO's paper carries the highest ratings, Aaa/AAA.

Thrift institutions, either directly or indirectly through special purpose financing corporations, secured some of their debt obligations in order to enhance the credit standing of the paper. The securities are backed by eligible collateral such as federally insured or guaranteed mortgages and deeds of trust on real property, Government National Mortgage Association Certificates, Federal National Mortgage Association Certificates, Federal Home Loan Mortgage Corporation Certificates, and conventional mortgages. These secured issues are obligations of the thrift or the special purpose subsidiary, not of any special trust, and do not constitute deposits or savings accounts. The security is still owned by the thrift, although pledged for repayment of the debt created. Proceeds from the sale of the secured bonds and notes (not from the sale of mortgages) are used by the thrift for general purposes. If, following a default, the proceeds from the liquidation of the pledged property are insufficient to pay the entire amount of the bonds, the bondholders would then become general unsecured creditors of the issuer to the extent of the deficiency ranking on a parity with other general unsecured creditors.

The eligible collateral is held by a trustee and periodically marked to market to ensure that the market value has a liquidation value in excess of the amount needed to repay the entire outstanding bonds and accrued interest. If the collateral is insufficient, the issuer must, within several days, bring the value of the collateral up to the required amount. If the issuer is unable to do so, the trustee would then sell collateral and redeem bonds. Another collateralized structure allows for the defeasance or "mandatory collateral substitution" which provides the investor assurance that it will continue to receive the same interest payments until maturity. Instead of redeeming the bonds with the proceeds of the collateral sale, the proceeds are used to purchase a portfolio of U.S. government securities in such an amount that the cash flow is sufficient to meet the principal and interest payments on the mortgage-backed bond. Because of the structure of these issues, the rating agencies have assigned triple-A ratings to them. The rating is based on the strength of the collateral and the issues' structure, not on the issuers' credit standing.

Equipment Trust Financing: Railroads

Railroads and airlines have financed much of their rolling stock and aircraft with secured debt. The securities go by various names such as equipment trust certificates (ETCs) in the case of railroads, and secured equipment certificates, guaranteed loan certificates and loan certificates in the case of airlines. We will look at railroad equipment trust financing first for two reasons: (1) the financing of railway equipment under the format in general public use today goes back to the late nineteenth century, and (2) it has had a superb record of safety of principal and timely payment of interest, more traditionally known as dividends. Railroads probably comprise the largest and oldest group of issuers of secured equipment financing.[14]

---

[14] See Michael Downey Rice, *Railroad Equipment Obligations* (New York, NY: Salomon Brothers, 1978). This book, privately published and sponsored by the investment banking firm of Salomon Brothers, gives a good historical and legal background on the instrument. It does not, however, incorporate the effects of the Bankruptcy Reform Act of 1978, which became effective October 1, 1979.

Exhibit 3: Ratings of Debt Securities
of Selected Railroad Companies (January 1, 1990)

| | ETC Ratings | | | Senior Public Debt | |
Company	Moody's	S & P		Moody's	S & P
Atchinson, Topeka & Santa Fe	Aa3	A	General Mortgage	A3	BBB
Baltimore & Ohio Railroad	Aa2	A+	First Consolidated Mortgage	A2	BBB+
Burlington Northern RR	Aa3	A+	Consolidated Mortgage	A3	BBB+
Louisville & Nashville	Aa2	A+	First & Refunding Mortgage	A2	BBB+
Missouri Pacific Railroad	Aa1	AA+	First Mortgage	A1	A+
Southern Railway	Aaa	AAA	First Consolidated Mortgage	Aa2	AA

Source: *Moody's Bond Record* and *Standard & Poor's Bond Guide*, March 1994.

Probably the earliest instance in U.S. financial history in which a company bought equipment under a conditional sales agreement (CSA) was in 1845 when the Schuylkill Navigation Company purchased some barges.[15] Over the years secured equipment financing proved to be an attractive way for railroads — both good and bad credits — to raise the capital necessary to finance rolling stock. Various types of instruments were devised — equipment bonds (known as the New York Plan), conditional sales agreements (also known as the New York CSA), lease arrangements, and the Philadelphia Plan equipment trust certificate. The New York Plan equipment bond went the way of the dodo bird in the 1930s. The Philadelphia Plan ETC is the form used for most, if not all, public financings in today's market.

The ratings for equipment trust certificates are higher than on the same company's mortgage debt or other public debt securities. This is due primarily to the collateral value of the equipment, its superior standing in bankruptcy compared with other claims, and the instrument's generally self-liquidating nature. The railroad's actual creditworthiness may mean less for some equipment trust investors than for investors in other rail securities or, for that matter, other corporate paper. However, that is not to say that financial analysis of the issuer should be ignored. Exhibit 3 compares the ratings on equipment trust certificates of a number of railroad companies with the ratings on some of their other public debt. In some cases, the differences between the two securities are slight; in others they comprise a complete rating grade.

Equipment trust certificates are issued under agreement that provide a trust for the benefit of the investors. Each certificate represents an interest in the trust equal to its principal amount and bears the railroad's unconditional guarantee of prompt payment, when due, of the principal and dividends (the term *dividends* is used as the payments represent income from a trust and not interest on a loan). The trustee holds the title to the equipment, which when the certificates are retired, passes to, or vests in, the railroad. But the railroad has all other ownership rights. It can take the depreciation and

---

[15] Arthur Stone Dewing, *The Financial Policy of Corporations* (New York, NY: The Ronald Pres Company, 1926), p. 178.

can utilize any tax benefits on the subject equipment The railroad agrees to pay the trustee sufficient rental for the principal payments and the dividends due on the certificates, together with expenses of the trust and certain other charges. The railroad uses the equipment in its normal operations and is required to maintain it in good operating order and repair (at its own expense). If the equipment is destroyed, lost or becomes worn out or unsuitable for use (that is, suffers a "casualty occurrence") the company must substitute the fair market value of that equipment in the form of either cash or additional equipment. Cash may be used to acquire additional equipment unless the agreement states otherwise. The trust equipment is usually dearly marked that it is not the railroad's property. One equipment trust agreement states:

> *Section 4.6.* The Railroad agrees that at or before the delivery to the Railroad of each unit of the Trust Equipment, there shall be plainly, distinctly, permanently and conspicuously placed and fastened upon each side of such unit a metal plate bearing the words [Missouri Pacific Equipment Trust, Series No. 22, Chemical Bank, Trustee, Owner and Lessor]..., or such words shall be otherwise plainly, distinctly, permanently and conspicuously marked on each side of such unit, in either case in letters not less than one-half inch in height. Such plates or marks shall be such as to be readily visible and as to indicate plainly the Trustee's ownership of each unit of the Trust Equipment. In case... such plates or marks shall at any time be removed, defaced or destroyed, the Railroad shall immediately cause the same to be restored or replaced. The Trust Equipment may be lettered "Missouri Pacific Railroad," "Missouri Pacific Lines, "M.P." or with the name, insignia, emblem or initials of any Affiliate which... is authorized to use the equipment... for convenience of identification of the leasehold interest of the Railroad therein. During the continuance of the lease... the Railroad shall not allow the name of any person, association or corporation to be placed on any of the Trust Equipment as a designation which might be interpreted as a claim of ownership thereof by the Railroad or by any person, association or corporation other than the Trustee.[16]

Immediately after the issuance of an ETC the railroad has an equity interest in the equipment that provides a margin of safety for the investor. Normally, the ETC investor finances no more than 80% of the cost of the equipment and the railroad the remaining 20%. The Union Pacific Railroad Company's 8¾% Equipment Trust No. 1 of 1987 issued January 28, 1988, was for $101,200,000, equal to 80% of the original cost of the equipment financed. This equipment consisted of 75 Dash diesel-electric road freight locomotives with a cost of $83,668,950 (cost per

---

[16] Missouri Pacific Railroad Equipment Trust Series No. 22, Equipment Trust Agreement Dated as of October 15, 1982, between Chemical Bank Trustee and Missouri Pacific Railroad Company.

locomotive, $1,115,586), 25 diesel-electric road freight locomotives with a cost of $29,357,500 (cost per locomotive, $1,174,300), and 345 center partition bulkhead flat cars costing $13,467,906 ($39,037 each) for a total of $126,494,356. Although modern equipment is longer-lived than that of many years ago, the ETC's length of maturity is still generally the standard 15 years (there are some exceptions noted below). Assuming a 20-year equipment life with straight line depreciation, there will be a positive margin of equity in the trust at normal maturity date. Actually, however, much of the equipment can remain in service for thirty to forty years without a major overhaul.

The structure of the financing usually provides for periodic retirement of the outstanding certificates. The most common form of ETC is the serial variety. It is usually issued in 15 equal maturities, each one coming due annually in years one through fifteen. The Atchison, Topeka and Santa Fe Railway Company Equipment Trust, Series AA, dated February 15, 1994, consists of 15 serial maturities of $3,795,000 due each February 15 from 1995 through 2009. The certificates were reoffered at par by J. P. Morgan Securities Inc., the underwriter, in April 1994 at yields ranging from 4.25% for the one-year piece to 7.57% for the February 15, 2009 maturity. Consolidated Rail Corporation issued its 1988 Equipment Trust Certificates, Series A, with serial maturities of unequal principal amounts due annually October 15, 1991 to October 15, 2004. There are single-maturity (or "bullet maturity") ETCs such as the previously mentioned Union Pacific 8 ¾% Equipment Trust No. 1 of 1987. This 7-year issue did not have a sinking fund and matured on January 15, 1995. There are also sinking fund equipment trust certificates where the ETCs are retired through the operation of a normal sinking fund, one fifteenth of the original amount issued per year. Thus the Louisville and Nashville Railroad Company's 12.30% Equipment Trust Certificates, Series 10, due February 1, 1995 (original issue $53,600,000), had an annual sinking fund of $3,575,000, designed to retire 93.4% of the issue prior to maturity.

The standing of railroad or common carrier equipment trust certificates in bankruptcy is of vital importance to the investor. As the equipment is needed for operations, the bankrupt railroad's management will more than likely reaffirm the lease of the equipment because, without rolling stock, it is out of business. One of the first things the trustees of the Penn Central Transportation Company did after the firm filed for bankruptcy on June 21, 1970, was to reaffirm its equipment debt. On August 19, the court issued the required equipment debt assumption orders.[17] There were outstanding about $90.7 million of equipment trust certificates, $442.9 million of conditional sales agreements, and unexpired lease rental payments on other contracts of $594 million. It was not until the end of 1978 that investors and speculators started to recover something from the other Penn Central obligations. Cases of disaffirmation of equipment obligations are very rare indeed. But if equipment debt were to be disaffirmed, the trustee could repossess and then try to release or sell it to others. Any defi-

---

[17] Rice, *Railroad Equipment Obligations*, p. 125.

ciency due the equipment debtholders would still be an unsecured claim against the bankrupt railway company. Standard gauge, non-specialized equipment should not be difficult to release to another railroad.

The Bankruptcy Reform Act of 1978 provides specifically that railroads be reorganized, not liquidated, and subchapter IV of Chapter 11 grants them special treatment and protection. One very important feature found in Section 77(j) of the preceding Bankruptcy Act was carried over to the new law. Section 1168 states that Section 362 (the automatic stay provision) and Section 363 (the use, sale, or lease of property section) are not applicable in railroad bankruptcies. It protects the rights of the equipment lenders while giving the trustee the chance to cure any defaults.[18] Railroad bankruptcies usually do not occur overnight but creep up gradually as the result of steady deterioration over the yeas. New equipment financing capability becomes restrained. The outstanding equipment debt at the time of bankruptcy often is not substantial and usually has a good equity cushion built in.

Equipment debt of noncommon carriers such as private car leasing lines (Trailer Train, Union Tank Car, General American Transportation etc.) does not enjoy this special protection under the Bankruptcy Act. Standard & Poor's says that it accordingly rates this debt only as the senior security of the lessor. Signal Capital Corporation through its Pullman Leasing Company division (a noncommon carrier) leases rail freight cars to shippers and railroads and finances the equipment through the issuance of equipment trust certificates. In 1988, Signal Capital issued $100 million of 9.95% Certificates due February 1, 2006, to reduce short-term borrowings incurred to finance the railcar leasing division. The ETC agreement provided for the sale, assignment and transfer to the trustee of 5,156 freight cars with a depreciated final cost of at least $125 million. None of the equipment would have been in use prior to January 1, 1975! The prospectus states:

> In the event of bankruptcy or reorganization of the Company or any sublessee, the rights of the trustee to repossess or dispose of equipment covered by the Trust would be subject to the effect of the federal bankruptcy laws upon enforcement of lessor's rights. These laws, among other things, impose automatic stays upon rights of repossession as against the Company and non-railroad sublessees; may invalidate lease termination

---

[18] Bankruptcy Reform Act of 1978, P.L. 95-598 (Chicago, IL: Commerce Clearing House). Section 1168 states in part,

> The right of a secured party with a purchase-money equipment security interest in, or of a lessor or conditional vendor of, whether as trustee or otherwise, rolling stock equipment or accessories used on such equipment, including superstructures and racks, that are subject to a purchase-money equipment security interest granted by, leased to, or conditionally sold to, the debtor to take possession of such equipment in compliance with the provisions of a purchase-money security agreement, lease or conditional sale contract, as the case may be, is not affected by Section 362 or 363 of this title or by any power of the court on enjoin such taking of possession....

clauses which become effective by reason of bankruptcy and certain other insolvency-related events; and allow a trustee in bankruptcy (or the Company or sublessee if it should be a debtor-in-possession) to assign or terminate an unexpired lease not-withstanding a provision in the Agreement or the sublease which prohibits, restricts, or conditions such assignment or termination.

Equipment trust certificates have even been issued in reorganization. An interesting example due to the dividend yields is the issue of Chicago & North Western Railway Company Trustees' Equipment Trust Certificate, 2½% of 1939. The $1,800,000 offering made on November 24, 1939, was sold at yields ranging from 0.45% for the December 15, 1940, maturity to 2.85% for the December 15, 1949, paper. The funds raised paid approximately 76.2% of the equipment's cost.

During the twentieth century losses have been rare and delayed payments of dividends and principal only slightly less so. Detroit, Toledo and Ironton Railway Company defaulted in December 1907 or June 1908 on $40,000 of 4½% Equipment Notes. The face value less a small amount of expenses was eventually realized.[19] The Seaboard Airline Railroad and the Wabash Railway Company required holders of maturing equipment obligations to extend their maturities for a short period or to exchange them for Trustees' or Receivers' Certificates of lower coupon. There were a couple of other delays of principal and/or dividend payments but they were often limited to the grace period. Due to the strong position of the lien on equipment and loans by the Reconstruction Finance Corporation (RFC) to some railroads, losses were minimal during the Great Depression. This is especially noteworthy in view of the sharp drop in commodity prices and traffic which resulted in a decline in the value of much of the equipment.

One railroad that defaulted and caused investors a loss was Florida East Coast Railway Company. In most Wall Street literature on equipment financing, this case appears only as a historical footnote; however, it is interesting even though it is history and laws have changed. The railroad overextended during the boom times of the 1920s but reality caught up with it and so FEC entered bankruptcy on September 1, 1931. In 1932 the road experienced difficulty in meeting its equipment obligations. In 1936 the receivers disaffirmed the lease and the equipment was sold in a public sale. After a subsequent sale of the equipment in 1937 and further court battles, a judgment was finally paid in 1944. The final payment came in 1950, nearly twenty years after the initial bankruptcy filing. In sum, after all expenses and fees were paid, the net recovery by the equipment certificate holder was between 68 and 70% of the claim.[20]

---

[19] Dewing, *The Financial Policy of Corporations*, p. 216.
[20] Richard S. Wilson, *Corporate Senior Securities* (Chicago, IL: Probus Publishing Company, 1987), pp. 48-52.

Airline Equipment Debt

Airline equipment debt has some of the special status that is held by railroad equipment trust certificates. Of course, it is much more recent, having developed since the end of World War II. Many airlines have had to resort to secured equipment financing, especially since the early 1970s. Like railroad equipment obligations, certain equipment debt of certified airlines, under Section 1110 of the Bankruptcy Reform Act of 1978, is not subject to sections 362 and 363 of the Act, namely the automatic stay and the power of the court to prohibit the repossession of the equipment. The creditor must be a lessor, a conditional vendor, or hold a purchase money security interest with respect to the aircraft and related equipment. The secured equipment must be new, not used.[21] Of course, it gives the airline 60 days in which to decide to cancel the lease or debt and to return the equipment to the trustee. If the reorganization trustee decides to reaffirm the lease in order to continue using the equipment, it must perform or assume the debtor's obligations which become due or payable after that date, and cure all existing defaults other than those resulting solely from the financial condition, bankruptcy, insolvency or reorganization of the airline. Payments resume including those that were due during the delayed period. Thus, the creditor will get either the payments due according to the terms of the contract or the equipment.

The equipment is an important factor. If the airplanes are of recent vintage, well maintained, fuel efficient and relatively economical to operate, it is more likely that a company in distress and seeking to reorganize would assume the equipment lease. On the other hand, if the outlook for reorganization appears dim from the outset and the airplanes are older and less economical, the airline could very well disaffirm the lease. In this case, releasing the aircraft or selling it at rents and prices sufficient to continue the original payments and terms to the security holders might be difficult. Of course, the resale market for aircraft is on a plane-by-plane basis and highly subject to supply and demand factors. Multimillion-dol-

---

[21] Some secured issues are not affected by Section 1110 of Federal Bankruptcy Code and thus would be treated as any regular secured creditor. This includes issues secured by used aircraft, engines and parts. If the bankrupt airline could use the aircraft, it could continue as a debtor-in-possession and the trustee would be prohibited from exercising its right of repossession. The secured creditor must be given "adequate protection," but the term has not been explicitly defined. It is generally meant to protect the interest of the secured debtor in the collateral. This may be accomplished by cash payments or the granting of additional security. Peoples Express Airlines, Inc., in its offering circular and consent solicitation of October 8, 1986, explained why its secured equipment certificates would not likely qualify for treatment under Section 1110:

> In view of the fact that all of the aircraft were originally acquired by the Company with the proceeds of other financings, the Company believes that in the event of... seeking relief under the Federal Bankruptcy Code,...the...limitations on remedies available to the Trustee would not be affected by Section 1110...which allows for repossession of Aircraft in certain instances. Accordingly, the Company does not believe that the Trustees will have the legal ability to realize upon the Aircraft collateral promptly after the institution of a bankruptcy case. Any delay in the exercise of the Trustees' legal may adversely affect the collateral value of the Aircraft.

lar airplanes have a somewhat more limited market than do boxcars and hopper cars worth only $30,000.

Most of the publicly offered equipment loans in the 1970s financed approximately 70 to 75% of the cost of new aircraft and related parts. The 25 to 30% equity was invested mostly by outside financial institutions which could take advantage of the depreciation deduction and the investment tax credit. These issues generally had maturities of 15 to 16 years. Some of the equipment deals done in the 1980s had maturities out to 23 or so years. But in many cases the debt portion of the financing amounted to 50 to 60% of the equipment's cost, providing a greater equity cushion. The lease agreement required the airline pay a rental sufficient to cover the interest, amortization of principal, and a return to the equity participant. The airline was responsible for maintaining and operating the aircraft, as well as providing for adequate insurance. It must also keep the equipment registered and record the equipment trust certificate and lease under the Federal Aviation Act of 1958.

In the event of a loss or destruction of the equipment, the company may substitute similar equipment of equal value and in as good operating condition and repair and as airworthy as that which was lost or destroyed. It also has the option to redeem the outstanding certificates with the insurance proceeds. In 1975, a portion of the Trans World Airlines 10s of 1985 was redeemed due to the destruction of one of the Boeing 727-231 aircraft securing the loan. A problem could arise under Section 1110 in the case of a bankrupt airline with outstanding ETCs secured with substituted equipment. More recent ETC financings have stated that the owner trustee as lessor should be entitled to the benefits of Section 1110 with regard to the initially delivered aircraft and equipment. But the prospectuses go on to say that "it is doubtful whether, after an Event of Loss to an Aircraft or Engine or a voluntary substitution of an engine by Piedmont, any replacement aircraft or engine subjected to the lien of the applicable Equipment Trust Agreement would have the benefits of Section 1110."[22]

An important point to consider is the equity owner. If the airline runs into financial difficulty and fails to make the required payments, the owner may step in and make the rental payment in order to protect its investment. The carrier's failure to make a basic rental payment within the stipulated grace period is an act of default but is cured if the owner makes payment. The Piedmont Aviation prospectus says:

> In the event Piedmont fails to make any semi-annual basic rental payment when due under a lease, and as long as no unrelated event of acceleration under the related Equipment Trust Agreement shall have occurred and be continuing, within 15 days of the expiration of the grace period for rental payments the Owner Participant or the applicable Owner Trustee may furnish to the Equipment Trust

---

[22] Prospectus for $89,600,000 Piedmont Aviation, Inc. 1988 Equipment trust Certificates, Series D, E, F and G, dated September 23, 1988, p. 23.

Trustee... the amount of such rental payment, together with any interest thereon on account of the delayed payment thereof, in such event such Equipment Trust Trustee and the holders of outstanding Certificates of the Series to which such failure relates may not exercise any remedies otherwise available under such Equipment Trust Agreement or such Lease as the result of such failure to make such rental payment, unless such failure is the fourth consecutive or seventh cumulative failure to make such rental payments. The Owner Participant of the Owner Trustees may also cure any other default by Piedmont in the performance of its obligations under the leases that can be cured by the payment of money.[23]

Thus, a strong owner lends support to the financing, and a weak one little.

Airline equipment debt should be considered by many investors but it pays to investigate before investing. Do not be misled by the title of the issue just because the words secured or equipment trust appear. Investors should look at the collateral and its estimated value based on the studies of recognized appraisers compared with the amount of equipment debt outstanding. Is the equipment new or used? Do the creditors benefit from Section 1110 of the Bankruptcy Reform Act? As the equipment is a depreciable item and subject to wear, tear and obsolescence, a sinking fund starting within several years of the initial offering date should be provided if the debt is not issued in serial form. Of course, the ownership of the aircraft is important as mentioned above. Obviously, one must review the obligor's financials as the investor's first line of defense depends on the airline's ability to service the lease rental payments. Failure to do adequate research and digest what has been studied could lead to a costly and possibly unwise investment.

Many investors have probably wished that they had more closely read the prospectus of Peoples Express Airlines, Inc., 14⅜% Secured Equipment Certificates due April 15, 1996, and dated April 17, 1986. Full of certain risk factors, it shows the company's heavy leverage and recent lack of fixed charge coverage. It points out that the aircraft to be secured are used, ranging in age from 4.5 to 18.0 years, and with estimated useful lives from 12.0 to 20.5 years, as well as the possible impairment to the trustee's right to repossess the aircraft in the event of default. All in all, investors were buying a weak security. The truth was revealed all too quickly. Less than six months later — before the first interest payment was made the company informed its creditors that they had to make concessions in order for Texas Air Corporation to proceed with its acquisition of Peoples. Probably the most hurtful concession was that requesting the equipment certificate holders to exchange their old paper for new with interest rates 2¼ percentage points less. Thus, the 14⅜% owners would get new certificates with a 12⅛% interest rate. While buyers paid $1,000 per certificate on delivery on April 24, 1986, the worth

---

[23] Ibid., p. 29.

was only about $700 each on September 12, and a somewhat better $800 each on October 3. But, that 14⅜% coupon was certainly attractive in April!

A borrower can pledge any type of asset for a loan in order to obtain lower cost monies, if the security is satisfactory to the lender. In some cases, the lender's claim or access to the property is somewhat moot insofar as the debtor, even in bankruptcy, will continue to use the collateral under court supervision. A mortgage could be closed off and unsecured financing utilized, as with New York Telephone Company, Illinois Bell Telephone and some others. Expenses associated with issuing unsecured debt are usually less than those of secured obligations, and the mortgage may be considered an anachronism to many observers of the financial scene. But in other cases, a borrower may be unable to get any financing unless the security is adequate. Thus, it may be necessary for one to "hock the family ranch" in order to get the financing.

UNSECURED DEBT

We have discussed many of the features common to secured and unsecured debt. Take away the collateral and we have unsecured debt. In this connection, the two other Cs of credit — character and capacity — become increasingly important.

Unsecured debt, like secured debt, comes in several different layers or levels of claim against the corporation's assets. But in the case of unsecured debt, the nomenclature attached to the debt issues sounds less substantial. For example, "General and Refunding Mortgage Bonds" may sound more important than "Subordinated Debentures," even though both are basically second claims on the corporate body. In addition to the normal debentures and notes, there are junior issues; for example, General Motors Acceptance Corporation, in addition to senior unsecured debt, had public issues designated as senior subordinated and junior subordinated notes, representing the secondary and tertiary levels of the capital structure. The difference in a high-grade issuer may be considered insignificant as long as the issuer maintains its quality. But in cases of financial distress, the junior issues usually fare worse than the senior issues. Only in cases of very well-protected junior issues will investors come out whole — in which case, so would the holders of senior indebtedness. Thus, many investors are more than willing to take junior debt of high-grade companies; the minor additional risk, compared to that of the senior debt of lower-rated issuers, may well be worth the incremental income.

Looking at General Motors Acceptance Corporation's Senior Subordinated Notes, 14⅜% due April 1, 1991, we see that they "are subordinate in right of payment... to all indebtedness for borrowed money... now outstanding or hereafter incurred, which is not by its terms subordinate to other indebtedness of the Company." The Junior Subordinated Notes, 8⅛% of April 15, 1986, say that they are subordinate and junior, with the remaining wording similar to that of the senior subordinate debt. The junior debt subordination wording further implies that in the event of bankruptcy or insolvency proceedings, liquidation, reorganization or receivership, all principal, premium (if any) and interest on superior or senior and senior subordinated indebtedness will be paid in full before any payment is made on junior subordinated indebtedness. Many of these legal proceedings actually involve negotiation and compromise between the various classes of creditors. Even junior creditors can receive some consideration, although, under strict application of priority, they normally may be entitled to little or nothing.

Subordination of the debt instrument might not be apparent from the issue's name. This is often the case with bank and bank related securities. Chase Manhattan Bank (National Association) had some 8 ¾% Capital Notes due 1986. The term "Capital Notes" would not sound like a subordinated debt instrument to most inexperienced investors unfamiliar with the jargon of the debt world. Yet capital notes are junior securities. The subordination section of the issue's prospectus says, "The indebtedness... evidenced by the Notes... is to be subordinate and junior in right of payment to its obligations to depositors, its obligations under banker's acceptances and letters of credit and its obligations to any Federal Reserve Bank and (except as to any Long Term debt as defined ranking on a parity with or junior to the Notes) its obligations to its other creditors...." This issue was debt of the bank and thus had prior claim on the assets of the bank in case of receivership, conservatorship or the like, over and above the claim of the Bank's sole shareholder (and the creditors of that shareholder), the Chase Manhattan Corporation.

Credit Enhancements

Some debt issuers have other companies guarantee their loans. This is normally done when a subsidiary issues debt and the investors want the added protection of a third-party guarantee. The use of guarantees makes it easier and more convenient to finance special projects and affiliates although guarantees are extended to operating company debt. Examples of third party (but related) guarantees include US West Capital Funding, Inc. 8% Guaranteed Notes due October 15, 1996 (guaranteed by US West, Inc.). The principal purpose of Capital Funding is to provide financing to US West and its affiliates through the issuance of debt guaranteed by US West This guarantee reads: "US West will unconditionally guarantee the due and punctual payment of the principal, premium, if any, and interest on the Debt Securities when and as the same shall become due and payable, whether at maturity, upon redemption or otherwise. The guarantees will rank equally with all other unsecured and unsubordinated obligations of US West." Citicorp has guaranteed the payment of principal of interest on a subordinated basis for some of the debt issues of Citicorp Person-to-Person, Inc., a holding company providing management services to affiliates offering financial and similar services. PepsiCo, Inc. has guaranteed the debt of its financing affiliate, PepsiCo Capital Resources, Inc., and The Standard Oil Company (an Ohio Corporation) has unconditionally guaranteed the debt of Sohio Pipe Line Company. The Seagram Company Ltd., a Canadian corporation, has "unconditionally guarantee[d] the due and punctual payment of principal and interest on the [9.65% Debentures of Joseph E. Seagram & Sons,

Inc., an Indiana corporation], when and as the same shall become due and payable, whether at the maturity date, by declaration of acceleration or otherwise."

There are also other types of third party credit enhancements. Some captive finance subsidiaries of industrial companies enter into agreements requiring them to maintain fixed charge coverage at such a level so that the securities meet the eligibility standards for investment by insurance companies under New York State law. The required coverage levels are maintained by adjusting the prices at which the finance company buys its receivables from the parent company or through special payments from the parent company. These supplemental income maintenance agreements, while usually not part of indentures, are very important considerations for bond buyers.

Another type of support agreement is found in the BellSouth Capital Funding Corporation's 9¼% Notes due January 15, 1998. This support agreement between the company and its parent, BellSouth Corporation, stipulates that the parent (1) agrees to cause BellSouth Capital to maintain a positive tangible net worth in accordance with generally accepted accounting principles; (2) will provide the necessary funds to pay debt service if the subsidiary is unable to meet the obligations when due; and (3) shall own, directly or indirectly, all of the outstanding voting capital stock of the subsidiary throughout the life of the support agreement. In addition, in case of a default by the parent in meeting its obligations under the default agreement, or in the case of default by the subsidiary in the payment of principal and/or interest, the holders of the securities or the trustee may proceed directly against the parent. However, they do not have any recourse to or against the stock or assets of the parent's telephone subsidiaries.

Another credit enhancing feature is the letter of credit (LOC) issued by a bank. A LOC requires the bank to make payments to the trustee when requested so that monies will be available for the bond issuer to meet its interest and principal payments when due. Thus the credit of the bank under the LOC is substituted for that of the debt issuer. For example, in February 1988, Holiday Inns, Inc., a subsidiary of Holiday Corporation, issued $200 million each of 8⅝% Notes due 1993 and 9% Notes due 1995. The principal and interest on the notes are payable by drawings under an irrevocable, direct-pay letter of credit issued by The Sumitomo Bank, Limited, acting through its New York City branch. The notes also carry the guarantee of Holiday Corporation. These credit enhanced securities were rated Aaa by Moody's Investors Service while Holiday Inns unsecured senior debt is rated B1, hardly investment grade. The adjusted capitalization of Holiday Corporation at the time of the offering showed $250 million of short-term debt, $2,385 million of long-term debt, and a stockholders' deficit of $766 million. The LOC is not given out gratis. In addition to an initial fee for granting the LOC, Holiday Inns must pay an annual fee and a drawing fee for each payment made thereunder. Both Inns and the parent must reimburse the bank for all payments made under the LOC. These reimbursement obligations are secured by first mortgages/deeds of trust on certain hotel/casino properties and first priority interests in certain related properties in Nevada. Sumitomo was also named the trustee of the notes. Interest savings for the company were estimated at a substantial 200 basis points. In other words, the interest rates on the debt would have been around 10⅝% and 11%, respectively, and the total cost increased by $8 million annually or some $48 million over the life of the notes.

Insurance companies also lend their credit standing to corporate debt, both new issues and outstanding secondary market issues. Financial Security Assurance (FSA) has unconditionally and irrevocably guaranteed the scheduled payments on new issues such as Columbus Southern Power Company's 8⅝% First Mortgage Bonds due 1996 and County Savings Bank 10.15% Bonds due 1998. In the secondary market FSA has applied its *TAGSS* program (*Triple-A Guaranteed Secondary Securities*) to numerous blocks of bonds issued by Texas Utilities Electric, Commonwealth Edison and Georgia Power, among others. The ratings on these enhanced securities are Aaa/AAA, not the rating that would be on the securities if they were "stand alones." FSA usually requires that the issue to be insured must be investment grade on its own merits and also be collateralized so as to reduce the insurer's risk of loss. The investor in these issues gets a greater degree of safety through the higher rating and protection against the underlying issuer's credit deterioration. In addition, the issue's liquidity could be enhanced as more investment firms may be willing to make a market in the insured bonds. From the new issuers' perspective, the interest savings more than offset the cost of the insurance premium leading to a lower net interest cost. Certainly, utility rate regulators like to see companies under their supervision take steps to reduce their overall costs.

While a guarantee or other type of credit enhancement may add some measure of protection to a debtholder, caution should not be thrown to the wind. In effect, one's job may even become more complex as an analysis of both the issuer and the guarantor should be performed. In many cases, only the latter is needed if the issuer is merely a financing conduit without any operations of its own. However, if both concerns are operating companies, it may very well be necessary to analyze both, as the timely payment of principal and interest ultimately will depend on the stronger party. A downgrade of the enhancer's claims paying ability reduces the value of the bonds.

Negative Pledge Clause

One of the important protective provisions for unsecured debt holders is the negative pledge clause. This provision, found in most senior unsecured debt issues and a few subordinated issues, prohibits a company from creating or assuming any lien to secure a debt issue without equally securing the subject debt issue(s) (with certain exceptions). Designed to prevent other creditors from obtaining a senior position at the expense of existing creditors, "it is not intended to prevent other creditors from sharing in the position of debenture holders."[24] Again, it is not necessary to have such a clause unless the issuer runs into trouble. But like insurance, it is not needed until the time that no one wants arrives.

A book on international lending says that "the chief value of such a clause is that no future loan can be secured without at the same time securing equally or ratably

---

[24] *Commentaries*, p. 350.

all other loans which contain the negative pledge clause. It is obvious that such a clause does not prevent the borrower from contracting other obligations in the future." It also points out a stronger version of the clause specifying that if the issuer should pledge revenues as security for a new loan, the older loan would have priority as to the pledged security.[25] One negative pledge clause section reads as follows:

> The Company and its Restricted Subsidiaries will not create, incur, assume or suffer to exist any mortgage, pledge or other lien or encumbrance upon any Principal Property or any shares of capital stock or indebtedness of any Restricted Subsidiary, whether now owned or hereafter acquired, if after giving effect thereto the aggregate principal amount of indebtedness secured by any mortgage, pledge or other lien or encumbrance would be in excess of 5% of Consolidated Net Worth unless the Debentures will be secured equally and ratably with (or prior to) such other obligations, indebtedness or claims;... Exceptions include purchase money mortgages securing debt not exceeding the fair cost of the property, liens securing certain construction and improvement loans, liens in connection with government contracts, liens on the property of a restricted subsidiary at the time it became a restricted subsidiary, and certain liens in favor of an instrumentality of the United States, or any state or subdivision thereof to secure debt to finance the acquisition, construction or improvement of property.[26]

Another restrictive covenant has the following limitation on liens:

> FFC will not, and will not permit any Designated Subsidiary to, issue, assume, incur or guarantee any indebtedness for borrowed money... secured by a mortgage, pledge, lien security interest or other encumbrance upon any share of capital stock of any Designated Subsidiary unless the Securities... shall be secured equally and ratably with such Debt.[27]

---

[25] John T. Madden and Marcus Nadler, *Foreign Securities* (New York, NY: Ronald Press Company, 1929), pp. 162, 163.

[26] Prospectus for $150,000,000 Harris Corporation 10⅜% Debentures due 2018, dated November 29, 1988. The 5% allowance for secured debt used to be a standard indenture provision. However, with the weakening of indenture protection afforded bondholders over the last decade, this limitation has also been expanded in a number of cases. For example, Eastman Kodak Company's 9⅛% Notes due 2004, issued in October 1988, allows secured debt up to 10% of consolidated net tangible assets. Recent issues of The May Department Stores Company permits liens to amount to up to 15% of consolidated net tangible assets; it formerly had been a 5% limitation.

[27] Prospectus for $150,000,000 *Fireman's Fund Corporation* 9⅝% Debentures due 2016, dated October 16, 1986.

Negative pledge clauses are not just boiler plate material added to indentures and loan agreements to give lawyers extra work. They have provided additional security for debtholders when the prognosis for corporate survival was bleak. International Harvester Company and International Harvester Credit Company had negative pledge clauses that became operative when they secured sorely needed bank financing.

As we have seen, corporate debt securities come with an infinite variety of features yet we have just scratched the surface. We will look at many more in subsequent chapters. For now, the reader should realize that participation in the corporate bond ring involves careful analysis and study. Failure to do one's homework — whether one is a trader, an investor, an investment banker, or a salesman — may lead to disaster.[28] While prospectuses may provide most of the needed information, the indenture is the more important document. Read it and don't be afraid of its length and complexity.

---

[28] Ileen B. Malitz, *The Modern Role of Bond Covenants* (Charlottesville, Virginia: The Research Foundation of the Institute of Chartered Financial Analysts, 1994). The concluding paragraph of this recommended study of bond indentures of issues offered between 1960 and 1991 says:

> The lesson for creditors is to require protection or be willing to accept the consequences if debt value declines. Creditors cannot have it both ways. They must make a choice between high yield and decreased risk. Each potential creditor must decide which is more important and live with the decision.

CHAPTER 3

Maturity

The date stated in a bond's title may not always mean that the security will mature as specified. This chapter looks at the maturity characteristics of corporate debt, from retractable and extendible issues to bonds with puts; these features allow the holder to alter the stated maturity date. We will also look at the trend of maturities of new issues over the recent past.

WHAT IS MATURITY?

Webster's defines maturity as being full-grown, ripe, or fully developed; or a being perfect, complete or ready.[1] While these definitions might apply to some bond market participants, we are interested in the financial definition: the coming due of a security, i.e., the termination or the end of a period of a note, debenture, bond or other obligation. A debt issue's maturity is fully set forth in the indenture and is usually part of the issue's title. For example, we might refer to "May 10⅞s of '18" for The May Department Stores Company 10⅞% Debentures due September 1, 2018, or the "long bond" to mean the most recently issued and longest-maturing bond of the United States Treasury. Most people assume that the issue's principal will be paid on the maturity date and interest will cease to accrue after that date. But this is not really so; the maturity is the latest date at which the principal amount will be paid. In a majority of cases (at least those of investment-grade or higher-quality issues), the maturity date probably should be taken with a grain of salt. Often the issuer can retire or redeem an issue prior to maturity (i.e., prematurely). In other cases, the bondholder can get the principal back upon request before the stated maturity date due to special features in the bond contract.

---

[1] *Webster's New Universal Unabridged Dictionary*, 2d ed. (New York, NY: Dorset & Baber, 1983).

Obviously, when working with time spans we can use all sorts of mea-surements. The bond world usually is concerned with short-term, intermediate-term, and long-term bonds. Some use these descriptions without fully understanding what they mean; various bond market practitioners and the-oreticians might give different estimates of maturity. As a starting point, let us regard any debt obligation due within one year as the equivalent of cash items. Commercial paper is in this category, since its maturity cannot be more than 270 days from the date of issuance. Also included is any debt, regardless of its original time to maturity, that is scheduled to be retired within 12 months from the date of inquiry.

One of the authors informally surveyed analysts, traders, salesmen, and bond portfolio managers in order to get their viewpoints on the time span for the maturity of bonds due beyond one year. To this select group, short-term debt meant issues with maturities of from one to five years, though several said that two years was their outside limit and one tolerated issues due up to seven years. A majority said that intermediate-term corporate debt matures within five to ten years of issuance. Some held out for 12-year issues and one even included issues with maturities as long as 15 years. Long-term bonds, then, would be those with maturities longer than those of intermediate-term issues. Some would include a category between intermediate and long-term, but the market generally thinks in terms of only three maturity categories.

For our purposes, we will consider short-term corporate debt as that having maturities from one to five years. Intermediate-term debt is debt that matures in more than 5 years and goes out no more than 12 years. Finally, long-term debt matures in more than 12 years.

LONG-TERM DEBT

What is considered long-term today may have been relatively short-term in another generation. Over the years investors' perceptions of bond maturity have undergone substantial changes. If one asked if any long-term bonds have been issued recently, the reply would be yes; however, using the definitions of a half century ago, the answer may have been "no," with a few exceptions. Dewing's classic work says this about bond maturity:

> The length of their life varies greatly according to the credit
> market at the time of issue, the prejudices of investors, the type
> of security behind the bonds, and the character of the business
> in which the issuing corporation is engaged. A classification of
> periods is little more than approximate; yet such phrases as
> "short-term" and "long-term" have crept into the vocabulary of
> finance. Without holding too rigidly to the limits given, one
> may say that obligations which mature in less than five years

are the nature of notes, meaning by note merely a short-term bond in which the safeguards described in the indenture under which they are issued refer much more to the temporary credit of the corporation than to the ostensibly permanent character of its property. Bonds which run from five to fifteen may be conveniently designated as short-term, while those that run from fifteen to forty years may be called medium-term bonds. Those which will not mature for more than forty years should be called long-term bonds and belong to a special class because of the difficulty of projecting conceptions of property value into the distant future.[2]

Probably no corporate bond market participant today would agree with Dewing's maturity classification. There is no doubt that a bond with a maturity greater than forty years is in the long-term category, but most would take exception to Dewing's short-term and intermediate-term views.

Today's bond investors are little aware of a truly long-term bond. Yet such bonds do exist. In 1988, Swedish Export Credit Corporation issued $150 million 9⅛% debentures maturing in 2038, the first 50-year public issue sold in the U.S. market in an untold number of years. Many investment banking firms were reluctant to participate in the offering, feeling that the market would not be receptive to such a long maturity. But the managing underwriter, along with two others, went ahead with the offering which was reported 85% sold at the end of the first day of marketing. This should be viewed as a commendable performance considering the maturity.

There has been a smattering of other 50-year issues including $200 million Texaco Capital Inc. 7½% Guaranteed Debentures due 2043 and not callable for twenty years. Tennessee Valley Authority has come to the market with several 50-year bonds, the first in 1992. TVA's chief financial officer felt that its liabilities ought to be more closely matched with its 50 to 70 year assets. That year also presented a window of opportunity for a few issuers selling century bonds, issues with maturities of 100 years. The first of these was the $300 million The Walt Disney Company 7.55% Senior Debentures due July 15, 2093, callable starting in 2023. This was followed the next day with $150 million of noncallable The Coca-Cola Company 7⅜% Debentures due July 29, 2093. A couple of months later the New York branch of ABN AMRO Bank N.V. issued $150 million of noncallable 7⅛% subordinated deposit notes due October 15, 2093. These issues apparently filled investor appetites for super long-dated paper (at least for the time being) since interest rates rose shortly after the last issue was sold. The window slammed shut as shorter bonds with more conventional maturities took front stage.

---

[2] Arthur Stone Dewing, *The Financial Policy of Corporations* (New York, NY: The Ronald Press Company, 1941), p. 180.

U.S. investors can buy a perpetual issue of Canadian Pacific Limited, listed on the New York Stock Exchange. ("Perpetual" means that the debt can be outstanding indefinitely and thus has no maturity). The issue is called 4% Perpetual Consolidated Debenture Stock. Despite the word "stock" in the title, it is debt. *According to Moody's Transportation Manual*, the debenture stock is a perpetual obligation of the Company constituting "... a first charge on the whole of the undertaking, railways, works, rolling stock, plant, property and effects of the company." This issue is truly perpetual as it is cannot be called or redeemed by Canadian Pacific. As it has no maturity, there can be no yield-to-maturity; current yield (the 4% interest rate divided by the market price) is the appropriate yield measurement for this security.

In November 1986, Citicorp, the large bank holding and financial services company, sold a $500 million perpetual issue overseas. This was supposedly a first for a U.S. banking concern, although other foreign banks have sold similar undated debt securities. Citicorp views the perpetuals as equity for regulatory capital purposes but as debt for Internal Revenue Service purposes. The tax authorities have viewed debt without maturity as equity and thus have not allowed interest expense to be deducted for income tax purposes. But this particular issue can be redeemed at Citicorp's option starting in 1991, at the option of the holder in 2016, and annually thereafter. On redemption in 2016 or later, however, the holder will get in exchange not cash but securities, such as common stock, perpetual preferred stock or other marketable permanent capital. This optional redemption on the holder's part apparently caused the Internal Revenue Service to consider the issue as debt. In contrast to the Canadian Pacific perpetuals, the Citicorps are not thought of as truly infinite securities, since they can be redeemed by either party.

Is a perpetual security too long? Then what about the Green Bay and Western Railroad Company's Income Debentures? The Class "A" and Class "B" debentures are due only when the railroad is sold or reorganized!

In mid-1992 only $3,000 par amount of Series "A" debentures was outstanding out of an originally authorized $600,000. Class "B" debentures outstanding were $6,298,000 out of an authorized $7,000,000. While these interesting items are not perpetual issues, they come pretty close. For one thing, they are not callable. Also, the disposition of the income is quite unique. After operating expenses are paid, then 2½% of the par value may be paid on the Class "A" debentures and then 2½% on the common stock (based on $100 par value). The two securities then share, on a pro rata basis, up to an additional 2½% (5% in total). Any excess earnings may be declared and distributed to the holders of the Series "B" debentures with no limitation upon the directors' approval. This is a case of a debenture ranking behind common stock in the disposition of earnings and yet can receive a payment limited only by the prior year's earnings, whenever such a distribution is declared at the discretion of the Board of Directors. The right to distribution is not cumulative. But of course, management is elected by the common shareholders, and they have the final say.

Between 1904 and 1934, payments on the "A" debentures and stock were between 2½% and 5%; in 1935 they were 2½% on the debentures and 1% on the stock; in 1936 and 1937, both issues received a payment of 7½%; nothing was paid in 1938; and 5% was paid on both securities from 1939 to 1978. As the Class "B" income debenture payments come from what is left over and also must be declared by management, they have been relatively meager, ranging from zero in 1921, 1932 to 1936, 1938 and 1939, 1946 to 1948, 1950, 1953, 1955, and 1961 to 3% in 1965. *Moody's Transportation Manual* for 1988 says that payments in the 1970s were 2% for 1970 to 1972, ¼% for 1973, 1% for 1974, ¾% for 1975, and ½% for 1976.

In 1979, Green Bay and Western was sued by some Class "B" debenture holders. Among the allegations was that the Company and its directors wrongfully withheld distributions from the securities holders, and continued to withhold distributions through 1991 even though there were sufficient earnings from which payment could have been made. For example, GB&W earned $852,463 in 1989, $1,692,458 in 1990, and $786,360 in 1991. A settlement of the lawsuit was reached in 1987 but it was rejected by the court in early 1988, in part due to exorbitant legal fees charged by the plaintiffs' attorneys. As of June 30, 1992, the case was still pending. However, several months earlier, the Board of Directors of the railroad declared a distribution of $216,135 to its security holders payable on May 1, 1992, as follows: common stock, $90,025 ($5.00 per share); Class "A" debentures, $150 ($50 or 5% per debenture), and Class "B" debentures, $125,960 ($20 or 2% Per debenture).

The Class "A" debentures and the common stock share equally in liquidation on a pro rata basis up to their par value. Also, upon the sale of the railroad, 75% of the stockholders must agree to accept the par value ($100 per share) for their stock. Any remaining balance of liquidation proceeds go to the Class "B" debenture holders.[3] The capital structure has been described as the "English recapitalization" and "a railroad which cannot be placed in receivership or undergo financial difficulty as long as it can earn enough to pay its operating expenses."[4] Finally, the following poem (attributed to S.C. Barnett, a reporter from the Green Bay Press-Gazette) has been written about the Series "B" debentures:

---

[3] In addition to the description of the issues in *Moody's Transportation Manual*, see Ray Specht and Ellen Specht, *The Story of the Green Bay and Western*, Bulletin 115, October 1966, The Railway and Locomotive Historical Society.

[4] Ibid, p. 28.

THE SONG OF THE B'S
By Homer

I've classed among my foolish ventures
My purchase of Class B: debentures;
Those bonds which say in language deft,
"With all else paid, you get what's left,
(Unless the Board makes declaration
It's needed for depreciation!)"

But once in many years, I find
The gloomy cloud is silver-lined;
The long-dead-ghost perambulates,
The eagle sh--er defecates,
And there I see, upon my desk
A Winthrop letter, labeled "Esq."

I feel a kinship, quite complete,
With mighty figures of "The Street:"
The railroads' thundering symphony
Is earning dough for them — and me!
And midst its tones, like some great organ,
I'm one with Vanderbilt and Morgan

I've got my bonds, I'm glad I've held 'em,
But payments STILL are goddam seldom![5]

For investors who feel more confident with a definite maturity, financial history provides a few examples. Still outstanding and paying are the 4% First Mortgage Gold Bonds of the Toronto, Grey & Bruce Railway Company dated January 1, 1884, and maturing June 14, 2883. The bonds come only in coupon form in denominations of £100 sterling. The coupons (40 to a sheet and enough for 20 years) are payable in Montreal (in Canadian dollars, as payments in gold are restricted) or London (in sterling). According to *Moody's Transportation Manual*, the company's properties were leased to the Ontario & Quebec Railway Company for 999 years at an annual rental equal to interest on 4% first mortgage bonds. On January 1, 1884, the lease was transferred to the Canadian Pacific Railway Company, now Canadian Pacific Limited. The bonds are truly long-term as they are not callable for life. Canadian Pacific said that of the £719,000 outstanding, it owns £307,900.[6]

---

[5] Ibid, p. 29.

[6] Letter to one of the authors, March 24, 1981. These bonds are listed on the London Stock Exchange and are also quoted in Glasgow.

Of a somewhat shorter maturity (but at least of a U.S. company) are the Elmira and Williamsport Railroad Company's 5% Income Bonds due October 1, 2862. The bonds were guaranteed as to interest by the Northern Central Railway but were assumed by the Pennsylvania Railroad Company in 1914 for 999 years from 1863, and eventually became an obligation of the Penn Central Transportation Company. While not subject to call, the bonds were paid in full ($1,468 representing principal and accrued and unpaid interest) in late 1978 upon the reorganization of Penn Central.

Another relatively long bond also involved in the Penn Central reorganization is the West Shore Railroad Company's 4% First Mortgage Bonds due January 1, 2361. The noncallable bonds were issued in 1886, guaranteed by the New York Central and Harlem River Rail Road Company, and eventually assumed by Penn Central on February 1, 1968. The lien was on 306 miles of track from Weehawken, New Jersey to Buffalo, New York, a historic line dating back to early American railroading. Penn Central's reorganization plan provided that each $1,000 principal amount of West Shore 4s receive $140 in cash, $131 principal amount of Penn Central Corporation's 7% Series "A" General Mortgage Bonds due 1987, $265 principal amount of Series "B" Bonds due 1987, 19.8 shares of Series "B" Convertible Preference Stock, and 8.92 shares of common stock.

The Decline of the Long-Term Bond Market

Today one will find few truly long-term bonds such as the above. Certainly, an occasional issuer such as the Swedish Export Credit Corporation or Walt Disney may attempt an offering when the market's window of opportunity beckons. Even the aforementioned Citicorp perpetual can be called. In 1985 one major business publication said, "The long-term corporate bond is beginning to look like an endangered species.... The mainstay of the credit markets only ten years ago, fixed-rate issues with maturities of twenty years or more shrank... and shriveled.... The long-term fixed rate sector is now speculative and not a financing market...."[7] The decline was attributed to many factors, including the high inflation and soaring interest costs of the seventies which wrought havoc on the values of long-term debt instruments. Investors wanted instruments of shorter maturity and less volatility. For example, insurance companies changed emphasis from the traditional whole-life policy with its focus on the long-term investment of reserves and the buildup of cash values to the more short-term-oriented term life and other policies designed more for pure insurance purposes than for savings and investment.

Companies used to finance their long-term assets with long-term debt and short-term assets, such as receivables and inventories, with commercial paper and bank loans. If they borrowed long, they invested long; if they borrowed short, they invested short. In effect, corporate financial officers would try to match the maturity of their assets with their liabilities. If they borrowed short and invested long, they could face a crisis at maturity. They might not have the liquid assets available to pay

---

[7] Elizabeth Kaplan, "The Waning of the Long-Term Bond." *Dun's Business Month* (June 1985), pp. 40-42.

the loan when due, and refinancing might be very difficult due to adverse market conditions. A well-run and structured corporation with sound practices and financial policies will not face a crisis at maturity, as it will have managed its cash flow carefully and in accordance with solid principles.

One way to look at asset life is in terms of a company's depreciation policies. The lower the depreciation as a percentage of gross plant, the longer the assets' book lives. Most new-issue debt of the Bell Telephone system, both before and after the divestiture, typically has had 40-year maturities. Of course, depreciation measurements may not tell the whole story. If the plant has been under-depreciated due to obsolescence, the debt's maturity may exceed the asset's life. In the telephone industry, copper wire may last for 40 or more years — but with fiber optic cable available, will it continue to be used and useful? Is the copper wire today worth what it is carried at in the company's financials? Perhaps telephone debt should have shorter maturities more closely matching asset life in this age of rapid technological change.

If a company's long-term growth prospects are good, lenders may be more willing to lend to it on a longer-term basis. However, the decadent decade of the seventies with stagnation and low-to-no-growth attitudes of many public officials and big business leaders contributed to the shortening of investors' maturity preferences. Even if borrowers would be better served by longer-term loans, it is investor demand that must be satisfied if financing is to be obtained at relatively reasonable cost.

With our society's great emphasis on the short-term — ranging from debt financing to managing corporate income statements for quarterly results to youngsters with their newly minted degrees (but without a good foundation in the basics of business and ethics) wanting to become overnight millionaires — it is no wonder that government leaders and major businesses have failed to provide the inspiration needed for America's premier place in the world. The deficit is always going to be cured in the next few years. New laws will shortly lead to a better life (but will botch things up in the long run). The general attitude is "What are you doing for me right now? Let's get ours while we can." While people want action, what is needed is thought. Companies cannot adequately plan for the future if they must constantly be concerned with rolling over maturing debt. This short-term viewpoint does little to improve soundness of one's bond investment.

Recent Changes

The 1970s witnessed many changes in the maturity characteristics of corporate bonds. In many cases, the stated maturity was shortened to suit the investors' needs. In others, the effective maturity of the bond could be shortened or retracted by the investor or the issuer. Still others permitted the parties to lengthen or extend the maturity.

There are few truly extendible bonds in the marketplace, i.e., issues whose maturities may be extended at the issuer's option. Most investors would not buy bonds which give the issuer the sole right to lengthen the maturity unless they got something in return. The few bonds have been mostly issued by speculative grade companies such as Turner Broadcasting and Texas Air Corporation (now defunct). For example,

Texas Air's Senior Increasing Rate Extendible Notes provided for their maturity on each interest payment date commencing August 15, 1986, unless the company extended the maturity to the next interest payment date. Issued in February 1986 with an initial interest rate of 12.50%, the rate increased by 50 basis points per quarter during the first year (payments due on the 15th of May, August, November, 1986, and February 1987), and by 25 basis points per quarter starting May 15, 1987 with the final maturity no later than February 15, 1991.

The increase in the coupon rate is the extra consideration Texas Air paid for the right to extend maturity; the investor is getting something in return. However, since this can be pretty expensive money, Texas Air had the right to pay off the whole issue on any maturity date, extend the whole issue's maturity to the next interest payment date, or extend only part of the issue and redeem the balance of the bonds at the early maturity date. The minimum amount of bonds whose maturity may be extended is $25 million. The scheduled interest rate would be 14½% for the quarter starting February 15, 1987, rising to 15½% on February 15, 1988 and finally to 18¼% for the quarter starting November 15, 1990, and payable February 15, 1991. Turner Broadcasting has only extended the maturity on part of its increasing rate extendible notes, redeeming a large portion at the maturity dates in late 1986.
15½%

BONDS WITH PUTS

Most bonds with "extendible" (or "extendable") in their titles are considered mislabeled by some; they should be called retractable bonds, since the issuer has the right to shorten the maturity from that stated. This is, in effect, an exercise of the company's right to call the bonds. Many variable-rate issues grant the company the right to call the bonds at a number of dates prior to the final maturity. For example, The CIT Group Holdings, Inc. had an extendible note issue with a final maturity of March 28, 1996. The coupon was 7⅝% to March 28, 1990, at which date CIT elected to redeem the bonds (retraction of maturity) even though it could have set a new interest rate, interest period and redemption terms. This latter action is generally referred to as extending the maturity. But the terminology is not really all that important as what is retractable to one is extendible to the other.

This bond had another interesting feature, one that was not often used until the mid-seventies — a put. This provision gives the investor the option to either ask for repayment on a certain date(s) prior to the stated maturity or to hold the bond to either the next put date (if any) or maturity. In the case of the above CIT issue, the holder had the right to put the notes back to the issuer on March 28, 1990 (the date at which the new interest rate and terms would commence), or to hold them until the next put date when the opportunity for redemption occurs once again. This option is not a separate instrument but embedded in the bond contract itself. The valuation of embedded options is discussed in Section II.

In most cases, bond investors are at the issuer's mercy. They have loaned money for what they expect to be a certain number of years, but this period could very well be shortened if the issuer decides to call the bonds. A call or premature redemption often occurs when the situation is advantageous for the borrower and less attractive for the lender, namely in periods of lower interest rates when the lender would have to reinvest the proceeds at yields that more than likely would reduce the overall rate of return (or at least the promised rate of return at the time of the initial investment). Chapter 9 will discuss price compression of higher coupon bonds in a lower interest rate environment. In periods of high interest rates when bond prices are depressed, few issuers have any interest in retiring their debt. However, holders of optional maturity bonds or bonds with puts can turn the tables in their favor. If the coupon rate is below the going market rate, investors need not hold the debt until maturity or even sell it in the market place; they can turn it back to the issuer for repayment at the principal amount and reinvest the proceeds in a security having a current market interest rate. The issuer will usually cancel the repurchased bonds but some issues provide for a remarketing of the put bonds through an investment banker to other investors.

The right to put the bonds back to the issuer is an important option which the bondholder should not forget. Bondholders should be aware of the period during which the issuer or trustee must be notified. If the notification is not properly given, the holders will continue to own the bonds, which may be to their detriment. Besides a loss in value, they might be left owning a much less marketable security. Generally, the put option, once exercised, cannot be revoked. But there are some cases of floating rate notes providing that if the interest coupon is increased after bonds have been put but prior to the effective put date, the holder may revoke the put request and have the bonds returned. The lead time for notification varies from as few as four to fifteen days before the put date to as long as six to eight months.

The importance of heeding the put date cannot be overstressed. For example, in 1979 Beneficial Corporation sold $250 million of debentures with a coupon of 11½% to January 15, 1984, and 9% thereafter to maturity on January 15, 2005. The put notification period was from September 15 through October 14, 1983. The bonds were worth close to par at that time as they could be redeemed on January 15, 1984. However, for those who did not exercise the put the market price plunged; a few investors were left holding a now 9% note due in 21 years. The 9% notes traded at about 71 in late 1984, quite a penalty for negligence. Less than $6.5 million were outstanding.

Put Bonds with a Morbid Touch

Some put provisions have certain restrictions on the holder's right of redemption. For example, a few issues provide that not more than a certain amount of bonds will be repurchased from any holder at any one put date. In addition, there may be an aggregate limitation on the total amount of bonds which may be redeemed at any one time. CP National Corporation's 15¼% Debentures due 1997 provide for an annual put subject to not more than $25,000 principal amount from any debentureholder and not more than $500,000 principal amount in aggregate.

Some issues have a death redemption benefit; to enjoy this put you have to be deceased! The legal representative of a deceased holder or the surviving joint tenant may tender their bonds to the issuer for redemption. In some cases these puts have priority over the requests of living debtholders. In the case of The Cato Corporation 10½% Subordinated Debentures due 1996, the death benefit is only applicable to the initial beneficial owner of the debentures. The death benefit provisions are mostly found in smaller issues which have generally been underwritten by regional and local investment banking firms. It can provide an estate with a market for the bonds which might otherwise be difficult to sell.

Poison Puts

About 1986, in reaction to the increased merger and acquisition activity, some companies incorporated "poison puts" in their indentures. These were designed to thwart unfriendly takeovers by making the company proposed to be acquired unpalatable to the acquirer. All too often companies have been taken over or drastically restructured and debt substantially increased with the result that the bond ratings get lowered and bond prices decline. The common shareholder might come out all right but the bondholders do not. Bondholders consider this an unfair transfer of wealth from one class of investors to another.

Basically, poison put provisions may not deter a proposed acquisition but could make it more expensive. In addition, uncertainty is increased as the put payment is not made, in most cases, until 100 days after the change in control occurs. Thus, the management has no way of knowing exactly how many bonds will be tendered for redemption. Of course, if the board of directors approves the change in control, i.e., it is a "friendly" transaction (and most takeovers are friendly if the price is right), the poison put provisions do not become effective. The designated event of change in control generally means either that continuing directors no longer constitute a majority of the board of directors or that a person, including affiliates, becomes the beneficial owner, directly or indirectly, of stock with at least 20% of the voting rights. In a couple of cases (such as in ITT Corporation's 7⅞% Notes due 1993 and Kerr-McGee Corporation's 9¾% Debentures due 2016) a rating change is also part of the requirement to set the put in motion.

The prospectus for ICN Pharmaceuticals, Inc. Debenture offering commented on the Change-in-Control Put as follows:

> The Change-in-Control Put may deter certain mergers, tender offers or other present or future takeover attempts and may thereby adversely affect the market price of the Common Stock. Since a Change-in-Control Put may deter takeovers where the person attempting the takeover views itself as unable to finance the repur-

chase of the principal amount of Debentures which may be delivered to the Company for repurchase upon occurrence of such
Change-in-Control. To the extent that the Debentures are repurchased pursuant to the Change-in-Control Put, the Company will be
unable to utilize the financing provided by the sale of the Debentures. In addition, the ability of the Company to obtain additional
Senior Debt based on the existence of the Debentures may be similarly adversely affected.[8]

These poison puts lacked teeth and in 1988 investors got particularly upset at
the continuing activity in corporate restructurings. It was the leveraged buyout of RJR
Nabisco Inc. that was "the straw which broke the camel's back." The whole industrial
bond market was affected as bond buyers withdrew from the market and new issues
postponed. Trading of industrials in the secondary market nearly came to a standstill
as prospectuses and indentures were checked and rechecked for protective covenants.
Bond analysts sharpened their pencils and did event risk studies to try to identify
companies which appeared vulnerable for some type of restructuring. Investors
demanded better covenants in public issues and, in some cases, got them. New poison
put language was developed and incorporated in the new indentures. Essentially, if
both a designated event and a rating downgrade to below investment grade occur
within a certain period, the company is obligated to repurchase the bonds at par. It
does not matter if the takeover is friendly or hostile. One issue provided that if the
market value of the debentures was less than par due to the event and rating downgrade, it could elect to redeem all of the issue at par. If it failed to redeem the bonds, it
would have to reset the interest rate to such a level which would have resulted in the
bonds being worth par on the day after the downgrading date.[9]

MEDIUM-TERM NOTES

Medium-term notes (MTNs) are new-issue debt instruments offered continuously
over an extended period of time. An extension of commercial paper issuance, maturities normally range from 9 months to 15 years, although some may be as short as 6
months. In recent years an increasing number of programs have set the maximum
maturity at 30 years. From 1972 to 1982, the major captive automobile finance companies accounted for most of the issuance and offered their medium-term notes
directly to the public. But with the advent of shelf registrations by the Securities and
Exchange Commission and Rule 415 providing the issuer of public securities greater
flexibility than before, medium-term note programs took on a new life. Issuers made

---

[8] Prospectus for $100,000,000 ICN Pharmaceuticals, Inc. 12⅞% Sinking Fund Debentures due July 15,
1998, dated July 17, 1986.

[9] Moody's Investors Service issued two interesting special comments on the topic of event risk. These are
"Indenture Protection and Event Risk," November 18, 1988, and "Event Risk: Moody's Amplified Its
Views on Indenture Protection Issues," January 5, 1989.

plans with the major Wall Street investment banking firms to market their medium-term notes as agents of the issuer on a best efforts or a reasonable efforts basis.[10] In addition, in order to broaden the market for the securities, investment bankers make a secondary market in the MTNs of the issuers for which they act as agent. Providing increased liquidity and needed marketability, this gives investors another outlet for their MTN investments in case circumstances change since they would no longer be locked-in until maturity.

According to a March 1994 study by Leland E. Crab of the economic staff of the Board of Governors of the Federal Reserve System, total issuance of medium-term notes by all US corporations was slightly less than $5.5 billion in 1983 (virtually all by financial corporations.) In 1993, issuance was $85.7 billion of which 67.3% was sold by finance companies, banking firms, securities brokers, and other financial institutions. The remaining 32.7% was issued by utilities, manufacturing and other nonfinancial borrowers. In 1993, 205 corporations tapped the MTN market (68 financial and 137 nonfinancial), up from 12 in 1983 (10 financial and 2 nonfinancial). Since the end of 1989 outstandings grew from $76 billion of 217 issuers to an estimated $210.4 billion from 365 issuers. This latter amount includes of 47 finance companies with some $45.2 billion, followed by three auto finance companies with $33.3 billion, 104 manufacturing companies with $30.9 billion, 83 electric, gas and water utilities with $28.2 billion, seven securities brokers with $21.8 billion, and 32 banking firms with $19.6 billion. In the 1983 through 1993 period, a total of 435 different companies issued MTNs raising some $415.6 billion. Again, nonfinancial issues outnumbered financial issuers, 271 to 164. This is an investment grade market; only 1.1% of the $416 billion was rated Ba and lower. Aaa-rated paper was 5.0% of the total, Aa-MTNs was 21.5%, A-rated paper about 56.5%, and Baa issues 15.9%.

According to one observer, the growth of MTNs came at the expense of commercial banks and their term loans. The cost to the issuer is often less than term loans at many banks. "Many large corporate borrowers have as good or better credit ratings than all but a very few of the banks lending in this market. Moreover, for large borrowers the banks no longer have any special expertise in assessing the creditworthiness of potential borrowers. Much of the relevant information is public and readily available to any potential investor."[11] The cost to the issuer of MTNs is generally less than with a conventional note issue. Agents' commissions typically range from 0.125% to 0.75% of the principal amount, depending on the maturity of the note. Costs of conventionally underwritten debt issues can run higher.

An issuer with an active MTN program will post the rates for the maturity ranges it wishes to sell. Generally, the maturity ranges might be from nine months to one year, from one year to 18 months, from 18 months to two years, and then annually

---

[10] Some prospectuses of issues contain wording such as "The Notes are being offered on a continuing basis by the Company through [the agents] who have agreed to use their best efforts to solicit purchasers of the Notes." Others may have slightly different phraseology such as "Offers to purchase the Notes are being solicited (or on a reasonable best efforts basis) from time to time by the Agents on behalf of the Company." Is a best-efforts basis better than a reasonable (best) efforts basis?

[11] Ben Weberman. "Watching $40 Billion Walk Out the Door," *Forbes* (October 20, 1986), pp. 33-34.

out to the final maturity date. Depending on the issuer, the note may have a fixed rate or a variable rate. Fixed rate interest payments are typically on a semiannual basis with the same interest payment dates applicable to all of the notes of a particular series of an issuer. Of course, the final interest payment is made at maturity. Interest on floating rate and variable rate MTNs may have more frequent coupon payments. If the interest rate market is volatile, posted rates may change, sometimes more than once a day. The notes are priced at par which appeals to many investors; they don't have to be concerned about amortizing premiums and the accretion of discounts. Any change in new rates will not affect the rates on previously issued notes.

The purchaser may usually set the maturity as any business day within the offered maturity range, subject to the borrower's approval. This is a very important benefit of MTNs as it enables a lender to match maturities with its own specific requirements. As they are continuously offered, an investor can enter the market when his needs require and will usually find suitable investment opportunities. With underwritten issues, the available supply, both in the new issue and secondary markets, might not be satisfactory for the portfolio's needs. A particular series of medium-term notes may have many different maturities but all will be issued under the same indenture. The bulk of the notes sold have maturities of less than 5 years with the 2- to 3-year range the most preferred. The notes generally are noncallable for life, although some issuers have leeway to add redemption features to unsold notes.

The medium-term note market is primarily institutional with individual investors being of little import for a couple of reasons. For one, the majority of issues require a minimum purchase of $100,000. Also, commissions on MTNs are less than on many other competing investments and individual salesmen would more than likely steer their clients to investments which are more rewarding to their pocketbooks. Banks and bank trust departments are the biggest holders of MTNs, followed by thrift institutions, insurance companies and nonfinancial corporations. Commercial banks and thrifts have used medium-term notes as part of their arbitrage activities. They might borrow in Europe or get funds through term certificates of deposit and reinvest the monies in higher yielding MTNs with similar maturities, taking the spread between the two instruments. Of course, if they needed funds to meet increased loan demand, the MTN secondary market provides an outlet.

Not all medium-term notes are sold on an agency basis; some have been underwritten. C.I.T. Financial Corporation issued $200,000,000 of 8% Medium-Term Notes due March 1, 1989, at a discount price of 99.875% on February 27, 1986. A few weeks later through a different set of underwriters, it issued $100,000,000 of 7.75% notes due April 15, 1993. These notes are redeemable at the issuer's option on and after April 15, 1991. Equitable Life Leasing Corporation sold 12.62% Medium-Term Notes with a final maturity of November 1, 1988. This issue is interesting in that the Company makes level monthly payments representing interest and principal repayment. Equitable also issued serial medium-term notes with each series maturing every six months. Finally, United States Steel Corporation sold 9% Intermediate-Term Notes due in 1992.

Exhibit 1: Outstanding Issues Classified by Term to Maturity
1900 to 1944 ($ Million/% of Total)

Year	Total Outstanding	Over 1, to 5 Years	Over 5, to 15 years	Over 15, to 30 Years	Over 30, to 50 Years	Over 50 Years
1900	$5,882.7	$252.3	$775.0	$1,388.6	$2,149.5	$1,337.3
		4.29%	12.83%	23.62%	36.54%	22.73%
1916	$15,957.1	$1,116.8	$3,030.4	$4,949.8	$4,909.9	$1,950.2
		7.00%	18.99%	31.02%	30.77%	12.22%
1928	$25,352.0	$2,209.2	$6,110.9	$10,643.0	$3,853.6	$2,535.3
		8.71%	24.10%	41.98%	15.20%	10.01%
1936	$22,081.9	$1,376.3	$6,059.8	$8,941.1	$3,198.4	$2,506.3
		6.23%	27.44%	40.49%	14.48%	11.36%
1944	$19,687.0	$1,140.0	$5,092.3	$10,028.8	$1,538.5	$1,895.4
		5.79%	25.87%	50.90%	7.82%	9.63%

Note: Excludes issues due within one year and those for which information is
lacking. Data are for January 1.
Source: W. Braddock Hickman, *Statistical Measures of Corporate Bond Financing Since 1900*
(Princeton, NJ: Princeton University, 1960), Table 40.

MATURITY DISTRIBUTION
IN THE CORPORATE BOND MARKET

Over the years there have been a number of studies on the maturity distribution of the
bond market. Of major importance is the work of Hickman covering most of the first
half of this century.[12] Exhibit 1 is condensed from his study. Note that well over 50%
of the outstanding corporate debt at the turn of the century had maturities longer than
30 years. About $3.5 billion out of the total of $5.9 billion matured after 1930 with
nearly 23% due in more than 50 years. There were 96 issues amounting to $1,214.7
million due in 1975 and beyond but the bulk of these consisted of railroad debt. By
1916, debt maturing in more than 30 years amounted to 43% of the total outstanding.
In 1928, it was 25%, in 1936 about 26%, and in 1944 around 17%. (Hickman's study
does not go beyond 1944.) Much of this decline in the extreme long-term outstanding
has been more than likely due to the extinguishment of debt through bankruptcy and
reorganization.

From 1900 to 1943, the number of issues and par amount of super long-
term offerings (30 years and longer) declined. In the 1900 to 1907 period, Hickman
tabulated 1,692 new super long-term issues with a par value of $4,090.1 million.
The length of maturity of new offerings generally declined in importance over each
succeeding period (the exception being 1924 to 1931). In 1940 to 1943, only 6.35%
of the issues offered were 30 years or longer in maturity. This amounted to $674.7
million or a touch more than 11% of the total par amount offered. The five years in
the 1900 to 1943 period with the greatest volume of these super long-term issues
are shown in Exhibit 2. Exhibit 3 presents the par amount of offerings classified by
term to maturity.

---

[12] W. Braddock Hickman, *Statistical Measures of Corporate Bond Financing Since 1900* (Princeton, NJ:
Princeton University Press, 1960).

Exhibit 2: Top Volume Years for Super Long-Term Offerings
1900 to 1943 (Par Amount, $ Millions)

Over 30, to 50 Years		Over 50, to 75 Years		Over 75 Years	
1927	$1,111.5	1903	$173.9	1922	$219.8
1928	902.8	1939	158.1	1930	125.3
1901	854.4	1936	106.6	1900	107.8
1931	770.3	1924	105.1	1915	101.5
1930	767.2	1930	88.3	1902	100.3

Source: W. Braddock Hickman, *Statistical Measures of Corporate Bond Financing Since 1900*
(Princeton, NJ: Princeton University Press, 1960), Table 94.

Exhibit 3: Par Amount of Offerings
Classified by Term to Maturity
1900 to 1943 ($ Millions/% of total)

Period of Offerings	Total	Over 1, to 5 Years	Over 5, to 15 years	Over 15, to 30 Years	Over 30, to 50 Years	Over 50 Years
1900-1907	$8,592.5	$659.1	$726.9	$3,116.4	$3,270.2	$819.9
		7.67%	8.46%	36.27%	38.06%	9.54%
1908-1915	$9,249.1	$1,510.4	$918.0	$3,651.8	$2,536.7	$632.2
		16.33%	9.93%	39.48%	27.43%	6.83%
1916-1923	$12,138.0	$2,076.0	$3,594.6	$4,676.7	$1,263.1	$527.6
		17.10%	29.61%	38.53%	10.41%	4.53%
1924-1931	$20,764.7	$1,565.0	$4,059.0	$9,415.7	$4,873.6	$850.5
		7.53%	19.55%	45.35%	23.47%	4.10%
1932-1939	$13,533.0	$610.1	$3,793.3	$7,888.1	$840.9	$400.6
		4.51%	28.03%	58.29%	6.21%	2.96%
1940-1943	$6,115.5	$55.3	$1,600.4	$3,785.1	$494.9	$179.8
		0.91%	26.17%	61.89%	8.09%	2.94%
1900-1943	$70,392.8	$6,475.9	$14,693.1	$32,533.8	$13,279.4	$3,410.6
		9.20%	20.87%	46.22%	18.87%	4.48%

Source: W. Braddock Hickman, *Statistical Measures of Corporate Bond Financing Since 1900*
(Princeton, NJ: Princeton University Press, 1960), Table 94.

Exhibit 4: Average Maturity of Investment-grade Corporate Bonds (Years)

Year	Merrill Lynch Corporate Master Index	New Issues	Moody's Composite Corporate Bond Average (%)
1988	13.57	11.05	10.18
1987	14.27	12.54	9.91
1986	15.00	15.79	9.71
1985	15.08	12.86	12.05
1984	15.50	9.87	13.49
1983	15.83	15.37	12.78
1982	17.42	12.90	14.94
1981	17.55	15.70	15.06
1980	18.16	18.42	12.75
1979	18.23	22.01	10.12
1978	18.52	23.10	9.07
1977	18.72	22.83	8.43
1976	18.80	20.39	9.01
1975	19.07	17.99	9.57
1974	20.08	19.93	9.03

Maturity Composition of Today's Corporate Bond Market

One of the authors conducted a study of the maturity composition of the corporate bond market during the 1974 to 1988 period (see Exhibits 4, 5, and 6). Exhibit 4 illustrates the maturity decline in the outstanding and new-issue investment-grade corporate bond sectors. The Merrill Lynch Taxable Bond Index, Corporate Master, which includes all investment-grade corporate issues with $10 million or more outstanding, had an average maturity of 20.08 years at the end of 1974. This has steadily declined to under 19 years at the end of 1978, under 18 years at the end of 1981, less than 16 years at the end of 1983 and 14¼ years at year end 1987. The average maturity approximated 13 years and seven months at December 31, 1988. The average maturity of new issue investment grade corporate issues declined as interest rates rose into the double-digit area starting in 1979. The low point was reached in 1984 when maturity averaged only 9.87 years.

Exhibit 5 shows the breakdown of investment-grade new issue volume by maturity classification. Through 1980 long-term issues (maturities of 12 or more years) constituted over half of the volume. Short-term debt was insignificant with less than 10% of the volume for any year prior to 1982. In that year short-term offerings increased substantially, rising to 21.48% of the investment grade offerings. In 1984 long-term new issues were only 14.39% of all investment-grade corporates.

Exhibit 5: Percentage Distribution of Volume —
New Issue Investment-grade Corporate Offerings
by Maturity Classification

Year	Short-term 1-5 Years (%)	Intermediate-term >5 and <12 Years (%)	Long-term > 12 Years (%)
1988	39.67	37.34	22.99
1987	32.35	40.00	27.65
1986	22.65	34.51	42.84
1985	30.26	38.34	31.40
1984	42.74	42.87	14.39
1983	28.00	31.55	40.45
1982	21.48	45.80	32.72
1981	7.02	51.01	41.97
1980	8.98	38.90	52.12
1979	2.78	25.27	71.95
1978	8.75	23.71	67.54
1977	6.39	14.70	78.91
1976	7.34	26.36	66.40
1975	1.73	41.80	56.47
1974	5.64	28.18	66.18

Exhibit 6: Average Maturity of Corporate New Issues
by Industry Classification: All Rating Categories
(Selected Years)

Industry	1988	1987	1986	1985	1981	1978	1974
Telephone	16.00	23.60	27.54	29.35	26.50	37.24	31.87
Electric	18.55	19.14	21.91	23.60	16.87	25.49	20.39
Gas and Water	15.68	14.82	19.77	12.44	12.81	17.77	16.00
Industrials	11.70	14.26	15.56	14.25	17.79	19.79	19.87
Finance	7.52	7.32	8.26	6.41	11.55	16.82	10.48
Banks & Thrifts	6.58	8.34	7.57	8.21	6.38	15.87	17.87
Transportation	11.21	16.43	16.18	15.29	17.28	18.00	19.85
International	15.12	13.87	19.38	12.72	11.35	17.83	22.69

It should be noted that if an issue has a put exercisable at the option of the holder, the maturity is considered to be the first put date, not the nominal stated maturity. Also, medium-term note offerings under a best-efforts basis are not included in the figures.

Exhibit 6 indicates the average maturity for new-issue investment-grade offerings by industry classification. The industry with the longest maturity debt on average is telecommunications, although, as far as new issues are concerned, it lost that status in 1988. Bell System issuers have traditionally used relatively long-term bonds in their financing activities with maturities up to forty years. Electric utilities have also been among the issuers of long maturity debt in the 30 to 35 year range. But investor demand for shorter maturities affected even the utility industries. In 1981 the average new telephone and electric issue was of considerably shorter maturity than several years prior. Industrial companies, another traditional user of long-term funds, had to shorten the maturities of their new-issue offerings. The average maturity has come down from slightly under 20 years in 1974 to 11.79 years in 1988. The average maturity of bank and thrift issues has fallen by more than half from 17.87 years in 1974 to 6.58 years in 1988. Finance company issues have also experienced a sharp reduction in average maturity, especially since 1978. Was this new-issue trend because investors want shorter maturity issues due to the difficulties these financial institutions faced in the eighties? Were investors concerned about the quality of the loans held by these lenders? After all, consumer loans to residents of troubled areas, loans to overextended farmers, borrowings by third world nations which will never have the capacity nor the character to repay, and loans for corporate decapitalizations gave investors good reason to avoid the long end of the market. Shorter-dated issues provide investors with greater peace of mind due to their reduced volatility than do long issues, with all other things being equal. The effect of maturity on price volatility is explained in Section II.

Investors seeking refuge in a shorter maturity of a troubled issuer should not receive much comfort. The shorter maturity structure of corporate debt increases pressures on corporate financial managers. The more frequent refinancings needed to replace a heavier volume of maturing debt also adds to management's burden and to the pressures and distortions in the bond market. More of a corporation's cash flow may have to be directed away from potentially profitable investments, research and development activities to the repayment of obligations as they become due. We have often heard corporations and other borrowers say that while their assets exceed their liabilities, they are in a temporary cash bind because of maturing debt obligations.

CHAPTER 4

Interest Payments

A main factor affecting a bond's value is the nature of the coupon or interest payments. This chapter reviews the many variations of interest payments ranging from zero and nominal interest rates to those which fluctuate periodically based on an index or other measurement. The effect of interest payments on the price, yield and price volatility of a bond is covered in greater detail in Section II.

GENERAL CHARACTERISTICS

Investors lend money and in return they expect to receive some form of consideration, usually periodic payments in the form of interest, for the use of that money. The most common form of interest rate is one which is set for the life of the issue, the so-called straight or fixed coupon. Since the early seventies the floating rate or variable coupon bond has attracted increased investor demand. These bonds, where the interest rate fluctuates over the life of the issue, are more fully described below. Sometimes the debt instrument provides for no periodic payment of interest at all but a lump sum payment at maturity; thus the zero coupon issue. Bond market convention calls these payments coupons even though all bonds now sold in the United States are in registered form. Interest payment or interest rate would be the more accurate terminology. Coupon, of course, is a term carried over from years ago when bonds were sold with coupons attached representing the interest payments to be made over their lives. So when you hear a trader ask "What's the coupon on that bond?" take it to mean "What is the interest rate?"

Timing of Interest Payments

Most debt issues sold in the United States provide for the payment of interest twice a year at six month intervals. If the interest rate on a bond is 10%, then each $1,000 bond will have two payments of $50 each every year. In the case of medium-term

85

notes, interest is paid semiannually and at maturity if the maturity date does not coincide with the interest payment date; this is called a "short coupon." Another type of short coupon is found on some new issues where interest might accrue from the date the trade settles, that is, the date payment is made by the purchaser to the underwriter. For example, if a new issue is sold with a settlement date of September 15 but with interest payment dates of March 1 and September 1, the price of the bond may not include interest from September 1. In this case, the first interest payment on March 1 will represent interest on the use of the money for 5½ months, that is from September 15. If the offering terms call for the purchaser to pay the offering price plus accrued interest from September 1 until the settlement date of the transaction, then the first interest payment due on March 1 will be a full coupon payment of six months.

An example of a bond with a long first coupon is the $100 million issue of Mitchell Energy & Development Corp. 5.10% Senior Notes due February 15, 1997. The notes were offered at par on January 20, 1994, with interest accruing from the settlement date (also know as the "dated date") of January 27. Interest is payable each February 15 and August 15 starting with the August 15, 1994 payment. This first interest payment represents more than six and one-half months of interest earned from January 27 through August 15. Subsequent payments will represent only the six months earned between payment dates.

Thus, semiannual payments may be each January and July 1, or March and September 15. In many bond publications these would be abbreviated as J&J1 and M&S15. The first or the fifteenth of the month are the more common interest payment dates although there are a number of issues which pay at the end of the month or some other odd date. For example, John Deere Credit Company had several fixed-rate issues with interest payments due on April 30 and October 31, and others with interest payment dates on the first or fifteenth of the month. Illinois Bell Telephone has several debenture issues with interest payments dates such as J&D10, F&A18, and A&O22.

Bonds with only one interest payment a year (annual coupons) are the norm for issues in the overseas markets but they are seldom issued in the United States. However, this does not mean that they don't exist. Ford Motor Credit Company sold several issues in the public market which pay interest only once each year. For example, its annual adjustable rate notes due March 31, 1997, pay interest only on March 31; the normal semiannual payments would likely be March 31 and September 30. Upon emerging from reorganization in 1984, Wickes Companies, Inc. issued 12% Debentures due January 31, 1994. The interesting feature about this issue is that interest was paid annually on January 31, 1986, (accruing from February 1, 1985) and 1987 and then it changed to semiannual payments commencing July 31, 1987. Bond issues with more than two interest payments a year are also fairly scarce. There are a number of domestically issued floating rate notes with quarterly interest payments such as Chemical Banking Corporation due March 11, 1996, with payments due on March, June, September and December 10. Few straight or fixed coupon bonds pay other than semiannually. However, CP National Corporation 10.375% Debentures of 1991 and its 16.50% Debentures due 1996 pay interest on the last day of May, June, September and December.

Bonds with monthly interest dates are infrequently encountered. However, in August 1982 General Motors Acceptance Corporation sold $60 million of Notes due September 1, 1997. The issue was divided into two tranches or parts with the only difference the interest rate and the frequency of the interest payment. The 12.90% Notes totalled $54,350,000 and paid interest March 1 and September 1. The balance of $5,650,000 was 12.50% notes with interest payable on the first of each month starting October 1. The prospectus said, "The lower stated interest rate on the Notes with interest payable monthly... reflects in part the earlier and more frequent payment of interest on the Monthly Notes than on the Notes with interest payable semiannually...."

Are these two rates equivalent? The buyers of the 12.50% monthly notes receive $10.41667 per $1,000 each payment or a total of $125.00 a year. The 12.90% semiannual issue pays $64.50 every six months or $129.00 annually. Are the buyers of the monthly payment notes getting $4.00 less per note per year? The answer is yes, they are getting paid less. But also, the two yields are not equivalent. Compounding, a very important element to investment returns, will be illustrated in Chapter 9. But briefly, the concept of yield to maturity involves some basic assumptions such as the interest earned from an investment will be reinvested at a rate equal to the purchase yield of that investment. As a matter of fact, interest on interest for long-term bonds can account for a substantial portion of the total return from the investment. Of course, no one knows the exact reinvestment rates which will be obtained in the future. If the reinvestment rate averages more than the purchase yield, then the actual total return will be greater. If the actual reinvestment rate averages less than the purchase yield, the actual total return will be less than that initially expected. Thus, promised rates of return as expressed through yields to maturity may not be the realized rates of return.

Normally, interest payments (as well as principal payments) due on Sundays and holidays are paid on the next business day without additional interest for the extra period. Indentures might have a clause covering this in the covenant section or in the miscellaneous provisions article. Beneficial Corporation has the following provision:

Section 14.03. Payments Due on Sundays and Holidays.
In any case where the date of maturity of principal of or interest on any Securities or the date fixed for redemption of any Securities shall be a Sunday or legal holiday or a day on which banking institutions in the State of New York are authorized by law to close, then payment of interest or principal and premium, if any, may be made on the next succeeding business day with the same force and effect as if made on the date of maturity or the date fixed for redemption and no interest shall accrue for the period after such date.[1]

---

[1] Indenture dated as of June 15, 1983, between Beneficial Corporation and Bankers Trust Company, Trustee, Providing for the Issuance of Debt Securities.

Payment and Record Date

Since most corporate bonds are now in registered form, interest is paid to the holder by check on the interest payment date. The interest check is normally mailed on the business day preceding the interest payment date to the holder of record. The record date, usually fifteen days prior to the payment date, is the date the trustee prepares the list of bondholders entitled to the approaching interest payment. The interest for the General Motors Acceptance Corporation issues described above is payable to holders of record on the 15th of the month preceding the interest payment date. The record dates for the semiannual payments are February 15 and August 15. Interest payments for bonds in coupon or bearer form are collected in a fashion similar to the clearance of checks. The investor deposits the coupons with his bank for collection through the banking system from the issuer's bank or paying agent. The agent checks the coupons to see that they are in order and then will credit the depositor's bank or correspondent for eventual credit to his account.

There may be instances when corporations of shaky credit standing will not be able to make the interest payment on time. In such situations the regular interest record date is void and any purchaser of the bonds after that date may receive the interest when paid and if the new owner is a holder of record on the required date. When the company obtains the necessary funds, a new record date will be established for that interest payment. Let us assume that August 31 is the original record date and the interest payment date is September 15. Funds are not on hand and thus the interest payment is not made on September 15. Several weeks later monies become available allowing payment to be made. A new, special record date will be set for the late interest payment, generally no more than 15 nor less than 10 days prior to the new payment date. Holders of record on that new date, not the old date, will be entitled to the interest payment. Section 307 of the registered version of the Model Debenture Indenture makes provision for the payment of defaulted interest.

ACCRUED INTEREST

The purchase of a coupon bond usually requires the payment of an amount equal to the agreed-upon sales price (including commission, if any) plus the interest which has accrued from the last interest payment date to the settlement date of the transaction. If the bond is an income bond or in default — that is, not currently paying interest — then there is no accrued interest and none will be paid. The bond is said to "trade flat" when it does not trade with accrued interest. The seller is entitled to accrued interest only if the bond is in good standing. If one sells a bond that settles after the interest record date and before the interest payment date (i.e., the seller is still a holder of record) the purchaser will have paid the seller accrued interest up to the date of settlement. As the purchaser is entitled to the full interest payment on the payment date, the seller (or his broker/dealer) will attach a due bill to the bonds which assigns the rights for the upcoming interest payment to the purchaser. For sake of argument, let us assume that the accrued interest for the trade settling after the record date is $55 and that a full six months interest is $60. The purchaser has paid the record holder the proper amount accrued, namely $55. The seller's broker gives a due bill for the $60 interest payment to the purchaser so that he will be paid when the interest payment is received by the seller. Thus, the seller has received his $55 of interest and the buyer has the $5 he is owed for the rest of the interest ($60 due bill less the $55 accrued interest paid at purchase). If the corporation fails to make payment after the record date, the due bill becomes void and the new holder is entitled to received nothing from the seller. He now has the right to receive payment from the company.

Some speculative grade bond investors have found out a hard fact of life: They bought bonds and paid the accrued interest only to have the issuer fail to meet the next interest payment when due. The seller received payment including accrued interest at the time the transaction settled but if the new holder were to sell, the price would probably be lower and no accrued interest would be received. In addition, the investor now has no assurance that it will ever be paid in full because bankruptcy is more likely. This adds substantially to the monetary and psychic cost of a junk bond. It is difficult to admit that one has been duped, to acknowledge that one's timing was wrong. The issuer defaulted shortly after the investment was made and the new holder hasn't yet seen any return when one was expected. This was dramatically noted in mid-June 1989 when Integrated Resources announced that it would halt interest payments and seek an accommodation with its various lenders; it could no longer rollover its maturing commercial paper. Trading in the debt securities went from "with accrued interest" to "flat." One publicly traded senior subordinated note, the 13⅛s of 1995 with interest due each January and July 15, had just about five months of accrued interest when trading went to the flat status; this is equal to nearly $55 per $1,000 note.

A calendar year has 365 days (or 366 days in the case of a leap year) but for purposes of computing corporate bond interest a year consists of only 360 days. Each month in a corporate bond calendar is 30 days whether or not it is February, April, or August. A 12% corporate bond will pay $120 per year, equal to $10 per month. Interest will accrued in the amount of $0.33333 per day. The accrued interest on a 12% bond for 3 months is $30; for 3 months and 25 days, $38.33, and so forth. The corporate calendar is referred to as 30/360. Day count conventions will be explained in Chapter 9.

Interest Variations

Most corporate bonds are the "plain vanilla" type, just a semiannually paying issue with the same interest rate throughout its life. But starting in the seventies, new tools became available allowing financial engineers, the Doctors Frankenstein of finance, to devise increasingly complex new structures and features for investors and issuers.[2] Some of these variations or unconventional features are beneficial in that they allow firms to offset increased finance risks of one type or another; these received a warm response from various market participants and have lasted since they served the needs of both sides of the transaction. These include floating rate and variable rate securities and zero coupon bonds. Others that had little value were discarded. In some cases only one or two issues could be sold as they apparently did not fulfill the current needs of investors. In this category are such issues as money market notes, dual coupon debentures, and maximum reset notes and debentures. As long as there is interest rate, exchange rate and other financial volatility, as long as the world is a risky place, there will be continual development in financial instruments, whether we like it or not. We will look at a number of these creations by the modern day offspring of Mary Shelley.

Currencies

Most bonds sold in the United States are denominated in legal tender dollars, and the interest is paid in dollars. (We were inclined to say "good, old-fashioned" dollars until we remembered that dollars now represent little except good faith. They are not backed by specie and they do not constitute a promise to pay anything. Look at a dollar bill and just wonder what it really means!) This makes sense as the funds raised are mostly used to finance activities within this country. Monies required for financing of foreign subsidiaries and other nondomestic purposes can be raised overseas in international and local markets, and through banks and other lending institutions. Even dollars can be raised outside the borders of the United States in the Eurodollar market. Starting in the early 1980s some American companies sold issues in the United States denominated in foreign currencies and "faux-currencies," as both fixed coupon and floating rate issues. For example, in March 1985, Hercules Incorporated sold 10⅛% Bonds due March 15, 1992, for 50 million European Currency Units (ECU).[3] The purchasers could pay for the bonds in ECU or in U.S. dollars; if paid for in dollars, such payments would have to be converted into ECU through the agent of the underwriters.

---

[2] In its December 8, 1986 issue, *Barron's National Business and Financial Weekly* carried an interview with James Rogers, a private investor and professor of finance at the Columbia University Graduate School of Business. Rogers said, in part:

> But since no economy in the world is near as strong as the financial markets, all this money has been flowing into financial assets all over the world. Investment bankers are staying up late, trying to come up with and invent new financial instruments to soak up all this money that's sloshing around. I keep up a little bit with these things, even in my retirement, but there are financial instruments now that I have never heard of. Some of the things they have created in the Eurodollar market — I just don't know what's going on anymore. And I've got former students who are out there trading interest-rate swaps and mortgage-backed securities and foreign currency swaps, and they don't have a clue as to what they're doing. They don't have a clue on what the ultimate ramifications, or who the ultimate creditor is, or anything else about these things. All they know is it's trading and they're making a lot of money.
>
> In sum, many market participants have an insufficient understanding of the risks associated with their activities.

[3] The European Currency Unit (ECU) is a "faux-currency" as it is not money in circulation such as the pound sterling or the United States dollar. There is no central bank issuing ECU notes although financial institutions issue travelers' cheques and other financial instruments denominated in ECU, and it is increasingly recognized in international transactions. The ECU is a synthetic, composite, or basket currency, consisting of specific amounts of currencies from each of the member nations of the European Economic Community. One ECU was worth approximately U.S. $1.30 in March 1995.

The ECU bonds were issued in registered form to U.S. buyers; foreign buyers could get bonds in coupon form. Only bearer (coupon) bonds can be exchanged for registered bonds; registered bonds cannot be exchanged for the coupon form. One interesting point is that the registered bonds are not callable for life. But the coupon bonds can be called at the option of the company at any time in the event of certain changes in the United States tax laws which would cause the company to pay additional amounts in respect of bearer bonds. If called, the holder can avoid having his bonds redeemed by exchanging coupon for registered bonds. Principal and semiannual interest payments are in ECU but may be paid in dollars for registered bonds at the holder's option. The actual dollar amount to be received will depend on the exchange rate prevailing two business days preceding payment. If the ECU ceases to exist, the indenture provides that payment will be in the dollar equivalent of the ECU as determined by a major bank to be selected by the trustee. It would be based on the composition of the ECU on the last day that the ECU was used.

Bonds have also been issued in the United States in real foreign currencies such as the New Zealand dollar (NZ$), the Australian dollar (A$) and the Canadian dollar (C$), by such companies as Chrysler Financial Corporation, Citicorp, and Security Pacific Corporation. Generally, interest and principal payments will be converted into U.S. dollars unless the holders want to receive the foreign currency. The holders bear any costs in connection with the currency conversion, which are deducted from such payments. Semiannual interest payment dates are not the usual first or 15th of the month but odd days such as the third, nineteenth, or twenty-second. Holders of large amounts may receive their payments by wire transfer from the trustee instead of by check. The governing law for the issues is New York statutes. In the event of a legal action any judgment would likely be made in U.S. dollars but the prospectuses state that it is unclear as to whether or not the exchange rate between the foreign currency and the U.S. dollar would be taken into account.

Foreign currency issues can provide investors with another avenue for portfolio diversification, but they aren't without risk. As a matter of fact, another risk element is assumed in these bonds — currency or exchange risk — in addition to the usual credit or business risk and interest rate risk. With foreign exchange risk we do not know what the value of our interest payments will be after the payment is exchanged for U.S. dollars, nor, for that matter, do we know the U.S. dollar value of the principal of our investment at maturity, the sale date, or any date in between. True, this could apply to many investments, but the added element of currency risk just makes the problem increasingly more complicated. For this reason many individual investors might be better served by investing in these bonds through mutual funds and other intermediaries, rather than buying them directly. Large, knowledgeable professional investment managers have the staffs, resources and contacts necessary to follow and analyze international economic and political activity and the resulting effects on the currency markets. They can also engage in hedging transactions to reduce the exchange risk if they deem it necessary. But even the most sophisticated investment manager can misread, misinterpret, and make errors in judgment.

The high nominal interest rates on some of these issues should not disguise the currency risk. If the foreign currency depreciates, it will be converted into fewer U.S. dollars. If the foreign currency appreciates vis a vis the U.S. dollar, it will be converted into more dollars. For example the Australian dollar was worth U.S. $0.90 at the end of December 1983, dropped to U.S. $0.65 at the end of 1986, rose to U.S. $0.86 in December 1988, and was worth U.S. $0.78 at the end of 1994. Conversely, the United States greenback would have been able to purchase $1.11 of Australian dollars at the end of 1983, $1.54 at year-end 1986, $1.16 two years later, and $1.29 in December 1994. In early 1989 *Barron's noted that even skilled professionals can find the currency markets hazardous.*

Yields are up Down Under, but the Australian dollar is down. That combination adds up to hefty losses for American investors who have flocked to Aussie fixed-income investments in their global quest for the highest yields.

The Australian dollar plunged to 82.35 U.S. cents, from its 1989 high, touched Monday, of just over 89 cents. Most of the decline followed Thursday's report that the nation's current account deficit widened dramatically in January, to A$1.54 billion from $924 million in December. (Estimates called for an unchanged deficit in the current account which counts trade and service flows.)

For U.S. investors in Australian bonds, the double-whammy of a plunging currency and surging interest rates [Australian government bond yields rose 150 basis points since the beginning of the year] was devastating. For instance, *First Australian Prime Income Fund*, a closed-end fund that invests in Down Under debt, plummeted in heavy trading. It was the most active issue trading on the American Stock Exchange Friday, closing at 8¹³/₁₆ from 9⅜ last week, a 6% loss. That was more than double its 3% total return for January, which placed First Australia Prime Income seventh among closed-end bond funds last month, according to data from Lipper Analytical Services. Last week's losses also took a hefty chunk out of the robust returns of 28.50% in the 12 months ended January 31, when the A-dollar was rising while rates were falling.[4]

Dual Coupon Issues

With the exception of floating rate debt whose interest payment might vary as often as weekly due to changes in the underlying financial benchmark, most bonds have one interest rate for life. However, there are some issued with an interest payment which automatically changes after it has been outstanding for awhile. Beneficial Corporation's Debentures due 2005 had an 11½% interest rate to January 15, 1984, and 9% rate

---

thereafter. This is called a *stepped-down* interest rate. Others have increasing interest rates; these are known as *dual coupon* or *stepped-up* coupon issues. In September 1982, The Charter Company proposed to issue $100 million of Dual Coupon Subordinated Debentures due 2002. Preliminary pricing talk indicated that the interest rate for the first five years would be 7%, increasing to 9½% for the final 15 years. The bonds were to be priced at 50% of face value, raising $50 million before underwriting fees. Instead of this offering, Charter sold $60 million face amount of 14¾% Subordinated Debentures due 2002. It defaulted on its interest payments two years later. Another dual coupon issue resulted from the reorganization of Wickes Companies. It issued 20-year debentures due January 31, 2005, with interest accruing at a 7½% rate from February 1, 1985, until January 31, 1994, and at a 10% rate thereafter to maturity.

In February 1986, the herd instinct resurfaced once again in Wall Street as American Express Credit, Gannett Company, Hertz Corporation and Household Finance Corporation each sold a $100 million issue with stepped-up coupons, all within three weeks of each other. These noncallable issues had interest rates of 8.40% to 8.50% for the first five or six years, stepping-up in 1990 or 1991 to 9.30% to 9.55% to the maturity date. The bondholders had the right to put the notes back to the issuer on 30 to 60 days prior notice to the change in coupon.

A number of lower-rated companies have issued increasing rate or progressive rate notes in which the interest rate is raised by a fixed number of basis points periodically, usually 25 or 50 basis points each quarter. These issues have no ceiling or cap on the maximum interest rate which can ultimately be set (except, possibly, state usury laws) and so they can become pretty costly. This should encourage the debtor to redeem the notes at the earliest possible time, if at all possible.

Participating Bonds

A bond which can participate in the fortunes of an enterprise over and above the coupon rate is called a *participating bond*. We are not referring to convertible issues which may rise in price because the underlying common share price increases, but to those issues which share in the company's profits or participate in the appreciation of certain assets. Not too many have been issued. Of interest to students of American financial history is the Union Pacific Railroad Company/Oregon Short Line Railroad Company 4% Participating Gold Bonds due August 1, 1927, because of its involvement with the historic antitrust case of the Northern Securities Company, a railroad holding company. The bonds, dated August 1, 1902, were secured by common stock of the Northern Securities Company. Besides requiring an annual 4% interest payment beginning in 1903, the holders were to receive an additional amount equal to any dividends and interest in excess of 4% paid on the collateral, namely the common stock of Northern Securities. On March 14, 1904, the U.S. Supreme Court rendered a decision in the Northern Securities case under the Sherman Antitrust Act which prohibited the company from receiving dividends from railroad stock it owned. The decision also put "an end to the holding company as a legal instrumentality for the attainment of monopoly [powers]."[5]

---

[5] William Z. Ripley, *Trusts, Pools and Corporations* (Boston, MA: Ginn and Company, 1916), p. 491.

Therefore, Northern Securities could not pay dividends on its shares and the participating feature of the bonds was rendered meaningless. They were redeemed at 102.50 on February 1, 1905.

Another type of bond may participate in any appreciation of certain real estate. In 1982, The Koger Company, a real estate operating concern, sold $30 million of Real Estate Appreciation Notes due June 1, 2000. The notes had a fixed 9% rate to June 1, 1988, at which time the coupon was reset to 8%. The next reset was to be on June 1, 1994, when the rate would be the greater of 8% or the capitalization rate used by the independent appraisal company in appraising the company's properties. In addition, on these dates the principal amount of the notes may be increased by the amount of additional interest accrued to the preceding December 31 based on an increase in the appraisal of the company's properties. Fixed interest is payable on this increase in the principal amount. However, the final reset never occurred since the company defaulted in 1991. It reorganized in 1993 and issued common stock to the bondholders.

In 1982, Hovnanian Enterprises, Inc. issued 16⅞% Participating Senior Subordinated Debentures due May 15, 1994. The fixed rate is paid quarterly but on each May 15 an additional sum may be paid based on a percentage of the company's pre-tax net income, as defined. As long as Hovnanian Enterprises has earnings and the bonds are outstanding, an additional amount will be paid. Extra payments of 3% were made annually. The company repurchased the entire issue in May 1991. In the case of Northern Pacific's 15% Subordinated Participating Debentures due February 15, 1998, additional interest was payable if the adjusted earnings of the company exceed certain levels, but only up to an additional $60 per debenture. The additional amount may be paid in cash or additional debentures. Again, this became a moot point when the company defaulted in 1991.

Income Bonds

Much maligned, held in low esteem, and seldom encountered nowadays are income bonds, a hybrid security superior in the capitalization ranking to preferred equity but generally of a subordinated status as debt. Today, one would think that with all of the varieties of debt instruments being created, and the burgeoning market for speculative grade bonds, the positive features of income bonds would appeal to at least some issuers and investors. But as time marches on, the income bond recedes into the depths of financial memory. Most of the outstanding income bonds issued have been created as a result of financial reorganizations. Some observers feel that the stigma of financial failure attached to these obligations is the reason why they have been shunned by issuers and investors alike.

Income bonds came out of the railroad reorganizations of the 19th century. Interest payments were contingent, not fixed, and would only be paid if earned. But earnings can be juggled and "interest disbursements often depended on the judgment of the board of directors who were likely to reflect the interests of the stockholders who elected them rather than the income bondholders who were creditors of the corporation. As a result, the board might favor directing earnings towards enlarged expenditures for maintenance of property and equipment rather than toward income bond payments." [6] Because of this, a carefully worded definition of earnings, and a requirement that interest be paid if earned, are necessary protective features. Also, interest payments, if not earned and paid, should be cumulative without limitation.

Failure to pay interest (if unearned) on an income bond is not an act of default and would not, in and of itself, be a cause for bankruptcy. Failure to pay interest on other obligations or failure to meet other terms of the income debt agreement may be grounds for legal proceedings. It is this factor that is important to both parties to the contract; it lessens the financial burdens on a company in times of financial stress. By not being required to pay interest when it does not have earnings, the management of the company under temporary difficulty may be able to gain enough time to straighten things out for the benefit of the creditors and equity owners. It is this feature that makes income bonds similar to preferred stocks; failure to pay preferred stock dividends, whether or not earned, is not an act of default although it is an indication of financial problems. Dividends can be suspended at management's whim. While dividends are payable from after-tax net income, income bond interest, while contingent, is payable from pre-tax income and so the net cost to the issuer is reduced. But income bonds occupy a creditor position in case of bankruptcy while preferred shares are in an equity position.

There are only a score or so of income bonds in the public markets today. Most are railroad issues, a number of which are in arrears on their payments. About half have annual interest payments and the rest provide for semiannual or even quarterly payments. The bonds trade flat and have a record date for registered holders. Like preferred stocks, they will trade "ex-interest" a week prior to the record date. Some companies publish interest payment notices in the financial press prior to the interest payment date but one can often fail to notice these. A reliable source for income bond payments is a special section in the *Standard & Poor's Called Bond Record*.

Besides being issued as part of bankruptcy reorganizations, income bonds and debentures have been issued to replace preferred stock, for the refunding of higher interest rate income bonds and to raise capital for general corporate purposes. They have been issued with warrants with the income debenture usable in lieu of cash of the exercise price of the warrant. One major issuer of the 1960s and 1970s was Gamble-Skogmo, Incorporated, which first sold them through its own securities sales organization and then through an outside regional securities firm. The bonds were offered mostly on a best-efforts basis to thousands of investors in middle America.

Income bonds can be used in mergers and acquisitions instead of preferred stock and junior debt. They can have any type of feature as more conventional issues, such as being convertible or participating. They can be designed with features such as sinking funds and call provisions, and be of any priority and security. They

---

[6] Sidney M. Robbins, *An Objective Look at Income Bonds* (Boston, MA: Envision Press, 1974), pp. 6-7. Another interesting article endorsing the use of income bonds in corporate capital structures is Leo Barnes' "A Do-It-Yourself Way to Cut Taxes," *Business Week* (May 5, 1975), pp. 21-25.

can be designed with debt-like features so as to satisfy the Internal Revenue Service that they are debt instruments, not equity (or "debtquity" as some refer to junk bonds). Certainly, an income obligation of a creditworthy issuer should find a receptive market and be generally evaluated as any other senior security. The income obligation of a speculative grade issuer should be viewed as no worse than much of the other similar debt outstanding. While the certainty of interest payment is less than with conventional debt, at least the investor may received some cash flow from the investment; that is more than can be said for low grade zero coupon issues. But as with all securities, it is important for the investor to know the terms of the issue so that a proper bond analysis can be made.

Missouri Pacific Railroad Company (MoPac) has several issues of income bonds outstanding. Two issues are general income mortgage bonds and one is an income debenture. The income mortgage bonds are rated A3 by Moody's and the income debentures Baa1. All three issues are rated A by Standard & Poor's. These securities were issued in the 1956 reorganization of the company. The bonds are secured by a general mortgage on all properties and assets of the railroad, subject to the rights of the first mortgage. Interest has been paid on a timely basis to date. Interest is payable to the extent earned from available net income (as defined) up to the stated amount, and cumulative up to 13½% (three years of unpaid interest).[7] The Board of Directors, in its own discretion and subject to the limitation that the funds are not required for needed and desirable betterments, may, out of lawfully available monies, make payment of the accumulated and accrued interest on the bonds. But past due interest on the Series B bonds cannot be paid unless the unpaid interest on the Series A bonds has been paid or set aside for payment. The interest on the debentures is not cumulative but, again, may be paid at the discretion of the Board, whether or not earned, provided the senior issues have been taken care of.

Hudson & Manhattan Railroad Company issued an interesting income bond in 1913 called the "Five Per Cent. Adjustment Income Bonds due February 1, 1957," with interest payable April and October 1 and at maturity. Issued under a plan of readjustment of the company's debt, each $1,000 principal amount could also be paid in pounds sterling in London at the rate of £205/11s per $1,000 bond (a dual currency bond). Interest was noncumulative prior to January 1, 1920, but cumulative after that date. The company entered bankruptcy proceedings in December 1954, and emerged from reorganization January 1, 1962. The income bond holders received only 3½ shares of class "B" stock. In September 1962, the company was taken over by the Port of New York Authority in condemnation proceedings resulting in the eventual payment of $531.60 per class "B" share.

In October 1981, the trustee of The Curtis Publishing Company's 6% Income Debentures due 1986 notified the Company that it was in default since it had not made the interest payments due April 1 and October 1, 1981 (plus some earlier

---

[7] For a fairly complete definition of available net income and the disposition of income, see *Moody's Transportation Manual* (New York, NY: Moody's Investors Service, Inc.)

payments), even though it had net income for 1979, 1980 and 1981. In fact, the unpaid principal amount for the debentures at the end of 1981 amounted to $943,000 and the accrued interest to $870,000. The company claimed that because it had an accumulated deficit it could not pay interest on the debentures even if earned unless ordered to do so by the court. The company's counsel opined that it would violate Pennsylvania law to pay the interest as debt issued in exchange for stock (as in this case) was considered stock for purposes of the law and any interest payments would be considered as dividend payments. Also, dividends were prohibited as long as there was an accumulated deficit.

In 1983, Curtis reached an agreement with the trustee under which a standby letter of credit of a national bank was issued covering interest obligations on the debentures for 1980 through 1983. It agreed to build up cash reserves to pay the principal at maturity on October 1, 1986. The payments due during the disputed time, from the beginning of 1980 through April 1, 1983, were paid with interest on the past due amounts. It is interesting to note that while payments due from October 1, 1983 (coupon number 54), to the April 1, 1986, coupon were earned and available for payment, most holders, according to a company spokeswoman, did not send in their coupons for collection.

Original Issue Discount Bonds with Coupons

Original issue discount bonds (OIDs) are those that have been deliberately priced at less than par value because their interest rates at issuance are below current market levels. For tax purposes, the OID may be ignored if it is less than 0.25% of the par value times the number of years to maturity. If a five-year bond is originally offered at 98.75 or higher, no OID is deemed to exist. The cutoff point for a 10-year bond is 2½ points or 97½ and higher, 95 for a 20-year issue, and so on. In the case of many speculative grade issues, the interest coupons may appear to be fairly current, but if the issuer were to sell a bond priced at par, the interest rate would have to be even higher. In some cases, management's reluctance to have a high coupon on the books may be the reason for the issuance of a bond at an original issue discount. Also, the actual out-of-pocket cash interest expense outlay is less for a deep discount OID than for a bond with only a moderate discount or a full coupon.

While OIDs are not a phenomenon of the eighties, the deep discount issues took the market by storm in 1981 and 1982, especially in the investment grade area. Prior to this time most original issue discount bonds were issued by speculative grade companies. While some investment grade OIDs were issued on a private placement basis in 1980, the first public issue of this era was offered on March 10, 1981; $175 million par value of Martin Marietta Corporation's 7% Debentures due March 15, 2011, sold at 53.835 to yield 13.25% to maturity. This was quickly followed by a number of other issues of General Motors Acceptance Corporation, J.C. Penney Company and Transamerica Financial, among others. By the end of the year nearly $7 billion par value ($3.3 billion of proceeds) was issued. Most of these had interest rates in the 5½% to 7% range.[8] However, certain changes in the tax laws made issuance after May less attractive to many companies, and volume fell drastically. Since then, the majority (but not all) of original issue deep discount bonds have been issued by companies with debt quality ratings below investment-grade.

Original issue deep discount debt offered corporations a number of advantages. The interest cost was less than full coupon debt for several reasons; some have placed the savings over conventional fixed coupon debt at 50 to 100 basis points. Investors were willing to make this yield sacrifice because it enabled them to lock in the return on the discount portion of the investment, and reduce the reinvestment risk on the coupon portion in case interest rates declined. Most coupon OIDs were currently callable, but this provision was not too meaningful. Thus, these issues afforded considerable protection from premature redemption compared with current coupon issues for few companies would want to call a six or seven percent coupon bond at 100, especially when rates are higher than the coupon rate. In addition, the issuer could amortize the original issue discount for tax purposes on a ratable or pro rata basis over the life of the issue and utilize the compound interest or economic interest method for financial reporting purposes.

In the early years of the issue, the amount deducted or amortized for tax purposes exceeds that of the interest method. The company reduces its nearby tax burden and increases cash flow; the amortization of the discount, although called interest expense, is not a cash outlay. Cash flow is important to the issuer and it has the use of this additional money until the debt is repaid. The 1982 tax law change made the tax reporting and financial reporting methods the same for subsequent new issues of original issue discount debt, namely the economic or true interest basis. Under this method the amortization of the original issue discount steadily increases over the years by the rate at which the bond was issued. It reduces the cash flow benefit in the early years from original issue deep discount bonds but it does not eliminate it. The accretion of the discount is still a noncash charge to the income statement.

Some have said that because the interest imputed by the discount is taxable, it would discourage many potential buyers. This is true for investors who, unless in a low marginal tax bracket, must pay taxes on the accreted discount even though it is not cash interest. Individuals generally would be better off in tax-advantageous investments such as municipal bonds.[9] However, one must not overlook the fact that the main buyers of taxable corporate bonds are not taxable individuals for their own accounts but institutions with little or no tax liabilities such as pension funds, including individual retirement accounts, and other self-directed plans. These original discount issues provided those investors with a debt instrument well suited their needs.

---

[8] Ford Motor Credit Company issued $100 million of 1% Original Issue Discount Notes due August 15, 1990, at 63.52 to yield 10.571% to maturity. The current yield was 1.574%, not too substantial. General Motors Acceptance Corporation also issued 1% Notes due October 22, 1990, on April 27, 1987. The yield to maturity was 7.45% and the current yield 1.243%. Specially designed for large institutional investors, the minimum denomination was $5 million for the Ford Credits and $1 million for GMAC.

While the 1982 tax changes dampened the incentive of investment-grade companies to issue new deep discount bonds, there were several other reasons. In times of high interest rates, investors look for ways and instruments with which to lock in yields and their promised returns. Interest rates peaked in mid-1982, making subsequent OID investments somewhat less appealing to many investors. In a lower interest rate environment, compounding or interest on interest is less important than when yields are high. Investors may hesitate to invest in what seems like a relatively low-guaranteed rate of return if they think that rates will rise again and thus enable them to reinvest at higher yields. Also, the lower interest rates reduce cash flows for corporate issuers and the resulting tax advantages, making OIDs less attractive from their viewpoint.

ZERO-COUPON BONDS

The ultimate in original issue deep discount bonds is the bond with no coupon or periodic interest payment, called the *zero-coupon bond* or *zero* for short. This is really just the principal portion of an issue, similar to stripping away the coupons from a coupon bond. Remove the coupons and what is left? Only the principal portion due at some future maturity date. There is nothing special about a zero coupon bond. It has the advantages of the original issue discount bond but even more so, offering complete lack of reinvestment risk as there is nothing to reinvest. Call protection is even greater than with coupon OIDs, in most cases. Some are noncallable for life but most are currently callable at par. Others are similar to municipal zero coupon bonds as they are callable at a premium to the accreted value. While most are bullet issues, that is bonds with one maturity and no provision for periodic retirement as with a sinking fund, a few issuers have opted for serial maturities. For example, PepsiCo Capital Resources, Inc. sold $850 million of zeros due annually from April 1, 1988, to April 1, 2012.

It was only a matter of weeks after the first OID was issued for the zero coupon corporate OID to hit Wall Street. On April 22, 1981, J.C. Penney Company, Inc. offered $200 million principal amount zero coupon notes due May 1, 1989, at 33.247 ($332.47 per $1,000 bond) for a yield to maturity of 14.25%. (Six days earlier it had issued $200 million of 6% Debentures due in 2006 for a 14.85% yield.) The next issuer came to market two months later on June 24 when General Motors Acceptance Corporation issued $750 million principal amount of discount notes due July 1, 1991. The price was 25.245 for a 14.25% yield to maturity. In 1981

---

[9] There are only three zero coupon bonds, called deferred interest debentures, on which taxable holders pay no taxes on the accreted interest, although they could incur some capital gain tax liability. Issued in 1982 through recapitalizations under the tax code, the issues are Exxon Shipping Company's Guaranteed Deferred Interest Debenture due September 1, 2012, General Motors Acceptance Corporation Deferred Interest Debentures due December 1, 2012, and another issue due June 15, 2015. The debentures are callable at any time, in whole or in part, at the principal amount plus accrued interest computed on a straight-line basis.

$2.475 billion par value ($778 million of proceeds) of zeros were issued. In 1982 another $6.89 billion ($1,652 million of proceeds) came to market. Since then, new issue activity greatly diminished as it did for deep discount coupon OIDs.

While these issues were new to the corporate bond market, the concept of a zero coupon debt instrument is well-established with American investors. They have bought noninterest bearing Series "E" and Series "EE" United States savings and war bonds for years. Interest is paid in a lump sum along with the original purchase price at maturity.

Many term savings certificates and accounts can be viewed as just another form of a zero coupon bond. An investor buys the certificate or makes a deposit at a stated interest rate for a certain period of time. The interest is not paid out but allowed to be reinvested and compounded until maturity. Overseas they might call these "capitalization certificates" or bonds or deposits with capitalized interest. Late in the War of the Rebellion (also known as the War of Secession to our southern friends), the Federal government issued circulating legal tender compound interest Treasury notes in denominations of $10, $20, $50, $100, $500 and $1,000. The notes accrued interest at a rate of 6% compounded each six months (3% per period) and were repayable at the end of three years. The obverse of the note stated: "Three years after date the United States will pay the bearer... dollars with interest at the rate of six percent compounded semi-annually." The reverse side had the following: "By Act of Congress this note is a legal tender for... dollars but bears interest at six per cent compounded every six months though payable only at maturity as follows [here is found the accrued interest and the worth of the note at the end of six semi-annual periods]... This sum $... will be paid the holder for principal and interest at maturity of note three years from date." In April 1879, the Treasury issued refunding certificates in $10 denominations that accrued interest at a 4% annual rate for an indefinite period. But in 1907, Congress stopped the accrual of interest when it reached $11.30 for each $10 certificate.

In bankruptcy, the claim of an original issue discount bond, whether it has a coupon or no coupon, is not the principal amount of $1,000 but the accreted value up to the date of bankruptcy; this is the original offering amount plus accrued and unpaid interest. These bonds, especially zero coupon issues, have been sold at deep discounts and the liability of the issuer at maturity may be substantial. Thus, there is the accretion of the discount but this is not put away in a special fund for retirement purposes. There are no sinking funds on most of these issues. One hopes that corporate managements properly invest the proceeds and run the corporation for the benefit of all investors so that there will not be a cash crisis at maturity. The potentially large balloon repayment creates a cause for concern among investors. It is most important to invest in higher quality issues so as to reduce the risk of a potential problem. If one wants to speculate in lower rated bonds, then that investment should throw off some cash return.

Many investors have been confused by yields and returns of zero coupon bonds. There is no current return, as zero divided by the price is zero. Yet one of the authors has heard from many bond market participants that they bought a zero with a current return of 20% or 25%. That is impossible under conventional fixed income mathematics. Where these investors went wrong is to assume that the accretion of the original issue discount is a dollar return or yield and have divided that amount by the price of the security. This is a bookkeeping matter only, not cash in the pocket. A $500 investment that will grow to $1,000 in five years produces a gain of $500 or 100% of the original amount invested. Some might say that the return is 20% annually. This method of calculation is specious and out of step with accepted bond world conventions. Other investors have confused simple interest with compound interest, the generally accepted investment measurement. While the results may look good, they are incorrect and could lead to false conclusions.

An important point for the bond investor is whether the total cash flow or return from a zero will be greater or less than that from a coupon bond over the same time span. To make this determination one must estimate what could be earned on coupon reinvestment over the investment horizon. If the estimated return on the coupon bond is greater than that of the zero, then the coupon issue may be the preferred investment. In high interest rate markets, the zero with its automatic compounding, is probably the more attractive investment. In low interest rate environments, where the compounding effect is less and the probability of higher interest rates greater, the coupon bond might be the better. While forecasting is one of the more difficult tasks to do with any degree of accuracy, it is necessary for making intelligent investment decisions. As with all senior security investments, these forecasting decisions must be continually made and monitored as circumstances change. Generally, bond portfolios should not be static but changed as time and outlook dictates. Individual issues and sectors get overvalued and undervalued from time to time, and zero coupon securities are no exception.

Zero/coupon Deferred Interest and Payment-in-Kind Bonds (DIBs and PIKs)

A hybrid zero coupon bond is the deferred interest bond (DIB), also known as the zero/coupon bond (zero *slash* coupon). Issued through exchange offers, leveraged buyouts, recapitalizations or mergers, as well as being conventionally underwritten, these are generally (but not always) subordinated issues of lower rated industrial firms. They have been issued by companies such as Colt Holdings Inc., Container Corporation of America and Owens-Corning Fiberglas Corporation, and there was even the Deferred Interest Third Mortgage Bond of Public Service Company of New Hampshire. Most of the issues are structured so that they do not pay cash interest for the first five years. At the end of the deferred interest period cash interest accrues, generally between 13 and 18%, and paid semi-annually to maturity, unless the bonds are redeemed earlier. The deferred interest feature allows newly restructured, highly leveraged and other companies with less than satisfactory current cash flows to defer the payment of cash interest over the early life of the bond. Hopefully, when cash interest payments start, the company will be able to service the debt. If it has made excellent progress in restoring its financial health, it may be able to redeem or refinance the debt rather than have high interest outlays.

A variation of the deferred interest debenture is the pay-in-kind (PIK) debenture. With PIKs, cash interest payments are deferred at the issuer's option until some future date. Instead of just accreting the OID as with DIBs or zeros, the interest rate is paid out in smaller pieces of the same security, namely other pieces of the same paper. The option to pay cash or in-kind interest payments rests with the issuer, but in many cases the issuer has little choice as provisions of other debt instruments often prohibit cash interest payments until certain tests are satisfied. The holder just gets more pieces of paper, but these at least can be sold in the market without giving up one's original investment; DIBs and zeros do not have provisions for the resale of the interest portion of the instrument. Again, an investment in this type of bond, as it is issued by speculative grade companies, requires careful analysis of the issuer's cash flow prospects and ability to survive.

Harcourt Brace Jovanovich, Inc., issued $250 million of 14¾% Subordinated Pay-In-Kind Debentures due September 15, 2002, on September 18, 1987. The PIKs were issued in registered form only in minimum denominations of $1,000 and multiples thereof, with cash interest accruing from September 15, 1992, payable March 15, 1993, and each six months thereafter. HBJ has the option of paying any interest payment not exceeding $100 to any holder in cash. Additional PIKs issued in lieu of cash payments may be issued in any denomination. Thus, the holder would receive a 14¾% debenture (or the in-lieu cash payment) in the denomination of $73.75 every six months for each $1,000 face amount of PIK debenture. Each PIK payment would increase on every interest date as in compound interest, with the holder getting an increasing amount of paper (unless previously sold), since the base or principal amount is increasing every six months. The holders of these deferred interest securities, if they were deemed to have been issued with original issue discounts for tax purposes, would have to pay income taxes on the accretion of any OID. The tax treatment of PIKs appears to be rather complex.

Obviously, tax laws, regulations, and their interpretation change over time; investors should therefore consult with their tax consultants who are familiar with each individual's particular tax situation and type of instrument for appropriate advice.

Debt with Variable Coupons

Late in 1973 an innovation appeared in the U.S. bond market with the introduction of the floating rate note (FRN). Instead of a fixed coupon rate, the interest rate fluctuated at 1½% (150 basis points) over the prime lending rate, subject to the minimum rate of 8% and a maximum rate of 12%. Only two issues totalling $35 million were issued that year, but in 1974 activity picked up with 11 issues amounting to some $1.3 billion being sold. Ten of these had the coupon based on the secondary market yields for 3-month U.S. Treasury bills. For the next three years not one variable coupon issue came to the public market. In 1978 only one offering for

$200 million was made, followed by a jump to 18 issues for $2.7 in 1979. A few other benchmarks for rate determination purposes were tried. Underwriting volume slipped again until 1982, when it resurged, hitting a peak of more than $17 billion in 1985.

Investor demand was stimulated by increasingly volatile bond markets. Market participants wanted an instrument with an income stream that would rise when other interest rates increased, one that offered some protection against interest rate volatility. Issuers with floating rate assets could now have a counterbalance on the liability side of the balance sheet. Both parties could better match their assets and liabilities from an interest rate standpoint. Many of the issues also offered some principal protection against any sustained downturn in market prices through the use of puts. Cash managers have increasingly used floating rate notes as a high-quality substitute for other short-dated instruments in the core portion of their portfolios. One reason is the better yields on these securities. Another reason for their popularity is that transaction costs are reduced because of the less frequent rollover of maturing short-term paper.

The term "floating rate note" or "floaters" covers several different types of securities with one common feature: Interest will vary over the life of the instrument. The rate may be based on a financial benchmark such as the London Interbank Offered Rate (LIBOR) or the U. S. Treasury bill auction rate, or it can be determined at the issuer's discretion. Some have been based on nonfinancial benchmarks such as the price of gas, oil and copper, or the volume of stock trading on the New York Stock Exchange.[10] Floating rate debt usually has coupons based on a short-term money market rate or index that reset (change) more than once a year, such as weekly, monthly, quarterly or semi-annually. One of the earliest and largest issues based on the interest yield equivalent of the 3-month U.S. Treasury bill was Citicorp's Floating Rate Notes due June 1, 1989, issued in July 1974. Interest was reset and payable each June 1 and December 1; in addition, investors had the right to require the company to redeem the notes at par on those dates. Another is Wells Fargo & Company's Floating Rate Subordinated Capital Notes due August 1, 1996, resetting weekly at $\frac{1}{16}$ of 1% over the 3-month LIBOR rate and payable quarterly. This is an example of a "mismatched" floater, that is, the interest resets a number of times during the period based on the benchmark rate applicable to the whole period. The interest rate is based on 3-month LIBOR, not one-week LIBOR.

---

[10] An example of an interest-indexed issue is Presidio Oil Company's Senior Subordinated Gas Indexed Notes due February 15, 1999. The notes pay interest each February, May, August and November 15, subject to a minimum base rate of 13¼% and a maximum rate of 18%. Additional interest may be paid after August 15, 1989 if the 12-month moving average of the gas index price exceeds $1.75 per million British thermal units. The additional interest is 2.5 basis points for each $0.01 by which the gas index exceeds $1.75. These notes are somewhat like participating bonds in that the holder participates in the upward price movement of the company's main commodity. The Bloomberg service notes that the following additional payments were made in 1993 and 1994: August 15, 1993, 13.425%; November 15, 1993, 13.85%; February 15, 1994, 14.05%; May 15, 1994, 13.925%; August 15, 1994, 14.125%; and, November 15, 1994, 13.90%.

"Adjustable-" or "variable-rate" debt include those issues with coupons based mostly on a longer-term index and reset not more than annually. This category includes those issues based on the one-year and longer Treasury constant maturity rate as published by the Board of Governors of the Federal Reserve System.[11] Some issues may have such terms as the interest rate, the interest period and the redemption features determined by the issuer periodically during the note's life. In effect, the corporation has issued a series of short to intermediate-term securities, of which only the first has known provisions. All have puts available to the holder, for without them, the investor would be at the issuer's mercy.

Volume Comment

Exhibit 1 shows that more than 560 variable rate debt issues have been underwritten in the 1973-1991 period with a total par value of close to $98 billion. This excludes floating rate medium-term notes and certificates of deposit. Banks, bank holding companies and thrift institutions have issued the greatest amount of floaters, some $34 billion or 37% of the total. This shouldn't be surprising considering that these floating rate liabilities are a partial match for some of their floating rate assets. In second place with $30 billion (31%) are finance companies such as the captive automobile finance subsidiaries and stock brokerage firms. Industrial and transportation companies with $29 billion issued account for about 29% of the amount issued. Other issuers include sovereign nations, international financial institutions such as the International Bank for Reconstruction and Development, branches of foreign banks and utilities.

Exhibit 2 shows that the most popular benchmark or rate determination classification is the U.S. Treasury bill rate, either the auction of new issues or the secondary market. Close to $24 billion of this type has been issued through the end of 1991. In nearby second place, are those issues where the interest rate is based on the Treasury constant maturity and the somewhat similar category where the rate is determined by the issuer. In third place are LIBOR-based issues.

---

[11] The Federal Reserve Statistical Release H.15 (519), *Selected Interest Rates*, describes the Treasury constant maturity series as follows:

> Yields on Treasury securities at "constant maturity" are estimated from the Treasury's daily yield curve. This curve, which relates the yield on a security to its time to maturity, is based on the closing market bid yields on actively traded Treasury securities in the over-the-counter market. These market yields are calculated from composites of quotations reported by five leading U.S. Government securities dealers to the Federal Reserve Bank of New York. The constant yield values are read from the yield curve at fixed maturities, currently 1, 2, 3, 5, 7, 10, and 30 years. This method permits estimation of the yield for a 10-year maturity, for example, even if no outstanding security has exactly 10 years remaining to maturity.

Exhibit 1: Floating Rate Debt by Industry Type (1973-1991)

Year	Banks & Thrifts ($)	Number of Issues	Finance & Related ($)	Number of Issues	International ($)	Number of Issues	Industrial Transportation & Others ($)	Number of Issues	Utilities ($)	Number of Issues	Total $Million	Total Number of Issues	% of Total Amount Issued	% of Total Number of Issues
1991	2,650.0	10	1,050.0	6	-	-	2,248.7	10	-	-	5,948.7	26	6.10	4.63
1990	2,670.0	10	2,973.6	16	-	-	1,816.5	6	325.0	7	7,785.1	39	7.98	6.95
1989	2,205.0	8	4,125.0	14	-	-	4,757.4	29	250.0	1	11,337.4	52	11.62	9.27
1988	3,695.0	19	6,889.7	31	-	-	2,691.0	19	-	-	13,275.7	69	13.61	12.30
1987	1,825.0	15	1,031.6	5	-	-	1,516.0	9	125.0	1	4,497.6	30	4.61	5.35
1986	3,768.6	19	2,514.2	16	-	-	1,436.3	8	-	-	7,719.1	43	7.91	7.66
1985	3,934.8	38	4,425.0	31	553.5	4	7,630.6	22	575.0	5	17,118.9	100	17.55	17.83
1984	5,295.0	42	3,315.0	26	2,500.0	5	5,052.0	30	275.0	3	16,437.0	106	16.85	18.89
1983	3,710.0	20	1,025.0	9	100.0	1	300.0	4	100.0	1	5,235.0	35	5.37	6.24
1982	350.0	3	1,890.0	13	-	-	775.0	7	-	-	3,015.0	23	3.09	4.10
1981	250.0	1	25.0	1	-	-	85.0	1	-	-	360.0	3	0.37	0.53
1980	250.0	1	250.0	1	-	-	52.0	1	-	-	552.0	3	0.57	0.53
1979	2,041.5	14	250.0	2	-	-	400.0	2	-	-	2,691.5	18	2.76	3.21
1978	200.0	1	-	-	-	-	-	-	-	-	200.0	1	0.21	0.18
1977	-	-	-	-	-	-	-	-	-	-	0.0	0	0.00	0.00
1976	-	-	-	-	-	-	-	-	-	-	0.0	0	0.00	0.00
1975	-	-	-	-	-	-	-	-	-	-	0.0	0	0.00	0.00
1974	$1,160.0	8	10.0	1	-	-	157.5	2	-	-	1,327.5	11	1.36	1.96
1973	-	-	35.0	2	-	-	-	-	-	-	35.0	2	0.04	0.36
Total	$34,004.9	209	$29,809.1	174	$3,153.5	10	$28,918.0	150	$1,650.0	18	$97,535.5	561		
% of Total	34.86	37.25	30.56	31.02	3.23	1.78	29.65	26.74	1.69	3.21				

Source: *Floating and Variable Debt and Bonds with Optional Maturities*, Merrill Lynch Capital Markets, 1989 and *The Fitch Bond Book*, Fitch Investors Service, Inc., 1992.

Exhibit 2: : Floating Rate by Benchmark Type (1973-1991)

Year	Prime, Commercial Paper, Federal Funds, and Other Money Market Rates ($)	Number of Issues	LIBOR ($)	Number of Issues	Treasury Bills ($)	Number of Issues	Treasury Constant Maturity or Rate Determined by Issuer ($)	Number of Issues	Other including stepped-up coupons, miscellaneous indices and adjustments ($)	Number of Issues	Total ($)	Total Number of Issues
1991	1,400.0	6	-	-	2,925.0	15	-	-	1,623.7	5	5,948.7	26
1990	3,787.0	16	1,661.5	9	-	-	225.0	1	2,111.6	13	7,785.1	39
1989	3,890.0	12	3,271.9	16	500.0	2	225.0	3	3,450.5	19	11,337.4	52
1988	4,579.0	22	1,200.0	6	1,700.0	7	2,585.0	10	3,211.7	24	13,275.7	69
1987	1,025.0	11	825.0	5	-	-	1,395.0	6	1,252.6	8	4,497.6	30
1986	300.00	1	1,400.0	10	2,185.0	8	2,160.0	11	1,674.1	13	7,719.1	43
1985	290.0	4	8,237.4	42	2,803.5	19	5,476.0	30	312.0	5	17,118.9	100
1984	2,000.0	3	2,950.0	26	5,012.0	34	6,050.0	41	425.0	2	16,437.0	106
1983	100.0	1	400.0	2	3,585.0	23	1,150.0	9	-	-	5,235.0	35
1982	-	-	-	-	1,000.0	7	2,015	16	-	-	3,015.0	23
1981	-	-	-	-	-	-	335.0	2	25.0	1	360.0	3
1980	-	-	-	-	250.0	1	250.0	1	52.0	1	552.0	3
1979	-	-	-	-	2,441.5	17	250.0	1	-	-	2,691.5	18
1978	-	-	-	-	200.0	1	-	-	-	-	200.0	1
1977	-	-	-	-	-	-	-	-	-	-	0.0	0
1976	-	-	-	-	-	-	-	-	-	-	0.0	0
1975	-	-	-	-	-	-	-	-	-	-	0.0	0
1974	7.5	1	-	-	1,320.0	10	-	-	-	-	1,327.5	11
1973	35.0	2	-	-	-	-	-	-	-	-	35.0	2
Total	$17,413.5	79	$19,945.8	116	$23,922.0	144	$21,116.0	131	$14,138.2	91	$97,535.5	561
% of Total	17.85	14.08	20.45	20.68	24.53	25.67	22.67	23.35	14.50	16.22		

Source: *Floating and Variable Debt and Bonds with Optional Maturities*, Merrill Lynch Capital Markets, 1989 and *The Fitch Bond Book*, Fitch Investors Service, Inc., 1992.

Review of the Terms and Features

Because financial engineers have created debt instruments with a variety of terms, investors and other market participants should carefully review the prospectus and offering documents of issues in which they are interested, especially floaters.

Only a few of the issues have sinking funds requiring the periodic retirement of a portion of the bonds. Unlike conventional debt, many have call features permitting the company to redeem the bonds only on specific dates, often the date on which the holder may put the bond. Others have fairly standard call features and a fair number are not callable at all. The put feature varies, with some permitting the holder to require the company to redeem the bonds on any interest payment date. Others allow the put to be exercised only when the coupon is adjusted. In cases of extendible notes where the new terms, including the coupon and the interest period are reset only every few years, the put may be used only on those dates. Of course, the time required for prior notification to the issuer or its agent varies from as little as four days to as much as a couple of months. For example, Transamerica Commercial Finance Company's 8⅝% Extendible Notes due June 15, 1997, with interest reset dates of June 15, in 1991 and 1994, are redeemable by the company at par, and may be put by the holder, only on those interest reset dates. Fifteen days prior notice is required for the put to be exercised.

Most of the issues sold in the United States are payable in U. S. dollars. But there are also issues denominated in ECU, Australian dollars and New Zealand dollars. In most cases, the coupon is set at a certain premium to the base or benchmark rate. For those based on the Treasury constant maturity, it might be at a minimum percentage of the base rate (and may be set higher at the issuer's discretion). For example, Primerica Corporation's Extendible Notes August 1, 1996, were scheduled for an interest rate change on August 1, 1987. The coupon was 13.25%, but as interest rates were considerably lower, the corporation set the rate from August 1, 1987, through July 31, 1992, at 8.40%, about 105% of the five-year Treasury constant maturity of 8.00%. The minimum percentage under the indenture was 102.5%. Apparently this rate was not satisfactory to the holders and many notes were either put back to the company during the first two weeks of July or the holders threatened to do so. In any event, several days prior to the commencement of the new rate and interest period a notice appeared in the newspaper of record announcing that the company "... is exercising its option under the terms of the Extendible Notes due 1996 to establish an interest rate higher than the rate previously announced..." The rate was increased to 8.875%, equal to 110.9% of the Treasury constant maturity. The notice further stated, "Holders of the Notes who have previously elected repayment of their Notes may revoke such election (and thereby become entitled to receive the increased interest rate)...." by notice "... to the Company or the Trustee no later than 5:00 P.M., New York City time on the first business day following publication of this Notice."

In other cases the rate might be set at a certain number of basis points above or below the base rate, as the case may be. Many 3-month LIBOR-based issues have the rate set at LIBOR plus ⅛ or ¼ of 1% (12.5 or 25 basis points), while some 3-month Treasury bill-based issues are spread from 100 basis points to as much as 450 basis points over the base rate. The spread over the base rate tends to be high for relatively low yielding indices and lower for higher yielding ones, all other things being equal. In certain cases the spread may be a discount from the base rate. In general, the progression of the benchmark rates from the lowest spread to the highest starts with the prime rate, followed by LIBOR, federal funds, commercial paper, certificates of deposit to the 11th District cost of funds, and finally Treasury bills often having the widest spreads. The 11th District index is a weighted average of interest costs for thrift liabilities in the 11th district of the Federal Home Loan Bank System.

Some issues provide for a change in the spread from the base rate at certain intervals over the life of the floater. For instance, the coupon for Citicorp's floater due September 1,1998, was based on the interest yield equivalent of the market discount rate for 6-month Treasury bills plus 120 basis points from March 1, 1979 through August 31, 1983, and then 100 basis points over the base rate to August 31, 1988. It then declined to 75 basis points over, subject to 6½% minimum coupon. The issue was redeemed on September 1, 1993. *Step-down floaters* have the same characteristic of a lower spread as maturity approaches. Chemical Banking Corporation's two-year Step-Down Floating Rate Notes due July 18, 1990, have a 25 basis point premium to the 1-month commercial paper index for the first year, declining to a 20 basis point premium in the second year. Some issues are on an either or basis. One such example is Barclays-American Corporation Floating Rate Subordinated Notes due November 1, 1990. Interest is payable quarterly and calculated monthly at the higher of (i) the prime rate minus 125 basis points or (ii) the 30 day commercial paper rate plus 25 basis points. Other issues have their coupon rates determined through a Dutch auction procedure or remarketing process, with the applicable interest rate the one at which all sell orders and all buy orders are satisfied.

One usually expects that as interest rates rise, the coupon on the floater will increase, and as rates fall, the coupon will decrease. This makes sense to most people, but there are some issues that might even confuse many bond professionals. With yield curve notes the interest rate is reset and payable twice a year based on a certain percentage rate (depending on the issue) *minus* the 6-month LIBOR rate. For example, the General Motors Acceptance Corporation's Yield Curve Notes due April 15, 1993, are based on 15.25% minus 6-month LIBOR. If LIBOR is at 8%, the rate on the notes would be 7.25%. If LIBOR increases to 10%, the yield curve note drops to 5.25%, and if LIBOR falls to 6%, the yield curve note would have a rate of 9.25%. It appears that only those investors who are bullish on the direction of interest rates would care for these issues. Another type of issue for interest rate bulls are the maximum reset notes and debentures. The two issues (one of each) which came to market in late 1985 were not warmly received by investors according to some traders. The initial coupon rates were 10.625%. Interest is adjusted and payable semiannually, and if, at the interest determination date, 6-month LIBOR exceeds 10.50%, then the interest rate for the period will be reduced from 10.625% by the amount of the excess, with the minimum rate being zero percent. With LIBOR at 12%, the rate on these notes would decline to 9.125%. *At least if LIBOR exceeds 21⅛% the holder will not have to pay the issuer anything.*

Some of the issues have floors below which the interest rate can not go. A number of the LIBOR-based issues have minimum rates of 5.25%. Others have declining minimums such as the Citicorp's due September 1, 1998. The minimum rate is 7.50% through August 31, 1983, then 7.00% through August 31, 1988, and then 6.50% to maturity. Certain issues have ceilings or maximum rates, often because of state usury laws. Many issues state that the maximum rate is 25% due to New York State's usury law but holders of $2.5 million or more of an issue are exempt from this. Some issues of Texas bank holding companies had a 17% maximum rate. In 1974, Crocker National Corporation sold $40 million of floating rate notes due 1994 with a 10% maximum rate due to uncertainties with California law. For several years the coupon rate was below the ceiling but in 1979 interest rates shot up, restricting the interest to 10%. As the notes had a put feature, many investors put the bonds back to the company and reinvested the proceeds in more attractive instruments. Had there been no put option, those investors would have been out of pocket for a number of years. One should certainly relate the ceiling rate with the spread over the base rate: Is the spread satisfactory enough to compensate for the limit to the income stream in case rates rise, or is the ceiling too close to the base rate?

Several floating rate issues have both a floor and a ceiling, which together are called *collars*. Baltimore Gas & Electric Company issued a couple of floaters in 1985 with collars. Based on the 91-day Treasury bill auction rate (bond equivalent basis) the spreads are 110 basis points for one and 112.5 basis points for the other. The collars are 8% and 12%, and 7.90% and 11.90%, respectively. These appear to be relatively narrow bands within which the interest rate may vary but the lower ceiling is offset to some extent by the higher floor. Other issuers of collared floaters include California Federal Savings and Loan Association, Citicorp, and Student Loan Marketing Association.

The Market for Floaters

Individual investors found the first series of floating rate notes quite appealing. The two-year delay in the put feature was a small negative, but it was used to mollify the thrift interests which did not view these retail debt instruments kindly. They feared an outflow of deposits to these new securities. From the investor's viewpoint, they were, at worst, two-year instruments and then six-month instruments once the puts became effective. Price fluctuations were relatively narrow because of the put. When the second batch of floaters hit the market in 1979 they were also warmly received by investors. Many investors did not care that the new generation of floating rate paper did not have any puts. They thought that as long as the coupon rate was adjusted every six months the bonds would naturally stay around par. How mistaken they were! There was nothing to keep them at par when all around was changing. The spread was fixed at market levels which existed at the time bonds were initially priced by the investment bankers. They did not have puts and, as interest rate movements became increasingly more volatile later in the year, their prices sank. These new issues were just intermediate to longer-term securities with a coupon that happened to fluctuate. If the credit quality of the issuer deteriorated, prices would be reduced. Because of rapid movements in interest rates, the rates, when reset, were often below the market rates. Prices had to adjust for this gap between the floater rate and the market rate. The semiannual coupon change did not provide the needed support. In the January 1980 to June 1981 period, based on end-of-week prices on the New York Stock Exchange, Citicorp's June 1, 1989, floater with a put had a price range of only 96 to 103¼. In comparison, floaters without puts had wider price fluctuation. Manufacturers Hanover floating rate notes of May 1987 moved between 86¼ and 101½, while Chase Manhattan's due in 2009 had a low of 82 and a high of 100½.

In early 1980, as interest rates fell sharply, the floaters that were hurt the most in the preceding few months, moved rapidly from the low 80s and 90s to the par area. For example, the Chase Manhattan 2009s went from 86 to about 100 in 15 weeks. But retarding some prices were the investors who wanted to get even; they wanted to get rid of an investment that had not measured up to their initial unreal performance expectations. After the rally, prices took another tumble as rates once again rose. This history shows how important the put feature can be. Of course, it also helps if you know the risks and rewards of the specific instruments one happens to be investing in.

Many investors in the floating rate note market are financial institutions with floating rate liabilities of one sort or another. Other investors use floaters as substitutes for money market instruments, although those without put features are not perfect substitutes for short-dated instruments. Money market funds have been large buyers of floaters with puts within one year. They have been used as hedges against rising interest rate markets. If interest rates are thought to be on the increase, floaters with frequent resets should provide increasing income. Their defensive characteristics should lend them price stability. A mismatched floater might be suitable. Resetting weekly to increasingly higher levels with interest payable quarterly or semi-annually, the holder is not locked into one rate for three or six months. LIBOR has historically been at higher levels than Treasury bill rates and the relationship between the two should be analyzed prior to investing. If the spread between the two is relatively narrow, and one's interest rate outlook is cautious, then LIBOR-based floaters might be considered so as to take advantage of a possible widening of the spread relationship.

Investors looking for a decline in interest rates may prefer floaters with less frequent resets (such as extendible notes) and deferred resets (so as to maintain the higher coupon for as long as possible). Of course, large investors don't have to limit themselves to just what is available in the domestic market; the supply of floating rate paper in the foreign markets is considerable. The major investment firms with their worldwide trading capabilities, participate in these markets 24 hours a day.

CHAPTER 5

Debt Retirement

The main reason corporations retire their debt prior to maturity is because declining interest rates make it economical. The issuer may substitute new and lower cost debt for older issues with higher interest rates, or may redeem the debt through cash on hand built up through the retention of earnings, the sale of assets, or the proceeds from new equity issues, among others. The lower debt expense may lead to improved earnings and cash flow. Other reasons include the desire by the issuer to eliminate restrictive or onerous covenants from its indenture and to improve or change the corporation's capital structure, so as to increase its financial and managerial flexibility. Describing the various call features found in corporate bond indentures, this chapter is important for anyone who wants to value the embedded options found in callable bonds. The techniques for doing so are explained in Section II.

THE IMPORTANCE OF KNOWING
A BOND ISSUE'S REDEMPTION TERMS

Without knowledge of financial history, many bond market participants are thus unprepared when events occur in the market that are similar to past events. This is especially true when interest rates decline, particularly from lofty levels. Being unfamiliar with the financial past, traders and investors do not understand what may happen under present or future conditions. Portfolios and trading positions have been structured based on considerations that may have been appropriate at one time, but may now be inadequate under changed conditions and outlook. In many cases, investors' eagerness for increased yield makes their bond holdings vulnerable to premature retirement. This, coupled with an unfamiliarity with the issue's terms, makes bond investment riskier than it ought to be. Investors should read the prospectuses and indentures of the issues they own, especially for the higher-coupon bonds. Redemption provisions vary from issue to issue, even among those of the same company and under the same general indenture. How often do you hear someone say, "I don't have time to read a pro-

111

spectus"? This is not an adequate response and market participants must take the time to diligently study their holdings' provisions in order to be able to take proper action at the appropriate time.

The importance of knowing the terms of bond issues, especially those relating to redemption, cannot be overstressed. Yet there have appeared numerous instances of investors, professional and others, who acknowledge that they don't read the documentation. For example, the following statements were attributed to some stockbrokers: "But brokers in the field say they often don't spend much time reading these [official] statements," "I can be honest and say I never look at the prospectus.... Generally, you don't have time to do that", and "There are some clients who really don't know what they buy.... They just say, 'That's a good interest rate.'"[1] The following are from legal decisions involving debt redemptions:

> Although she received prospectuses for her investment, plaintiff... never read any FPL [Florida Power & Light Company] prospectus or other description of the 10⅛ bonds before she purchased the 10⅛ bond...

> ... did not possess or read any FPL prospectus describing the 10⅛ bonds before he purchased the... bonds... in the after market.

> ... did not read or rely on prospectuses when buying bonds in the after market....

As the Fifth Circuit Court also pointed out in *Alabama Power*:

> ... it is reasonable (for the issuer) to assume that investors who (purchase) their bonds would familiarize themselves with the conditions under which they were issued, and particularly the terms of redemption, by reading the few short paragraphs on the face of the bonds.

> The plaintiffs offered little, if any, evidence of their own due diligence in making their investment decisions, which respectively involved a reckless disregard for, or deliberate inattention to, the contents of the FPL prospectus, which none of them read or consulted, as well as an apparent and knowledgeable willingness to 'gamble' on the part of the more sophisticated investor,...[2]

> We note initially that bondholders are charged with knowledge of the contents of the trust indenture where the bond certificate refers to the terms of the indenture.[3]

---

[1] "The Lessons of a Bond Failure," *The New York Times* (August 14, 1983).

[2] Samuel Lucas, et. al., Plaintiffs, v. Florida Power & Light Company, Defendant. Final Judgment, 77-4009-Civ-SMA, United States District Court, Southern District of Florida, October 31, 1983.

A professional analysts' journal stated:

> To infer that all money managers and other analysts do not read prospectuses is a quantum and incorrect leap, yet uneasy feelings exist about the number that do. Why read a prospectus, 10K or any other fully disclosed information? Is someone out there saying something and analysts not listening? One would surmise that, if prospectuses contained value, they would be read. Is there a delusionary safe harbor in believing too strongly that all known information is reflected in market prices and well diversified portfolios insure against all but market risks?[4]

Retirement of debt before the stated maturity is not a new phenomenon. James Grant said, "At the turn of the century the risk to bondholders was default... or the early redemption of sound securities...."[5] It occurs periodically whenever interest rates decline. Hickman stated:

> During periods of rising interest rates few issues are called, many are paid off at maturity, and though realized yields may rise with money rates, call premiums may be insufficient to offset default losses, and substantial capital losses may result. In periods of falling money rates the reverse appears to be true: few issues are paid off at maturity, many are called, and even though default losses may be substantial, call premiums may be more than sufficient to offset them, and capital gains may occur.[6]

Recent periods of major debt redemption activity include 1963, 1975 through 1978, 1984 to 1987, and 1991 through 1993. Times of generally declining interest rates, they provided ample opportunity for corporations to rid themselves of high-coupon debt. Indeed, with interest rates dropping to the lowest level in decades, investment-grade bond calls were more than $84 billion in the first ten months of 1993.[7] Bond calls are common, and yet they have caused the unwary investor much consternation over the years. Investors have suffered un-

---

[3] Judgment, Harold Harris, Continental Casualty Company and National Fire Insurance Company of Hartford, etc. Plaintiffs-Respondents, v. Union Electric Company, Defendant-Appellant, St. Louis Union Trust, et al., Defendant-Cross Appellant. Missouri Court of Appeals, Eastern District, June 16, 1981.

[4] Charles A. D'Ambrosio, "When's the Last Time You Read a Prospectus?" *Financial Analysts Journal* (September-October 1983), p. 10.

[5] James Grant, *Bernard M. Baruch, The Adventures of a Wall Street Legend* (New York, NY: Simon and Schuster, 1983), p. 55.

[6] W. Braddock Hickman, *Corporate Bond Quality and Investor Experience* (Princeton, NJ: Princeton University Press, 1958), p. 87.

warranted losses of principal that might have been avoided had they heeded one warning: Know the terms of the bond contract. Remember that investors are parties to the bond contract even though they may have purchased the issue in the secondary market long after the bonds were first publicly offered. The subsequent buyer is as much a party to the bond contract as is the initial purchaser; he succeeds to the contract.

It is common knowledge that bond market participants are unaware of indenture provisions, especially those relating to redemption and the options given to the issuer. Bondholders often have mistaken ideas as to what a corporation may do when it comes to debt retirement. It should always be kept in mind that corporate managements generally do not have bondholders' interests at heart; they are elected by, and beholden to, the owners of the business, namely the common shareholders. Their duty is to increase shareholder wealth, not that of bondholders. They do not owe any fiduciary duty to bondholders, their only responsibility is contractual.

WHY THE CONCERN ABOUT PREMATURE REDEMPTION?

Some might ask, "Why is there all the concern about premature bond redemption?" After all, we get our money back and can reinvest it. But *that* is the concern: In most cases, a company will call its high-coupon bonds when interest rates are lower; therefore, investors lose their high income and must reinvest the bond proceeds in a lower interest rate environment. The promised yield expected at purchase may be reduced. While lower interest rates may reduce the interest-on-interest component of the expected total return from a bond, at least many investors still expect to get the relatively high interest payment coming in. But corporations are run by managements who do what individuals often try to do. If they see an opportunity to reduce their expenses by calling high-coupon debt, they will usually do so. If homeowners rush to refinance their home mortgages when rates drop, why can't companies refinance their outstanding high-cost debt?

Besides suffering a decline in interest income and the resulting interest-on-interest, the bonds are called at prices which are often lower than recent market prices. The call price may be at a premium to par but the redemption price may be only par. Examples of calls at levels well below the prevailing market price of the bonds are presented later in this chapter.

Yield-oriented investors are among those often hurt by premature bond redemptions. They are attracted by the relatively high yield to maturity without realizing that this is most likely due to one of two reasons: increased risk of default or increased risk of call. Seldom is the high yield due to inefficiencies in the market. Whenever a bond offers above-average yield, the investor should ask why. One does not usually get something for nothing in the financial markets.

---

[7] Andrea del Galdo and George O. Williams, *1993's Record Refundings*, Special Report, Fitch Investors Service, Inc., November 15, 1993.

CALL AND REFUNDING PROVISIONS

A company wanting to retire a debt issue prior to maturity usually must pay a premium over the par value for the privilege. The initial call premium on long-term debt traditionally has been the interest coupon plus par or the initial reoffering price (in some cases it is the higher of the two). Thus, a 30-year bond initially priced at 100 with a 10% coupon may have a call price of 110% for the first year, scaled down in relatively equal amounts to par starting in year 21 to maturity. Anheuser-Busch Companies, Inc. offered $200 million of 10% debentures in mid-1988 at 100% of par; the maturity is July 1, 2018. Exhibit 1 shows the redemption schedule for the bonds. Note that the initial call price is equal to the coupon plus the reoffering price. Subsequent redemption prices are in decrements of 50 basis points (0.5 of 1%) to par starting July 1, 2008. Some issues only show the call premium such as 8.583%, 8.154%, 7.725%, instead of the whole price.

The prices shown in Exhibit 1 are called the *regular* or *general redemption* prices. There are also special redemption prices for debt redeemed through the sinking fund and through other provisions such as the maintenance and replacement fund, with the proceeds from the confiscation of property through the right of eminent domain, and through the release and substitution of property clauses. The special redemption price is usually par, but in the case of some utility issues it initially may be the public offering price, which is amortized down to par (if a premium) over the life of the bonds. Carolina Power & Light Company's 9¾% bonds due May 1, 2004, have a special redemption price that is a discount. The bonds, issued in 1974 at 99.75, have a special redemption price starting at 99.75 and accruing to par for the final year starting May 1, 2003. This price can be used for redemptions for the improvement fund, the maintenance and replacement fund, or with the proceeds of released property. In other instances, the special redemption price is the same as the regular redemption price. This makes the debt redemption somewhat more costly for the issuer and provides the bondholder an additional premium. Rules of thumb for corporate bond characteristics applicable a generation ago cannot be safely used today; there are too many exceptions for one to be able to ignore the documentation. In the case of shorter-maturity debt, the initial call premium will usually not be the full coupon but some fraction thereof, scaled down to par; it may even be par for the issue's life.

The Anheuser-Busch debentures are currently callable — that is, the company may redeem the bonds at any time at the above general redemption prices subject only to the ten-year prohibition against lower cost refunding. Other issues may not be called for any reason for a certain number of years. For example, there is usually a five-year noncallable period for long-term debt of the former members of the American Telephone and Telegraph Company family. Therefore, the call price at the time the bond may first be called is not par plus the coupon, but the amortized price in five years after issuance obtained by the par plus the coupon calculation. If the telephone bond had the same coupon and reoffering price as the Anheuser issue, the initial call price would be 107.5 for the 12 months beginning July 1, 1993.

Exhibit 1: Redemption Schedule for Anheuser-Busch Companies, Inc.
10% Sinking Fund Debentures due July 1, 2018

Redemption
The Debentures will be redeemable at the option of the Company at any time in whole or in part, upon not fewer than 30 nor more than 60 days' notice, at the following redemption prices (which are expressed in percentages of principal amount) in each case together with accrued interest to the date fixed for redemption:

If redeemed during the 12 months beginning July 1,

1988	110.0%	1999	104.5%
1989	109.5%	2000	104.0%
1990	109.0%	2001	103.5%
1991	108.5%	2002	103.0%
1992	108.0%	2003	102.5%
1993	107.5%	2004	102.0%
1994	107.0%	2005	101.5%
1995	106.5%	2006	101.0%
1996	106.0%	2007	100.5%
1997	105.5%	2008 and	
1998	105.0%	thereafter	100.0%

provided, however, that prior to July 1, 1998, the Company may not redeem any of the Debentures pursuant to such option, directly or indirectly, from or in anticipation of the proceeds of the issuance of any indebtedness for money borrowed having an interest cost of less than 10% per annum.

Source: Prospectus dated June 23, 1988.

In 1979 some of the Bell System companies attempted to change the call price formula. Instead of basing the premium on the initial coupon, it was arbitrarily set at half of the coupon rate. On August 21, 1979, Northwestern Bell Telephone offered $300 million of 9½% bonds due in 37 years at 99.7 with the initial call price after five years at 104.75. Other affiliates tried the same call price formula over the next several months, but investors did not care for it. The lower call price meant that interest rates did not have to decline as much in order for the company to profitably refund the debt, and thus vulnerability to call was increased. In addition, if the bonds were called, investors would be receiving substantially less than under the older formula. The experiment was unsuccessful and the more traditional call pricing resumed.

There is another type of call pricing formula called a "make-whole" or "yield maintenance" premium. Usually found in privately placed debt issues, some public offerings also have them. The make-whole is designed to protect the investors' original yield to maturity by being an amount such, that when added to the principal amount and reinvested at the redemption date in U.S. Treasury securities having the same remaining life, would provide a yield to maturity equal to the original yield on the called issue based on the initial offering price. The premium is generally the sum of the present values of the remaining scheduled payments of principal and interest discounted at the appropriate Treasury yield. A specific Treasury issue may be called for by the indenture or the formula may call for the use of the proper maturity from the Federal Reserve Statistical Release h.15 (519). Thus, the lower the Treasury bond's yield, the greater will be the call premium to the investor and the more costly to the issuer. That is probably the main reason make-wholes are found in very few public debt issues. So-called "sophisticated" private placement buyers demand and can get make-wholes. The public bond buyer doesn't yet have that clout. But the make-whole is a reasonable type of provision as the investor will have to reinvest the redemption proceeds in a lower interest rate environment.

A few of the issues might have a certain period during which they have call protection. For example, Eastman Kodak's 9.95% Debentures due July 1, 2018 are callable on and after July 1, 2003 at par plus a make-whole premium. However, most issues with make-whole calls are immediately callable. Albertson's, Inc. 6⅜% Notes due May 1, 1995, are callable at any time at 100% of the principal amount together with accrued interest plus a make-whole premium. Both of these issues were publicly offered.

However, there is a word of caution with issues that are redeemable at a "make-whole redemption amount." In this type of redemption the redemption amount may be less than the principal amount. In the examples mentioned above the premium is added to the principal amount. However, in the case of Stanford University's 6⅞% Bonds due February 1, 2024, the redemption price is just the net present value of the remaining scheduled principal and interest payments discounted at the appropriate Treasury yield. There is no mention of par plus or the principal plus the make-whole premium.

If a debt does not have any protection against early call, then it is said to be a *currently callable issue*, as is the Anheuser issue. But most new bond issues, even if currently callable, usually have some restrictions against certain types of early redemption. The most common restriction is that prohibiting the refunding of the bonds for a certain number of years. Aware of the dangers of generalizations, industrial company long-term debt issues often had ten years of refunding protection while electric and gas utilities normally provided five years.[8] Many telephone, bank and finance issues provide deferred call provisions. Both call prohibitions and refunding prohibitions may be for a certain number of years or for the issue's life. Bonds that are noncallable for the issue's life are more common than bonds which are nonrefundable for life but otherwise callable.

Many investors are confused by the terms *noncallable* and *nonrefundable*. Hess and Winn said: "The terms 'noncallable' and 'nonrefundable' are often used rather loosely as interchangeable entities, although from a technical stand-point they have different meanings."[9] Call protection is much more absolute than refunding protection. While there may be certain exceptions to absolute or complete call protection in some cases (such as sinking funds and the redemption of debt under certain mandatory provisions), it still provides greater assurance against premature and unwanted redemption than does refunding protection. Refunding prohibition merely prevents redemption only from certain sources, namely the proceeds of other debt issues sold at a lower cost of money. The holder is only protected if interest rates decline, and the borrower can obtain lower-cost money to pay off the debt. The Anheuser bonds cannot be redeemed prior to July 2, 1998, if the company raises the funds from a new issue with an interest cost lower than 10%. There is nothing to prevent the company from calling the bonds within the ten-year refunding protected period from debt sold at a higher rate (although it normally wouldn't do so) or from funds obtained through other means. And that is exactly what Anheuser did. Between December 1993 and June 1994, it called $68.8 million of these relatively high-coupon bonds at 107.5% of par with funds from its general operations.

Some prospectuses specifically clarify refunding and redemption. For example, Cincinnati Gas & Electric Company's prospectus for the 10⅛% First Mortgage Bonds due in 2020 states,

> The Offered Bonds are redeemable (though CG&E does not contemplate doing so) prior to May 1, 1995 through the use of earn-

---

[8] On May 8, 1969, the Securities and Exchange Commission issued a release which modified its policy regarding refunding protection provisions for first mortgage debt of companies subject to its jurisdiction under the Public Utility Holding Company Act of 1935. Prior to that date, those subject issues had to "be redeemable at the option of the issuer at any time upon reasonable notice and with reasonable redemption premiums, if any." The modification allowed issuers to include in their indentures provisions prohibiting the refunding of those new bonds with the proceeds of lower cost debt securities for a period of not more than five years. These companies had to pay higher interest costs than other utility companies due to the lack of refunding protection. This SEC modification placed the utility holding company subsidiaries on a more equal footing with other nonholding company operating utilities. The release also stated:

> Heretofore, the general redemption prices of first mortgage bonds have been considered reasonable... whenever such redemption prices commence, immediately following the issuance of such bonds, at an amount equal to the sum of the coupon rate plus the public offering price and decline each year thereafter by equal amounts to the principal amount at the beginning of the last year prior to maturity. No change in this policy is authorized. Therefore, when the five-year period of nonrefundability authorized herein expires, the general redemption price at which the bonds may then be called will be the same as it would have been if there had been no restriction on refundability.

[9] Arleigh P. Hess, Jr. and Willis J. Winn, *The Value of the Call Privilege* (Philadelphia, PA: University of Pennsylvania, 1962), p. 24. The publication presents an interesting historical background of bond calls, including corporate, government, and municipal.

ings, proceeds from the sale of equity securities and cash accumulations other than those resulting from a refunding operation such as hereinafter described. The Offered Bonds are not redeemable prior to May 1, 1995 as a part of, or in anticipation of, any refunding operation involving the incurring of indebtedness by CG&E having an effective interest cost (calculated to the second place in accordance with generally accepted financial practice) of less than the effective interest cost of the Offered Bonds (similarly calculated) or through the operation of the Maintenance and Replacement Fund.

Refunding means to replace an old bond issue with a new one, often at a lower interest cost. In the Florida Power & Light case the judge said;

> The terms "redemption" and "refunding" are not synonymous. A "redemption" is simply a call of bonds. A "refunding" occurs when the issuer sells bonds in order to use the proceeds to redeem an earlier series of bonds. The refunding bond issue being sold is closely linked to the one being redeemed by contractual language and proximity in time so that the proceeds will be available to pay for the redemption. Otherwise, the issuer would be taking an inordinate risk that market conditions would change between the redemption of the earlier issue and the sale of the later issue.[10]

Corporations generally prefer to issue callable bonds for the flexibility they offer in financial management. If interest rates decline or other circumstances change, they can get out of the debt contract with minimal cost. On the other hand, investors prefer noncallable bonds for their guarantee of certain cash flow for a fixed period; this allows them to plan accordingly. But borrowers and lenders often must compromise; thus, we get the bond that is noncallable or nonrefundable for only a part of the issue's promised life span. In the early sixties, electric utilities offered issues with five years refunding protection at rates of 15 to 25 basis points less than issues with no refunding protection, all other factors being the same. Investors were willing to reduce their yield for the additional protective feature.

Beginning in early 1986 a number of industrial companies issued long-term debt with extended call protection, not refunding protection. A number are noncallable for the issue's life such as Dow Chemical Company's 8⅝% debentures due in 2006 and Atlantic Richfield's 9⅞% debentures due in 2016. The prospectuses for both issues expressly prohibit redemption prior to maturity. These noncallable-for-life issues are referred to as "bullet bonds" in Wall Street.

---

[10] Lucas et al. v. Florida Power & Light Company, Final Judgment, paragraph 77.

Other issues may also be nonredeemable by the issuer for the life of the bonds but they may provide the holder with the right to require the company to re-purchase the bonds at a specific date or dates. For example, Eastman Chemical Company's 7⅝% debentures due in 2024 have a put at par plus accrued interest on June 15, 2006. In order to exercise the put, the holder much make an irrevocable notification to the company at anytime from April 15 through May 15, 2006. The 6⅝% first mortgage bonds of Arizona Public Service Company are also noncall-able for life unless all other of its first mortgage bonds have also been redeemed within twelve months of a merger or consolidation or in the case of certain other transactions involving the transfer of substantially all of the mortgaged property.

According to Standard & Poor's *CreditWeek*, "The first wave of noncall long-term bonds gave issuers 20 to 25 basis points savings on their financing costs.... Now companies are lucky if investors give up 10 to 15 basis points for a noncall fea-ture."[11] Of course, interest rates dropped considerably in early 1986. Call protection is a more valuable option when interest rates are high, which is precisely when lend-ers prefer noncallable issues. When interest rates are low, call protection is less meaningful, making fully call-protected bonds less attractive to investors.

Redemption dates are usually stated as "on or after" a certain date. In some cases, however, the bonds may only be redeemed on certain dates, often the interest payment dates. Prior notice must be given — usually 30 to 45 days preceding the re-demption date. Of course, if the bonds are listed on a securities exchange, the ex-changes must also be notified. For a fully registered bond, the redemption notice is sent directly to the registered holders; a printed notice in the financial press is not required, although it would aid market participants. If the bonds are in coupon form, a printed notice in the financial press listing the serial numbers of the bonds to be called is necessary.

Some speculative grade bond issues started to appear in 1992 granting the issuer a limited right to redeem a portion of the bonds during the noncall period if the proceeds are from an initial public stock offering. In a few cases, proceeds from a secondary stock offering are also a permissible source of funds. Called "clawback" provisions, they merit careful attention by inquiring bond investors. According to Merrill Lynch's High Yield Securities Research Department, an increasing number of high yield issues have clawbacks. In the nearly three-year period ending June 30, 1994, of the almost 700 high yield issues in its sample, close to 25% came with claw-backs. The percentage of the issue that can be retired with stock proceeds ranges from 20% to 100% with the clawback period usually limited to the first three years after issuance. The redemption prices are around 110% of par, give or take a couple of points. Investors should be forewarned of clawbacks since they can lose bonds at the point in time just when the issuer's finances have been strengthened through ac-cess to the equity market. Also, the redemption may reduce the amount of the out-standing bonds to a level at which their liquidity in the aftermarket may suffer.

---

[11] "'Vanilla' Bonds Suit Investor Tastes," *Standard & Poor's Credit Week* (August 4, 1986), p. 16.

Bonds can be called in whole (the entire issue) or in part (only a portion). A few issues, such as the Alaskan Housing Finance Corporation, permit optional redemption only in whole. The method of redemption is usually stated as "by such method as it shall deem fair and appropriate" or "fair and equitable," and is left to the discretion of the trustee. Most directly or privately placed issues provide for pro rata redemption in case of partial calls. This means that all holders will have the same percentage of their holdings redeemed (subject to the restrictions imposed by the minimum denominations). Very few publicly issued bonds have pro rata redemption features; rather, the redemption is done "by lot." This is, essentially, the random selection of bonds through the use of computer programs.[12] One public issue with a pro rata redemption feature is Equitable Life Leasing Corporation's $100 million of 9⅛% Senior Notes due 1990. The prospectus says, "The Notes are subject to redemption semi-annually on each December 4 and June 4 commencing on December 4, 1988 in $20,000,000 equal aggregate principal amounts. The Notes will be redeemed pro rata among the holders of Notes to the extent practicable and otherwise by lot. The Notes will be in fully registered form and will be in denominations of $1,000 or integral multiples thereof."

In 1991, Knight-Ridder, Inc. issued $160 million 8½% Amortizing Notes due 2001 providing for pro rata retirement of the issue. The Company was required to retire 25% of the initial principal amount of each outstanding note ($1,000 per note) each September 1, 1998 through 2000, leaving 25% of each note due at maturity on September 1, 2001. Thus, after the first payment there will be a total outstanding amount of $120 million with each note having a par value of $750. The next amortization payment will reduce the par value to $500 per note and the total outstanding to $80 million, and the next to $250 and $40 million, respectively.

Often, the documentation states that the redemption is subject to the deposit of the redemption monies with the trustee on or before the redemption date. If funds are not at hand, the redemption notice becomes void and has no effect. An announcement of the intention to redeem debt also has no effect until an official notice has been issued and the funds given to the trustee. In March 1987, Wickes Companies announced plans to redeem in December $200 million of 12% sinking fund debentures. Subsequently, interest rates climbed and bond prices fell so that at the end of September it withdrew the redemption plans; market conditions made it undesirable for the company to proceed with the redemption.

According to the New York Stock Exchange, trading in nonconvertible bonds that have been called in whole ceases when funds are available for payment with the trustee. In the case of a partial call, bonds which have been called for redemption are no longer "good delivery" for the settlement of trades. The exception is when trades are specifically in the called bonds. Once a bond has been called, the few that do trade are, in effect, substitutes for short-term paper. Active bond portfolio managers should

---

[12] Descriptions of the bond selection process may be found in Robert I. Landau, *Corporate Trust Administration and Management* (New York, NY: Columbia University Press, 1985), pp. 161-163, and *Commentaries On Indentures* (Chicago, IL: American Bar Foundation, 1971), pp. 497-499.

be alert as to which of their bonds have been called so that trades settle promptly and without any problems caused by the delivery of "bad" bonds.

General Electric Capital Corporation also reneged on a planned redemption of $500 million of its Reset Notes due March 15, 2018. The bonds had an 8% coupon rate for the three years ended March 15, 1994. On January 26, 1994, GECC notified the noteholders that it would redeem the issue on March 15 at par. This was within the required 30 to 60 prior notice period. Money market investors now bought the notes as a short-term investment due within a matter of weeks. In early February, the Federal Reserve started to boost interest rates and on February 15 the Company switched gears and canceled the proposed redemption. Instead, it decided to reset the new interest rate based on the indenture at 108% of the three-year Treasury rate in effect on the tenth day preceding the date of the new interest period of March 15.

All of a sudden investors held notes that had a below market rate coupon and a long maturity of 24 years, not an above market rate coupon for a short-term maturity of six weeks or so. *The Wall Street Journal* reported that the notes dropped from par to 98 ($1,000 to $980 per note). Obviously, investors were infuriated and they protested to the Company. On March 8 the new interest rate of 5.61% was announced in the financial press. On the very next day GECC announced a tender offer for the notes commencing March 17. It would buy them back at par plus accrued interest on April 15. This bailed out many investors who had faith in the Company's original redemption announcement. It seems that one can not even trust the highest-rated issuers to play fair and square anymore.

Refunding is the primary cause of bond redemptions, as companies can increase shareholders' wealth by substituting lower-cost debt for higher-cost debt. There are many different ways in which issuers estimate the savings which can be achieved through refunding, but refunding is basically a capital budgeting procedure. One calculates, on an after-tax basis, the net present value of the expected savings over the life of the issue to be refunded and subtracts from that figure the costs of the transaction to obtain the net advantage for the refunding. The discount rate used is the after-tax yield on the new debt based on semiannual payments (assuming a conventional bond). It should be noted that the issue's call premium and related expenses are deductible from the current year's income taxes, thus reducing the cost of the refunding. Expenses associated with the new or refunding issue must be amortized over the issue's life. If the net advantage of the refunding is greater than zero, a refunding opportunity exists.[13]

Because the call premium and certain other costs are written off for tax purposes in the year incurred, the transaction may result in a loss for financial reporting purposes. But that should not override the economics of the transaction. Many utility

---

[13] A comprehensive review of debt retirement and the analytical framework are found in John D. Finnerty, Andrew J. Kalotay and Francis X. Farrell, Jr. *The Financial Manager's Guide to Evaluating Bond Refunding Opportunities* (Cambridge, MA: Harper & Row, 1988). This book covers discounted cash flow methodology, tax and accounting considerations, refunding of premium and discount debt, sinking fund issues, tenders, exchange offers, defeasance and the refunding of preferred stock.

companies have been urged by their regulators to use all available means for reducing their interest costs. As further encouragement, the companies should be assured that they will not have to absorb the loss on the transaction in the year incurred, but can amortize it and other related costs (net of the tax benefits) over the new securities' lives for rate-making and reporting purposes. However, as a member of the staff of the Public Utilities Commission of the State of California stated in 1983, "if there is a clear-cut opportunity for a utility to effect substantial interest savings through refinancing and it fails to act promptly, there is ample justification for a rate-making adjustment imputing a lower interest rate as a penalty."[14]

The optimal timing of a refunding may be difficult, for once done the opportunity to achieve further savings is gone; the issuer will have given up the call option. An issuer should decide whether to refund now or wait until rates are lower. If rates are expected to be lower, the issuer must determine whether they will be low enough to make the delay worthwhile. If a refunding is done now, the costs of the new bond issue are locked-in until the new refunding or call-protected period has expired.

The refunding of high-cost debt in a lower interest rate environment should come as no surprise to any investor. Any one who faithfully reads the financial press ought to be aware of current interest rate levels compared to those on the bonds he owns. Also, some companies have issued press releases and other reports discussing vulnerable issues. On March 18, 1986, Public Service Electric and Gas Company issued a release, "PSE&G Announces Potential Redemption of High Interest Rate Debt Issues." Listing seven high coupon issues (12% and higher) with a total outstanding principal amount of $482.28 million and the dates on which they are eligible for redemption, the release said, in part,

> The Company estimates that $132 million of interest costs would be saved through these refundings over the remaining lives of the redeemed bonds ($38 million on a 'present value' basis) based on a 9% refunding rate. Another benefit would be a reduction in the embedded cost of long-term debt by about 65 basis points. The interest coverage ratio would also be improved, thereby enhancing the credit standing of the Company.

OUTRIGHT REDEMPTIONS

For want of a better term we will use *outright redemptions* to mean the retirement of debt at the general redemption price. The proceeds for the outright redemption need

---

[14] Letter dated June 13, 1983, to Members and Conferees, National Association of Regulatory Utility Commissioners (NARUC) from John J. Gibbons, Chairman NARUC Staff Accounting Committee. Mr. Gibbons was also the Assistant Director and Chief Accountant, Revenue Requirements Division of the California Commission.

not come from lower cost borrowings, nor is the redemption triggered by the maintenance and replacement fund, the sinking fund, or the release and substitution of property provisions found in bonded debt. Outright redemptions are also known by some as "cash calls," but this term could also be applied to other types of debt calls. The point to remember is that they can occur at any time unless there are call prohibitions; investors should not be lulled by a nonrefunding provision.

In 1973 Bristol-Myers Company redeemed at 107.538 $25 million of its 8⅝% debentures due 1995. Issued in 1970, they traded as high as 111 in 1972 and were about 108-109 when the call was announced. A number of holders, including institutional investors and at least one Wall Street corporate bond dealer, were confused by the call, having mistaken "nonrefundable" for "noncallable." The bonds were nonrefundable for 10 years but were currently callable. In 1977, NCR. Corporation redeemed all of its 9¾% debentures due 2000 at 107.88. Still within the ten-year nonrefunding period, the bonds were trading at 111 to 111.5 at the time the call was announced. NCR was in a strong cash position, with projected cash flow substantially in excess of expected capital spending plans. This redemption helped to improve NCR's balance sheet and reduced leverage. In the opinion of these companies' management, their debt offered them better returns than investment in plant and equipment.

Archer-Daniels-Midland Company (ADM) presents an interesting case. On May 12, 1981, the company sold $250 million of 7% debentures due May 15, 2011, and $125 million of 16% sinking fund debentures, also maturing on May 15, 2011. Both issues were currently callable, the 7% to original issue discounts at par and the full coupon 16s at a premium. The 16% debentures also had the standard 10-year prohibition against lower-cost refunding. Subsequent to these offerings A-D-M raised money in 1982 and 1983 through lower-cost borrowings. It also sold common equity on January 28, 1983, raising more than $131 million, and again on June 1, 1983, raising another $15.45 million. At 6:19 P.M. on June 1, 1983, the Dow Jones Capital Markets News Wire Service announced that the company would redeem on August 1, at 113.95 plus accrued interest of $33.78, all of the outstanding 16% sinking fund debentures due May 15, 2011.

The corporate bond market was in an uproar. This call was well within the 10-year refunding protected period. One investment banking firm sued to bar the redemption, claiming that "investors expected the debentures to continue on the market until 1991 (which) kept the trading value of the debt at about $1,250 per $1,000 face value and misled investors into believing the debentures would continue to be traded... it wouldn't have purchased the debentures if it believed Archer-Daniels would redeem the bonds so soon."[15] People don't often sue in debt redemptions unless they stand to lose money. Here, the plaintiff lost money. Several weeks before the call, it purchased $15,518,000 face amount of the debentures at 125.25 each, and the day be-

---

[15] "Morgan Stanley Sues Over Archer-Daniels' Plan to Redeem Debt," *The Wall Street Journal* (July 11, 1983).

fore, another $500,000 principal amount at 120.[16] If these bonds were held to the call date, the principal loss would have been nearly $1,784,000.

The company said that the proceeds for this redemption came from the sale of the common stock. The shelf registration prospectus dated March 22, 1983, may have indicated that the high-coupon debt might be in jeopardy when it said in the use of proceeds section, "The proceeds will be used, as required, for general corporate purposes, including working capital, capital expenditures and possible acquisitions of, or investments in, businesses and assets, *and the repayment of indebtedness originally incurred for general corporate purposes*" (emphasis added). The debenture prospectus said that "The proceeds will be used, as required, for general corporate purposes." This is part of the standard boilerplate found in many financing documents. The plaintiff claimed that A-D was not allowed, by the issue's terms, to call the bonds from lower-cost funds and it pointed to the 1982 and 1983 debt financings. It contended that the money raised from the common stock sales was little more than a subterfuge for circumventing the refunding protection provided in the indenture. It also alleged securities fraud by A-D-M, as the company did not reveal its own interpretation of the redemption language and would contemplate redemption if it felt that doing so was in its own best interests.

The court upheld A-D-M's right to call the sinking fund debentures with the proceeds from the sales of common shares saying the redemption was within the company's legal rights and in accordance with the indenture. It pointed to the strict "source" of funds argument which came up several years earlier in the case of the redemption of preferred stock with the proceeds of common stock.[17] The Archer-Daniels decision was an important event in modern corporate bond world, as it substantially eroded the effectiveness of standard refunding provisions.

The story didn't end with the 1983 call. Investors don't readily forget the times that they lost money, especially if they felt that they might have been "bamboozled." One year later, on August 6, 1984, A-D-M sold $100 million of 13% sinking fund debentures due August 1, 2014, at a price of 97.241. The new bonds, also with the standard ten-year refunding protection, were not well-received as only about 70% of the issue was sold by the underwriters at the original offering terms. When the managing underwriter terminated syndicate underwriting restrictions, the bonds immediately sold off. As *Bondweek* (August 13, 1984) said, "A-D-M Re-enters Market With a Thud," and "... the offering never really got off the ground. Street officials said that without a doubt A-D-M's controversial move last year was a factor in the poor reception of its issue last week in the midst of an otherwise bullish market."

On January 9, 1986, A-D-M sold $100 million of 10¼% debentures due January 15, 2006. The price the company paid to reenter the corporate bond market and the good graces of institutional investors was that these bonds were noncall-

---

[16] Morgan Stanley & Co., Incorporated, Plaintiff, v. Archer-Daniels Midland Company, Defendant. Opinion 83 Civ. 5113, United States District Court Southern District of New York, July 29, 1983.

[17] The Franklin Life Insurance Company v. Commonwealth Edison Company, United States District Court, Southern District of Illinois, May 19, 1978.

able for life. In April, 1986, the company attempted to rid itself of the then high-coupon 13s. Instead of calling the bonds at below-market prices as it had nearly three years earlier, it tendered for them with a bid above the market. Archer-Daniels probably had enough of Wall Street lawyers for awhile.

SINKING AND PURCHASE FUNDS

A sinking fund is a provision allowing for a debt's periodic retirement or amortization over its life span. It can also require the periodic deposit of funds or property into a reserve for the loan's eventual retirement or the maintenance of the value of the collateral securing it; this is called an *improvement fund* or a *sinking and improvement fund*. It is more common to have the sinking fund applied to the current extinguishment of debt and not to have the funds build up for use at maturity.

Were debt viewed as permanent, sinking funds would not be needed. Thus the huge United States Government debt does not have any sinking fund. Of course, some might say that with Treasury bills rolling over every week and the frequent note and bond maturities, a sinking fund, even if desirable, would be unnecessary. To reduce debt, the Treasury would only have to sell a smaller amount at each auction. However, much corporate debt generally has been viewed as less than permanent. Early U.S. railroad issues came with sinking funds, but in the last half of the nineteenth century, railroads sold many secured and very long-term issues with no sinking funds. Railroad promoters, financiers and investors apparently viewed the properties as lasting forever. But starting in the early twentieth century, as industrial corporations became more prominent with unsecured debt financing, the importance of sinking funds increased. Investors thought that provision for the periodic retirement of debt before the assets became economically worthless would be preferable to nonamortizing issues. This could strengthen an issuer's credit by prohibiting an unwieldy sum to become due and payable all at once at maturity. This final payment is called a *balloon*. The security provided by tangible assets was less important as investors realized that much property depreciates, deteriorates, depletes and becomes obsolete. Debt service and security would be better provided from cash flow and operations, or, in some cases, from the pledging of unfunded property in lieu of the debt retirement.

Sinking funds in various forms have probably existed for as long as people have borrowed money from one another and worried about the ultimate repayment. A sinking fund was proposed for government debt during the reign of England's William the III in the late seventeenth century.[18] References to measures for reducing the Crown's public debt are found in Mackay's narrative of the South-Sea Bubble scandal:

---

[18] F. Corine Thompson and Richard L. Norgaard, *Sinking Funds: Their Use and Value* (New York, NY: Financial Executives Research Foundation, 1967).

Upon the 22nd of January, 1720, the House of Commons resolved itself into a committee of the whole house, to take into consideration that part of the King's (George I, the Elector of Hanover) speech at the opening of the session which related to the public debts, and the proposal of the South-Sea Company towards the redemption and sinking of the same.[19]

In George Washington's administration, Alexander Hamilton, the first Secretary of the Treasury, developed a plan for the reduction of the country's debt. But many government attempts at using sinking funds for debt reduction purposes fell short of the goals.

A variety of sinking fund types are found in publicly issued debt. The most common is the *mandatory specific sinking fund*, requiring the periodic redemption of a certain amount of a specific debt issue. This type is found in most longer-term industrial issues and some electric utility bonds. Bell System debt has no sinking funds. The 10¾% May Department Stores Company Debentures due 2018 has a typical mandatory specific sinking fund as follows:

The Company will provide for the retirement by redemption of $12,500,000 of the principal amount of the Debentures Due

---

[19] Charles Mackay, *Extraordinary Popular Delusions and the Madness of Crowds* (New York, NY: L. C. Page & Company, 1932 reprint), p. 49. Originally issued in 1841, this book became popular after being recommended by Bernard M. Baruch nearly 60 years ago. In discussing the speculative madness of the time, Mackay comments on one of the "bubbles" as follows:

> But the most absurd and preposterous of all, and which showed, more completely than any other, the utter madness of the people, was one started by an unknown adventurer, entitled, 'A company for carrying on an undertaking of great advantage, but nobody to know what it is.' (p. 55).

This appears to be similar to the blind investment pools of the mid-1980s. Mackay also wrote something which sounds as though it could appear in today's financial press after the insider trading scandals:

> The public mind was in a state of unwholesome fermentation. Men were no longer satisfied with the slow but sure profits of cautious industry. The hope of boundless wealth for the morrow made them heedless and extravagant for today. A luxury, till then unheard of, was introduced, bringing in its train a corresponding laxity of morals. The overbearing insolence of ignorant men, who had arisen to sudden wealth by successful gambling, made men of true gentility of mind and manners blush that gold should have power to raise the unworthy in the scale of society. The haughtiness of some of these 'cyphering cits,' as they were termed by Sir Richard Steele, was remembered against them in the day of their adversity. In the parliamentary inquiry, many of the directors suffered more for their insolence than for their peculation. One of them, who, in the full-blown pride of an ignorant rich man, had said that he would feed his horse upon gold, was reduced almost to bread and water for himself; every haughty look, every overbearing speech, was set down, and repaid them a hundredfold in poverty and humiliation. (pp. 71-72).

2018 on June 15 of each of the years 1999 to and including 2017 at the principal amount thereof, together with accrued interest to the date of redemption. The Company may also provide for the redemption of up to an additional $25,000,000 principal amount... annually,... such optional right being noncumulative. The Company may (1) deliver outstanding Debentures Due 2018 (other than Debentures Due 2018 previously called for redemption) and (2) apply as a credit Debentures Due 2018 which have been redeemed either at the election of the Company or through the application of a permitted optional sinking fund payment, in each case in satisfaction of all or any part of any required sinking fund payment, provided that such Debentures Due 2018 have not been previously so credited.[20]

The above tells us that the Company must retire 5% of the $250 million issue each year starting June 15, 1999 (one year after the refunding protection expires). Four or five percent is customary for longer-term industrial bonds. With bonds of shorter maturities, sinking funds, if provided, may retire a greater percentage of the issue on each sinking fund date. Owens-Corning Fiberglas Corporation's 11¾% Senior Subordinated Debentures due 2001 have an annual 20% sinking fund requirement starting in 1997. (Utility issues often have smaller sinking funds.) The May Company payments retire 95% of the issue prior to maturity, leaving $12,500,000 as the final amount due on June 15, 2018. Many investors erroneously call this a 100% sinking fund, implying that the entire issue is retired prior to maturity. However, the required sinking fund sinks only 95% of the issue, leaving a $12,500,000 balloon payment. The company has the right to increase sinking fund payments by another $25,000,000, for a total of $37,500,000. This is a "triple-up" option. More often, issues have a "double-up" option allowing the retirement of bonds in an additional amount equal to the mandatory requirement. Usually the issuer may deliver debentures acquired by it instead of paying cash and calling the required bonds at par. In high interest rate periods, when the bonds are trading below par, companies would normally prefer to buy the bonds through open market purchases instead of calling them at the higher price; this can lend price support to the bonds. In times of lower interest rates, open market purchases are costly and unnecessary. The company can merely deposit cash with the trustee for a par call; this could depress the bond's price. Thus, depending on the coupon rate relative to the current market rate, a sinking fund may have varying affects on the bond's price and liquidity.

---

[20] Prospectus for The May Department Stores Company's $250 million of 10¼% Debentures Due 2018, dated June 8, 1988.

Over the years, a number of institutional investors have played "the sinking fund game;" these have become known as "sinker sockers." In this scheme, one or a few investors attempts to control or corner an issue, i.e., buy up the available floating supply of a deep discount bond with a currently operating sinking fund or with one due to start within a couple of years. This does not mean that they must own 100% of the bonds, only a substantial portion of the available supply. Many bonds may be "locked up" in certain investment accounts due to restrictions on their sale at prices lower than their cost. These investors have often purchased the bonds at the time of the original offering at much higher prices. Even if the sinking fund collectors do not control every outstanding bond, they can make life difficult for corporate financial managers. After a company has cleared the market of tradable bonds for the sinking fund, the only remaining ones are those held by the sinking fund collectors. Therefore, the company needing bonds to satisfy the sinking fund must strike a bargain with the bonds' owner at a price at or close to the sinking fund call price. Thus, the investor stands to reap an extra reward.

Of course things can go wrong. Investors may have to sit with an underperforming asset for several years until its scarcity value becomes known. During that time, the credit quality may decline or the investor's objectives may have changed. One portfolio manager with a major eastern trust bank reportedly tried to corner some bonds of a steel company. However, the steel company, an important client of the bank, became aware of the plan and was perturbed; it stopped doing business with the bank. A number of companies have become painfully aware of sinking fund collectors and, as a result, try to keep their sinking fund activities and information (amounts outstanding and to be retired) as secret as possible.

There is also the *nonmandatory specific sinking fund*, the most prevalent type in electric utility company issues. The $100 million 7½% bonds of Public Service Electric and Gas Company due on March 1, 2023, require the retirement of $2½ million principal amount of bonds each March 1, 1994, through 2022. The company may satisfy the sinking fund, in whole or in part, by delivering bonds acquired through open market purchases or other means, by paying cash to the trustee who will call bonds for redemption at 100, or by the utilization of unfunded property additions or improvements at 60% of their cost. Property credits so utilized cannot be further employed under the mortgage.

Utilities are usually considered consumers of capital, for they engage in large, ongoing construction projects. As they need to borrow fairly regularly, the application of property credits helps to reduce the demands on the capital markets. (It makes no sense to pay off debt on the one hand only to have to go back to the market to raise the money that was just paid out.) Utilization of property credits conserves cash and still helps to maintain the integrity of the collateral behind the bonds. In some cases, a company may be able to authenticate and simultaneously cancel new bonds specifically authorized for this purpose. This usually is done against unfunded property additions and thus reduces the amount of new debt the company can issue.

A slight variation of the property sinking fund is found in the indenture of Continental Telephone Company of California's 7⅝% first mortgage bonds due December 31, 1997. The requirement is 1% annually of each outstanding series of bonds. The funds must be held by the trustee as part of the mortgaged property and paid back to the company as reimbursement for 100% of the amount of available net property additions. If not paid out, the funds may be used to repurchase or call bonds. Any funds remaining in the trust after five years must be used to retire debt.

One cannot always rely on what is stated in a company's financial reports. In May, 1977, some holders of New England Power Company's 10⅞% bonds due 2005 were surprised when the company announced the redemption on the following July 1 at 101.55, of $2.4 million of the outstanding $80 million issue. The bonds had the usual utility sinking fund provisions, namely, 1% annually, cash, bonds or property credits at 60%. The indenture also provided that an additional 2% ($1,600,000) could be retired. Surprised investors, having read the company's 1976 annual report, would have concluded that property credits would be used and bonds would not be called. A footnote to the financials said that "the company may elect to satisfy its annual sinking fund obligations of $3,850,000... by evidencing to the Trustee net additional property in amounts not less than $6,417,000 in 1977.... For the sinking fund requirement due in 1977 the company intends to so elect." Because of declining interest rates, the company did a complete about-face in less than a matter of weeks after the annual report was issued. Thus, the sinking fund obligation was satisfied with the high coupon bonds and property additions. In 1978 the company also retired $2.4 million of the 10⅞s. High-coupon bonds in a lower interest rate environment are vulnerable to call even if the issuer promises not to do so.

Specific sinking funds apply to just the named issue. There are also *nonspecific sinking funds* of both the mandatory and nonmandatory variety. The nonspecific sinking fund, also known as a *funnel, tunnel, blanket,* or *aggregate* sinking fund, is based on the outstanding amount of a company's total bonded indebtedness. If mandatory, the sinking fund must be satisfied by bonds of any issue or issues selected by the company. If nonmandatory, the company may utilize certain property credits in fulfilling the sinking fund requirement. Nonspecific sinking funds are found in the indentures of 17 companies. Three of these — Baltimore Gas & Electric, Ohio Edison, and Pacific Gas & Electric — have mandatory funnel sinking funds. The other 14, including the subsidiaries of the Southern Company and Northeast Utilities, have nonmandatory funnel sinking funds.

In most cases the redemption price for bonds called under the funnel sinking fund is par, but Pacific Gas & Electric's and Southern California Edison's operate at the general or regular redemption prices. Pacific Gas has usually chosen to retire its low-coupon issues trading at discounts. The funnel sinking fund may be deceptive. Usually 1% of all bonds outstanding, this can amount to a large requirement, especially if the total amount is applied against a single issue. For example, if bonded debt of $3 billion consists of issues ranging in size from $50 million to $200 million, the annual funnel requirement is $30 million; this equals 15% to 60% of any one issue. When interest rates and cash needs are high, companies normally utilize unfunded property additions if they are able to do so. But actual bond retirement provides a way to redeem high coupon debt (usually at par) when interest rates are down. In some cases, however, a maximum of 1% of a specific issue may be retired in any one year if the call is within five years of issuance (the refunded protected period). The Southern Company (among others) had to place this restriction in its subsidiaries' indentures after the funnel calls of the early 1970s. Thus, while there is a limit on the amount of the bonds that can be redeemed in the first five years, once that period has expired, investors should be careful. An issuer could apply the maximum amount possible to the retirement of the bonds at par and then call any remaining ones at the regular redemption prices.

Most sinking funds operate annually, but some, such as Pacific Gas & Electric's are effective semiannually. Again, most sinking funds are based on a specific percentage of the original amount issued, or a fixed amount of bonds which remains the same until the entire issue is retired. But other issues' sinking fund payments may increase periodically. Each payment may be higher than the preceding one, or payments might be level for several years, then step up for another few years, and so forth. There are even some sinking funds that increase for several years and then decrease for a few more years.

Because of the risk of exhausting gas supplies, some gas pipeline company indentures provide for the acceleration of the sinking fund in the event that estimates of the reserve lives of the companies' proven gas reserves decline. ANR Pipeline Company (formerly Michigan Wisconsin Pipe Line Company) has such a provision. The prospectus for the 10⅝% First Mortgage Pipe Line Bonds due April 15 1995, states,

> Indenture will provide in substance that in the event that an independent engineer's certificate of reserve life, which the Company is required to file with the Trustee prior to May 1 of each year, shows a reserve life for the Company's controlled proven gas reserves of less than eight years and a date of exhaustion of reserve life earlier than any sinking fund payment date then in effect, the next two sinking fund installments shall each be increased.... However, if the reserve life shown in any such certificate is less than four years, all sinking fund installments falling due subsequent to the year in which such certificate is filed shall become payable on December 31 of such year.

Thus, the sinking fund payments can be increased, but if future certificates subsequently show an improvement in the gas supply, the sinking fund will be adjusted once again. Transcontinental Gas Pipe Line Corporation was required to accelerate the sinking funds of at least five of its mortgage bond issues and one debenture issue in the 1970s for at least five years in a row.

There are other types of sinking funds but they are seldom encountered in public U.S. corporate debt. Sinking funds can be on a contingent basis, i.e., based on a certain level of corporate earnings or expressed as a percentage of earnings or cash flow. This type may be found in some of the financially weaker companies (such as one emerging from bankruptcy or reorganization), requiring that part of the cash flow be directed towards debt retirement. If there are no earnings or a lack of adequate cash flow, there is no sinking fund requirement. Missouri-Kansas-Texas Railroad Company's 5% Prior Lien Series E bonds due 1990 had a 1% sinking fund with the deposits to be made from earnings in excess of $1 million. That company's 5½% Subordinated Income Debentures due in 2033 have a noncumulative sinking fund payable from available income, if any.

Another type of sinking fund found in Canadian provincial debt issues sold in the United States is called the *invested* or *Canadian* sinking fund. This is really a fund of cash and securities set aside to provide monies for debt retirement at maturity. Usually the funds can be invested in the same bonds, other bonds of the issuer, Canadian government bonds, and certain other permitted investments. Some issuers have utilized this type of fund to help support the market for existing bonds at the time of a new issue's sale by purchasing the outstanding bonds from holders at an attractive yield spread from the new issue if the proceeds were used to buy the new bonds.

A few issues may have a *purchase fund.* In some cases, it may operate prior to the start of the sinking fund; in others, there may be no sinking fund. Although the purchase fund may seem like a sinking fund, it does not operate when the debt's market price is above par. The purchase fund may require that the issuer, through its agent, attempt, on a best efforts basis and in good faith, to purchase each year a certain amount of bonds at par or less, in public and private transactions. This may lend market support to the bonds and encouraged some investors to buy the bonds who ordinarily might not do so.

One such purchase fund, found in Harnischfeger Corporation's 15% Notes due April 15, 1994, requires an annual purchase fund of 5% of the original issue in the event the notes' market price is less than par for 60 consecutive calendar days. This purchase fund is cumulative and remains in effect until satisfied, but there may be no more than one such purchase obligation in any one year. The prospectus says:

> The purchase agency arrangements have been designed to provide a limited measure of market liquidity for the Notes and in certain circumstances to result in the retirement prior to stated maturity of a portion of the outstanding Notes. There can be no assurance that such arrangements will, in fact, support market liquidity for the Notes or result in the retirement of any Notes.

> The purchase agency arrangements are not equivalent to a sinking fund, mandatory redemption feature or similar provision... In the event that the market price of the Notes is equal to or greater than 100% of the principal amount thereof for even one day within each 60 consecutive calendar day period, the purchase agency arrangements of the Note Indenture will not become operative. Prospective

purchasers should be prepared to hold any Notes to be purchased by them until maturity in 1994, optional redemption, if any, by the Company or sale in the open market or otherwise.

In 1986 the *annuity note* appeared. Basically a level debt service arrangement similar to a home mortgage, each periodic payment is applied to interest and principal. Ford Motor Credit Company issued Series 1 of its Annuity Notes in September 1986. The minimum denomination was $100,000, repayable in 20 equal quarterly install- ments of $5,933.28 each March 1, June 1, September 1, and December 1, starting De- cember 1, 1986. The first installment consisted of $1,791.45 of interest and $4,201.83 of principal. The last installment, on September 1, 1991, consisted of only $105.47 of interest and $5,887.81 of principal. This type of security eliminates any large balloon payment at maturity and helps the company to better match its liabilities with its auto- mobile receivables. Some investors needing periodic return of principal, especially those pension funds with heavy payments to retired benefices, have been thought to be among the purchasers of these notes.

MAINTENANCE AND REPLACEMENT FUNDS

Until March 23, 1977, few in the investment community knew — or cared — what a maintenance and replacement fund (M&R) was. On that date the exact nature of this little known, never used, but standard provision was made abundantly clear when Flor- ida Power & Light Company announced its intention to deposit $64.8 million in cash with the trustee of its 10⅛% bonds due March 1, 2005 (issued March 13, 1975) to sat- isfy the maintenance and replacement fund requirement. (The maintenance and re- placement fund is also known as the maintenance and renewal fund, the maintenance fund, and the replacement fund.) The cash was used for the September 2, 1977, re- demption of $63.7 million of the outstanding $125 million bond issue at the special re- demption price of 101.65. The regular redemption price at that time was 110.98, and the refunding-protected period would not expire until March 1, 1980, when the regular redemption price would be 109.76. Prior to the March announcement, the bonds were trading around 111; afterwards, they fell immediately to 101.

The M&R provision was first placed in bond indentures of electric utilities subject to regulation by the Securities and Exchange Commission under the Public Utility Holding Company Act in the early 1940s. It remained in the indentures even when some of the companies no longer were subject to regulation under the act. Property is subject to wear and tear, and the replacement fund supposedly helps maintain the integrity of the property securing the bonds. One writer said, "A re- placement fund is designed to force actual annual expenditures for new property or the reduction of bonded indebtedness."[21] It differs from a sinking fund in that the

---

[21] John M. Stuart. "A Re-examination of the Replacement Fund," *Public Utilities Fortnightly* (May 23, 1968), p. 3.

M&R only helps to maintain the value of the security while a sinking or improvement fund is designed to improve the security behind the debt. It is similar to, but
more complex than, a provision in a home mortgage requiring the home owner to
maintain his property in good repair.

A maintenance and replacement fund requires a company to annually determine the amounts needed to satisfy the fund and any shortfall. (Not all utility indentures provide for them, and some companies have eliminated or sharply modified
them in recent years.) The requirement is based on a formula, usually 15% or so of
adjusted gross operating revenues, but some are based on a much smaller percentage
(such as 2% to 2½%) of depreciable mortgaged property or a percentage of bonded
debt. The difference between what is required and the actual amount expended on
maintenance is the shortfall. The shortfall is usually satisfied with unfunded property
additions, but it can be satisfied with cash or, in some cases, maintenance and replacement fund credits from prior years. The cash can be used for the retirement of debt or
withdrawn upon the certification of unfunded property credits.

Inflated fuel costs in the 1970s increased the M&R requirements of those
funds based on a percentage of revenues beyond what was previously adequate. In
some cases, unfunded property additions might be insufficient to satisfy the shortfall.
Companies may be unable to obtain the necessary operating permits and other licens-
es for some nuclear plants, which would make such property ineligible for use as unfunded property. Also, the amount of available property additions may be inadequate
due to declining construction outlays resulting from reduced demand for electric power. But the M&R certainly grants most companies the right to retire debt. Some issues
restrict the amount of bonds that may be redeemed through the M&R fund. Investors
should be skeptical of companies saying that they have no intention of retiring debt
through the M&R provisions — they may be forced to do so by the economics of the
situation, as Florida Power & Light was. Of course, the company's cash position is an
important determinant of whether or not it is financially able to call the bonds. As we
have seen, cash can be raised if doing so makes sense, and refunding limitations almost always relate to redemptions at the general, not the special, redemption prices.
Also, some companies may be reluctant to utilize an M&R call for fear of angering
their investors. But again, if the company is pressured by regulatory authorities, it may
have no choice but to comply. Also, the initial trauma of the M&R calls of the late
1970s is over; investors today are more aware of the possibility of such calls and can
usually position themselves accordingly.

What caused Florida Power & Light to resort to a maintenance and replacement fund call? In January 1977, the public service commission began rate hearings
as it was interested in FP&L's cost of debt and ways to reduce it. It was suggested
by the company's financial people that a debt retirement through the maintenance
and replacement fund was one way to reduce interest costs. This testimony was giv-
en on March 23 and a press release issued, but the right not to redeem the bonds was
reserved. In June, the commission issued an order granting FP&L a $195.5 million
rate boost, based on the assumption that half of the 10⅛s would be retired and sub-

stituted a 9% rate. It projected that annual interest savings of more than $500,000 would be passed through to customers. "Once the Florida Public Service Commission factored these retirements into its cost of capital calculations, the company had little choice, but to go ahead and exercise the special redemption option."[22] The 1983 court decision said that all the benefits from the redemption would be passed through to the ratepayer whether or not the bonds were called. The company's shareholders received none of the savings.[23]

Florida Power and Light's redemption broke the ice. Several others followed, most notably Carolina Power & Light Company. In 1977 and 1978, Carolina deposited with its trustee nearly $79 million under similar M&R provisions. In June 1978, it called for redemption $46 million of the privately held 11⅛% bonds due 1994 and $32.7 million of the publicly held 11s of 1984 at par, the special redemption price. Carolina was sued by its bondholders, including an insurance company which negotiated the first Carolina Power & Light Mortgage dated May 1, 1940; it contained an improvement fund and a maintenance and renewal fund that could be satisfied with fundable property or bonds. The courts have upheld the issuers' rights to redeem debt through such provisions. But companies should ensure that their offering documents clearly spell out special redemption features to avoid accusation of concealing important information. It is also incumbent upon bond buyers to know the terms of the issues they own. "Investors beware! We have the right to redeem our debt in any way that our contract allows. We will do it the cheapest way in order to benefit our ratepayers and shareholders."

After the 1977 to 1978 period, maintenance and replacement fund calls receded into the background as interest rates rose. It wasn't until 1985 that these redemptions again occurred to any noticeable degree. By that time investors should have been at least somewhat familiar with these provisions even though they still disliked them. The legal considerations were out of the way, and the provisions have become a fact of life. But par calls are especially painful as the following two examples show.

On May 5, 1986, Houston Lighting & Power Company redeemed $117,056,000 of its 12⅜% first mortgage bonds due March 15, 2013, through the replacement fund provisions, leaving about $8 million outstanding. The call price was par but the bonds were trading at 115 or so just before the redemption was announced in early April.

On May 31, 1988, Central Maine Power Company redeemed at par $25.5 million of its Series F 12¼% General and Refunding Mortgage Bonds due May 1, 2013, under the renewal and replacement fund covenant. The sad part about this story is that many investors complained that they did not realize this issue was subject to the covenant as they assumed that the First Mortgage Bonds were still outstanding. After all, the prospectus for the subject 12¼s said that "The maintenance covenant

[22] "Early Redemption of Outstanding High Coupon Bonds — A Welcome Relief for Ratepayers." (Speech by William D. Talbott, Director, Accounting Department, Florida Public Service Commission, presented at the Fifth Institutional Investors Bond Conference, New York, October 21, 1977.)
[23] Lucas et al. v. Florida Power & Light Company, Final Judgment.

contained in the First Mortgage... will remain in effect until the First Mortgage is dis-charged, and upon such discharge the renewal and replacement fund provisions of the General Mortgage will become effective." If the investors, especially those with fidu-ciary responsibilities, had done a responsible job of proper research, something as el-ementary as looking at the annual report each year, they would have known that the First Mortgage Bonds no longer existed. The annual report for the year ended Decem-ber 31, 1986, stated: "The First and General Mortgage dated June 1, 1921, was dis-charged in December, 1986 in connection with the call for redemption of all outstanding bonds thereunder. Upon such discharge, the General and Refunding Mortgage succeeded the First and General Mortgage as the senior general lien on sub-stantially all of the Company's properties and franchises." It goes on to say, in refer-ring to the General and Refunding Mortgage Bonds, "Bonds may also be redeemed under certain conditions by means of cash deposited with the trustee under various provisions of the mortgage indenture."[24]

REDEMPTION THROUGH THE SALE OF ASSETS AND EMINENT DOMAIN

Bondholders want the borrower to maintain and preserve the value of the collateral securing the debt. The fact that the debt may be overcollateralized does not necessar-ily mean that management has free rein over the use and disposition of the excess collateral and any proceeds therefrom. But the lender has no right to impose undue restrictions on the borrower's ability to sell plant and property if doing so is deemed desirable from the standpoint of sound business practices. The secured lender has the right to adequate protection. If a company has $100 million of bonded debt outstand-ing secured by $200 million of plant, property and equipment, the $100 million sur-plus collateral provides additional protection for the bond owner. If the company feels that it is prudent to sell some of the property securing that debt, it should be allowed to do so (release the property from the mortgage lien) and substitute either cash or other property so that the total value of the collateral will not be reduced. The cash can be used to retire bonds or buy additional collateral. This type of situation is covered by *release and substitution of property clauses.*

---

[24] See *Bondweek*, Vol. IX, No. 14, April 11, 1988, for more flavor about this redemption. The replacement fund call was only part of the total redemption that May 31. The Company also offered to repurchase up to $34 million of the bonds through a Dutch auction procedure; it repurchased $18.8 million at 103.98% of par. The Company's treasurer said, "We want to give holders an option without alienating them." The tender and the possibility of the replacement fund redemption was announced in March. The bonds fell to par from about 109 to 109½ before getting back to 104 to 105. One manager was quoted as saying that "It caught all holders by surprise. No one really knew they were eligible to be taken out at par." This is just another example disproving the notion many have that bond investing is easy, a "no-brainer." Proper bond investment requires continual research, an inquiring mind, and common sense.

The release and substitution of property clause of Arizona Public Service as described in its prospectuses is fairly clear.[25]

> When not in default under the Mortgage, the Company may obtain the release from the lien thereof of (a) property that has become unserviceable, obsolete or unnecessary for use in the Company's operations, provided that it replaces such property with, or substitutes for the same, an equal value of other property and (b) other property that has been sold or otherwise disposed of, provided that the Company deposits with the Trustee cash in an amount, or utilizes as a credit net Property Additions acquired by the Company within the preceding five years and having a fair value (not more than Cost), equal to the fair value of the property to be released.

Arizona has utilized this method of debt redemption a couple of times. In late 1984, it retired $100 million of its 16% First Mortgage Bonds due 1994 at 100, with the proceeds from the sale of its gas distribution assets. In early 1987, it redeemed $150 million of its 11½% First Mortgage Bonds due June 1, 2015, also at par. The proceeds for this redemption came from the sale and leaseback of its portion in the Unit #2 of the Palo Verde nuclear power plant. These bonds had been issued only in June of 1985.

There have been cases in which companies sold plant, deposited the funds with the trustee, and then later decided not to redeem debt. In March 1984, Georgia Power Company sold some property and deposited funds with the trustee. It could have used the funds to purchase or redeem bonds or could have withdrawn them against delivery of bonds or shown that unfunded property additions existed after withdrawal. The fear of high-coupon bond redemption hung over the market for a couple of months until, on May 31, the company said it would not redeem any debt. Georgia decided against the call because of uncertainties in the financial markets. It pointedly stated that if it had future asset sales, its options regarding the funds would remain open.

Of course, investors are hurt most when their high-yield, premium-priced bonds are called at par or the special redemption price, and most electric utility mortgage issues use the special redemption price for these special calls. A few provide for the regular redemption prices including Florida Power & Light Company, Duke Power Company and Southern California Edison Company, among others. System Energy Resources 14% First Mortgage Bonds due November 15, 1994, are not optionally redeemable by the Company but they are redeemable with the proceeds of released property at 125% of their principal amount, a rather high call premium which should

---

[25] Prospectus for $100,000,000 of Arizona Public Service Company First Mortgage Bonds, 11½% Series due November 1, 2015, dated November 21, 1985.

ease any investor ill-will in case the bonds have to be called. Of course, par is the price for certain other redemptions. The Company has also used the par price for released property redemptions of other high-coupon issues such as its 16% and 15⅜% First Mortgage Bonds due 2000. Because the redemption prices used in any special redemption may vary between issues of the same company, prudent investors should carefully review the bonds' documentation to ascertain the call prices and the issues' vulnerability to special call.

Unsecured debt usually has no special redemption prices or requirements for prepayment in the event of asset sales. However, there may be exceptions, especially in the case of some sub investment-grade debt. Remember, do not confuse call protection with refunding protection. Redemptions of unsecured debt do occur within the refunding-protected period where the funds came from the sale of assets. In December 1983, Internorth, Inc. announced a February 1, 1984, call of $90.5 million out of $200 million of its 17½% debentures due August 1, 1991, at the regular redemption price of 112.32. The refunding-protected period ran until September 30, 1988. However, the proceeds were obtained from the sale of its Northern Propane Gas Company unit. On October 1, 1984, it redeemed another $23,875,000 of these 17½% debentures at 109.86 with funds obtained from the 1983 sale of two tanker ships.

The sale of assets to an affiliated company will not prevent debt redemption through the release clauses. Wisconsin Michigan Power retired $9.9 million of its 9¼% bonds due 2000 in February, 1977, at 100.97. On June 30, 1976, the company sold its gas business for $16.9 million to Wisconsin Natural Gas Company, an affiliate. The gas company got some of the money through bank borrowings. Of the proceeds, $16.5 million was deposited with the trustee under the release and substitution of property clause and a portion of the funds released to the company against certified property additions. The balance was used to redeem the high-coupon 9¼s, as interest rates had declined to the point where management thought it was in the company's best interest to do so.

Another similar transaction between affiliates occurred eight years later. This resulted in South Carolina Electric and Gas Company's (SCE&G) redemption of its 16% First Mortgage Bonds due June 1, 2011, at par on March 1, 1985. At the end of 1984, a new holding company called SCANA was formed that had two subsidiaries, SCG&E and the South Carolina Generating Company. SCG&E sold a coal-fired generating plant to its affiliated generating company for $80 million. It used these funds to par call the 16% bonds, which recently had been trading at 116. Some have called this unfair dealing and even a sham transaction. The lesson for investors is to be wary of debt redemption in times of lower interest rates.

Many utility bond issues contain provisions regarding the taking or confiscation of assets by a governmental body through its right of eminent domain or the disposition of assets by order of or to any governmental authority. In a number of cases, bonds must be redeemed if the company receives more than a certain amount in cash. Washington Water Power Company must apply the proceeds of $15 million or more to the retirement of debt. The redemption price may be either the special or regular, depending on the issue. In 1984, Pacific Power & Light

Company sold an electric distribution system to the Emerald People's Utility District for $25 million. It applied these proceeds to the redemption of half of the outstanding 14¾% Mortgage Bonds due 2010 at the special redemption price of 100. This issue was not the highest-coupon bond outstanding in the company's capitalization. There were some 18s of 1991, but these were exempt from the special provisions for the retirement of bonds with the proceeds from property sold to governmental authorities. More recently, in April 1988, Utah Power & Light Company retired some 13% bonds due 2012 with funds obtained from the condemnation of some of its property in Kaneb, Utah, and the sale of electric assets to a couple other cities.

NET WORTH, MERGER, AND OTHER REDEMPTIONS

The great increase in merger and acquisition activity, including leveraged buyouts and other corporate restructurings, has caused some companies to include other special debt retirement features in their indentures. For example, the *maintenance of net worth clause* is included in the indentures of many lower-rated bond issues of the 1980s. In this case, an issuer covenants to maintain its net worth above a stipulated level. If its net worth falls below that specified amount for a certain period (usually two consecutive quarters), the company must begin redeeming its debt at par. The redemptions, often 10% of the original issue, are mostly on a semiannual basis, and must continue until the net worth recovers to an amount above the stated figure. In many cases, the company is only required to "offer to redeem" the stated amount. An offer to redeem is not mandatory on the bondholders' part; only those holders who want their bonds redeemed need do so. In a number of instances in which the issuer is required to call bonds, the bondholders may elect not to have bonds redeemed. This is not much different from an offer to redeem. It may "protect" bondholders from the redemption of the high-coupon debt at lower interest rates. However, if a company's net worth declines to a level low enough to activate such a call, it would probably be prudent to have one's bonds redeemed.

The minimum net worth requirement varies from approximately 45% to 65% of the issuer's net worth at the time the debt was issued, depending on the company. The definition of net worth, or net tangible assets, will also vary among issuers. The prospectuses talk about generally accepted accounting principles and frequently include only common shareholders' net worth, but some also include preferred stock. Intangible assets, such as goodwill, patents, trademarks, and unamortized deferred charges, normally are excluded from the calculation of tangible net worth. But again, definitions vary among issues. The prospectus for Coastal Corporation's 11¾% Senior Debentures due June 15, 2006, defines consolidated net worth as:

> ... the total consolidated stockholder's equity (exclusive of any Mandatory Redemption Preferred Stock) of such person and its subsidiaries determined on a consolidated basis in

accordance with generally accepted accounting principles, except that there shall be deducted therefrom all intangible assets (determined in accordance with generally accepted accounting principles) including, without limitation, organization costs, patents, trademarks, copyrights, franchises, research and development expenses, and any amount reflected as treasury stock; provided, that goodwill arising from acquisitions and unamortized debt discount and expense, whether existing on the date of the indenture or arising thereafter, shall not be deducted from total consolidated stockholders' equity.

Obviously the definition is very important, and one cannot always rely on the prospectus since it may include no definition or only an incomplete one. This was important for the holders of Minstar Inc.'s 14⅞% Senior Subordinated Notes due 1995. The $300 million issue was publicly sold in April 1985, and one year later the company announced the call of $30 million at par due to the net worth clause (they were otherwise not callable until April 1, 1990). The notes were trading around 113 ($1,130 each) prior to the call announcement. Minstar subsequently redeemed another $30 million in September 1986 and purchased an additional $126.6 million of notes in the open market, recording an extraordinary loss of $13.5 million on the debt extinguishment. Also, in the annual report for the year ended December 31, 1986, the company recorded as current maturities of long-term debt $60 million of notes subject to this mandatory redemption in 1987. Here again an indenture provision was used to retire some high-cost debt and caught investors off guard. Analysts and investors relying on the prospectus could come up with no close approximation of tangible net worth. The prospectus stated: "Tangible Net Worth generally means consolidated shareholders' equity, less, among other things, goodwill, patents, trademarks, service marks, trade names, copyrights, organization or developmental expenses and other intangible items."

The indenture for the notes defines tangible net worth as follows:

Tangible Net Worth means the consolidated equity of the common stockholders of the Company and its consolidated subsidiaries less their consolidated Intangible Assets, all determined on a consolidated basis in accordance with generally accepted accounting principles. For purposes of this definition "Intangible Assets" means the amount (to the extent reflected in determining such consolidated equity of the common stockholders) of (i) all write-ups (other than write-ups resulting from foreign currency translations and write-ups of tangible assets of a going concern business made within twelve months after the acquisition of such business) subsequent to December 31, 1984 in the book value of any asset owned by the company or a consolidated subsidiary, (ii) all investments in unconsolidated subsidiaries and in persons which are not subsidiaries, and (iii) all unamortized debt discount and expense, unamortized deferred charges, goodwill, patents, trademarks, service marks, trade names. Copyrights, organization or developmental expenses and other intangible items, all of the foregoing as determined in accordance with generally accepted accounting principles.[26]

Note item (ii) above and the reference to investments. Minstar had substantial investments in marketable equities with value, yet the indenture was written so as to make then valueless. They had to be eliminated in the calculation of tangible net worth. It is interesting to note that the use of proceeds section of the prospectus stated that the monies "will be added to the Company's general funds to be used for acquisitions, investments, and general corporate purposes." It said that the company "makes significant investments in securities of other companies." Thus, investors who initially purchased the bonds were effectively reducing tangible net worth to the extent that investment securities were purchased with the proceeds. Also, this could allow a company with a similar definition and operations to rid itself of some high-coupon debt at par just by making more investments! Of course, Minstar's published annual report made no mention of what tangible net worth amounted to according to the indenture's definition at December 31, 1985.

There are a few other ways companies can (or must) extinguish debt prior to maturity. The issues of some finance companies and others with a considerable amount of accounts receivable have provisions allowing the issues to be redeemed if the receivables decline below a certain amount. While not mandatory, this provision can protect debtholders from a weakening of credit due to a substantial decline in the issuer's asset base. It allows the issuer to reduce its debt burden, assuming that it still has the wherewithal to do so. Of course, if the company elects to redeem debt, it will most likely choose from the higher-coupon issues. This provision has been infrequently invoked — if ever — by major debt issuers. A call could occur if there were a serious recession and receivables declined by a substantial amount. It could also be activated if a company sold or transferred receivables to another corporation as part of a reorganization, restructuring or liquidation.

The debt of some foreign companies sold in the United States may be subject to premature redemption in the event of certain situations that normally would not affect conventional domestic issues. In December 1983, The Swan Brewery Company Limited sold US$135 million of 14⅞% Limited Subordination Debentures due December 15, 1998. The issue requires Swan to redeem a specific percentage of the outstanding debentures (subject to certain credits) if the average of the U.S. dollar noon

---

[26] Minstar, Inc. $300,000,000 of 14⅞% Senior Subordinated Notes due 1995, Indenture, dated as of April 1, 1985, Norwest Bank Minneapolis, N. A. Trustee.

buying rates for Australian dollars over certain six-month periods is less than those stated in the prospectus. The redemption is on a pro rata basis, but holders may elect not to have their bonds redeemed. Another provision, also subject to election by the debtholder, allows the company to offer to redeem the entire issue if the Australian government requires the withholding of taxes and other governmental charges from payments to the debenture holders.

TENDERS

Another debt retirement method is the *tender*. While it may be more costly for the borrower than a straight cash call, it allows debt to be retired even if it is noncallable. Also, tenders don't force the holder to give up the bonds. To encourage holders to tender their bonds, the issuer must offer a price above what others are willing to offer, namely a buyback price above the market. The premium which Mountain States Telephone & Telegraph Company offered for its 11⅝% Debentures in the March 1986 tender "was determined by calculating the tender price that would provide a yield-to-first-call comparable to the yield an investor could realize by investing in U.S. government agency issues over the same time horizon."[27]

Tenders are not limited to only issues selling above par. In 1983, Diamond International Company tendered for its 8.35% debentures due in 2006 at 77½, and Black & Decker Manufacturing Company tendered for its 8.45% notes due 1985 at 98. In 1985, Burlington Northern Railroad Company made an unsuccessful tender at 53½ for Northern Pacific Railway Company's 4% Prior Lien Railway and Land Grant Gold Bonds due 1997, and at 39 for Northern Pacific's 3% General Lien Railway and Land Grant Gold Bonds due 2047. The bonds, issued in 1896, are not callable for life. The mortgages do not provide for their modification or for the release of certain collateral, namely some valuable natural resource-laden properties Burlington Northern wanted to commercially develop. The tender was part of a plan to obtain the release of the property by substituting government bonds in a trust to ensure the payment of principal and interest when due for the remaining untendered bonds; this is an in-substance defeasance (discussed shortly). Bondholders sued, as they thought a higher price should have been offered. A federal judge barred Burlington from proceeding, and the company withdrew the offer. Burlington subsequently negotiated a settlement (effective in early 1988) with the bondholders and paid them what some called a "hold-up" premium of $147.50 per $1,000 1997 bond and $456.30 per 2047 bond. In return, the bondholders release from the lien of the mortgage millions of acres of land and mineral rights.

Each summer the Baltimore Gas & Electric Company asks for tenders to satisfy the funnel sinking fund on its mortgage bonds. In some cases the tenders are accepted and in other cases it is more advantageous for the company to repurchase bonds in the open market, or to even have the trustee call the bonds at the special redemption prices.

---

[27] See Finnerty, Kalotay and Farrell, *Evaluating Bond Refunding Opportunities*, p. 38.

Most tenders allow a company to retire debt at a fixed or predetermined price, and rather quickly since tenders are usually open for only a limited time. A simple open-market purchase of bonds usually occurs over a longer period, leaving the purchaser subject to changes in market conditions. Open-market purchases may prove to be less costly than a tender offer if interest rise and prices decline, but it is less likely to permit a company to achieve its debt retirement goals. Of course, the market can go against the company using a fixed-price tender offer, with the result that few bonds are repurchased. Therefore, in recent years, an increasing number of issuers are using a "fixed-spread tender offer" which allays its interest rate risk during the tender period. In this type of tender the purchase price of the bond is based on the yield to maturity of some other issue (most often a U.S. Treasury issue) maturing on or close to the first refunding or call date of the subject corporate bond plus a fixed spread expressed in basis points.

For example, on December 14, 1993, Southern New England Telephone Company tendered for its 9.60% Medium-Term Notes, Series A, due February 15, 2030 and not callable until February 15, 1995, then at $1,067.50 per note. The tender price is that resulting from the yield to maturity based on the bid price of the 5.50% U.S. Treasury Note due February 15, 1995 (the first call date on the Southern New England Notes) plus 0.10% (ten basis points). Based on the yield of the Treasury note on December 10, 1993 of 3.81%, the yield and purchase price of the Southern New England paper would have been 3.91% and $1,128.41, respectively, and a fairly substantial premium over the first call price. The large premium was worth it to the Company because the net present value of the interest savings over the life of the retired bonds compensated it for the loss of the of call option two years down the road.

With the Dutch auction tender, the sellers rather than the buying company set the prices they wish to receive. At the end of the tender period, the buyer reviews all of the tenders received and determines the highest price it is willing to pay. It then buys all of the bonds tendered at and below the maximum acceptable tender price. The Dutch auction allows the market to set the tender price.

Proceeds for a tender can come from any source. On December 3, 1986, The May Department Stores Company sold $150 million of 9⅛% debentures due 2016. The use of proceeds section says that the new funds would be used to retire some short-term debt that had a weighted average interest cost of 5.8% and matured before January 1, 1987. Yet, on December 11 the company announced the tender for $100 million of its 11⅞% debentures due April 15, 2015, at 112.04. Holders need not tender their bonds, and the company is within its rights to offer to repurchase them even within the refunding-protected period.

Several years later May Department Stores utilized another type of tender tactic which raised the ire of a number of bondholders and cost the Company and Morgan Stanley, its investment banker, a fair amount of money. On October 1, 1992, May sold $200 million par value of 8⅜% Debentures due in 2002, netting nearly $198 million. Settlement for the bonds was October 8. According to the prospectus, the proceeds were to be used "for the purchase of the Company's other indebtedness," among other things. On October 6, May, through its investment banker, initiated a tender offer for all of its $175 million of outstanding 10⅞% Debentures due 2018. May offered to buy the bonds at a price of 109.16, only a slight premium over the call price of 108.70. The bonds had been trading near 110 at that time. Holders were given two weeks to tender at this slight premium, and if they didn't, May would call the untendered bonds at the regular redemption price. This type of "gun-to-the-head" tender is called *simultaneous tender (offer) and call*, or STAC for short.

The interesting thing about this strong-arm tactic is that the bonds would be called even though the issue still had six years remaining of refunding protection. While it had just sold an issue with a coupon 250 basis points less that the called bonds, May said it wasn't a refunding but a redemption with so-called "clean cash" obtained when it dissolved its share of a real estate partnership.[28] May reported a nonrecurring gain of $298 million on this transaction. However, according to the Form 10-Q quarterly report filed with the Securities and Exchange Commission for the period ended August 1, 1992, the nonrecurring gain did not provide cash. The cash wasn't "clean" and the Company did not have a discrete, segregated equity fund in place from which the redemption could be made. If the cash were clean, then there would be no reason for May to offer any premium over the regular redemption price. In fact, the new bond issue had all the appearances of a refunding bond. It was closely linked to the 10⅞% Debentures since it was issued just days before the start of the STAC and these proceeds were available for the tender and call. Some think that the issuance of the new bond was a real blunder.

Some $77 million of the 10⅞s were tendered and the remaining $88 million were called. Investors strongly resented this coercive tactic of May and Morgan Stanley, feeling that it was improper to use the threat of a cash call in order to induce them to tender their bonds at only a slight premium. In addition, to add fuel to the fire, on November 13, 1992, May announced that it was calling for redemption $85 million of its $250 million 10¾% Debentures due 2018 at a price of 108.60.

Certainly, proceeds of the new issue could be used for the tender part of the transaction, but it was a violation of the indenture of the 10⅞s and the 10¾s to refund the bonds. After all, the pertinent redemption sections of the prospectuses bar refunding of the 10⅞s prior to September 1, 1998, and the 10¾s prior to June 15, 1998. Taking the 10⅞s, the prospectus states: "... provided, however, that the Company may not redeem the Debentures prior to September 1, 1998, as part of a refunding or anticipated refunding operation by the application, directly or indirectly, of the proceeds of Indebtedness for money borrowed which shall have an interest cost to the Company of less than 10.975% per annum." Virtually identical wording is also used for the 10¾% Debentures.

---

[28] The Employees Retirement System of Alabama et al., Plaintiffs, vs. The May Department Stores Company and Morgan Stanley & Co., Defendants. Fourth Amended and Restated Complaint, Case No. CV 92-2726-R, Circuit Court for the Fifteenth Judicial Circuit, Montgomery County, Alabama, March 5, 1993.

Just because May did not call these transactions refunding operations doesn't mean that they aren't. They had all the attributes of refundings. A group of investors representing $156 million of bonds filed a legal action against May and Morgan Stanley seeking compensatory damages in excess of $25 million and punitive damages of $100 million based on the following causes of action: 1) Violation of the Trust Indenture Act; 2) breach of contract; 3) conversion; 4) malicious breach of the implied covenant of good faith and fair dealing: bad faith; 5) tortious interference with contract; 6) fraud, misrepresentation and deceit, and 7) violation of state securities acts.

The suit was settled in August, 1994, just prior to coming to trial. The plaintiffs won $28 million and were allowed to keep the redemption premium. A May spokesman said: "We believe that the transaction was a fair and legitimate means of retiring high-cost callable debt." The Company settled to avoid further litigation and costs, citing "uncertainty in jury trials dealing with complicated financial transactions." The lead plaintiff said that the settlement "... sent the right message that this is wrong and bondholders are going to sue if you do it. STAC violates the terms of an indenture. It was a tactic that created fees for Wall Street."[29] Score one for the good guys!

In general, it makes good sense for investors to consider tender offers because if enough bonds are repurchased, the few remaining could very well become virtually unmarketable, or at least, very illiquid. If listed, they could be delisted. Traders will not ordinarily take into their positions bonds which can't be readily resold. Also, with fewer bonds outstanding the holder is more likely to lose a greater percentage of its holdings through the sinking fund. In September 1983, Northern States Power Company (Minnesota) received tenders at 119.75 for about $65.6 million out of $75 million of its 15¾% mortgage bonds due 2011. Some $9.4 million remained in public hands. The sinking fund was 1% or $750,000 each year, cash, bonds or property additions. On October 31, 1983, the company called for the December 1 sinking fund — $750,000 of the bonds, or nearly 8% of the then outstanding amount. Thus, in less than two months holders lost some 19¾ points — the difference between the tender price and the sinking fund call price. Similar amounts were retired in subsequent years at par and the remaining balance was retired on December 1, 1986, at 112.21.

DEFEASANCE

Defeasance is included as a type of debt extinguishment even though the bonds remain outstanding. There are two types of defeasance transactions. One is called *economic* or *in-substance defeasance* and the other is *legal defeasance* or *novation*. Until the early

---

[29] See Bloomberg Business News for the following stories on the settlement: DJ, 8/22/94, "May Stores, Morgan Stanley Settle Refinancing Lawsuit," BBN, 8/22/94, "May Stores, Morgan Stanley Settle Bond Suit for $28 Mln.," and BBN, 8/22/94, "Rates of Return: Chalk Up Another Investor Victory," Another interesting article is Benjamin J. Stein, "STACked Deck, Bondholders Get Tough Over Tender Deal," *Barron's* (June 21, 1993), pp. 14-15.

1980s, defeasance was rarely used for public corporate debt. There had been cases of privately placed debt in which the issuer reached an agreement with all of the lenders under which they would release the borrower from the indenture in return for ample consideration, typically an acceptable package of securities. A corporation with public debt could do little to defease its obligations, although municipal obligations provided for legal defeasance for a number of years.

In 1983, the Financial Accounting Standards Board (FASB) narrowly approved the *Statement of Financial Accounting Standards No. 76* "Extinguishment of Debt, An Amendment of APB Opinion No. 26," providing for the defeasance of corporate debt.[30] Effective for transactions entered into after December 31, 1983, it applies only to debt with specific maturities and fixed interest rates. In this type of defeasance, an irrevocable trust is established to service the principal and interest payments on the debt issue being defeased. The assets of the trust must consist of essentially risk-free monetary assets in the currency in which the debt is denominated and with a cash flow timed to very closely match that of the defeased obligation. For U.S.-dollar payable debt, these qualified assets include cash, direct obligations of the U.S. government, debt guaranteed by the U.S. government, and securities that are backed by U.S. government obligations as collateral under an arrangement in which the collateral's interest and principal payments flow directly to the security holder. As some securities can be paid prior to the stated maturity or have partial principal payments that may be paid before the final maturity, they are not essentially risk free from a timing standpoint and thus are not eligible for inclusion in the trust assets. Many issues of U.S. Government sponsored enterprises (also known as agencies) also are ineligible, as they are not guaranteed by the United States. The debtor must be virtually assured that it will not be required to make any future payments in regard to the defeased debt.

An economic defeasance removes the debt from the corporation's balance sheet but leaves the borrower still liable under all of the indenture provisions until the debt is actually extinguished. It must abide by any covenants, as economic defeasance is not provided for in indentures. Because of the debtor's continuing obligation under the indenture, the transaction must be disclosed in the notes to the financial statements for as long as the debt remains outstanding. The debtor remains liable for

---

[30] Statement of Financial Accounting Standards No. 76, "Extinguishment of Debt, An Amendment of APB Opinion No. 26," November 1983. This statement was approved by only a four-to-three vote. The three dissenting members said:

> ... they do not believe the extinguishment of debt accounting and resultant gain or loss recognition should be extended to situations wherein the "debtor was not legally released from being the primary obligor under the debt obligation." They believe... that "a liability once incurred by an enterprise remains a liability until it is satisfied in another transaction or other event or circumstance affecting the enterprise." ...Dedicating the assets might ensure that the debt is serviced in timely fashion, but that event alone just matches up cash flows; it does not satisfy, eliminate, or extinguish the obligation. For a debt to be satisfied, the creditor must be satisfied. (p. 5).

tax reporting purposes since it pays income taxes on the income of the trust and takes a deduction for the interest expense. Also, when the trust terminates at the defeased debt's maturity, taxes also must be paid on the increase in value between the cost of the trust's assets and the maturity value. But any fees paid to investment bankers for advice and any trustee fees normally will be considered tax deductible expenses at the time they are incurred.

A novation, or legal, defeasance removes the debt from the balance sheet for financial reporting purposes, frees the corporation from any indenture terms (with a few minor exceptions), and eliminates any further tax consequences. In order to obtain this, the indenture must make provision for legal defeasance. In January 1981, Union Carbide Corporation registered a proposed $200 million offering whose indenture contained such a provision. The issue never came to market as investors, being overly wary, thought this was another method by which a company could prematurely retire debt. However, after in-substance defeasance got the nod of approval from the Securities and Exchange Commission in 1983, most indentures of publicly offered corporate bonds included legal defeasance language.

For several years, the defeasance provision was viewed as a pledge rather than a sale or exchange of property and thus a transaction was not taxable. More recently, the indenture language was modified to take note of regulations treating defeasance as a debt redemption prior to maturity in exchange for property deposited in a trust, a transaction subject to federal income taxes. Defeasance sections of prospectuses have thus been modified. The following from the May 5, 1989, prospectus for General Motors Corporation 9¾% Notes due May 15, 1999, is one such example.

> The Corporation, at its option, (i) will be discharged from any and all obligations in respect of the Notes (except for certain obligations to register the transfer or exchange of Notes, replace stolen, lost or mutilated Notes, maintain paying agencies and hold monies for payment in trust), or (ii) will not be under any obligation to comply with certain covenants applicable to the Notes..., if the Corporation deposits with the Trustee, in trust for the holders of the Notes, (A) money or (B) obligations issued or guaranteed by the United States of America which through the payment of interest thereon and principal thereof will provide money, in each case in an amount sufficient to pay all the principal of (and premium, if any) and interest on the Notes on the dates such payments are due in accordance with the terms of the Notes. To exercise the option described in (i) above, the Corporation is required among other things, to deliver to the Trustee an opinion of nationally recognized tax counsel to the effect that holders of Notes will not recognize income, gain or loss for Federal income tax purposes as a result of such deposit and discharge and will be subject to Federal income tax on the same amounts and in the same manner and at the same times as would have been the case if such deposit and discharge had not occurred.

Section (i) above is often called "defeasance and discharge" while section (ii) is referred to as "covenant defeasance." It is important to note that provisions may vary among issues and a few do not provide for tax opinions as the General Motors issue. In such cases where a defeasance transaction occurs, the result would be a taxable transaction under current rules and regulations. Investors subject to Federal income taxes should consult with tax counsel if purchasing or trading defeased bonds to see if there might be a tax liability.

While the trusts are irrevocable they are not inviolable, as a considerable number provide for the withdrawal and substitution of collateral sufficient to satisfy the payment obligations. It was reported that withdrawals were made in 1986 when some companies bought back and retired portions of their defeased debt and sold a corresponding share of the Government securities withdrawn from the trusts. This was an economic way of taking advantage of the tax laws, which would shortly change. The loss taken on the repurchase would be partially offset by the high 46% income tax rate, while the capital gain on the sale of the Treasuries would be taxed at 28%. This caused some accounting experts to consider whether the whole issue should be reexamined. The initial FASB bulletin took into account the possibility of the repurchase of defeased debt and said that it should be viewed as though "the debtor is making an investment in the future cash flows from the trust and should report its investment as an asset in its balance sheet. The debtor should not be considered to be reextinguishing its debt. Thus, no gain or loss should be recognized from such purchase of those debt securities."[31] It did not consider that the "irrevocable" trusts could be violated even if provided for.

In 1982 there were several economic defeasance transactions. Kellogg Company defeased its 9⅝% Notes due October 1, 1985, by paying $65.6 million in cash to the Morgan Guaranty Trust Company, which arranged for a group of companies to assume the principal and interest payments for the $75 million issue. The transaction was also guaranteed by a Morgan Guaranty letter of credit. Exxon Corporation defeased its 6% debentures due 1997 and the 6% debentures due 1998. The trust portfolio consisted of federal government and agency securities. These transactions were allowed to stand as economic defeasances, since they occurred before FASB No. 76 took effect. Since the beginning of 1984 a number of other companies defeased debt including Atlantic Richfield Co., The Cincinnati Gas & Electric Company, and City Investing Company.

Normally, defeasance transactions occur when interest rates are high, a company has lower-coupon debt outstanding, the prices of Treasury securities are depressed, and the issuer is in an ample cash position. Also, the benefits of investing in a trust of Treasury securities should outweigh investment in new plant and equipment. Among the advantages of defeasance is the boost it can give to reported earnings due to the difference between the par value of the defeased bonds and the cost of the trust assets. United States Steel Corporation (now USX Corporation)

---

[31] Statement of Financial Accounting Standards No. 76, p. 14.

issued an earnings release on July 30, 1985, stating that it retired $192 million of debt in the first half of the year, including defeasing $168 million of the 4⅝% subordinated debentures due 1996. The total extinguishment resulted in an extraordinary gain of $38 million net of income tax of $32 million. These earnings are "below the line" and should not be used in calculating the financial ratios popular with corporate bond analysts; they are nonoperating, noncash, and nonrecurring.

The debt is also removed from the books, leverage should decrease and other debt-related measurements should show improvement. This could lead to a better credit evaluation of the company, especially if it is a novation. The repayment risk that had been associated with the predefeased debt is, to all intents and purposes, eliminated. Defeasance reduces the chance of the issue's price being run up in a repurchase program, but at times it may be more expensive. Obviously, it should be undertaken only after all alternative methods of debt redemption have been analyzed. The benefits to the balance sheet and income statements are one-time occurrences. Finally, with an in-substance defeasance, nothing really has changed as the company is still legally liable for the debt.

How have the rating agencies reacted to defeasance transactions? When the previously mentioned Union Carbide issue was proposed, Moody's Investors Service in its Bond Survey of February 2, 1981, stated, "When and if such a transaction (defeasance) occurs, payment of the bonds becomes assured, Moody's would raise the rating for these debentures from Aa to Aaa." Standard & Poor's Corporation commented that it would rate legally defeased issues AAA in consideration of the quality of assets in the trust and the matched flow of funds to debt service requirements. Examples of legally defeased issues raised to the S&P "AAA" rating category include Cameron Iron Works Inc. 11½% Notes due 1991 (formerly rated "BB+") and Leaseway Transportation Corporation's collateral trust notes ("B+").

Obtaining the highest rating for an in-substance defeased issue requires overcoming some concerns about bankruptcy and the effects on the trust estate pledged to service the debt. Standard & Poor's commented:

> Therefore, in order for S&P to rate in-substance defeased debt 'AAA', opinions of counsel are required indicating that:
>
> - The automatic stay provisions of the Bankruptcy Code (Section 362 (a)) would not apply in the event of the company's bankruptcy.
>
> - Section 549 of the code, which could void or impair the timely use of escrowed funds to pay debt service, would not apply in the event of the company's bankruptcy.
>
> - Deposit of assets into the escrow account will not constitute a preference with respect to the company in the event of the company's bankruptcy within 90 days after such deposit.

In addition, S&P must be assured that the defeased debt will be free from any risks associated with cross-default provisions that would tie the default and acceleration of the defeased issue to a default on other debt of the company.[32]

CONCLUSION

The level and trend of interest rates are among the more important factors in a company's decision whether or not to retire its debt, be it through a sinking fund, refunding or defeasance. An issuer will redeem its debt when it is to its own advantage, not the debtholder's. If necessary, the issuer may use the protective provisions of the indenture against the bondholder. Other factors considered are the company's cash position and ability to raise the needed cash, its future cash requirements and financing plans, and, in the case of some utility companies, its ability to certify property additions or specifically authenticated bonds as credits for certain redemptions. Of course, we must not leave out the tax factor as another important consideration. Issuers must consider the impact of any redemption on its relationships with creditors, the investment community, the regulatory authorities and, most important, its shareholders and customers. Circumstances and attitudes do change. Just because a firm has established a pattern for the satisfaction of sinking fund and other indenture provisions, and may have waited until the refunding-protected period passed, does not mean that it will continue to follow these patterns and methods. The greater the difference between the interest costs on the outstanding debt and the present level of interest rates (and the savings to be achieved), the more a company is compelled to use whatever means it can to retire debt.

Finally, the reader may find these definitions about call and redemption of interest.

> Call feature: A device that allows the only good bond you ever owned to be taken away from you.

> Call protection: Something that exists only in the mind of the naive investor.[33]

---

[32] Roy Taub and Neil Baron, "Bond Defeasance Nears FASB Approval," *Standard & Poor's CreditWeek*, November 78, 1983, p. 550.

[33] Maurice Joy, *Not Heard on the Street* (Chicago, IL: Probus Publishing Company. 1986), p. 17.

CHAPTER 6

Convertible Bonds

Convertible bonds are debt instruments with an embedded equity participation feature. They allow investors to participate in both interest rate and stock price movements, although the latter may have a greater price influence. As with the case of conventional debt securities, the term *bonds* is used in its generic sense. There are few true convertible bonds outstanding as most are notes and debentures. We will use bond interchangeably with note and debenture. This chapter explains many of the special features of convertibles. The option's approach to convertible bond evaluation is discussed in Chapter 12.

WHAT IS A CONVERTIBLE BOND?

A convertible bond can usually be exchanged or converted at the option of the holder into a fixed number of shares of common stock (and sometimes other securities).[1] Price appreciation in the underlying common stock will usually be reflected in the market price or value of the convertible. Referred to as hybrid securities, they combine elements of senior securities with those of junior equity. While of primary appeal to common stock buyers, there are times when they may be attractive to traditional bond investors as well. Being equity substitutes, they are more affected by individual company news and events than by interest rate and economic factors.

---

[1] While most convertibles may be exchanged for common stock, there are issues convertible into straight debt, cash and/or other securities; most of these have been created out of mergers and acquisitions. One such example was Avco Corporation's 5.50% Convertible Subordinated Debentures due November 30, 1993, convertible originally into 18.52 shares of common stock at $54 a share. In 1985 Textron acquired Avco for $50 per share and the terms of the outstanding convertibles were changed so the bonds were entitled to receive the cash value offered for the underlying security, namely $50 times 18.52 shares or $926 per bond.

Convertibles are not new to the twentieth century. Dewing notes that convertibles of one type or another have been around since at least the seventeenth century.[2] In our corporate history they were used by some infamous characters such as James Fisk, Jr., Daniel Drew and Jay Gould in their battles for the Erie Railway with Commodore Cornelius Vanderbilt in the 1860s.[3] Most often convertible bonds have been issued for legitimate corporate purposes by companies in sound financial condition. Many well-known corporations have utilized this form of financing including American Telephone and Telegraph Company, Eastman Kodak, International Business Machines, Greyhound Corporation, and Union Pacific Corporation, among others.

An estimate of the size of the outstanding publicly issued convertible market can be gleaned from Standard & Poor's *Bond Guide* for September 1994. It presents details of some 473 convertible bond issues with an outstanding par value of approximately $56.8 billion. However, eliminating smaller issues with less than $10 million outstanding as well as those convertible into cash and or straight debt, reduces the estimated number of converts as investment candidates to 384 with a par value of $55.7 billion. Of these, 39 were zero coupon convertibles with a par value of $21.7 billion. At the same time the September 1994 issue of the Merrill Lynch *Convertible Securities Review* gave details of 406 regular domestic and Euro convertible bonds including 40 zero coupon issues. The market value of the regular coupon issues was approximately $38.8 billion and the value of the zeros was $11.6 billion.

---

[2] Arthur Stone Dewing, *The Financial Policy of Corporations*, Volume 1, 5th ed. (New York: Ronald Press Company, 1953). He states:

> Conversion from one type of security into another has existed in England for a long period of time. Scott mentions the case of an early London Water Company in which King Charles I was allowed to convert his stock into bonds. (p. 256)

[3] George Wheeler, *Pierpont Morgan and Friends: The Anatomy of a Myth* (Englewood Cliffs: Prentice-Hall, Inc., 1973). In discussing Daniel Drew's three methods of twisted finance, Wheeler describes the first method, which consisted of violations of the New York State railway act, as follows:

> That law permitted the roads to issue bonds to raise money `to complete, equip and operate' the line. To help sustain the value of the bonds, a `sweetener' was allowed in which the buyer could convert the bond into a share of common stock. The theory was that the buyer would pay a better price for the bond and thus maintain its value if he knew that later, when the stock rose above par, he would have an additional profit through the conversion feature. But Drew had his own theories. He had the company issue the bonds in violation of the legislative provisions that they were only to be brought out for the specific purposes cited, and he immediately used the convertible feature despite the fact that the stock was far below par value.

CONVERTIBLE BOND PROVISIONS

As with any security, investors should analyze the terms of the convertible in which they are interested, especially before the investment is made rather than when trouble looms. There are always exceptions to general statements and a knowledge of these exceptions may mean the difference between profit and loss. While indentures may be the best source of information about the terms of the issues, they may not be readily available. Therefore, prospectuses will have to do even though they are summaries of the indenture and do not profess to be complete. The statements are qualified in their entirety by reference to the indentures.

The first part of the security description gives the maturity, interest record and payment dates, the issue's size, denominations and form of ownership, and other pertinent information. The next section discusses the status or ranking of the security. Convertible debentures are mostly subordinated in the right of payment to the senior debt and are designated with subordinated in the issue's title. Seldom will the most senior level of debt in the capitalization structure include a convertible issue. One exception was Dana Corporation's 5⅞% Convertible Debentures due in 2006 which ranked on a parity with all of the other senior debt of the company. Some companies might issue convertible debentures or notes, but upon closer inspection they will prove to be junior to most other issues.

The next section of the offering circular covers conversion rights, giving the price and number of shares into which the security is convertible, and the procedure for converting or exchanging the bonds. The conversion price for a majority of issues is usually set at 15% to 25% above the common's closing price on the day the offering was priced. Some issuers have the right to lower the conversion price to induce or force the holder to convert. There have been issues in which the conversion price increases during the life of the conversion privilege. This is designed to encourage early conversion if the stock's price increases. If the security is convertible into a fraction of a share, cash is normally paid instead of issuing fractional shares.

In most cases the bondholder receives common shares of the issuing company, but some convertible debentures are exchangeable into common shares of another company. The shares received may be those of the parent company such as Ford Motor Credit Company's 4.50% convertible subordinated debentures due November 15, 1996, and the 4⅞s of 1998, both exchangeable for the shares of Ford Motor Company. In other cases the shares may constitute an investment of the issuer. One such example is Pennzoil Company's 6½% Exchangeable Senior Debentures due January 15, 2003, exchangeable at $42.0628 into 23.774 shares of Chevron Corporation. Pennzoil may pay the holder converting the debentures cash in lieu of issuing Chevron's shares. Dividends paid on the underlying stock belong to the issuing company as long as it is the owner of the underlying shares. However, certain types of special or liquidating dividends and distributions remain with the associated shares and are distributed when an exchange occurs. The shares are held by an escrow agent who also acts as agent for the exchange of the debentures.

An investor in exchangeable issues must be concerned about two companies covered by one investment. These are (a) the issuing company which has the responsibility of servicing the debt, and (b) the company into which stock the security is exchangeable. You want both to remain healthy and prosper so that there is little chance of the interest or dividend not being paid on a timely basis and that the market value of the underlying equity increases so to make the exchangeable senior security more valuable. If the issuing corporation fails to meet its obligations, default and bankruptcy may follow. The exchangeable security holder is left in a general unsecured (or even subordinated) creditor status even though the underlying stock might be of a very sound company. The exchangeable holder does not have the right to these shares. The shares may be considered impaired and are likely to be deemed assets of the bankrupt's estate, which, along with the corporation's other assets, may be used to satisfy general creditors claims.

The conversion section provides information about the adjustment of the number of shares to be issued upon conversion or exchange in cases of stock splits, dividends, reverse splits, recapitalizations, issuance of warrants, assets and other securities. Without anti-dilution provisions, only the naive would buy convertibles as a company may split its stock and the convertible holder would receive only the old number of shares upon conversion. The Pennzoil prospectus states: "If Chevron should issue any Chevron Common Stock in subdivision or by way of stock dividend, the exchange rate will be proportionately increased, and if Chevron shall effect a combination of Chevron Common Stock, the exchange rate will be proportionately reduced...."

If the conversion occurs after the interest payment date and before the record date, adjustments are not made for the accrued interest. Because of this, the conversion price of the underlying stock may be greater than is first apparent. Convertible bonds trade like other bonds, namely at a certain price plus accrued interest to the settlement date. If you sell the bond in the open market you get the accrued interest, but if you convert you lose the accrual.

However, if an investor converts between the interest payment record date and the end of the day before the payment date, he may or may not have the right to the interest payment due on the payment date; it all depends on the terms of the particular issue. Often, securities surrendered for conversion during those dates must be accompanied with a check for the full amount of the interest to be received on the payment date. In some other cases, the interest will be paid to all holders of record even if they had converted prior to the payment date.

Most issues allow conversion to begin immediately after issuance but, from time to time, one runs across a bond with a delayed conversion feature. Most conversion rights expire at maturity or the redemption date, or a couple of weeks before, but a few may lose the conversion privilege several years before maturity. Dana Corporation's 5⅞% debentures of 2006, lost their convertibility on December 15, 1993. After that date the bonds were just straight debt securities. Holders of $146.7 million converted their debentures into common shares worth about $1,090 per debenture. The remaining $3.3 million of unconverted debentures were called for redemption on March 1, 1994, at $1,000 plus accrued interest of $12.40 per debenture. Failure to convert when the issue has been called means a loss but time and again investors fail to convert when it is in their interests to do so as demonstrated by the Dana issue. Bond investment is not a passive activity; it requires investors to remain alert to market events which may have an impact on their portfolios.

As with straight debt, a number of convertibles issued beginning in the late 1980s granted put options to the holders. Some issues provide that instead of paying cash for the put, the company may issue other securities. NeoRx Corporation's 9¾% Convertible Subordinated Debentures due 2014 had a change of control put option applicable before June 1, 1994. If a change of control (as defined) occurred the bonds may be put back to the issuer for $1,000. Instead of paying cash, the company has the option to pay the repurchase price in common shares valued at 95% of the average trading price for a specific period before the repurchase date. The terms of the put features are spelled out in the issuing documents. The put is a valuable feature allowing the holder to get out whole if the conversion privilege doesn't turn out to be as profitable as thought when the bonds were first purchased. The put, especially one exercisable only for cash, will act as a floor for the market price of the security. A put payable in cash is called a *hard put* while one payable in stock or other securities is called a *soft put*.

Until the early 1980s most convertible bonds lacked call protection; that is, they could be redeemed at any time at the issuer's option. Early in that decade some companies called their convertibles within a year after they were issued. A few were even redeemed before the first interest payment date. Some observers suggested that these early redemptions were "scams" in that the companies paid out little interest and through the forced conversions effectively sold common stock 15% to 25% above the market when the convertibles were first issued. On the other hand, if the issuing companies prospered from the good markets, so did investors. They had a higher yielding debt alternative for the equity providing some degree of market protection. While the bonds were called with large gains for the investors, they did not profit as much as the common shareholders. Nonetheless, gains were achieved and with less risk than an alternate investment in the underlying shares. The gains probably came sooner than investors first thought when the convertibles were purchased. These earlier-than-expected riches increased the rates of return. Certainly, investors would like to have such profitable "scams" day in and day out.

Since investors demanded some type of protection against early call, issuers began to add delayed redemption features to new convertible issues. Some issues have absolute redemption bars for a certain period of years, but many others provide conditional redemption protection. In the latter case, the issuer agrees that the bonds won't be called in the first two or three years unless the common stock trades at 130% to 150% of the conversion price for a certain period of time (often 20 trading days) before the redemption date. Thus, an early call ought not to harm the investor as the converts would be trading at good premiums over the redemption price. If the bonds were not called, it would normally mean that the underlying stock had not performed as well as anticipated.

Corporations usually call their converts to force conversion and not to redeem the securities for cash. There are times, such as the low interest rate period of 1985 to 1986, when cash calls occur. In these cases, some companies wanted to retire their more costly securities. However, one study said, "refinancing did not seem to be a motive behind these out-of-money convertible debt calls" in 1980 to 1984.[4] Investors usually have at least 30 days in which to convert their bonds after a redemption announcement. If a conversion is forced, investors may convert into common stock but they normally lose the accrued interest. Investors can sell the converts, in which case the accrued interest is theoretically paid. The bid will be higher than the call price or the conversion value less the accrued interest. In such instances the buyers (usually arbitraguers) adjust prices. Bids are reduced since they are not receiving the accrued interest even though they must pay it when purchasing bonds. Participating in the market to buy and convert the bonds and selling the resulting shares, they lock in a small but sure profit. Another course is to take the cash redemption price. This is likely to be done only if the call price plus the accrued interest is more than what investors would receive upon conversion or sale.

Convertibles can also be redeemed to satisfy sinking fund requirements. This can be a valuable feature when the issue is selling at a discount and a negative one when the convertible is trading above the sinking fund call price. Usually, the sinking fund can be satisfied with bonds previously redeemed or converted but not yet credited for sinking fund requirements. If these credits are not available, the company must purchase the requirement in the open market or call the securities.

CONVERTIBLE BOND CONCEPTS AND INVESTMENT CHARACTERISTICS

Many years ago we heard the saying that one should never buy a common stock without checking to see if a convertible was available. Upon investigation the convertible

---

[4] Sankarshan Acharya and Puneet Handa. "Early Calls of Convertible Debt: New Evidence and Theory." Working Paper Series Number 477, June 1988, Salomon Brothers Center for the Study of Financial Institutions. The study concludes:

> A significant percent (about 32%) of all the convertible bond calls [230], during 1980-1984, were made when they were out of [the] money. The median firm in the sample... called when the conversion value was 48.5 percent below the call price. We considered an economic setting in which the manager, who was assumed to maximize the value to common stockholders, did not find it optimal to call the out of [the] money convertible bonds if he was no more informed than the outside investors in the stock market. In the same setting we considered an asymmetry of information between the manager and the investors and showed the existence of an equilibrium in which the common stockholders' wealth could be improved by calling an out of [the] money convertible bond if the manager's private message indicated good future prospects of the firm. In this equilibrium, the stock price jumped upward on the announcement of call of an out of [the] money convertible bond.

may be a better alternative to an investment in the common shares. However, converts may not provide as much appreciation potential as the underlying common stock, but they may have a greater current return than the common. Also, the credit risk of a convertible bond is less than junior common shares. Some institutional investors are barred from investing in common stock; purchase of convertible debentures is one way around this prohibition. At times, when the bonds are selling near their theoretical investment value as a nonconvertible debt instrument, they may be viewed as near substitutes for straight corporate bonds (with a long-term option on the underlying common shares costing little or nothing).

Let's look at some of the terminology used in the convertible world along with a hypothetical issue's details for illustrative purposes. We will use Big Manufacturing Corporation's (BMC) convertible subordinated debentures with data from Exhibits 1 and 2.

Conversion price is the price of the common stock at which the debenture is convertible: $62.50 per share. It is also called the par conversion price.

Conversion ratio is the number of common shares that the bondholder receives through the exercise of the call option of the convertible or exchangeable bond. It is obtained by dividing the par value of the bond by the conversion price, thus: $1,000/$62.50 = 16 shares per $1,000 debenture.

Conversion parity price, also known as the *market conversion price*, is the market value of the convertible security divided by the number of shares into which it is convertible. Market conversion price is the effective conversion price for a buyer of the bond in the secondary market. Viewed as a break-even point, it is the price at which the common stock must trade in order for the conversion value to equal the market price of the convertible. Thus $760/16 equals a conversion parity price of $47.50. The common stock must trade at $47.50 in order for the total value of the underlying shares to be worth the convertible's current market price.

Conversion value is the market price of the common stock multiplied by the conversion ratio. Therefore, 16 shares times the market price of 34½ equals a conversion value of $552.

Conversion premium or *market conversion premium* is the market price of the convertible minus the conversion value. This may also be expressed in percentage terms with (a) the conversion premium divided by the conversion value or (b) the market price divided by the conversion value. Calculated on a per share basis, it is the market conversion price (conversion parity price) less the current market price of the stock. These values are calculated below for the BMC convertible:

	Per Bond		Per Share
Market price of debenture	$760.00	Market conversion price	$47.50
less: Conversion value	552.00	less: Current market price	34.50
equals: Premium	$208.00	equals: Market premium	$13.00
(a) $208.00/552 = 37.68%		$13.00/34.50 = 37.68%	
(b) $760.00/552 = 137.68%		$47.50/34.50 = 137.68%	

Exhibit 1: Big Manufacturing Corporation
5¾% Convertible Subordinated Debentures Due July 1, 2006

Issue date: June 22, 1981
Ratings: BB or equivalent by the major agencies
Interest payment dates: January 1 and July 1
Amount issued: $400,000,000
Amount outstanding (12/31/93): $360,000,000

Redemption: Currently callable at 102.02 through June 30, 1995, then at 101.73 through June 30, 1996, and at prices declining by about 0.29 annually to 100.00 on and after July 1, 2001.

Sinking fund: $20 million each July 1, 1992, through July 1, 2005, will retire 70% of the issue prior to maturity. Credit may be taken against the sinking fund obligation for debentures previously acquired, converted, or redeemed other than through the sinking fund, and the company has the noncumulative option to double payments.

Conversion: Convertible at anytime prior to maturity at $62.50 into 16 shares of common stock. The conversion privilege is protected against dilution as defined, and adjustments are made for cumulative changes of at least 1%.

Listed: New York Stock Exchange
Bond Ticker Symbol: BMC575

Exhibit 2: Big Manufacturing Corporation
Price Data and Dividend History

	Common Stock			5¾% C.S.D due July 1, 2006		
	Price	Indicated Dividend	Current Yield (%)	Price	Yield to Maturity (%)	Current Yield (%)
12/31/88	$30.375	$1.00	3.29	$637.50	10.25	9.02
12/31/89	26.125	1.00	3.82	572.50	11.63	10.04
12/31/90	26.625	1.10	4.13	688.75	9.64	8.35
12/31/91	21.500	1.20	5.58	635.00	10.78	9.06
12/31/92	29.750	1.20	4.03	718.75	9.49	8.00
12/31/93	29.250	1.40	4.79	703.75	9.94	8.17
12/31/94	34.500	1.40	4.06	760.00	9.07	7.57

The investor is paying a premium of $208 per bond ($13 per share) over the bond's conversion value for the right or option to convert into common stock for the life of the bond. This is a premium of 37.68%. In other words, the bond is selling at 37.68% above its conversion value.

Premium recovery period (also known as *premium payback period* or *break-even time*) is the length of time required to recover the dollar conversion premium through the difference between the higher income generated by the convertible and the dividend income on the underlying number of shares which could be purchased for the same cost as the convertible. This dollar-for-dollar calculation is important for determining the relative attractiveness of a convertible issue compared with the common stock. Usually, the higher the premium recovery period, the less attractive the convertible. Many investors view a recovery period of three years or less as desirable, purchasing the convertible when the premium recovery period is under three years and buying the stock when it is greater than three years. However, there could be other attractive convertibles with longer premium recovery periods. Each issue must be carefully analyzed within the context of the goals, objectives and risk parameters of the investment portfolio. The premium payback period does not consider the time value of money.

For the cost of the convertible bond ($760) an investor could buy 22.03 shares at the current market, ignoring commission charges.

Another calculation method uses the percentage premiums and yields. Thus, for the convertible debenture the formula is:

$$\frac{\text{Performance Premium} / (\text{Premium} + 100)}{\text{Yield Differential}} \times 100 = \text{Premium Recovery Period}$$

$$\frac{(37.68\%) / (37.68\% + 100\%)}{(7.57\% - 4.06\%)} \times 100 = \frac{0.2737}{3.51} \times 100 = 7.80 \text{ Years}$$

Investment or *straight bond value* is the theoretical value or worth of the bond but without the conversion privilege. All of the other features and terms remain the same including the capitalization ranking, redemption and sinking fund provisions, and maturity. The premium over straight or investment value is obtained by dividing the convertible's market price by its straight bond value. As interest rates change, so will the bond's straight value.

If a high premium recovery period makes an issue unattractive for the normal convertible buyer, who else might buy the bond and why? A traditional straight bond investor might find the BMC convertible debenture attractive, especially if it were selling close to or at the investment or straight bond value. In such a situation, one is getting a regular bond value with the conversion option thrown in for free. Bonds with large premiums over conversion value (out-of-the-money) and selling close to investment value are known as busted converts.

Let us assume that at the end of June 1994, the subject converts had a straight bond value equivalent to a yield to maturity of 10.00% or a dollar price of 70.68. With the bonds trading at 76, they are less than eight percent or 5.32 points away from the theoretical value as a nonconvertible bond. They are close to being, but not quite yet, busted converts. If the stock price of Big Manufacturing Corporation declines, the bonds would likely start getting some investment support as they approach the 70 level, all other things remaining the same. Certainly, lower interest rates and higher bond prices ought to mean increased support levels. However, investors should not be too complacent about these investment values. Things don't always remain the same and the market does not always behave the way one might think. Caution is advised in using straight bond values for there is no substitute for sound thinking when it comes to the art of investment.

There have been times when convertible prices went through these support levels "as a hot knife through soft butter." The late winter and early spring of 1966 was one such period when investment support levels "didn't amount to a hill of beans." At that time interest rates were rising and stock prices plummeting. Commercial banks were under pressure from the Board of Governors of the Federal Reserve System to reduce lending for speculative activities. Many banks withdrew their lines of credit to convertible bond speculators while others sought more collateral value to support the loans. Loans up to 90% and more were made against the market value of convertible bonds. Investment values declined due to rising interest rates; conversion values fell due to lower stock prices; speculative interest dried up resulting in declining market prices for convertible securities in general. The evaporation of the source of funds to fuel this speculative activity coupled with the calling of these bank loans added to the downward pressure on convertible prices as speculators raised cash to meet margin calls. It was an unpleasant time to have long positions in the convertible bond market. Some market participants went broke, a few convertible bond departments of Wall Street firms were closed, and a few commercial bankers were reprimanded by their superiors.

PRICE RISK

We have reviewed the type of price risk caused by a sharp decline in the price of the underlying common stock and where the bond is selling above conversion and investment value. Another type of price risk is due to the risk of call and the consequent forced conversion. The BM Corporation debenture has little risk of call in the immediate future since it is selling about 26 points below the 102.02 call price and the conversion value is only around 55. As the bond price rises above the par level, the risk of call and forced conversion increases. This is one reason conversion premiums tend to diminish, often being quite nominal or non-existent beginning around the 115 to 125 price level. The investor's risk at these levels in cases of a forced conversion is the amount of the conversion premium and, in many cases, the accrued interest, if any.

Another type of price risk touched upon earlier in this chapter and not caused by a drop in the common stock price or forced conversion, is that due to the issuer's voluntary redemption of the bonds. The driving force behind this type of call is the same as with straight senior securities, i.e. the desire to remove costlier securities from the balance sheet to enhance shareholders' wealth. Conversion isn't forced as investors would gain more by taking the redemption price than by exchanging the convertible for shares with a market value less than the redemption price. Admittedly, such redemptions are not all that common but they have caught investors unawares. They just couldn't imagine a call when the conversion value was less than par value. Such an act would not force conversion.

The spring of 1986 saw several redemptions of this type. National Medical Enterprises had an issue of $124 million of 12⅝% Convertible Subordinated Debentures due November 15, 2001. Convertible into 27.72 shares at $36.06, the bonds were trading on the New York Stock Exchange on April 8 at 114, and the common was selling at 24½ per share. The conversion value was $679.14 and the conversion premium $460.86 or 67.9%. Currently callable at 100, the convertibles were at a 14% premium over the redemption price. Before the next day's trading opened, the company announced the bond's call at 100 plus accrued interest to May 15. The stock closed on April 9 at 24⅝; it did not decline in price as there was little chance of the bonds being converted resulting in dilution to the current shareholders. However, the premium over the redemption price disappeared. On that day the converts traded between 100 and 101 and closed at 100, down 14 points overnight. The 14 point decline ($140 per $1,000 bond) meant that investors lost a grand total of $17,360,000 on the issue.

ZERO COUPON CONVERTIBLES

In 1985, investment bankers at Merrill Lynch & Co. added another "animal" to the menagerie of investment products offered by Wall Street firms. Liquid Yield Option Notes, known as LYONs (registered service mark of Merrill Lynch & Co., Inc.), joined their fellow CATS, TIGRs and other feline zero coupon investments. LYONs are zero coupon convertible securities combining a convertible feature with a put or series of puts. The securities received a favorable reception from many different types of investors including foreigners, pension funds and other tax-favored entities such as individual retirement accounts.

From the issuers' viewpoint, LYONs and their brethren issued by other firms provide a favorable long-term financing rate which is a less costly source of funds than regular convertible and zero coupon debt. There is no cash outlay for interest charges but the companies can take a tax deduction on their books for the original issue discount, thus aiding cash flow. Underwriting discounts charged on these issues (before deducting expenses paid by the issuer) range from 0.5% to more than 1.4% of the principal amount due at maturity (but payable when the payment is received from the buyers). Based on the lower discounted price to the investor, the underwriting fees amount to 2% to 3½% of the funds raised. Underwriting fees on investment grade conventional convertible debt generally amount to 1% to 2% of the principal amount, with higher fees for more speculative issues. However, if the issuers viewed the underwriting fee as excessive, then they would have sought an alternate and less expensive vehicle with which to raise capital.

None of the issues has a sinking fund but they have deferred call protection for approximately the first two years after issuance. In a few cases, however, if the market price of the common exceeds a certain percentage (50% to 73% depending on the issue) of the initial conversion price for a specified period prior to the start of the regular redemption period, the securities may be called. The call schedule for many of the earlier issues is the original offering price plus the redemption premium (initially at the offering yield scaled down annually to zero ten years after issuance) plus the accrued original issue discount. Newer issues offered since 1988 usually do not contain any redemption premium. The call price is just the original offering price plus the accrued interest computed at the original issue discount to the call date.

From time to time, holders have the right to require the issuer to redeem the LYONs at the holders' option. Most of the earlier issues provide for annual puts payable in cash (hard put) after a delayed starting date. These puts may require several months' prior notification to the issuer. The initial yield to the holders' put was several percentage points lower than the purchased yield but it increased each year by one percentage point until the original purchase yield is reached. This is similar to the redemption provisions of United States Series EE Savings Bonds. The put feature provides some stability or price protection to the bondholder in case of a rise in interest rates or a sharp decline in the stock's value. Zero coupon bond prices are much more volatile than the prices of coupon debt instruments and the put provides a floor for the investor. However, the put may come at an inopportune time when the issuer would rather not pay out the cash. This may be due to its poor financial condition. Maybe the issuer would rather retain the monies for other corporate purposes. Failure to make payment on a put is an event of default and, if not cured, may lead to bankruptcy proceedings. However, no payment under the put provisions may be made by the issuer if an event of default has occurred and has not been cured.

To get around some of the problems with an annual put payable in cash, most of the issues since 1988 provide for only one, or just several, put dates prior to maturity with the put price payable in cash, shares or, in some cases, notes (soft put). The put price does not include a premium but is only the original offering price plus the accrued original issue discount. The notes which may be paid in lieu of cash or stock on the put are interest bearing with a principal amount equal to the amount due at the put date; most have a maturity the same as the LYON. The interest rate on the put notes is set at a rate determined by the underwriter necessary for the notes to have an initial market value at or as near as possible to par. Of course, no assurance can be given the note will sell at such a price. If an issuer could not afford to pay cash on the exercise of the put, why would one want to take some more funny money of an obviously weak and suspect firm? That is the time one should consider the LYON's sale.

The initial conversion premiums generally range from 12% to 20% or so over the market price of the common at the time of issuance. The conversion rate is subject to the normal anti-dilution adjustments in cases of stock dividends, combinations, subdivisions and reclassifications. However, upon conversion, no adjustment is made for accrued interest or original issue discount as it is deemed to have been paid by the common stock received upon conversion. It is effectively lost. Therefore, while the number of shares into which the LYON may be converted is fixed, the conversion price is slowly and steadily increasing. Let us look at USF&G Corporation which issued on February 24, 1994, $220 million (par amount) of Zero Coupon Convertible Subordinated Notes due March 3, 2009. Convertible into 29.499 shares per note, the initial offering price of $512.98 results in a conversion price of $17.39, or a 21% premium to the 14⅜ price of the common stock when the notes were issued. The notes accrue interest at the rate of 4.5% (computed on a semi-annual bond equivalent basis). Five years after issuance and on the first put date they will be worth $640.82. On the next put date of March 3, 2004, they will be worth $800.51, and at maturity the value will, of course, be $1,000 per note. The conversion price thus rises to $21.72 ($640.82/29.499) at the 1999 put date and to $27.14 five years later. On the March 3, 2009 maturity date the implied conversion price is $33.90.

When analyzing LYONs for possible purchase, the conventional premium recovery period method isn't applicable as the bonds do not pay current interest. One has to look at the conversion premium, the fundamentals of the underlying stock, and the other terms of the issue in order to decide whether or not the LYON should be purchased. Keep in mind that if the stock does not move then the conversion premium is steadily increasing. It is for this reason that some convertible analysts feel that potential share dilution is limited. As time passes there is increasingly less incentive for holders to convert.

USABLE SECURITIES

Usable bonds are not convertible securities in the traditional sense discussed in the preceding sections. Instead, when combined with certain warrants, they become what are known as "synthetic convertibles."

A common stock purchase warrant is a longer term option giving the holder the right to buy shares at a fixed price for a certain time period. The length of the exercise period differentiates a warrant from a common stock option. An option usually has a life of under one year and is measured in months. On the other hand, a warrant's life is longer and is measured in years; in a few cases a warrant may be without any terminal date and is called a perpetual warrant. Atlas Corporation has perpetual warrants listed on the American Stock Exchange that give the holder the right to purchase common stock at $15.625 a share.

Warrants have been created out of corporate bankruptcy and reorganization, being given as part of the new company's securities in a recapitalization. Some have been issued with common shares while others were attached to straight bonds as a "sweetener" to make the securities more attractive to investors. When issued with other securities, the package is called a unit. After issuance the warrants generally may be detached from the other part of the unit and both traded separately. A bond which can be used instead of cash upon the exercise of the warrant is known as a usable security.

The conventional convertible bond combines into one instrument a straight fixed income obligation and a long-term option to buy stock. A synthetic convertible allows the two parts to be separated and freely traded, each on its own merits. As with a convertible bond, the warrant allows a delay in the issuance of the common shares from the time the warrant is issued to the time of exercise. The exercise of a warrant does not necessarily mean that debt is reduced for if the exercise price is paid in cash, the associated debt remains outstanding.

A usable bond trading below par effectively reduces the exercise price of the warrant. For example, if a warrant has an exercise price of $10 per share, the exercise of 100 warrants to purchase 100 shares of common stock requires $1,000 in cash. If the terms of the warrant provide that the exercise price may be paid in usable debt in lieu of cash, an investor would apply the usable security as long as it is selling below par value (taking into account any accrued interest). A usable bond trading at 80 reduces the exercise price from $10 to $8; in effect the investor is paying for his stock with a security worth 80 cents on the dollar.

Due to this usable feature, lower coupon discount issues might trade at lower yields to maturity (an higher prices) than would otherwise be the case if it were an ordinary straight issue. The premium over the normal pricing or valuation, or the demand for the usable bond, depends on several factors including the likelihood of the warrants being exercised and the time to the expiration of the warrants. The more likely the exercise of the warrants and the closer to their expiration, the greater the demand may be for the bond. Demand for the bond normally increases as the warrants' expiration date approaches assuming that the warrants will have value and thus will be exercised.

Another important factor is called "availability." This is the ratio of the amount of bonds outstanding compared with the amount of bonds required to exercise all of the warrants. Early in 1986 American Airlines, Inc. issued $200 million of 6¼% Subordinated Debentures due March 1, 1996, with 200,000 warrants to purchase 16.19 shares of AMR Corporation at $61.766 a share. If all warrants were exercised before the expiry date of March 1, 1996, AMR Corporation would issue 3,238,000 shares of common stock. The cost of these shares is $199,998,310, an availability factor of 100% and just in line with the total size of the issue. The warrant exercise terms allow the payment to be made in cash, check or "by the tender of the Debentures or by any combination thereof. For purposes of paying the exercise price of Warrants, Debentures will be valued at their principal amount, without credit for accrued interest, and applied only in integral multiples of $1,000 up to an amount not exceeding such exercise price."[5] Thus, $100,000 principal amount of debentures will pay the cost of 1,619 shares of common upon the exercise of the warrants.

---

[5] Prospectus for 200,000 Units of American Airlines, dated March 7, 1986, pp. 15-16.

If the common price rises, the warrants would likely be exercised, and they were. The warrants were subject to redemption or forced exercise on and after March 1, 1988, if the stock price equaled or exceeded 115% of the effective exercise price for a certain period before the date of the redemption notice. In the late summer of 1989 the price of the shares soared from the mid-60s to the mid-90s before hitting a high of 107⅜ in October; the warrants were called. Many, but not all of the warrant holders used the bonds to pay the exercise price. About $6 million were not so utilized and remained outstanding.

In 1983, Pan American World Airways, Inc. issued $100 million of 13½% Senior Debentures due May 1, 2003, with warrants to purchase 10,000,000 shares of common at $8 per share. The warrants' expiration date was May 1, 1993, subject to early redemption on May 1, 1986. The exercise of all the warrants required only $80 million face amount of the Debentures, or 80% of the issue, resulting in an availability factor of 125%. Thus, the amount of the bonds issued exceeded the amount needed for the exercise of all the warrants by 25%. Since the amount of bonds required to exercise the warrants in full was less than the amount issued, the potential demand from warrant holders would not be diminished and it is less likely that this issue would become based solely on this demand factor. It so happened that the bonds were overvalued and few, if any, of the warrants were exercised. The Company filed for bankruptcy under Chapter XI of the bankruptcy laws on January 8, 1991.

There are cases where there are not enough outstanding bonds to satisfy potential demand from warrant holders. In 1983 Western Air Lines, Inc. sold 90,000 units consisting of $90,000,000 10¾% Senior Secured Trust Notes due 1998, with 3,240,000 shares of common stock and warrants to purchase 9,000,000 shares of common. The immediately callable warrants exercisable at $9.50 (the Notes may be used instead of cash) expired June 15, 1993. Therefore, at issuance the availability factor was 105.3%. The principal amount of Notes outstanding ($90 million) exceeded the total exercise price of the warrants ($85.5 million) by $4.5 million. In 1985, the Company repurchased $13.9 million face amount of the Notes, reducing the outstanding amount to $76.1 million. Now the availability factor changed for the better to 89%. There were not enough bonds outstanding to satisfy the potential demand if all the warrants were to be exercised. Thus, any price up to fraction below par (leaving out consideration of accrued interest) should gladly be paid for the bonds by warrant holders wishing to exercise their rights.

TRADITIONAL CONVERTIBLE STRATEGIES

The Hedge

Convertibles are purchased by investors as alternatives to common stock when they have a positive outlook for the market and the shares. However, there are times when one may be bearish on the market in general and certain stocks in particular; short positions may then be justified. A short sale involves the sale of stock which is not owned in the hopes of buying back the shares (or covering) at some future date at lower prices. When stock is sold short, the shares must be borrowed from another owner to make delivery to the person who purchased the shares. To cover one's position and close out the short sale, the stock must either be purchased in the open market or obtained through the conversion of a convertible. As we mentioned that one should not buy a common stock without first seeing if there is a good convertible substitute, one should not short common stock without first checking if there is also a convertible for it. If the stock sold short also has a convertible, then investigate the convertible hedge for reducing the risk of having the market move against the short position, i.e., move above the sales price.

A convertible hedge involves a long position in the convertible security and a short position in the shares into which it is convertible. The hedge's purpose is to reduce or eliminate the loss if the common stock price goes up instead of down. For a convertible to be a candidate for the long side of a hedge, it should be trading close to or at its conversion value, ideally just at that point in the 115 to 130 price range where the conversion premium all but disappears. It should provide a greater yield than the underlying common so the interest income may be used to pay dividend payments on the shorted shares. Also, the greater the volatility of the shorted shares, the greater the chance for profit.

If the price of the underlying stock declines, the profit from the hedge will come primarily from a widening of the conversion premium. If the price of the underlying stock rises, the loss on the short position will be offset by the gain or the narrowing of the conversion premium on the long position in the convertible. Various names are given to convertible hedges depending upon the balance or imbalance between the common share equivalent of the long position and the common shares on the short side. A full hedge is where the long and short sides are equally matched. If the common stock moves up in price, it will be more or less evenly offset by the expected increase in value of the convertible. Exhibit 3 gives some details of a hypothetical convertible issue that we will use for illustrative purposes.

If the stock rises to 90 (an increase of 44%) in six months' time, we would get a loss on the short position of 27½ points a share for a total amount of $55,000. The bonds have to be worth a minimum of 180 (20 shares times $90) producing a profit of $55,000 which offsets the loss. In addition, we would have had to pay two quarterly dividends of $0.50 each or a total of $2,000 to the lenders of the stock which we shorted. However, we would have also received six months' interest, or $4,000, on the bonds thereby producing an overall profit of $2,000 on the hedge. In addition, some investors might be able to obtain a "short-sale rebate" from the broker representing interest on the proceeds of the short sale. However, not all brokers pay interest on cash balances from short sales. Had the hedge been entered into when there was still some slight conversion premium on the bonds, the gain on the bonds would have been reduced to the extent of that premium.

In a full hedge the long and short side is in balance. Thus we

Buy: $100,000 par value 8%   Cost: $125,000
     Convertibles at 125

Sell Short: 2,000 common shares at 62 1/2   Proceeds: $125,000

Exhibit 3: XYZ Company

8.00% Convertible Subordinated Debentures due June 1, 2009
Convertible at $50.00 into 20 shares of common stock

Price of common:	$62.50
Price of convertible:	$1,250
Conversion value:	$1,250
Conversion premium:	$0
Dividend per common share:	$2 per annum

What would happen if the common stock declined? Again, assume the stock dropped to 35, a decline of 27½ points over a six-month period. We have a gain on the short position of $55,000. The bond would also drop in price, but most likely not as much as the common. The conversion premium would start to reappear as the common declined. Let us assume that the bond dropped to 90. At this level the premium over conversion value is $200 ($900 - $700) or nearly 29%. At 90 we have a loss of 35 points in the bonds for a total of $35,000. Thus, the hedge produced a net gain of $20,000 (without much risk) before commissions, interest received and dividends paid out. A speculator engaging in these hedges only has to put up funds equal to the long position. Common stock can be shorted without any additional margin being required as long as the portfolio holds securities convertible into at least an equal amount of the stock sold short.

The full hedge produced profits on the downside with little risk. There are also partial hedges in which the two sides are not in balance. A half hedge with the hypothetical issuer would have involved the shorting of 1,000 shares and a quarter hedge the shorting of 500 shares, at the same time being long 100 bonds. The partial hedge may also produce profits on the downside, depending on where the long position starts to develop a premium over conversion value. It may also produce profits on the upside with reduced risk. Let us run through the numbers with a half hedge assuming that we are not as bearish as the fully-hedged investor. A rise in the stock to 90 produces a loss on 1,000 shares of 27½ points or $27,500. On the long side, the 100 bonds at a cost of 125 produces a $55,000 profit for a net gain of $27,500. On the downside, the short position of 1,000 shares shows a profit of $27,500. With a loss of $35,000 on the bonds, a net loss of $7,500 would result.

Actually, many speculators might start with a half-hedge and adjust the long and short sides depending upon market conditions and movement. For example, as the stock declined the short position might have been gradually increased or the long position decreased resulting in a more fully hedged and profitable situation. There are many variations that can be produced with a convertible hedge. Investors should be alert to the opportunities for profitable trading with reduced risk as they arise.

The convertible hedge was used in the 1940s and 1950s by an investment company managed by the gurus of security analysis, Benjamin Graham and David L. Dodd. Reviewing the annual reports of the Graham-Newman Corp. for the fiscal years ended January 31, 1950 to January 31, 1957, the year the company was liquidated, reveals several convertible hedges, both full and partial, throughout this period. We don't know how profitable they were nor what activity occurred between the reports but it interesting that intelligent investors such as these used the technique. Hedges included securities of companies such as Avco Manufacturing, Fedders-Quigan Corp., Gar Wood Industries, Tung-Sol Electric, Inc., Crucible Steel Co. of America, Allegheny Corp., American Airlines, American Cyanamid, Dow Chemical, National Container, Olin Mathieson Chemical, Pfizer & Co., Inc. and Granite City Steel. Some positions appeared on only the financial statements for one year while other positions were carried for more than five years. We believe that all the short positions involved hedges to some degree.

The prospectus for the Ellsworth Convertible Growth and Income Fund, Inc., dated June 20, 1986, mentions that the fund is allowed to "make short sales of securities which it owns or which it has the right to acquire through conversion or exchange of other securities." It goes on to say that it "may make a short sale in order to hedge against market risks when it believes that the price of a security may decline causing a decline in the value of a security... convertible into or exchangeable for such security.... The extent to which... gains or losses are reduced will depend upon the amount of the security sold short relative to the amount the Company owns, either directly or indirectly, and, in the case where the Company owns convertible securities, changes with the convertible premiums."

Convertible hedging is an appropriate technique for equity speculators engaging in short selling. It reduces the risk of loss if the stock price goes against the short position. It is important to act without emotion and to map out the upside and downside projections for both the long and short positions. A good chart of the historical prices and relationships of the convertible and the underlying stock is a valuable aid to convertible hedgers. It allows them to see where the securities have been so they can project where they might go in the future. It can also assist more active speculators as they vary the degree of the hedge.[6]

Writing Covered Calls

Another convertible strategy is the use of convertibles in a program of writing covered call options. A call option is a right to buy common stock at a predetermined price for a certain period, usually under one year. The issuer or writer of the call option is obliged to sell the underlying shares at the exercise price during the option period. This obligation terminates when the option expires or when the call is covered, i.e., repurchased. Few calls are exercised, as call owners usually sell profitable calls in the market. For writing the call option, the buyer pays the seller or writer a premium that is determined in part by the remaining life of the option, the exercise

---

[6] A convertible hedge strategy is described in Grant's *Interest Rate Observer*, Volume 9, No. 20, October 25, 1991. In the story "Never Lose," the portfolio manager calls his actions "statistical arbitrage," an activity designed "...to lock in a rate of return that does not depend on the direction of the market, or of interest rates... which he does not pretend to know."

price in relation to the common's price, and the volatility of the underlying stock. A covered option means that the option writer has the shares or securities convertible into the shares held in his account or portfolio. The options are written on the underlying common shares and not on the convertible securities.

Writing covered call options is done to enhance overall portfolio returns, not to maximize profits on individual issues. Better results are obtained in stable or rising equity markets than in declining markets. However, in a rising market calls may be exercised, thus restricting profit opportunities. This is offset, to some extent, by the option premiums received. To determine the number of convertible bonds needed to write calls, divide the number of shares to be received upon conversion of one bond into the number of shares for which the call option is being written. In the example in Exhibit 3, each bond is convertible into 20 shares. To write one covered call option for 100 shares, we need five bonds, and for 2,000 shares we need 100 bonds. As the bonds are selling at the conversion value of 125, any rise in the stock price should be fully reflected in the bond's price. On the downside we expect the conversion premium to reappear, thus reducing our loss. The bonds normally will decline at a slower rate than the underlying common. In addition, they offer a greater current yield than the stock, another advantage of many convertibles.

Therefore, for our 100-bond long position we can write 20 covered call options. Suppose a six-month option exercisable at 65 with the stock at 62½ has a premium of $375 per 100 shares. Let us look at the possible results of writing covered call options against the convertible and the underlying shares of our hypothetical company. Exhibit 4 shows that using convertibles instead of the underlying common stock in a program of writing covered call options may lead to better investment results. In this case there were smaller losses on the downside and greater gains when the stock rises.

Of course, the final results of covered call writing strategies depend on several factors including the income differential between the convertible and the common, the premium received for writing the call, the conversion premium, and the price action of the securities. This is a passive example. In actual practice, some investors might wish to limit their losses or take their gains at certain predetermined price levels by closing out or repurchasing the calls they had written.

Before attempting any covered call writing program, investors should go through simulations to see what the results might look like. Price history charts should be studied to get an idea of the past and a glint of future relationships between the common, the convertible and the option. There are investment services to assist investors in their call writing activities.

Convertibles are wonderful securities for investors who lack perfect foresight. If our crystal ball worked, we would only go with the investments that would always show profits; we wouldn't need securities providing some degree of downside protection. Few of us are perfect investors — and thus the need for convertible securities.

Exhibit 4: XYZ Company
Covered Call Option Data at Expiration Date
(Option is Exercisable at 65)

	$35	$50	$62½	$75	$90
Common Price	$35	$50	$62½	$75	$90
Convertible Price	$900	$1,100	$1,250	$1,500	$1,800
Option Value	$0	$0	$0	$10	$25
Cost of 100 convertibles	$125,000				
less: Option premium received	$7,500				
Net cost of convertible position	$117,500				
Profit (loss) on:					
convertible	-$35,000	-$15,000	$0	$25,000	$55,000
option	7,500	7,500	7,500	12,500	42,500
Profit (loss)	-27,500	-7,500	7,500	12,500	12,500
Interest income	4,000	4,000	4,000	4,000	4,000
Net profit (loss)	- $23,500	$3,500	$11,500	$16,500	$16,500
Rate of return on investment	-18.8%	-2.8%	9.2%	13.2%	13.2%
Cost of 2,000 shares of stock	$125,000				
less: Option premium received	$7,500				
Net cost of stock position	$117,500				
Profit (loss) on:					
stock	- $55,000	- $25,000	$0	$25,000	$55,000
option	7,500	7,500	7,500	12,500	42,500
Profit (loss)	-47,500	-17,500	7,500	12,500	12,500
Dividend income	2,000	2,000	2,000	2,000	2,000
Net profit (loss)	- $45,500	- $15,500	$9,500	$14,500	$14,500
Rate of return on investment	-36.4%	-12.4%	7.6%	11.6%	11.6%

CHAPTER 7

Speculative-Grade Bonds

The speculative-grade bond market was on a roller coaster in the late 1980s and the early 1990s. From the great heights of record new issue volume in 1989, the market all but fell into oblivion in 1990. The leading underwriter of this debt filed for bankruptcy and many of the major players including some institutional investors underwent legal prosecution (some might say "persecution") resulting in prison terms and the levying of huge fines. Market values dropped due to bankruptcies, forced selling into a weak market, and fear on the part of a vast number of market participants. Institutions which had been major investors in speculative bonds did an about face and curtailed their activities. Savings and loan associations were forced to divest themselves of their holdings. Yet, despite the feeling that the end-of-the-world was just around the corner, the market recovered to record new issue volume in just two years. Excesses had been purged, thoughtful investors returned seeking value and higher returns than those available in other market sectors during a period of declining interest rates. Today's speculative-grade bond market appears to be on a firmer foundation than just a few short years ago. While confidence has returned, the wise investor will still pay heed to the sound rules of investment and speculation.

WHAT ARE SPECULATIVE-GRADE BONDS?

Speculative-grade bonds are those rated below investment grade by the rating agencies, i.e., BB+ and lower by Duff & Phelps Credit Rating Co., Fitch Investors Service, L.P., and Standard & Poor's Corporation, and Ba1 and less by Moody's Investors Service, Inc. They may also be unrated, but not all unrated

171

debt is speculative. Also known as junk bonds, promoters have given these securities other euphemisms such as high-interest bonds ("HIBS"), high-opportunity debt, and high-yield securities.[1] While some of these terms may be misleading to the uninitiated, they are used throughout the investment world with "junk" and "high yield" the most popular. We will also use "junk" and "high yield' in this chapter. Speculative-grade bonds may not be high-yielders at all as they may not be paying any interest, and there maybe little hope for the resumption of interest payments; even the return expected from a reorganization or liquidation may be low. Some high-yield instruments may not be speculative-grade at all as they may carry investment grade ratings. The higher yields may be due to fears of premature redemption of high-coupon bonds in a lower interest rate environment. The higher yields may be caused by a sharp decline in the securities markets which has driven down the prices of all issues including those with investment merit. By using the term "high-yield securities" some may be attempting to whitewash the risks associated with these securities. But surely, an above average yield should denote extra risk to investors since there is "no free lunch" in the investment markets.

While the term "junk" tarnishes the entire less-than-investment-grade spectrum, it is applicable to some specific situations. Junk bonds are not useless stuff, trash or rubbish as the term is defined. At times, investors overpay for their speculative-grade securities so they feel that they may have purchased junk or worthless garbage. But isn't this also the case when they have overpaid for high-grade securities? There are other times when profits may be made from buying junk bonds; certainly then, these bonds are not junk but something that may be quite attractive. Also, not all securities in this low grade sector of the market are on the verge of default or bankruptcy. Many issuers might be on the

---

[1] High interest bonds ("HIBS") was applied to this type of debt in 1986 by the financial writer Ira U. Cobleigh. "Junk" is not of recent vintage as it was used in an article called "The Big Money in 'Junk' Bonds" which appeared in *Forbes* magazine, April 1, 1974. It said in part:

> What makes an issue a junk bond? While there is no precise definition, they typically come out of mergers or exchange offers. Some traders extend this definition to include the bonds of highly leveraged companies whose bonds are of questionable quality.

Columnist Ben Weberman, in the July 28, 1986 issue of *Forbes*, adds to the names of types of speculative-grade issues. *Gyrojunk* bonds are those that once were supported by large and real assets but due to reorganizations, divestitures and spin-offs, no longer have good assets supporting them. *Geriatric* issues are those of companies that once had some standing in industrial America and are now included in the Skid Row of industrial America. Others are *"borderline geriatrics... which are beyond middle age that have reconciled their aging to reality."* *Juvenile* junks are from younger issuers.

According to Martin S. Fridson in "Harold Fraine and the Rise of High Yield Research," *EXTRA CREDIT* (July/August 1993), Harold G. Fraine published the term "high yield bonds" in 1937 in "Superiority of High-Yield Bonds Not Substantiated by 1927-1936 Performance." This article appeared in *The Annalist*, New York Times Publishing Company, October 1937.

fringe of the investment grade sector. Market participants should be discriminating in the choice of their terminology.

Several types of issuers fall into the less-than-investment-grade high yield category including the following:

Original Issuers: These may be young, growing concerns lacking the stronger balance sheet and income statement profile of many established corporations, but often with lots of promise. Also called venture capital situations or growth or emerging market companies, the debt is often sold with a story projecting future financial strength. From this we get the term "story bond." There are also the established operating firms with financials neither measuring up to the strengths of investment-grade corporations nor possessing the weaknesses of companies on the verge of bankruptcy. Subordinated debt of investment grade issuers may be included here. A bond rated at the bottom rung of the investment grade category (Baa and BBB) or at the top end of the speculative grade category (Ba and BB) is known as a "businessman's risk "

Fallen Angels: Formerly companies with investment-grade rated debt that have come upon hard times with deteriorating balance sheet and income statement financial parameters are included in this category. They may be in default or near bankruptcy. In these cases, investors are interested in the workout value of the debt in a reorganization or liquidation, whether within or without the bankruptcy courts. Some refer to these issues as "special situations." Over the years they have fallen on hard times; some have recovered and others have not. One example of a fallen angel is Navistar International Transportation Company (formerly International Harvester Company). Its senior debt was rated A in 1976, fell to Caa in 1981, then recovered to investment grade Baa3 in 1989, only to become a fallen angel again in 1992 when it was downgraded to Ba2 and then Ba3. Chrysler Corporation is another issuer making the round trip from investment grade to noninvestment grade status and back again. Its senior debt fell from Baa in 1976 to Caa in 1981, and carried the A3 ranking in the fall of 1994. Others which have made the return trip include Long Island Lighting Company and Gulf States Utilities Company.

Restructurings and Leveraged Buyouts: These are companies which have deliberately increased their debt burden with a view towards maximizing shareholder value. The shareholders may be the existing public group to which the company pays a special extraordinary dividend with the funds coming from borrowings and the sale of assets. Cash is paid out, net worth decreased and leverage increased, and ratings drop on existing debt. Newly issued debt gets junk bond status because of the company's weakened financial condition. In 1988, The Kroger Co. declared a dividend of about $3.2 billion in cash and junior subordinated discount notes. Funds were obtained through bank borrowings with repayment to be made from asset sales and retained future cash flow. The proceeds did not go towards building the company, but towards its weakening and dismantling, at least over the intermediate term. Prior to the special dividend the senior debt was rated A2 by Moody's. It fell to B1 in 1988 and recovered to Ba1 where it stood at the end of 1994.

In a leveraged buyout (LBO), a new and private shareholder group owns and manages the company. The debt issue's purpose may be to retire other debt from commercial and investment banks and institutional investors incurred to finance the LBO. The debt to be retired is called bridge financing as it provides a bridge between the initial LBO activity and the more permanent financing. One example is Ann Taylor, Inc.'s 1989 debt financing for bridge loan repayment. The proceeds of BCI Holding Corporation's 1986 public debt financing and bank borrowings were used to make the required payments to the common shareholders of Beatrice Companies, pay issuance expenses, retire certain Beatrice debt, and for working capital.

THE HIGH-YIELD MARKET

The outstanding amount of publicly traded lower rated bonds is quite sizable. The junk market's size varies depending on one's source of data. Professor Edward I. Altman of the Salomon Center at New York University's Stern School of Business estimated the total outstanding amount at the end of 1994 was $235 billion, up from $181 billion at the end of 1990, $14.9 billion at year-end 1980, and $6.6 billion for 1970. Moody's Investors Service had about $237 billion of speculative-grade debt in mid-1994, up from $212.9 billion at the end of 1990. However, noninvestment grade debt represents less than 21% of the total Moody's rated universe of U.S. Corporate debt, down from the high of 25.4% at the end of 1989.

CS First Boston Corporation has even larger numbers for the high yield market as shown in the rather interesting Exhibit 2. It details the market growth from $81.2 billion at the beginning of 1986 to $294.3 billion at the end of 1994. The largest contributor to the increase of outstandings is new public issue activity, totaling $256.6 billion over the nine-year period. Registration of private placements under the registration rights provision added another $57.4 billion while net rating downgrades increased outstandings by $48.4 billion. The "other" category, primarily debt issued from bankruptcies and exchanges, added another $25.8 billion. Offsetting these various increases was some $175.1 billion of debt retirements. Note that First Boston's figures include split rated issues where either Moody's or Standard & Poor's rates the issue investment grade and the other agency has it in the speculative grade category.

Exhibit 1: Outstanding Moody's Rated Speculative-Grade U.S. Corporate Long-Term Debt, 1987 - 1994 (Par Value $ Billions)

End of	Baa Category as Percentage of Universe (%)	Ba1, 2, 3	B Category as Percentage of Universe (%)	B1, 2, 3	Caa and Lower	Caa and Lower Categories as Percentage of Universe (%)	Total Moody's Rated Speculative-Grade Debt	Speculative-Grade Debt as Percentage of Universe (%)	Total Moody's Rated Universe
1987	7.36	$55.80	10.19	$77.20	$13.40	1.77	$146.40	19.32	$757.90
1988	6.79	55.67	14.52	119.01	16.94	2.07	191.62	23.38	819.74
1989	6.44	57.49	15.06	134.31	34.34	3.85	226.14	25.35	892.03
1990	6.30	58.11	11.00	101.41	53.34	5.78	212.86	23.08	922.22
1991	7.77	77.07	7.69	76.21	55.16	5.56	208.44	21.02	991.53
1992	7.65	79.47	8.67	90.06	36.36	3.50	205.89	19.82	1,038.87
1993	7.86	86.86	9.87	109.07	28.97	2.62	224.90	20.35	1,105.15
June 1994	7.40	84.19	10.94	124.44	28.14	2.47	236.77	20.81	1,137.65

Source: *Moody's Bond Survey,* Volume 87, No. 39, September 26, 1994

Exhibit 2: Historical New Public Supply of Speculative-Grade Debt by Source, 1986 - 1994 ($ Billions)

	1986	1987	1988	1989	1990	1991	1992	1993	1994
Market Size @ Beginning	81.2	123.3	157.9	188.3	226.2	227.0	220.2	231.5	269.9
New Public Issues	34.2	28.6	27.8	24.9	0.7	10.1	39.6	55.9	34.8
Other[a]	4.9	2.3	4.6	7.8	0.5	0.0	5.7	0.0	0.0
Net Rating Downgrades (Upgrades)	8.9	8.5	-1.4	1.0	9.1	9.2	5.6	5.9	1.6
Debt Retirements[b]	-7.7	-11.8	-8.6	-7.7	-15.1	-26.2	-41.3	-35.2	-21.5
New Supply Sub-Total	40.3	27.6	22.4	26.0	-4.9	-6.9	9.6	26.7	14.9
Private Placements Registered (Est.)	1.8	7.0	8.0	11.9	5.7	0.0	1.8	11.7	9.5
Total Net New Supply	42.1	34.6	30.4	37.9	0.8	-6.9	11.4	38.3	24.4
Market Size @ End	123.3	157.9	188.3	226.2	227.0	220.2	231.5	269.9	294.3

a Includes new debt issued from completed bankruptcies and exchanges.
b Includes calls, tenders, open-market repurchases and bonds retired from completed bankruptcies and exchanges.

Source: *High Yield Handbook,* January 1995, CS First Boston Corporation

Exhibit 3: Speculative-Grade New Issue Activity, 1977 - 1994 (Par Value $ Millions)

Year	Amount ($)	Number of Issues	Average Issue Size ($)
1977	952	25	38.08
1978	1,464	50	29.28
1979	1,241	40	31.03
1980	1,351	40	33.78
1981	1,524	32	47.63
1982	2,548	42	60.67
1983	7,614	88	86.52
1984	14,688	132	111.27
1985	14,568	177	82.31
1986	34,189	223	153.31
1987	28,576	176	162.36
1988	27,671	157	176.25
1989	24,906	116	214.71
1990	682	6	113.67
1991	10,081	43	234.44
1992	39,586	236	167.74
1993	55,900	314	178.03
1994	34,755	179	194.16
Total	302,296	2,076	145.61

Note: Includes split-rated bonds, such as Baa3/BB+ or Ba1/BBB-.
Source: *High Yield Handbook*, January 1995, CS First Boston Corporation

Exhibit 3 shows data on new issue activity from 1977 through 1994. While 1977 is generally considered to be the inception of the modern day speculative-grade bond market, one only has to look at Exhibit 7 in Chapter 1 to realize that below investment grade issues were sold in prior years. The Merrill Lynch High Yield Research Group reports that in the 1970 to 1976 period there were 28 nonconvertible high yield debt issues publicly offered with a par value of $1.058 billion. Eleven of these issues were split rated, all of which had investment grade ratings by Moody's and noninvestment grade ratings by S&P. Most of the issuers had names that were readily known to most investors and the investment bankers were also recognized "Street" firms. Issues were sold by Tenneco, Inc.; Texas Eastern Transmission; B.F. Goodrich; Metro-Goldwyn-Mayer; Jersey Central Power & Light Company; Metropolitan Edison Company, and Savannah Electric & Power. Investment bankers were Eastman Dillon; Dillon Read; Goldman Sachs; Lehman Brothers; Halsey Stuart; White Weld & Co.; Kuhn Loeb; E.F. Hutton, and Salomon Brothers, among others.[2]

But 1977 is the starting point. Lehman Brothers underwrote three single-B-rated issues in March, raising $178 million. In early April, Drexel Burnham Lambert underwrote $30 million of 11.50% subordinated debentures due 1997 for Texas International, Inc.[3] Over the next several years volume ranged between $1.2 billion and

---

[2] Martin S. Fridson and Jeffrey A. Bersh, "What Caused the 1977-1978 Takeoff in High Yield Finance?" *EXTRA CREDIT* (November/December 1993).

[3] For the complete story of Texas International see Harlan D. Platt, *The First Junk Bond, A Story of Corporate Boom and Bust,* (Armonk, NY: M. E. Sharpe, Inc., 1994)

$1.5 billion. New issuance jumped 67% in 1982 compared with 1981 and nearly tripled again in 1983. It rose another 93% in 1984, was flat in 1985, and surged to a record $34 billion in 1986 fueled by increased speculative activity. But volume tapered off over the next three years in the face of increasing concerns about the health of the market and its participants. In 1989, 116 issues for $24.9 billion were publicly offered.

Concerns focused on the practices of some investment bankers as legal authorities investigated and prosecuted alleged insider trading activities, fraud and so-called "economic" crimes. Bankers being led away in handcuffs made prime time television news as did defaults and other financially stressful activities. The leading investment bank, Drexel Burnham Lambert and its high yield head, Michael Milken, came under fierce attack in Congress and by other government agencies. Milken's ties with Drexel were severed in December 1988 as the firm pleaded no contest to charges of securities law violations and paid $650 million in fines and damages. In February 1990, Drexel declared bankruptcy. The Justice Department continued its relentless pursuit of Michael Milken and finally, in April 1990, he accepted a plea bargain to six felony charges. He paid heavy fines and was sentenced to a prison term. Also, insurance companies and savings and loan associations, active investors in this asset class, came under fire. Junk bonds were blamed for the rising failures of savings and loan association although much of their other activity in real estate was more to blame. And Congress and the federal regulators are not entirely blameless for their past actions. So in 1989, Congress enacted The Financial Institutions Reform and Recovery Enforcement Act requiring S&Ls to mark their investment portfolios to market and to divest themselves of their holdings of junk bonds by 1994. The National Association of Insurance Commissioners tightened its regulations governing insurance company investments and imposed higher reserve requirements. These actions put further stress on the strained market.

In the face of the above calamities, the junk bond new issue market virtually disappeared in 1990, along with many participants. First Boston says there were six new issues for $682 million in 1990. Moody's figures show some $2.75 billion of new issues while Merrill Lynch records ten new issues with a par value of $1.397 billion. No matter what numbers one uses, there was essentially a wipeout of new issue activity. But the market recovered as participants regained their senses and confidence. Not every bad thing reported about junk bonds was true. Not all participants consorted with the devil. Many woke up and realized that there were good companies seeking to raise necessary capital and that the rewards were worth the risks. Investment bankers were willing to do fair deals and traders were willing to make competitive bids and offers. Distressed selling dissipated. Money flowed into high income mutual funds seeking to be put to work. In 1991, 43 new offerings were made totaling just over $10 billion par amount. In 1992, just under $40 billion was offered, and in 1993 another record was set: $55.9 billion par amount and 314 issues were sold.

The quality makeup of the high yield market has improved since the late eighties. While still primarily a single B-rated market, issues rated split CCC (Caa/B or B/CCC) and lower comprised some 9% of year end 1994's outstandings compared with 15% in 1988. Split-rated BBB (Baa/BB or Ba/BBB) and straight Ba and BB rated issues were 40% of the market versus only 13% in 1988. According to Merrill Lynch, new issues rated B- or lower were only 17.3% of 1994's volume and 15.6% of 1993's. The percentage of B- and lower new issues in 1987 was 59.3%, rising to 65.8% in 1988 and declining to 27.8% in 1989. It was zero percent in 1990. Again, senior debt as a percentage of high yield new issues ranged between 59% and 83% in the 1990 to 1994 period. In contrast, between 1986 and 1989, senior debt issues accounted for just 19% to 34% of new issue volume. Even the use of proceeds of new issues can be looked at as a quality-related measure. In the 1987 to 1989 period, debt issuance for acquisitions and leveraged buyouts was between 34.8% and 46.4% of total junk new issues, falling to zero percent in 1990 and between 2.4% and 3.1% for 1991 to 1993 and 7.5% for 1994. Similarly, use of new money for general corporate purposes (a catch all term) amounted to between 5.9% and 10.5% in 1987 to 1989 compared with 19.7% to 31.5% in the 1991 to 1994 span.

The large amount of the lower orders of corporate debt issued in the late 1980s led some to wonder if junk bond market participants perhaps had lost track of their senses. Creditors become less wary as the business cycle expansion moves along — in fact, they become more optimistic when they ought to become more cautious. Banks become less selective to whom they lend, and the terms of loans become less restrictive. Investment banking firms become less discriminating about their underwriting, they just want to get deals done. After all, they want to maintain or even increase their market share in the league tables of the leading underwriting firms. One way to do it is to finance every cat and dog that wants to come to market. Their investor customers will often buy what is offered without too much of a discerning eye.

With the decline in interest rates in the late eighties, investors wanting higher yields had to go to lower-rated securities. Not satisfied with the expected returns of Government bonds and investment-grade corporates, they wanted the higher yields offered by speculative-grade bonds (and the higher the yield the better). Above average yields denote above average risk but many investors apparently did not care. In return for high yield the investor assumes above average risk whether he accepts the fact or not. High yield to maturity or high current return may become no yield or return at all. Maybe the appropriate measurement should have been "yield to default" or "yield to reorganization." From 1984 into 1989, the market for speculative-grade debt was such that investors bought issues that probably would have never reached the marketplace a decade or two earlier. By mid-1989, there were signs that the market was beginning to take heed over junk bond quality. Some new issues were postponed or withdrawn, and the prices on many outstanding bonds declined in the face of several defaults and concern over the ability of the economy to avoid a recession. W. Braddock Hickman states:

> ... the trends in default rates are roughly comparable with trends
> in net and gross new financing, default rates tending to be high
> on securities issued during years of high financial volume and
> vice versa. This would seem to suggest that some issues, perhaps

those of marginal quality, can find a ready market only when the market is buoyant, and that in periods of market pessimism only the top grade issues can be placed....[4]

High-Yield Bond Performance and Default Rates

Without question, there have been disasters in the high-yield bond market just as there have been crashes in the equity markets. Prices of bonds suffered great declines as issuers went bankrupt, defaulted or tried to reorganize outside of the bankruptcy court. These actions do not mean that all is lost, as we shall see later. The investor holding Republic Steel, McLean Industries, Western Union, and Zapata Corporation debentures in mid-July 1986 would have felt as though all *was* lost. In the two-week period ending July 25, prices of these bonds dropped like a lead balloon after LTV's announcement that it would seek protection from creditors under the Federal bankruptcy laws. Republic Steel's bonds, part of the LTV group, were directly affected by the parent's bankruptcy. The declines in the other issues were due to the marginal nature of their operations and investors' perceptions that they might also have to file for bankruptcy. The Republic Steel 12⅛% debentures of 2003 dropped from 58⅝ to 18⅞, a decline of 68%, not including approximately $15 of accrued and unpaid interest. The Western Union 16s of 1991 went from 100 to 49½ before closing at the end of the period at 67, a price erosion of 33%. The Zapata 10⅞% subordinated debentures of 2001 fell *only* 18 points from 50 to 32, and the McLean Industries 12s of 2003 went from 70⅞ to 40.

The LTV bankruptcy was complex and long with the company finally reorganizing in the summer of 1994. The Republic Steel 12⅛s received 6.3 shares of new LTV common stock valued at 12⅜ a share, or a total value of $77.96 per $1,000 debenture. Western Union defaulted on the 16s and failed to pay them at maturity. Eventually the debentures were exchanged for new securities under a 1992 prepackaged bankruptcy filing and then, in April 1993, it filed for Chapter 11 bankruptcy. Zapata missed several years' interest payments on its bonds, then resumed payments in late 1988 only to suspend them again a year later. In 1990, it tendered for the bonds at $520 per $1,000 debenture. In 1991, it paid the past due interest on the outstanding bonds and in 1994 Zapata was still meeting interest payments when due. McLean Industries filed for reorganization in November 1986 and came out in May 1989. Holders of the 12s of 2003 received some preferred and common stock of the new company.

---

[4] W. Braddock Hickman, *Corporate Bond Quality and Investor Experience,* (Princeton, NJ: Princeton University Press, 1958), p. 109. Hickman also quotes from *Measuring Business Cycles,* a 1946 publication by Arthur C. Burns and Wesley C. Mitchell:

> After a severe depression industrial activity rebounds sharply, but speculation does not. The following contraction in business is mild, which leads people to be less cautious. Consequently, in the next two or three cycles, while the cyclical advances become progressively smaller in industrial activity, they become progressively larger in speculative activity. Finally, the speculative boom collapses and a drastic liquidation follows, which ends this cycle of cycles and brings us back to the starting point.

The summer of 1989 saw similar price action in the debt of Integrated Resources Inc. Exhibit 4 shows the price declines came in two distinct stages. The first shock was on June 14 when the company announced that its commercial paper dealers could no longer refinance or roll over maturing paper due to a lack of buyers and its bankers would not extend new credit. On June 15 it defaulted on close to $1 billion of short-term debt. It offered to exchange new secured debt with a longer maturity for this short-term paper but found no takers. The securities had been on Standard & Poor's *CreditWatch* list since January 2, 1989, with developing implications; it changed to negative on June 5. On June 14, S&P lowered the senior debt ratings from BBB to BB-, the subordinated debt from BBB- to B, and the commercial paper from A-2 to B. By the end of the week the senior debt was further downgraded to CCC+, the subordinated to CCC-, and the commercial paper to D. The week-to-week declines were impressive, both absolutely and relatively, with the largest percentage losses occurring in the subordinated debt. Investors who had done their homework on the company more than likely would not have been caught holding this high-yielding junk; only the greedy or those with hope in their hearts.

The story doesn't end at the end of June; there was an aftershock. Following the initial default, prices gyrated as speculators awaited news of restructuring plans. One plan would give senior creditors about 80 cents on the dollar in cash and securities. In mid-August, management cut the value of its assets and proposed a less attractive plan. Debt prices fell again as investors believed a bankruptcy filing was becoming increasingly certain with each passing day. Under such circumstances, Integrated's business would continue to deteriorate with creditors recovering even less. This August quake reduced the prices of some subordinated debt issues more than 40% to single-digit prices. Speculation was that senior creditors might recover about 70% of their claim and subordinated creditors about 30% within three years.

Integrated filed for bankruptcy protection in February 1990. In August 1994, four and one-half years later, the company was reorganized under the control of New York money manager Michael Steinhardt. Renamed Presidio Capital Corp., the organization plan provided that subordinated debtholders would receive about 55 cents for each dollar of claim, or shares of a separate entity that retained a small portion of Integrated's assets.

And the junk bond shocks continued. In one week in November, 1994, *The Wall Street Journal* reported that Grand Union Company's 12.25% notes due 2002 fell from about 64 to 44 when it announced it couldn't meet some scheduled interest payments because of continuing losses. F&M Distributors 11.50% notes due 2003 fell from 47 to 23 and then to 20 over two trading days. Again, operating losses were to blame and it said it wanted to restructure. F&M filed for bankruptcy on December 6. *The Wall Street Journal* reported the president of the company saying, "We were forced to take this action as a result of the severe financial restrictions placed on us by a highly leveraged balance sheet."

Adverse selection has led many investors to forgo the junk markets. However, most proponents of high-yield bonds feel that looking at the total picture instead of a few isolated cases gives a truer view of the merits and returns available from speculative-grade bonds.

Exhibit 4: Price Activity of the Bonds of Integrated Resources Inc.
Listed on the New York Stock Exchange, weeks ended June 23 and August 18, 1989

| | Week of June 19 - 23 | | | | | Week of August 14 - 18 | | | | |
| | | | | Week-to-week | | | | | Week-to-week | |
Issue	High	Low	Last	Price Change	Percent Decline	High	Low	Last	Price Change	Percent Decline
Senior Debt:										
10% due May 1, 1990	59.000	41.250	57.250	-42.250	-42.5	46.000	37.000	38.000	-9.000	-19.1
10¾% due May 1, 1992	66.375	37.500	57.250	-37.250	-39.4	46.000	36.000	37.375	-1.625	-4.2
11⅛% due May 1, 1994	70.000	40.125	55.250	-37.625	-40.5	45.500	36.250	37.125	-7.875	-17.5
Subordinated Debt:										
8⅜% due April 15, 1997	26.000	26.000	26.000	-30.000	-53.6	14.000	11.000	11.000	-7.000	-38.9
13⅛% due July 15, 1995	45.000	24.125	29.000	-43.000	-59.7	16.500	8.500	8.750	-7.250	-45.3
10¾% due April 15, 1996	35.000	20.750	26.375	-34.625	-56.8	16.250	9.000	9.000	-6.625	-42.4
12¼% due August 15, 1998	33.000	22.000	26.000	-39.875	-60.5	15.250	7.500	9.000	-6.750	-42.9

Note: Prices are expressed as a percentage of par.

Several major investment banking firms active in the high-yield market have indices measuring market performance. Exhibit 5 compares the total returns for the *First Boston High Yield Index* to the ten-year Treasury bond, the Shearson/Lehman Government Corporate Bond Index, the Standard & Poor's 500-Stock Index and the Composite Return of the Over-the-Counter Index. Total return includes interest income, principal gain or loss, and reinvestment of interest received.

The fourteen-year performance of the CS First Boston High Yield Index has been pretty respectable, with an average annual return of 13.77%. This is 248 basis point better than the average annual return on ten-year Treasury bonds and 189 better than the Shearson/Lehman Government Corporate Index. Even the average annual equity returns are less than the high yield average. There have been some years with stellar returns for all of the categories but they will move back towards the long term average over time. The high growth rates are not sustainable. Certainly, the 1991 to 1993 period was quite commendable. But the market was coming off two terrible years for the high yield business. There was a bull market in stocks as well as lower interest rates which helped companies and improved investor psychology. 1994 brought higher interest rates which took their toll. The annual return for high yield bonds fell from 25.87% for the 1990 to 1993 period to 11.16% for 1992 through 1994. The return on 10-year Treasuries dropped from 11.56% to 3.84% and the OTC index return fell from 28.1% annually to 8.21% for the same two time spans.

Exhibit 5: Comparison of the Total Rates of Return
for the High Yield Market to Selected Market Indices (1981 - 1994)

Year	CS First Boston High-Yield Index (%)	10-Year U.S. Treasury Bond Index (%)	Shearson/Lehman Government Corporate Index (%)	Standard & Poor's 500 Stock Index (%)	Over-the-Counter Composite Return (%)
1994	-0.97	-6.08	-3.51	1.32	-3.65
1993	18.91	11.94	10.98	10.08	14.01
1992	16.66	6.52	7.48	7.63	15.36
1991	43.75	16.46	16.15	30.48	59.82
1990	-6.38	6.81	8.29	-3.05	-12.99
1989	0.38	16.57	14.23	31.50	19.26
1988	13.65	6.11	7.59	16.44	15.42
1987	6.54	-1.92	2.55	5.20	-5.26
1986	15.63	19.89	16.52	18.67	7.36
1985	24.93	26.31	24.05	31.70	31.36
1984	10.69	12.93	16.62	6.20	-11.22
1983	13.91	3.50	9.27	22.60	19.87
1982	36.57	32.02	39.20	21.60	18.67
1981	8.96	4.85	2.95	-5.00	-3.21
Average 14-year Annual Return	13.77%	11.29%	11.88%	13.31%	10.33%
Three-Year Comparison, 1992 - 1994					
Value of $100 Investment	$137.37	$111.98	$115.10	$120.04	$126.72
Three-Year Compounded Growth Rate	11.16%	3.84%	4.80%	6.28%	8.21%
Return Spread vs. High Yield Index (basis points)	-0-	-732	-636	-488	-295
Five-Year Comparison, 1990 - 1994					
Value of $100 Investment	$184.87	$139.29	$144.77	$151.83	$176.22
Five-Year Compounded Growth Rate	13.08%	6.84%	7.68%	8.71%	12.00%
Return Spread vs. High Yield Index (basis points)	-0-	-623	-540	-437	-108
Ten-Year Comparison, 1985 - 1994					
Value of $100 Investment	$324.60	$276.18	$263.72	$382.30	$324.09
Ten-Year Compounded Growth Rate	12.50%	10.69%	10.18%	14.35%	12.48%
Return Spread vs. High Yield Index (basis points)	-0-	-181	-232	185	-2

Source: *High Yield Handbook, January 1992 and January 1995, High Yield Research Group, CS First Boston Corporation*

Total returns are just one way to evaluate portfolio performance. They are not short-term measurement or timing devices. Many investors use yield spreads ("risk premiums") as a guide to relative valuation in both the high-grade and speculative areas of the market. Spreads are an aid to answering such questions as: Should one increase participation in the speculative-grade market and reduce holdings of higher grade issues at this particular point in time? Is the market paying enough to justify the additional risk of more speculative-grade issues? Spreads are affected by many factors including perceived credit risk, bond characteristics, and market conditions. Spreads between high-grade and low-grade bonds may increase when interest rates are rising and during economic recessions periods of investor fear and uncertainty. During these times, investors often opt for stronger credits, bidding up their prices (lowering yields) while avoiding more risky debt issues.

Merrill Lynch's High Yield Research Group publishes yield spread data. Exhibit 6 presents the spread or yield difference history between Merrill's High Yield Master Index and the ten-year Treasury bond and the spread between its Double-B Corporate Index and its Single B Corporate Index. The average spread between the High Yield Index and Treasuries was 475 basis points. Eliminating the two highest and lowest spreads reduces the average to 462 basis points. The peak spread came in the quarter ended December 1990 when it was 933 basis points. The lowest spread of 276 basis points occurred in the first quarter of 1985 but it is an aberration since spreads steadily widened subsequently. Eliminating the out-of-line figure then makes the spread posted in 1994 as the lowest. These figures suggest that investor confidence was high and perhaps investors should exercise caution. A similar picture is seen in the Double-B versus Single-B figures. The average spread was 256 basis points and 237 without the extremes. Again, the market appeared cheapest in the fall of 1990 when all was gloom and doom.

Remember that this spread is an indication of the risk; it is additional payment (such as an insurance premium) to induce the investor to absorb such greater risk. Some reasons for these excess returns or risk premiums are suggested in a 1989 General Accounting Office report including:

- The market has been mispricing the bonds; it has been inefficient.
- The demand for high yield bonds has been artificially reduced because some classes of institutions, such as commercial banks, are restricted from investing in them.
- The high yield market is young compared to the market for investment grade bonds and must offer very attractive yields to secure capital.
- The yield spread includes a premium for liquidity risk.
- A portion of the yield probably reflects some expected future decline in the economy.
- Issuers have been optimistic about what they could earn on their investments, especially LBOs, and have been willing to pay high rates.[5]

---

[5] U.S. General Accounting Office, *High Yield Bonds — Issues Concerning Thrift Investments in High Yield Bonds* (Washington, D.C.: Superintendent of Documents, 1989) pp. 22-23.

Exhibit 6: High Yield Spread History
Merrill Lynch High Yield Master Index versus Ten-Year Treasury, Quarterly, 1985 through 1994

End of Quarter	Yield Spread (basis points)	End of Quarter	Yield Spread (basis points)
December-1984	347	March-1990	654
March-1985	276	June-1990	634
June-1985	372	September-1990	823
September-1985	345	December-1990	933
December-1985	409	November-1900	721
March-1986	486	June-1991	599
June-1986	445	September-1991	623
September-1986	481	December-1991	641
December-1986	502	March-1992	429
March-1987	434	June-1992	405
June-1987	390	September-1992	443
September-1987	357	December-1992	449
December-1987	442	March-1993	446
March-1988	436	June-1993	409
June-1988	407	September-1993	443
September-1988	415	December-1993	383
December-1988	405	March-1994	331
March-1989	423	June-1994	330
June-1989	528	September-1994	322
September-1989	557	December-1994	344
December-1989	645	Average Spread	475

Merrill Lynch Double-B Corporates versus Merrill Lynch Single-B Corporates, Quarterly, 1989 through 1994

End of Quarter	Yield Spread (basis points)	End of Quarter	Yield Spread (basis points)
March-1989	195	March-1992	151
June-1989	235	June-1992	165
September-1989	302	September-1992	182
December-1989	337	December-1992	192
March-1990	396	March-1993	178
June-1990	358	June-1993	150
September-1990	645	September-1993	204
December-1990	465	December-1993	161
March-1991	413	March-1994	158
June-1991	319	June-1994	151
September-1991	243	September-1994	163
December-1991	189	December-1994	184
		Average Spread	256

Source: *High Yield Market Year-End Update*, Merrill Lynch & Co., January 27, 1995.

It is this optimism that allowed them to obtain the funds for their speculative ventures. It is the optimism on the issuer side as well as on the investors' side. It takes two to make a transaction. In August 1989, Resorts International Inc. said it would stop paying interest to its bondholders and that it would submit a debt rescheduling or recapitalization plan to bondholders the next month. Management miscalculated, it was too optimistic as to what it could do. *The New York Times* quoted Merv Griffin, who purchased the company in November 1988, as saying, "Operating cash flows have been less because we underestimated the time and capital expenditures it would take to turn around the company's operations to generate increased profits. It has taken the company longer to sell non-operating real estate assets than originally expected." The president of Resorts said that the problems the company had when it was purchased were more than they expected. "It turned out to be something different than Merv envisioned he was buying. I will say that knowing what we now know, we wouldn't do the same deal. We discovered a lot in the way of problems after we got here." Resorts filed a Chapter 11 bankruptcy and worked out an exchange of debentures and notes for new securities. It emerged from bankruptcy in August 1990.

Of course, unwarranted optimism may lead to destruction. For example, Resorts International Financing's B3-rated 16⅝% Subordinated Debentures due September 1, 2004, were trading at 96½ at the end of 1988, with a 17.27% yield to maturity and a 17.23% current yield. Nine months later, trading flat (without accrued interest), they hit 30 before bouncing back to 34, and were without a current or yield to maturity. Even well-intentioned and knowledgeable professional investors can be too optimistic at times.

One high yield bond research arm of a major broker/dealer expressed its good feelings about these bonds in its year-end 1988 review. The report mentioned the analyst's optimism about management's ability to improve operating results. The company could also fund cash flow deficiencies through the sale of non-operating assets. It was the belief that Griffin had no incentives to default on this debt. Finally, as the bonds were trading at a 350 basis point premium over newly issued Griffin debt, this spread made the bonds attractive to some.

In retrospect, this turned out to be a bad call. The Resorts' bonds declined to 34 by the end of August 1989, a drop of 64.8%. The Griffin Resorts 13½% First Mortgage Bonds due November 15, 1995, and the 13⅞% Senior Secured Notes due May 1, 1998, suffered smaller losses. Both issues traded around 100 at year end 1988. By the following August 31, they were 70 and 67, respectively, down only a more modest 30% and 33%. Junk is perfidious, requiring diligent research on the part of investors. One should always be skeptical, but more about this later when we discuss ways to reduce the risks of investing in junk.

Professor Edward I. Altman of the Salomon Center of New York University is a leading scholar of junk bond default rates and mortality experience.[6] He defines the default rate as the dollar amount of defaulting bonds divided by the amount of outstanding high yield debt. His figures, shown in Exhibit 7, exclude convertible bonds and distressed debt exchanges. During the period of 1970 through 1994, the default rate ranged from a low of 0.158% in 1981 to a high of 12.080% in 1970 (the year the Penn Central default), averaging 3.144%. The average default rate weighted for the par amount of outstanding high yield debt is 4.240% for the full period. The par value amount of defaulted corporate straight debt securities didn't get above $1 billion until 1986 (the year of the LTV bankruptcy) when defaulted debt totaled $3.2 billion. The peak volume year was 1991 with $18.9 billion of defaults. Columbia Gas System, 1991's big bust, was rated Baa1 (investment grade) at the time of the default.

Companies have gone into bankruptcy and emerged only to default again. These two-time losers are teasingly referred to by Wall Street wags as "double dippers" or "Chapter 22s" (two times Chapter 11). Some of these issuers are: A.M. International in 1982 and 1992; Continental Airlines Corp. in 1983 and 1990; Lionel Corp. in 1982 and 1991, and Savin Corp. in 1986 and 1992. Emerging from bankruptcy usually means that the company has been rehabilitated and is now set for a new life. But just like some criminals after being released from jail, corporations also experience recidivism.

---

[6] Readers may be interested in other default rate studies including the following:

- Edward I. Altman and Scott A. Nammacher, "The Default Rate Experience on High-Yield Corporate Debt." *Financial Analysts Journal* (July/August 1985), pp. 25-41.

- Edward I. Altman, "Measuring Corporate Bond Mortality and Performance." *The Journal of Finance*, Vol. 44 No. 4 (September 1989), pp. 909-922.

- Paul Asquith, David W. Mullins, Jr., and Eric D. Wolff, "Original Issue High Yield Bonds: Aging Analyses of Defaults, Exchanges and Calls." *The Journal of Finance*, (Vol. 44 No. 4, September 1989) pp. 923-952.

- Leo C. Brand, Thomas Kitto, and Reza Bahar "1993 Corporate Default, Rating Transition Study Results." *Standard & Poor's CreditReview* (May 2, 1994).

- Jerome S. Fons, Lea V. Carty and Dana Lieberman, *Corporate Bond Defaults and Default Rates 1970 - 1994*, a special report of Moody's Investors Service, January 1995.

- Martin S. Fridson, "Defaulted Bonds: Supply, Demand and Investment Performance," Merrill Lynch & Co. Global Securities Research & Economics Group, March 29, 1994.

Exhibit 7: Historical Default Rates for Straight Debt Only 1970 to 1994

Year	Par Value Outstanding[a] ($ Millions)	Par Value Defaults ($ Millions)	Default Rates (%)
1994	235,000	3,148	1.454
1993	206,907	2,287	1.105
1992	163,000	5,545	3.402
1991	183,600	18,862	10.273
1990	181,000	18,354	10.140
1989	189,258	8,110	4.285
1988	148,187	3,944	2.662
1987	129,557	7,486 [b]	5.778[c]
1986	90,243	3,156	3.497
1985	58,088	992	1.708
1984	40,939	344	0.840
1983	27,492	301	1.095
1982	18,109	577	3.186
1981	17,115	27	0.158
1980	14,935	224	1.500
1979	10,356	20	0.193
1978	8,946	119	1.330
1977	8,157	381	4.671
1976	7,735	30	0.388
1975	7,471	204	2.731
1974	10,894	123	1.129
1973	7,824	49	0.626
1972	6,529	193	2.956
1971	5,805	82	1.413
1970	6,598	797	12.080
Arithmetic Average Default Rate:		1970 to 1994	3.144
		1978 to 1994	3.095
		1983 to 1994	3.853
Par Value Weighted Average Default Rate:		1970 to 1994	4.240
		1978 to 1994	4.282
		1983 to 1994	4.403

[a] Defaulted debt is excluded from outstandings.
[b] $1,841.7 million without Texaco, Inc., Texaco Capital, and Texaco N.V.
[c] The default rate is 1.345%.

Source: *High Yield Market Year-End Update*, Merrill Lynch & Co., January 27, 1995.

Debt mortality studies look at default rates as bonds age, similar to the way insurance actuaries look at human mortality. Standard & Poor's has conducted default and transition studies for a number of years and the general results are what one would expect. The higher a bond's initial rating, the lower the likelihood of default. For the thirteen years ending with 1993, the cumulative default rate for investment grade issues was 3.88% compared with 30.68% for speculative grade issues. Also, the lower the initial rating, the shorter the time period to default. It was 8.2 years from the time of the original AAA on two issuers to their default and 7.7 years for the nine originally-rated AA issuers In contrast, it took only an average of 3.8 years for the 160 initially-rated B issuers and 2.4 years for 26 originally-rated CCC issuers to knock on the bankruptcy court's door. There weren't any issuers rated A or higher that defaulted. However, there were five BBB issuers. Of the 143 issuers rated B-rated just prior to default, the average time to default was 1.8 years while it took CCC-rated issues only six months to default.

Another mortality study which caught the attention of the financial press in 1989 was written by three faculty members of the Harvard Business School, Paul Asquith, David Mullins and Eric Wolff. Known as *The Harvard Study*, it is an aging analysis of 741 junk bonds issued in 1977 through 1986. It found that 33.92% of the bonds issued in 1977 and 34.26% of those issued in 1978 had defaulted by the end of 1988. Bonds issued in 1979 through 1983 had mortality rates between 19.21% and 27. 56%, and bonds issued in 1984, 1985 and 1986 had mortality rates of 9.38%, 3.53% and 8.14%, respectively.

Care in the use of default and mortality rates must be exercised when examining the impact on a diversified portfolio. If the default rate is 5%, the portfolio's total return would not necessarily take a five hundred basis point loss. A loss of that magnitude would mean that the bond was purchased at par and became completely worthless upon default; the portfolio manager could not salvage anything from it. Defaults do not mean that a bond's price goes to zero. The prices of the various LTV Corporation issues one week after the filing of bankruptcy in July 1986, ranged from 19½ to 63⅛ for a simple average of 38.33. The debt included well-secured first mortgage bonds on a good steel plant to unsecured subordinated debentures. The average price one month before bankruptcy was 71.85 with a range of 56 to 90. The Altman study referred to in Exhibit 7 gives the average retention or recovery price on the 594 bonds used in the report for 1985 through 1994, as $40.95 per $100 bond. This is the price at the end of the month in which the bond defaulted. Secured debt had the highest prices — $59.26 — followed by senior unsecured debt averaging $50.81. Senior subordinated debt averaged $36.48 per bond and subordinated cash paying bonds had a recovery of $30.55. Non-cash pay subordinated debt had the lowest recovery values, only $18.73.

Since everyone doesn't buy bonds at par, the portfolio loss depends on the actual loss incurred or reported. In calculating default loss figures, Altman adds the principal loss the accrued coupon income; one assumes slightly less than six months interest on average but it varies depending on the last interest payment date and the coupon rate. Thus, the default loss to investors is (i) the default rate, times (ii) the loss of principal, plus (iii) the loss of coupon or accrued interest. For 1994, the default rate of 1.454% results in a default loss of 0.96% using the weighted average price after default of 39.9 (average loss of 60.1) and the weighted average coupon of 11.50%.

$$\text{Default rate} \times \text{Loss of principal} = \text{Loss from principal} + \frac{(\text{Coupon} \times \text{Default rate})}{2}$$

$$1.454\% \times 60.1 = 0.758 + \frac{(11.50 \times 1.454)}{2}$$

$$\text{Default loss for 1994} = 0.957\%$$

Hickman had several qualifications about the higher returns available from low-grade issues that bear repeating. He states:

> The major conclusion that investors obtained higher returns on low-grade issues than on high grades should not be accepted without proper qualification. For it cannot be emphasized too strongly that this finding emerges only when broad aggregates of corporate bonds are considered over long investment periods, and given the price and yield relationships that existed during these periods. In effect, the aggregate results reflect the experience of all investors over long periods, rather than that of any particular investor over any given short period.
>
> Another qualification is that realized yields and loss rates were not nearly so regularly related to quality as were promised yields and default rates. Because of the disparity in the performance of low-grade bonds, small investors (and many large investors that may have been inhibited from practicing the broadest type of diversification) would frequently have fared best by holding only the highest grade obligations. This conclusion follows both from the higher average default rate on low-grade securities and from the wider scatter of realized yields obtained on them over given periods.
>
> A third qualification is that realized yields were subject to extreme aberrations over time, since they reflected not only the risks of the business cycle but the state of the capital market as well. The average yields realized over selected periods of offering and extinguishment, or over selected chronological periods during which the issues were outstanding, indicate that the market usually overpriced low-grade issues (and underestimated default risks) at or near peaks of major investment cycles. As a general rule, low grades fared better than high grades when purchased near troughs and sold near peaks of the investment cycle; but by the same token, losses were heavy on low grades purchased near peaks and sold near troughs. The same is true of investments in declining as against growing industries. Low-grade issues of a declining industry rarely worked out as well as high-grade issues.[7]

---

[7] W. Braddock Hickman, "Corporate Bonds: Quality and Investment Performance," Occasional Paper 59. (New York: National Bureau of Economic Research, 1957), pp. 16-17.

WHO OWNS HIGH YIELD BONDS?

Buyers of speculative-grade bonds run the full range of the debt investor category. At the end of 1993 it was estimated that insurance companies held about 12% of the publicly outstanding high yield issues, down from an estimate of 30% in 1988. The latest holdings of speculatively-rated publicly issued debt was some $28.5 billion, equal to only 3.6% of the industry's total public bond portfolio. This is down from $32.6 billion or 4.8% of their public holdings in 1992. In that one year, holdings of the better grade BB issues rose 25% from $12.8 billion to $16 billion while the other categories declined. Lower rated bond holdings went from $19.8 billion to $12.4 billion. On the other hand, high yield mutual fund holdings of bonds increased from somewhat under $35 billion at the end of 1992 to $48.7 billion at the end of 1993. In January 1994, holdings hit a record $50.9 billion and then declined to $46.5 billion at the end of September 1994. However, it is estimated that total mutual fund holdings of high yield debt is a fair amount larger than the figures just mentioned since asset allocation funds, income funds, balanced funds, and general corporate bond funds also invest in these securities. For example, the August 9, 1994 issue of *The Value Line Mutual Fund Survey* reports data on 103 general bond funds. Of these, 53 had positions in less than investment grade debt. The average portfolio quality of the 53 was between A to AA. The high yield positions ranged from 1% of the portfolio to as much as 49%. 38 of the funds held high yield bonds equal to less than 20% of their total holdings, eight had between 20% and 29%, five had junk bond holdings comprising between 30% and 39% of the portfolios, and two had junk holdings amounting to 45% and 49%, respectively. Fund holdings in 1988 were estimated at about 30% of outstanding high yield issues.

Other major high yield investors include public pension funds, both public and private. Holding some 15% of the market in 1988, we estimate that 1994 positions are larger due to the perceived quality improvement in the marketplace. The search for yield can weaken portfolio managers' resistance to less than investment grade issues. Foreign investors, closed-end investment companies, unit investment trusts, securities dealers, and direct investment by individuals and corporations are other important participants in this market.

Individuals are an important category, both through direct purchases and indirectly through mutual funds, unit trusts and the like. In some experts' opinions, individuals should not participate directly in this market to any major extent. Many have individual retirement accounts, Keogh plans and other self-directed pension schemes that can build interest income on a tax deferred basis until the plan is liquidated. Should these funds be invested 100% in speculative grade securities? The answer is a resounding NO! These are retirement funds which should be prudently invested which means diversification among asset classes. Certainly, as one approaches retirement age, high yield bonds and more risky stock investments should be reduced and a more conservative investment posture taken. One should lessen the chances of adverse selection so diversification is a necessity. Most individual investors do not have portfolios large enough to permit adequate diversification of credit and market risk among individual bond issues. Also, many individuals do not have the right attitude for dispassionate investing; they don't buy when they should and they don't sell when they should. How often do we hear the excuse, "I don't want to take the loss." It really doesn't matter — the loss exists whether or not it is taken, and without the particular investment position the investor perhaps may be better able to think more clearly, rationally and without emotion.

Further, most have neither the time nor the knowledge and experience to adequately analyze the speculative bond market and individual issues. Besides reviewing the operations and credit status of the issuer, the terms of the issue have to be studied. It is not enough to look at an equity analyst's bullish opinion on the common stock of the company in question. If the investment is successful the shares can be worth many times the current price. Bonds on the other hand, can not trade far above par, and at maturity will not be worth more than par. Many equity analysts are unfamiliar with the nature of debt and may not be qualified to aid fixed-income investors. This is not to say that they should be ignored; equity analysts may often have important information about a company and an industry that is helpful to bond investors. However, one must be careful not to get swept away by the analyst's euphoria.

Since most individual investors can not achieve proper diversification, many turn to mutual funds. Mutual funds pool monies from many people and invest in securities. An open-ended fund normally must be prepared to sell and buy its shares when investors want to invest in or redeem their stock. Thus, the fund must usually keep some highly liquid investments on hand to meet normal redemptions. In times of higher than normal redemptions, they may have to sell investments. This can work to the investors' detriment as it will likely be the better class of junk the fund sells when it comes under pressure. It will often be the more liquid issues and stronger credits that go on the block while the fund has to retain the weaker credits for which there is less demand at what one considers reasonable prices. In fact, markets can become nonexistent when skies are cloudy and grey. A closed-end investment company does not face redemption pressures as it is not committed to buy and sell its shares. With a more stable capital structure there is less need for liquid reserves and a greater percentage of its assets can be working for the investor. In periods of poor junk bond markets with investors running for the exits, the additional selling pressure from mutual funds can exacerbate an already weak situation resulting in lower prices and lower net asset values.

Despite some of the concerns people may have with junk mutual funds, the important fact is that they can achieve the diversification individuals must have and the portfolio is under constant professional and, hopefully, experienced management. Prospective investors must do their homework and check out the fund's record and philosophy. Is the fund investing in the better or more conservative junk or is it investing solely for high yield at the expense of principal? In effect, is the dividend payment being paid only out of income or is it being maintained at the cost of capital? This investigation does not guarantee good results but it can reduce one's worry.

Also, funds provide for the automatic reinvestment of dividends into additional shares. This is another aid for the longer-term investor seeking to build assets through the periodic compounding of the reinvestment of dividends.

There are unit investment trusts for high yield bonds. A unit investment trust is another type of financial vehicle investing in a fixed portfolio of securities. The advantage here is supposed to be professional selection of the initial portfolio along with diversification (although often not as broad as with some open-end mutual funds and closed-end investment companies) and monthly interest payments. However, after the initial sale, management of the trust's holdings is usually less than with a continually managed mutual fund. The adverse financial condition of a portfolio investment may not require the sale of the security from the trust. The sponsor of the trust is usually empowered to direct the trustee to sell investments upon the occurrence of certain events, such as default or decline in price due to market or credit conditions, if the retention of the securities would be detrimental to the interest of the investors. Hopefully, the sponsor can and will act before "the horse is out of the barn."

In 1989, the risks of investing in unit trusts became apparent when Drexel Burnham Lambert ordered the liquidation of its *High Income Trust Securities* ("HITS"). Drexel decided to leave the retail securities business and wouldn't make a secondary market for the various units. Investors got *"HIT"* in several ways. They originally bought the units with a 4% sales charge. Then, the liquidation occurred before the bonds had a chance to mature and the sales were done in a less than robust market climate. With a forced sale, bidders either stayed away or submitted low-ball bids for many of the less liquid issues. Some of the bonds didn't receive any bids at all and final distributions on several trusts were delayed. Some of the units had defaulted bonds which, if the fund were actively managed, might have been sold before defaulting, not afterwards. The trustee said that the liquidated trusts had annual returns from 1.7% for the Series 12 trust to 10.8% for the Series 1 trust. The rates of return on these liquidated trusts were certainly not what the investors expected when they bought these investments which certainly turned out to be garbage or junk to many holders.

REDUCING RISKS IN A SPECULATIVE-GRADE PORTFOLIO

The 1989 General Accounting Office report on thrift junk bond investments said "... the high yield bond market, in its present size and form, has not been tested by a recession. A severe economic downturn might increase bond defaults, especially for those companies issuing bonds as part of leveraged buyouts."[8] Junk bond investors must realize there is default risk in holding these securities but it can be reduced and incremental yield obtained through careful selection of issues.

---

[8] U.S. General Accounting Office, *High Yield Bonds*, p. 3.

Exhibit 8: Collateralization Guidelines —
Imperial Savings Association 9⅜% Collateralized Notes due
September 15, 1990

	Maximum Percent of Market Value of Pledged Property Issued By Any One Issuer (%)	Maximum Percent of Market Value of Pledged Property in Any One Industry Category (%)
Moody's rating		
Aaa	100.0	100.0
Aa	20.0	60.0
A	10.0	40.0
Baa	6.0	20.0
Ba	4.0	12.0
B	3.0	8.0
Standard & Poor's rating		
AAA	10.0	50.0
AA	10.0	33.3
A	10.0	33.3
BBB	5.0	20.0
BB	4.0	12.0
B	3.0	8.0

Note: The referenced percentages represent maximum cumulative totals for the related rating category and each lower rating category.
Source: Prospectus dated September 24, 1987.

Adequate diversification is essential, and the lower down the quality ladder, the more diversified the portfolio should be. Exhibit 8 shows the diversification guidelines established by Moody's Investors Service and Standard & Poor's Corporation for the Imperial Savings Association's 9⅜% Collateralized Notes due September 15, 1990. The original issue size for any bond in the pool must be at least $100 million, but 20% of the speculative-grade sector may be from issues with an original issue amount of at least $50 million. Note that the higher quality the collateral, the less diversification required. For example, bonds rated Ba/BB from any single issuer cannot exceed 4% of the market value of the pledged property, and no more than 12% of the portfolio can be from any one industry. In the single-A category, the single issuer limit increases to 10%, while the industry concentration is 33% to 40%, depending on the rating agency. Such diversification helps protect against adverse selection. Of course, one should not modify one's own guidelines just because there are not enough qualified issues available for investment; just make do with the issues that fit.

As previously pointed out, one of the main advantages of investing in mutual funds is the diversity of their portfolios. Of the 51 funds Value Line classifies as "corporate high yield," 29 were diversified into eight to ten fairly broad industry sectors and thirteen funds were invested in five to seven different sectors. Even the fund with less sector diversification had diversification among issues. Only three funds held individual issues amounting to more than five percent of net assets. One fund had 5.21% of its assets in one issue, another fund 5.36%, and one fund 5.19% in one issue and 5.02% in another. This fund's ten largest holding comprised 45.64% of total net assets. Issue diversification in the other 48 funds was of no concern with many reporting the ten largest holdings comprising less than 20% of net assets.

Investors should limit the amount of subordinated debt in the portfolio. Subordinated debt of financially strong companies may are no problem, but as credit quality decreases, consideration should be given to senior debt over subordinated debt. Investors may permit subordinated debt if it is rated no lower than the Ba/BB category, implying that the senior debt may be investment grade. This may reduce the universe of possible investment opportunities, but it should be remembered that most investors in high yield instruments seek to minimize risk while still trying to achieve a better return. We are not seeking maximum short-term income regardless of the risk involved. Most senior unsecured issues have negative pledge clauses; subordinated debt issues generally don't. If a company runs into financial difficulty and needs additional financing, banks might provide the funds only if the new loan is secured by accounts receivable, inventory or certain other assets. If senior debt has a negative pledge clause then it, too, would fall under the security umbrella; subordinated debt would normally be excluded.

In the fall of 1981, the public debt securities of International Harvester Company and its finance subsidiary (now Navistar International Transportation Corporation and Navistar Financial Corporation) were selling at distressed prices after a period of operating losses. The bonds traded at levels suggesting that the companies were about to file for bankruptcy. Locked out of the commercial paper and long-term debt markets, they relied on more costly bank financing. The companies successfully negotiated with their banks a debt restructuring extending the parent's short-term debt maturities by two years. As part of the agreement, the parent pledged its fixed assets including plants and certain other properties but excluding inventories and receivables. The finance subsidiary's bank loans were secured by self-liquidating accounts receivable. The senior debt of both companies became secured as they contained negative pledge covenants. The parent's subordinated debt lacked any negative pledge and remained unsecured. If the restructuring failed, the public senior debtholders would at least have been on a parity with the banks with enhanced prospects of recovering much, if not all, of their investment; the subordinated debtholders did not obtain any greater protection or security; in fact, their position became weaker.

If an issuer has senior and subordinated debt outstanding, the senior should normally be preferred, all other things being equal. The senior issue's priority ranking may mean less price risk in case of bankruptcy. If there are several issues of senior debt outstanding, the one with the lowest dollar price generally is to be preferred, but keeping in mind the accrued interest to be paid at purchase. The idea is to reduce the risk of loss in case something unexpected occurs. An example is the bankruptcy of the LTV Corporation in July 1986. In bankruptcy, the claims of the various senior debt creditors against the bankrupt's estate would be approximately the same, namely principal plus accrued interest to the date of the filing of the bankruptcy petition. LTV (the parent company) had publicly held unsecured senior and subordinated debt. For example, the three senior unsecured issues (9¼s of February 1, 1997, 13⅞s of December 1, 2002, and the 14s of August 15, 2004) traded on a yield-to-maturity basis before bankruptcy. On June 6, six weeks before the filing, the closing prices of the three issues were 70, 90⅛ and 92, respectively. The promised yields to maturity were 14.96%, 15.55% and 15.30%, and the current returns were 13.21%, 15.23% and 15.22%. At the end of August, some six weeks after bankruptcy, the issues were trading at 35⅜, 37⅛, and 35⅝ respectively, down 49.5%, 58.8% and 61.3%. These prices were about 37% to 39% of the debtholders' claim, taking into account any original issue discount. When LTV emerged from bankruptcy in 1994, the holders of the 9¼s received securities worth $196.58 per $1,000 debenture, the holders of the 13⅞s received $194.52 per bond, and $201.02 was the value received by the 14% bondholders.

On June 6 the subordinated debt prices ranged from 58 for the 7⅞% Reset Notes due April 1, 1998, to 86 for the 5% Subordinated Debentures due January 15, 1988, a difference of 48.3%. On August 29 the prices of these issues were 21½ and 26½, down 63% and 67%, respectively. Before bankruptcy the issues were selling at 97.5% and 91.5% of the claim value; after bankruptcy they sold at 36.1% and 27.9%. Coming out of bankruptcy in 1994 the 7⅞% reset note holders got securities worth $61.22 per note while the 5% subordinated debt holders received securities valued at $66.03 per debenture.

Some investors believe that a short maturity bond is safer than a long-dated instrument. They are willing to buy it on a yield-to-maturity instead of on a more realistic basis. They assume that nothing can or will go wrong between the purchase and maturity dates. If the company does not go under, the short bond may very well provide a very attractive return. If the issuer defaults, there may be a big price drop. In 1985 and 1986, up to the date of LTV's bankruptcy filing, many market participants, especially individual investors and some unknowledgeable stockbrokers, said an attractive investment worth the risk was the LTV 5% subordinated debentures due January 15, 1988. After all, the bonds had only a couple of years to go until maturity, and perhaps the company would make a good exchange offer for them. Speculators thought nothing would happen to jeopardize their investment. Bankruptcy wasn't likely, as many expected steel industry conditions to improve over the next several years. The company was reducing operating losses from steel while its aerospace business was profitable. Were these speculators wrong! The bankruptcy filing struck like a bolt of lightning. The 5s of 1988 had a 15.12% yield to maturity on June 6, but investors didn't achieve it; the high yield caused by the short maturity lulled them into a quick loss overnight!

Another rule to follow is to limit, if not restrict completely, bonds that do not pay interest in cash. These include zero coupon bonds, deferred coupon debt (also called zero/coupons) and coupon issues with the interest payable at the issuer's option in cash, common stock, debt or a combination thereof. The later issues are also known as payment-in-kind bonds or PIK bonds. A zero coupon bond does not pay periodic interest and sells at a discount from face value. The return comes from the accretion of the difference paid for the issue and what one gets at redemption; there is no cash return before the final payment date. A deferred coupon (or zero *slash* coupon) bond is a combination of a straight zero and a regular coupon issue. For a certain period (typically four to five years) it will not pay any interest but, at a specific date in the future, interest payments will begin to accrue at a predetermined rate and paid semi-annually thereafter. An example is Ann Taylor, Inc.'s Senior Subordinated Discount Notes due July 15, 1999. Issued July 20, 1989, at 53.646% of par, interest did not accrue on the notes until January 15, 1994, payable starting July 15, 1994, at the rate of 14⅜%. This issue was called July 15, 1994.

Some financially weak companies have bonds permitting interest to be paid in shares of common stock. The shares delivered in place of cash are usually valued at between 75% and 90% of the average market price of the stock for a specified period before the payment date. This provision helps companies conserve cash. They have been issued or proposed by such firms as Petro-Lewis Corporation, LTV Corporation, Western Union Corporation, Sunshine Mining Company and Mesa Capital Corporation, among others. The bonds would normally trade with accrued interest if they have been paying cash interest; otherwise they trade flat, i.e., without accrued interest. Mesa Capital Corporation, for example, agreed with the New York Stock Exchange that its 12% Subordinated Notes due August 1, 1996, trade with accrued interest. Mesa may make payment in common stock only if it has given public notice at least 10 days before the start of the applicable interest period. If it pays stock interest, the notes will trade flat until the Exchange determines otherwise.

In speculative-grade bond investment, cash flow should come from the portfolio, not from bookkeeping accretions of invisible interest or blizzards of paper certificates. Investors should get some cash return from the investment and decide where and when to reinvest the interest payments — an option that non-interest-bearing securities don't offer. Also, if a company is so strapped for cash as to be unable to pay interest in dollars, it may be foolish to stay with the investment and take the big risk that the situation may not get any better.

Careful analysis is essential to reduce the risk of default in a speculative grade bond portfolio. The prospectuses of new issues must be diligently reviewed for the terms and nature of the issuer's business and industry. We trust that the underwriters have faithfully done their due diligence but that hasn't always been the case They have even been "bamboozled" by fraudulent promoters. Many new issue prospectuses, especially for lower-rated issues, have sections called "risk factors," "certain considerations," "investment considerations," or "risk and special factors" pointing out some of the possible risks to consider before making the investment. Sometimes these risks may be insignificant or just normal business hazards, but these sections often mention risks that some might not have considered. They are in prospectuses for a good reason and thus they should not be ignored.

Some of the risks mentioned in these special sections include the following:

1. The company might have a high debt-to-equity ratio. Often debt may be equal to eight, nine or more times equity. In a few cases, there might not be any equity. The large leverage could impair the issuer's ability to obtain additional financing in the future. The issuer may be more vulnerable to interest rate changes than it had been historically.

2. Restrictions have been placed on the company by its senior creditors (such as banks) that require the company to use proceeds from asset sales to repay them.

3. The company may have been experiencing operating losses. It may have a negative interest coverage ratio because earnings are inadequate to cover fixed charges. It is in a weak financial condition, and losses are expected to continue so long as depressed industry conditions persist. In addition to operating cash flow, the company may need additional funds in the future to pay the principal and interest on the securities being offered or outstanding. It may have to refinance its operations or sell some assets to meet these expected obligations. Based upon current operations and anticipated growth, the company does not expect that it will be able to generate sufficient cash from operations to make all payments under the credit agreements when due for the first two years following the leveraged buyout.

4. The subject issue is subordinated to other debt. Also, the issuer is a holding company and thus conducts its operations through subsidiaries. It relies principally on income from dividends from subsidiaries to supply the necessary funds for the debt service on its outstanding bonds. There might be restrictions on such upstreaming of dividends. Any right of the company or the debtholders to participate in the assets of any of the subsidiaries upon their liquidation or recapitalization is subject to the prior claims of the subsidiaries' creditors and preferred shareholders.

5. There may be no public market for the securities and a warning that none may develop.

6. The impact of interest rate fluctuations on the profitability of the issuer must be considered; that future performance is subject to prevailing economic conditions and business and financial factors, including those beyond control of the company.

7. In certain cases, the indenture does not restrict the payment of dividends.

8. Operating restrictions have been imposed on the company by regulatory authorities.

9. There may be income tax deficiencies due the Internal Revenue Service.

10. There may be contingencies due to the bankruptcy of a subsidiary and possible payments due the Pension Benefit Guaranty Corporation.

11. There is the risk of fraudulent conveyance liability. If a court, in a lawsuit by an unpaid creditor, finds that the issuer did not receive fair consideration or reasonably equivalent value for incurring the new debt, and the issuer was (i) insolvent, (ii) was rendered insolvent by reason of such transaction, (iii) was engaged in a business or transaction for which the assets remaining in the company constituted unreasonably small capital, or (iv) intended to incur or believed it would incur debts beyond its ability to pay such debts as they mature, it could invalidate the issuer's obligation under the new debt securities. The court could also subordinate the securities to existing and future debt, or take other action detrimental to the holders of the debt.

In the fraudulent conveyance sections of prospectuses, there are statements similar to the following from the prospectus dated August 10, 1994, for the offering of $70 million 13% Senior Subordinated Notes due 2002 of Health o meter, Inc. [sic] The proceeds of this offering were used to fund a portion of the cash required to conclude the acquisition of Mr. Coffee, inc. [sic], a producer of coffeemakers.

Management believes that neither the Company nor the Guarantors will be insolvent under the foregoing standards at the time the Notes and Guarantees are issued. There can be no assurance, however, as to what standard a court would apply to determine whether the Company or the Guarantors were "insolvent" as of the date of the Notes or the Guarantees were issued, or that, regardless of the method of evaluation, a court would not determine that the Company or the Guarantors were insolvent on that date. Nor can there be any assurance that a court would not determine, regardless of whether the Company or the Guarantors were insolvent on the date the Notes or the Guarantees were issued, that the payments constituted fraudulent transfers on another of the grounds listed above.

The Company and the Guarantors believe that based upon the forecasts and other financial information including pro forma financial statements reflecting the Acquisition, the Company and the Guarantors are and will continue to be solvent, that they will have sufficient capital to carry on their business and are and will continue to be able to pay their debts as they mature. Thus the Company and the Guarantors believe that in a bankruptcy case or a lawsuit by creditors of the Company or the Guarantors, the Notes and Guarantees should not be held to have been issued in violation of applicable federal or state fraudulent transfer laws. No assurance can be given, however, that a court would concur with the conclusions of the Company and the Guarantors in this regard.

Many new high yield issues are from privately-held companies, that is, the common stock ownership is held by a few people and thus the shares are not traded on a national securities exchange or in the normal over-the-counter market. Some have been issued by firms engaged in leveraged buyouts. If the securities are held by 300 or more persons, the company is considered a reporting one by the Securities and Exchange Commission, and must submit certain reports to the SEC. The prospectus for Dart Drug Stores, Inc., 12.70% Senior Debentures due 2001, stated that as it expected to have fewer than 300 debentureholders, it "... will not file reports with the Commission or furnish information to Debentureholders in accordance with the Exchange Act reporting requirements.... Pursuant to the Indentures, however, the Company must furnish annual and quarterly reports to Debentureholders containing financial statements and certain other information...."

Investors should make sure the indenture requires that quarterly financial statements with income statements and balance sheets and audited annual reports be sent to all debtholders of record, whether the company is a reporting one or not. The prospectus dated June 16, 1994, for the $200 million offering of 10⅞% Senior Subordinated Notes due 2004 of Plitt Theatres, Inc. and guaranteed by Cineplex Odeon Corporation states the following under the *Description of the Notes* section.

> Whether or not Plitt or Cineplex is required to file reports with the Commission, Plitt and Cineplex shall file with the Commission all such reports and other information as would be required to be filed with the Commission by the Securities Exchange Act of 1934, as amended, including, but not limited to, annual reports containing consolidated financial statements of Cineplex audited by its independent auditors, and quarterly reports containing unaudited condensed financial statements of Cineplex for each of the first three quarters of each fiscal year, in each case including summary financial information for Plitt. Plitt and Cineplex shall supply the Trustee and each holder of the Notes, or shall supply to the Trustee for forwarding to each holder of Notes, without cost to such holder, copies of such reports or other information.

These statements should also contain management's discussion of the operations and any other developments affecting the debtholders. They should discuss any of the financial ratios or tests that must be satisfied under the indenture including information about redemption if net worth declines, the use of maintenance and replacement funds, or certain coverage tests, among others. Often, bond investors don't even get these reports. Many publicly-held companies have shareholder meetings, talks with analysts, and public affairs meetings where fuller discussions of the firm's operations and outlook take place. Debtholders are often ignored when it comes to corporate communication. Many privately held companies release only the minimal amount of information necessary to satisfy the indentures, their lawyers, and the SEC; they don't have to respond to outside investor queries. Institutional investors are in a much stronger position to obtain what they need to analyze their private and public securities. Investment bankers may arrange meetings between the issuer and its bondholders, but individual investors don't get invited. This is another reason why individuals should invest in speculative-grade debt through professional money managers.

There are the traditional issuers of lower-rated publicly held companies — those not involved in the front page battles to avoid being taken over by financial wizards. These are the run-of-the-mill businessmen's risks. The proceeds from the issues might be used for regular business purposes, such as financing plant, equipment, research and development expenses, rather than blind pools, which some companies used to play the acquisition game. Traditional fixed income analysis can be used in these cases. Of course, leverage may be higher than with investment-grade issues (but probably lower than with leveraged buyouts), coverage of fixed charges may be lower, and many other financial measurements might appear weaker. But investors can analyze the business, get some sense of the value or worth of the assets (real, not blue sky), even under a worst-case scenario, and come to a decision that it is or is not a viable entity and the risk is or is not worth the potential reward. Such investigation is not one shot at the time of issuance or proposed purchase but a continual process. Investors should evaluate the fundamentals of the industry and the company, see where they are, and estimate where they might be in the future. They should look at cash flow and the firm's debt servicing ability.

After doing their preliminary work, investors must relate the value of the issue to other securities. Is the yield sufficient enough to compensate for the additional risk? Is it in line with comparably rated securities? If not, investors must find out why there is a difference. It could be that the market views the bond as better or worse than other similar issues.

DEFAULTED AND BANKRUPT ISSUES

A bankrupt issue may be more attractive than one that is not in bankruptcy. Certainly, issues of many marginal companies may appear overpriced for the risks involved. These should be analyzed and periodically reviewed on both an operating and liquidation or bankruptcy basis. Much of the analysis may involve educated guesswork as to what the assets might be worth in liquidation or reorganization. By so doing, investors will be prepared to step in or to avoid the issue if the company goes under. It is emphasized that this area of speculation is not for the faint at heart nor for the uninformed. To participate in distressed securities one must become familiar with the law and process of bankruptcy and creditors' rights. It is a complex area of the securities world.

When a company files for bankruptcy, many investors are forced to sell their positions. This is often the wrong time to do so. The market often cannot absorb the large amount of selling accompanying a bankruptcy filing. The securities may fall to levels far below what they are worth creating an opportunity for the knowledgeable speculator. Hickman says: "The conclusion appears unmistakable; on the average, investors who sold at default suffered unnecessarily large losses, and those who purchased obtained unusually large gains. It is unfortunate that many financial intermediaries were forced by their directors or by regulatory authorities to sell at that time."[9]

When one purchases a security of a company in bankruptcy, one is buying several uncertainties. You know your cost basis and you probably have an idea of what your claim is against the bankrupt's estate. You do not know how long it will be before a distribution is made. A few companies come out of bankruptcy in less than two years, while others take considerably longer. Two years is not considered a long reorganization period. It all depends on many factors including the complexity of the case; the friction between the various classes of creditors and claimants; the status of the company's current operations; management decisions, and other lawsuits pending against the bankrupt. Time is money, and the longer it takes to get a distribution, the lower the rate of return on the invested funds. You also do not know the exact value of what eventually will be paid or the breakdown of the distribution between cash (if any) and new securities. Essentially, you have bought a non-income-producing bond with an unknown future value and an indeterminate payout date.

The amount of the claim for unsecured debt is the face value of the security (or accreted principal amount for debt with an original issue discount) plus accrued and unpaid interest to the date of bankruptcy. Claims for unmatured interest are disallowed, and interest stops accruing on the date of filing. Thus, two issues of equal ranking may have different claims depending on the amount of accrued interest and accreted original issue discount.

The courts may allow a well-secured or over-secured claim (where the value of the collateral exceeds the amount of the debt) to accrue interest after bankruptcy is filed. This is supposed to give adequate protection for the interest of the secured creditor. Thus the claims of mortgage bonds that are well secured continue to increase until a settlement is reached. The first mortgage bonds and the general and refunding mortgage bonds of Public Service Company of New Hampshire had the interest payments reinstated within a few months of the bankruptcy. In some jurisdictions there is a question if under-secured creditors

---

[9] Hickman, "Corporate Bonds," p. 26.

can claim adequate protection. That is, does interest continues to accrue up to the value of the collateral even though the value is less than the full claim?[10] Where the collateral is worth less than the claim, the difference between the claim and the value of the collateral becomes a general unsecured claim against the bankrupt estate.

Let us look at the results of a few bankruptcies and what investors have received upon reorganization or liquidation.[11] We looked at four companies with both senior and subordinated debt outstanding to see how bondholders fared. Two dates were used for pricing: the end of the month before the bankruptcy filing and the end of the month after it. There were six senior debt and five subordinated debt issues for these companies. In some cases, the prices used were valuations or bid prices, not actual trades, and were those nearest the chosen dates. The senior debt had an average price of 49.73 the month before bankruptcy and a price of 33.92 the month after, a decline of about 32%. The five subordinated issues declined, on average, from 31.9 before bankruptcy to 14.2 a month later, representing a 52.5% drop in price. Cases where the debt rises in price when a company files for reorganization are rare, but it happens at times. This might occur when the issue's price has been pounded down to below what it may truly be worth by sellers who fear holding the bonds if a bankruptcy occurs. Braniff International 9⅛s of 1997 is an example in which the price was higher a month after bankruptcy.

Exhibit 9 summarizes the annualized returns of these securities from the date of theoretical purchase (the post-petition price) to the date of emergence from bankruptcy or the liquidation of the company. In most cases, cash is only part of the total package distributed to debtholders with the remaining portion a combination of debt and equity securities. Senior creditors normally have a greater portion of their distributions in cash than do subordinated creditors. W. T. Grant Company was liquidated and the total distribution was in cash. Braniff International paid part of the claim of its subordinated debtholders in discount travel scrip.

---

[10] "Bankruptcy Ruling Could Set Precedent For Deciding Secured Creditors' Claims," *Investor's Daily* (September 3, 1986), p. 2.

[11] The following studies concerning distributions to bondholders of bankrupt companies may be of interest to our readers. These are:

- Edward I. Altman, Allan C. Eberhart, Gail I. Hessol and Kenneth Zekavat. "Do Priority Provisions Protect a Bondholder's Investment?", A paper presented at The New York University Salomon Center's Conference on *The Dynamics of the Insurance Industry*, May 20-21, 1993. See also the similar Altman and Eberhart, "Do Seniority Provisions Protect Bondholders' Investments?", Working Paper Series S-94-12, New York University Salomon Center, Leonard M. Stern School of Business.

- Frank J. Fabozzi, Jane Tripp Howe, Takashi Makabe, and Toshihide Sudo, "Recent Evidence on the Distribution Patterns in Chapter 11 Reorganization," *The Journal of Fixed Income*, March 1993.

Exhibit 9: Summary of Distributions upon Settlement of Bankruptcy

BRANIFF INTERNATIONAL CORP.

Bankruptcy petition filed: May 13, 1982
Reorganization confirmed: December 15, 1983
Distribution: February 16, 1984

Issue	Pre-petition Price 4/30/82	Yield to Maturity	Annual Rate of Return to Distribution	Post-petition Price 6/30/82	Annual Rate of Return to Distribution	Distribution Value per $1,000	% Paid in Cash
10% Notes due 7/1/86	$438.75	37.22%	33.76%	$382.50	55.94%	$807.62	22.16
9⅛% Debs due 1/1/97	$355.00	26.31%	47.99%	$382.50	54.59%	$795.58	20.78
5% Sub Debs due 12/1/86	$290.00	40.27%	-53.38%	$50.00	24.64%	$72.04	No cash

DAYLIN, INC.

Bankruptcy petition filed: February 26, 1975
Reorganization confirmed: October 20, 1976
Distribution: October 20, 1976

Issue	Pre-petition Price 1/31/75	Yield to Maturity	Annual Rate of Return to Distribution	Post-petition Price 3/31/75	Annual Rate of Return to Distribution	Distribution Value per $1,000	% Paid in Cash
8.35% Debs due 4/15/97	$700.00	12.32%	-18.44%	$500.00	2.11%	$516.56	31.53
5% Sub Debs due 3/21/89	$220.00	25.77%	-59.67%	$195.00	-57.90%	$55.52	No cash

W. T. GRANT COMPANY

Bankruptcy petition filed: October 2, 1975
Liquidation order issued: February 12, 1976
Adjudicated a bankrupt: April 13, 1976
Distribution date for debentures: January 1, 1980, estimated due to several extensions of settlement offer.
Distribution date for sub debentures: April 29, 1983, after being extended several times.

Issue	Pre-petition Price 8/31/75	Yield to Maturity	Annual Rate of Return to Distribution	Post-petition Price 10/31/75	Annual Rate of Return to Distribution	Distribution Value per $1,000	% Paid in Cash
4¾% Debs due 1/1/87	$360.00	18.35%	25.72%	$150.00	55.76%	$967.90	100.00
4¾% Sub Debs due 4/15/96	$245.00	20.52%	-3.29%	$55.00	17.24%	$190.00	100.00

Exhibit 9: Summary of Distributions
upon Settlement of Bankruptcy (Continued)

WICKES COMPANIES, INC.
Bankruptcy petition filed: April 24, 1982
Reorganization confirmed: January 26, 1985
Distribution: December 20, 1984 (cash); January 28, 1985 (securities)

Issue	Pre-petition Price 3/31/82	Yield to Maturity	Annual Rate of Return to Distribution	Post-petition Price 5/31/82	Annual Rate of Return to Distribution	Distribution Value per $1,000	% Paid in Cash
8¼% Notes due 7/1/84	$650.00	31.08%	10.02%	$350.00	41.04%	$886.51	16.70
8⅞% Debs due 8/1/97	$480.00	19.74%	22.12%	$270.00	55.02%	$886.51	16.70
5⅛% CvSD Debs due 5/1/94	$300.00	21.68%	21.86%	$200.00	47.26%	$570.15	8.77
9% Cv Sub Deb due 5/1/99	$440.00	31.32%	5.98%	$210.00	44.66%	$570.15	8.77

Note: For further details on debtholder distributions for the above issues see
Richard S. Wilson, *Corporate Senior Securities,* (Chicago, IL: Probus
Publishing Company, 1987), Chapter 11.

The data show that greater returns go to those who bought after, rather than before the company filed for bankruptcy. The returns for pre-bankruptcy investment include accrued interest paid at the purchase date, except in those cases where there was an interest payment between the purchase and bankruptcy dates. Most of the prices of these securities reflected the companies' rather weak financial health just before bankruptcy. They were in the "twilight zone" of pricing, not high enough to create confidence that the issuers could survive but not low enough to reflect their possible rebirth. The high yields to maturity (an indication of expected return) pointed to the risks involved, yet many assumed those risks just at the wrong time. Also, most investors who purchased the senior debt after bankruptcy received greater returns than the subordinated debt buyers, as they had a greater portion of their claim against the bankrupt satisfied.

SUMMARY

Investment in speculative-grade debt can provide a portfolio with incremental returns over those available from higher-grade issues despite the increased risk of default. Careful analysis is imperative. Remember, bonds in general are securities with limited upside potential. Bond selection and investment is a negative art. Diversification among issuers is very important to reduce the negative impact of default on the portfolio. Again, as quality declines, the risk of default naturally increases, and bond prices become more subject to equity related events than to interest rate developments. Of course, investors should be most concerned with the company's survival and ability to meet its debt obligations on a timely basis. The mutual fund approach is strongly recommended for most individual and small institutional investors. Here one gets ample diversification and professional management — two features critical for success in the high-yield world of bonds.

CHAPTER 8

Corporate Debt Ratings

A bond rating indicates the default risk associated with a debt security. It is an assessment of the issuer's ability to meet the principal and interest payments in accordance with the terms of the debt contract or indenture. This chapter reviews the major debt rating agencies in the United States, the rating process, and the way ratings are used.

THE RATING AGENCIES

There is no official definition of a rating agency. The Securities and Exchange Commission (SEC) calls credit rating agencies "nationally recognized statistical rating organizations" (NRSROs.) These are companies whose securities ratings are used by market participants and regulators under various rules, regulations and procedures. To receive the coveted NRSRO designation, a firm must send a written request to the SEC. The Commission will investigate the applicant's organizational structure and the credentials of the management and the rating personnel. It will study the rating process and the procedures for after-rating surveillance. Although six firms have received NRSRO status, no formal guidelines have been issued as of the end of 1993. However, over the last couple of years, the SEC has indicated a desire to study the debt rating agency industry with a view towards increase regulation.[1]

---

[1] Vicky Stamas, "Rating Agencies Need Regulation and Standards, SEC Official Says," *The Bond Buyer* (April 14, 1992). See also "SEC may Enact Specific Standards for Credit Rating Agencies," *Bloomberg Business Newswire* (February 23, 1992).

One SEC commissioner wants a rating agency to meet several criteria. A rating agency should be nationally recognized by the users of ratings as issuing reliable and timely ratings. The rating process and methodology should be thorough and credible. Also, the rating staff and management should be free from any conflicts of interest, biases and external pressures. These are worthy goals but some observers believe that the free market should be the sole regulator. After all, if ratings are not accurate and timely, if the agency appears to be under outside influence, or if there are conflicts of interest or other factors affecting the credibility of an agency's ratings, then the market through investors and other intermediaries will stop using those particular rating agencies.

Rating agencies are registered investment advisers with the SEC under the Investment Adviser Act of 1940. Additional registration with the SEC may be satisfactory to some, but additional interference in the rating process through detailed regulation by the federal government is burdensome, costly, inefficient and counterproductive. As Brenton W. Harries, former vice president in charge of Standard & Poor's bond rating department in the late 1960s, said so succinctly: "We are regulated every day by the professionals who put their money where their mouth is when they invest in bonds that we rate, and if they think we're wrong, our business will die and suffer. If they think we're right and they put substance in us, that is the type of oversight and regulation which I think is best."[2]

There are four full-service nationally recognized statistical rating organizations in the United States: Duff & Phelps Credit Rating Co., Fitch Investors Service, L.P., Moody's Investors Service, Inc., and Standard & Poor's Corporation. There are also two limited service agencies specializing in banks and financial institutions, IBCA Inc. and Thompson BankWatch, Inc. [3] The full service firms offer default or credit risk ratings for the full range of senior securities including commercial paper, certificates of deposit and other short-term instruments, asset-backed and other structured transactions including collateralized mortgage obligations, and long-term debt issued by corporations and other business entities, governments and their subdivisions and agencies in the United States and around the world. Other services provided by the rating agencies include claims-paying ability ratings assessing insurance companies and their financial strength to pay policy and contractual claims, and servicer ratings assessing the capabilities of mortgage servicing companies. The agencies also provide fund credit ratings identifying the degree of credit risk in a mutual fund's investment portfolio, and fund stability ratings quantifying the potential volatility of the total return of fixed-income mutual

---

[2] "Profits, Racism, Quality of Life, and Other Issues Facing Rating Agencies." *The Bond Buyer* (February 28, 1993).

[3] There are also rating agencies in other countries including Argentina, Australia, Canada, Chile, France, Great Britain, Israel, Japan, Korea, Mexico and Sweden, among others. For a description of some of these see *Financial Times Credit Ratings International 1993 Directory,* Financial Times Newsletters, London, England. See also Richard D. Cacchione, "Rating Agencies in Developing Capital Markets," Fitch Investors Service, Inc. (July 1986).

funds. In addition, the agencies will provide credit opinions or credit assessments for firms needing ratings for transactions other than the raising of new money.[4] Brief descriptions of the rating agencies follow.

Duff and Phelps Credit Rating Co.

Duff and Phelps Credit Rating Co. (D&P) became a publicly-traded, New York Stock Exchange-listed company in late 1994 when its shares were distributed to the stockholders of its parent, the Chicago-based money manger, Duff & Phelps Corporation. The parent's origins go back to 1932 when it provided research on public utility companies. Since that time it has expanded into other areas including financial consulting, investment research and institutional investment management. In 1980, Duff entered the debt rating business as an outgrowth of its fixed income research activities. Achieving NRSRO status in 1982, it was the fourth of the full-service agencies to be so designated. In 1991, the fixed income rating and research services of New York City based McCarthy, Crisanti & Maffei, Inc., another NRSRO, were merged with those of D&P. Offices are located at 55 East Monroe Street, Chicago, Illinois 60603 (telephone: 312/368-3139) and at 17 State Street Plaza, New York, New York 10004 (telephone: 212/908-0200).

Fitch Investors Service, L.P.

Organized in 1913 as the Fitch Publishing Company by Francis Emory Fitch, it first issued *The Fitch Bond Book* in 1913. Known as the FBB, it was a compendium of detailed information about all currently outstanding bond issues at that time. Over the years, Fitch expanded its activities, first rating corporate debt in 1922 and publishing the ratings in the 1923 edition of The Fitch Bond Book. During the 1930s, Fitch worked with federal government regulatory officials on guidelines for investment by commercial banks in corporate securities. In 1960, the company sold most of its publications, rights to its rating symbols, and printing plant to Standard & Poor's Corporation, thus allowing it to concentrate on debt rating services. In 1989, the privately-held company was acquired by a new investor/management group which has greatly expanded it service and activities. The rating activities were reorganized into a limited partnership in January 1995. With regional business development offices in Dallas,

---

[4] Standard & Poor's has formalized its credit opinions into the Credit Assessment Service which is described more fully in *Standard & Poor's Credit Week* (February 22, 1993). These credit opinions represent implied or theoretical ratings for the company's senior unsecured debt. Companies may use these opinions in dealings with banks and other creditors, landlords, lessors and others needing to have an independent analysis of the firm's financial strength. In some cases, credit opinions may be issued to provide a company with the approximate rating that might be applied to a particular debt issue if it or its investment bankers were to pursue a formal rating. With a formal credit opinion or credit assessment, the agency undertakes a full rating analysis including due diligence meetings with management. An informal credit opinion will usually comment on the issuer based on financial reports and other material supplied by the issuer or its agents; due diligence is not necessarily complete and the usual plus or minus signs are not appended to the rating.

Tampa, San Francisco, and Chicago, the headquarters is located at One State Street Plaza, New York, New York 10004 (telephone: 212/908-0500 or 800/75-FITCH).

IBCA Inc.

IBCA Inc. is the U.S. rating subsidiary of IBCA Ltd., a part of the IBCA/Notation Groupe, the largest independent European rating agency. IBCA Inc. specializes in the ratings of financial institutions. The National Association of Insurance Commissioners recognizes IBCA's ratings of U.S. banks, insurance companies and other financial firms as well as those of non-U.S. issuers. The U.S. office is at Suite 1609, 420 Lexington Avenue, New York, New York 10017 (telephone: 212/687-1507).

Moody's Investors Service, Inc.

In 1900, John Moody founded John Moody & Co. and published *Moody's Manual of Industrial and Corporation Securities*. The second edition, which appeared in 1901, included railroad and public utility securities. The company expanded into the printing business in 1904, one about which Moody admittedly knew "practically nothing."[5] The firm became extended and went deeply into debt, getting caught up in the crash of 1907. Moody lost control of the company in 1907 and a Roy W. Porter became editor. Porter bought control in 1914, and in 1919 merged it with Poor's Railroad Manual Company forming Poor's Publishing Company.

In the meantime, John Moody made a fresh start through the formation of the New York City based Analyses Publishing Co. in 1908. The next year, 1909, saw the first edition of *Analyses of Railroad Investments,* introducing the system we now know and use for rating fixed income securities. The ratings, adopted from the mercantile and credit rating system in use since the 1800s by credit reporting firms, ran on a scale of Aaa (highest class) to E (very weak or defaulted). This was followed in 1910 by *Moody's Analyses of Investments* covering public utility and industrial companies. On July 1, 1914, Moody's Investors Service was incorporated, bringing together under one umbrella John Moody's financial publishing and investment service activities. In 1918, Moody's issued its manual of foreign and American government securities. In 1924, Moody's acquired the right from Poor's Publishing Company to the full use of the Moody name.[6] The company prospered during the roaring twenties and endured the troublesome thirties. Finally, in 1962, Moody's was acquired by The Dun and Bradstreet Corporation. Moody's headquarters is at 99 Church Street, New York, New York 10007 (telephone: 212/553-0500).

---

[5] For an interesting history of the early years of Moody's, see "Fifty Year Review of Moody's Investors Service," a speech given by John Moody, Chairman, in early 1950. There are excerpts from the speech in Livingston Douglas (editor), *Fixed Income Masterpieces, Insights from America's Great Investors* (Homewood, Illinois: Business One Irwin, 1993).

[6] Poor's acquired the right to the Moody name when it and the old John Moody & Company combined in 1919. However, the name could only be used in a limited way, namely, as a partial label on the title page in Poor's manuals. The manuals were titled *Moody's Manual of Railroad and Corporation Securities*. For instance, the 1914 edition was published by Moody Manual Company and the 1923 edition by Poor's Publishing Company.

Standard & Poor's Corporation

Standard & Poor's Corporation, known throughout the investment world as *S&P*, was formed through the 1941 merger of Poor's Publishing Company and Standard Statistics Company. S&P traces its history back to 1860 when Henry V. Poor published his *History of Railroads and Canals in the United States*. In 1867, the H.V. and H.W. Poor Company (later Poor's Railroad Manual Company) was founded and over the next fifty or so years expanded into industrial (1910) and public utility (1913) manual publishing and related financial advisory activities. In 1916, the firm began to rate stocks and bonds.[7] In 1919, Poor's Railroad Manual Company merged with John Moody & Company (see above).

The other part of S&P, the Standard part, can be traced to 1906 when Luther Lee Blake founded the Standard Statistics Bureau. In 1907, Blake hired John Moody to be the editorial supervisor of the Standard Bond Descriptions service providing daily updates on companies in Moody's Manual. Obviously, the relationship did not last with Moody going his merry way in 1908. However, Blake acquired the stock and bond card system of Roger Babson in 1913, and incorporated Standard Statistics Company in 1914. Standard Statistics began rating corporate securities in 1922.[8]

Poor's Publishing ran into trouble during the depression caused by expansion into the printing business with its consuming appetite for considerable sums of fixed capital investment. Paul Babson (Roger's cousin) gained control and removed Poor's from bankruptcy. In 1940, it sold its manual subscription list to Moody's Investors Service. However, still having a difficult time, it merged with Standard Statistics in 1941. Standard & Poor's Corporation was purchased in 1966 by McGraw-Hill, Inc. S&P makes its home at 25 Broadway, New York, New York 10004 (telephone: 212/208-8000).[9]

Thomson BankWatch, Inc.

The other limited service recognized rating agency is Thomson BankWatch, Inc., a member of the Thomson Financial Services group of companies owned by the Canadian-based Thomson Corporation. It provides ratings, research and consulting services on banks, insurance companies, securities firms, and other financial institutions. It maintains offices at 61 Broadway, New York, New York 10006 (telephone: 212/510-0300 or 800/852-1325).

As can be gathered from the brief history of the bond rating industry, the relationship amongst the major rating firms may be considered by some as somewhat incestuous, especially in view of S&P's ownership of the original John

---

[7] Gilbert Harold, *Bond Ratings as an Investment Guide*, (The Ronald Press Company: New York, 1938).

[8] There is some question whether Standard Statistics entered the corporate rating business in 1922 or 1923. Standard & Poor's says it was 1923 (see S&P *CreditWeek*, November 23, 1992, p. 39) but Harold (op. cit.) says it was 1922.

[9] For additional background information on Standard & Poor's Corporation, see "120 Years of Preserving the 'Right to Know,'" published circa 1984 by S&P.

Moody & Company and its 1960 purchase of Fitch's publications and ratings (see Exhibit 1). All four of the majors (along with Thomson BankWatch) have offices practically within sight of one another in lower Manhattan. Also, as with other specialized businesses, many analysts and other professionals have worked at more than one of the agencies during their careers.

WHAT ARE DEBT RATINGS?

A *bond rating* is an indicator of the potential default or credit risk associated with a particular debt security. It represents in a simplistic way the rater's assessment of an issuer's ability to meet the payment of principal and interest in accordance with the terms of the debt contract. Commercial paper ratings address the prompt payment of principal and interest on short-term obligations with original maturities generally not in excess of one year. The main emphasis in commercial paper ratings is the liquidity of the borrower enabling it to meet its obligations punctually. This liquidity factor takes into account cash and near cash items available internally as well as ready access to external sources of funds.

As there are only a handful of rating categories for a multitude of debt issues, securities having the same rating are of similar but not necessarily identical investment quality. The rating categories cannot fully reflect small nuances in the degree of risk between individual issues. Moreover, the character of risk varies from industry to industry and between corporate and other type of obligations. Ratings are not recommendations to buy or sell any security. While used by market participants to assist in the valuation of securities, they do not address the adequacy of the market price or the appropriateness of the security for any particular investor.

Debt Rating Symbols

Debt rating symbols or characters (see Exhibit 2 and Exhibit 3) are uncomplicated representations of more complex ideas. In effect, they are summary opinions. Fortunately for market participants, the major agencies use similar representations. In bond ratings the only difference is Moody's use of upper and lower case letters for some ratings (Aaa for Moody's compared with AAA for the others). But this similarity hasn't always been so.

Exhibit 4 shows the corporate bond rating scale used by Poor's Publishing Company in 1936. It ranges from the highest quality rating of A★★★★★applicable to United States Government obligations to as low as 'H'. However, corporate ratings generally were between A★★★ and D. Even after Poor's merger with Standard Statistics the S&P ratings were quite dissimilar from Moody's and Fitch. It was in late 1960 that S&P no longer was the odd man out as it bought the rights to the rating symbols of Fitch Investors Service, Inc. This standardized the industry's rating symbols and made life easier for bond market players. Exhibit 5 shows the old and new Standard & Poor's rating designations.

Exhibit 1: The Interrelationship of Moody's and Standard & Poor's

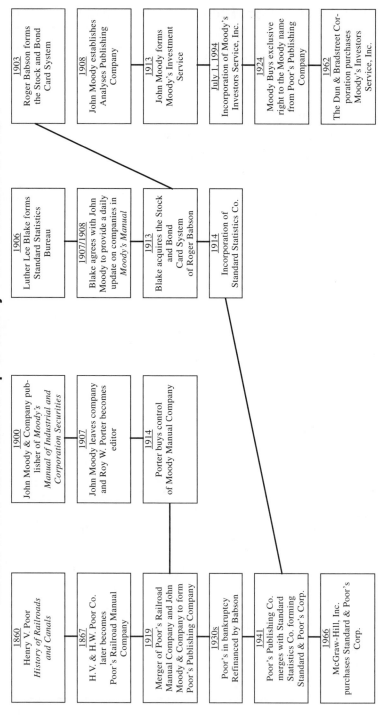

Exhibit 2: Scale of Debt Rating Symbols and Definitions

D&P	Fitch	Moody's	S&P	Summary Description
Investment Grade — High- Creditworthiness				
AAA	AAA	Aaa	AAA	Gilt edge, prime, maximum safety
AA+	AA+	Aa1	AA+	
AA	AA	Aa2	AA	High-grade, high-credit quality
AA-	AA-	Aa3	AA-	
A+	A+	A1	A+	
A	A	A2	A	Upper-medium grade
A-	A-	A3	A-	
BBB+	BBB+	Baa1	BBB+	
BBB	BBB	Baa2	BBB	Lower-medium grade
BBB-	BBB-	Baa3	BBB-	
Speculative — Lower Creditworthiness				
BB+	BB+	Ba1	BB+	
BB	BB	Ba2	BB	Low grade, speculative
BB-	BB-	Ba3	BB-	
B+	B+	B1		
B	B	B2	B	Highly speculative
B-	B-	B3		
Predominantly Speculative, Substantial Risk or in Default				
	CCC+		CCC+	
CCC	CCC	Caa	CCC	Substantial risk, in poor standing
	CC	Ca	CC	May be in default, very speculative
	C	C	C	Extremely speculative
			CI	Income bonds — no interest being paid
	DDD			
DD	DD			Default
	D		D	

Exhibit 3: Scale of Commercial Paper Rating Symbols and Definition

D&P	Fitch	Moody's	S&P	Summary Description
Duff 1+	F-1+		A-1+	Exceptionally strong credit quality
Duff 1	F-1	Prime-1	A-1	Very strong credit quality
Duff 1-				Strong credit quality
Duff 2	F-2	Prime-2	A-2	Good credit quality
Duff 3	F-3	Prime-3	A-3	Satisfactory credit quality
Duff 4	F-S		B	Speculative, non-investment grade
			C	Doubtful capacity for payment
Duff 5	D		D	Issues in default
		Not prime		Issues not falling within one of the prime rating categories

Exhibit 4: Poor's Corporation Ratings

A★★★★★★	Assigned to United States Government obligations exclusively.
A★★★★	Assigned to a few issues which, owing to peculiar conditions or exceptional developments, are more favorably situated than the average high class investment issue.
A★★★, A★★, A★	Investment bonds regarded as safe as to both principal and interest.
A	Investment bonds believed to be reasonably safe but not wholly free from possible adverse effects of changes in earnings.
B★★	Obligations which possess good security as to principal and a good margin of safety over interest charges over a period of years, but which need constant surveillance on the part of owners. These issues are often known as "business men's investments."
B★	Obligations wherein the speculative element has not begun to predominate. Principal is fairly secure but margin of safety over interest is usually small. Such issues are often known as of the "better-grade speculative" class.
B	Obligations wherein the speculative element begins to pre dominate. Principal and interest cannot be regarded as entirely safe. Such issues are only appropriate for persons who are attracted by chance of appreciation in market value.
C★★, C★	Obligations which contain little real equity in proportion to the element of risk involved. May also include some bonds in temporary default of interest.
C	Indicates serious default of principal or interest or similar unfavorable condition.
D★★, D★, D	Obligations wherein extremely little or no equity is visible. Such small equity, if it exists, will be indicated by the ★.
E, F, G, H	Not ratings in the strict sense of the word. These symbols indi cate theoretical priority of some securities over other securities of the same company, the highest of which is only entitled to the lowest rating assignable.

Source: *Poor's Corporation Ratings*, Poor's Publishing Company: New York, April Edition, 1936.

Exhibit 5: Old and New Standard & Poor's Rating Symbols

Old Symbol	New Symbol	Designation
A1+	AAA	Highest Grade
A1	AA	High Grade
A	A	Upper Medium Grade
B1+	BBB	Medium Grade
B1	BB	Lower Medium Grade
B	B	Speculative
C1+ - C1	CCC - CC	Outright Speculations
C	C	No interest
	DD - D	Best defaulted issues
D1 - D		In default

Source: *The Daily Bond Buyer*, November 21, 1960

Investors are accustomed to these simple alphanumeric symbols, often forgetting the more precise definition behind each one. They are subject to misuse and misinterpretation by many. While the symbols are essentially the same and the definitions somewhat similar, there are some differences. The appendix to this chapter presents the rating definitions of the four major agencies for long-term debt and short-term debt, respectively. In the A rating category, Duff & Phelps states that these issues have average but adequate protection factors. Fitch considers such issues as being of high-credit quality, while Moody's says such bonds possess many favorable investment attributes. S&P considers A-rated debt as having "... a strong capacity to pay interest and repay principal...." However, all four of the agencies consider A-rated bonds to be vulnerable to adverse changes in economic conditions.

There is a greater chance of confusion in the highly speculative grade category (Caa/CCC to C). For example, Duff & Phelps only uses the CCC designation for bonds with substantial risk characteristics while the other agencies have three rating designations in this category. Moody's does not have a D rating for defaulted issues. Instead, its Ca and C designations are applied to bonds in default of interest and principal payments while both Fitch and Standard & Poor's regards these issues only on the verge of default.

New to the symbolisms of the rating business are Standard and Poor's private placement ratings, introduced at the end of 1992. Similar to the designations used by the Securities Valuation Office of the National Association of Insurance Commissioners, they range from PPR1 to PPR6 with plus and minus modifications (see Exhibit 6).

The rating analysis is the same as for traditional ratings, but increased emphasis is placed on covenants and collateral in order to evaluate the risk of the ultimate loss of principal. Traditional S&P ratings are concerned with risk of default and timeliness of the of interest and principal payments. PPR ratings were designed with insurance companies and other active investors in the private placement market in mind. The choice whether or not to get a PPR rating or a traditional rating is left to the issuer.

Exhibit 6: Standard & Poor's Private Placement Ratings

PPR 1 and PPR 2	Private placements rated PPR 1 and PPR 2 are of high quality, exhibiting characteristics indicative of low ultimate loss. A PPR 1 rating indicates the highest quality with the lowest expected loss.
PPR 3	Private placements rated PPR 3 are of medium quality. The exhibit characteristics indicating moderate expected loss.
PPR 4 and PPR 5	Private placements rated PPR 4 and PPR 5 are of low quality, exhibiting characteristics indicating greater expected loss. A PPR 5 rating indicates more significant expected loss.
PPR 6	Private placements rated PPR 6 are of very low quality. A rating of PPR 6 indicates substantial expected loss.
Plus (+) or Minus (-)	PPR ratings may be modified by the addition of a plus or minus sign to show relative standing within the major categories.

Source: *Standard & Poor's CreditWeek*, December 7, 1992.

When the new rating scheme was first announced, some market participants were skeptical about the benefits to be derived from it. Some said that there was no need for the new ratings and others thought it would be confusing. By the beginning of 1994, there were still some doubters in the market but S&P managed to win a number over to their way of thinking. In June 1993, South Jersey Gas Company applied to Fitch, Moody's and Standard & Poor's for a rating on $35 million first mortgage bonds due 2013, a private placement under Rule 144a. Fitch rated the bonds BBB, Moody's gave them a Baa1, and S&P assigned a BBB+ to the issue, all lower medium grade ratings. At the same time, S&P also gave them a PPR-1 private placement rating, the highest quality. This was the first time that both types of ratings were applied to a debt issue. As one financial writer put it, "With two widely different ratings on the same issue, S&P is, in effect, giving new meaning to the term split rating." [10]

One should periodically review rating definitions in order to reinforce exactly what the symbols mean. But it is even more important to read the opinions of the rating agencies when they assign or review the rating in question. These opinions or credit assessments enable investors to more appropriately appraise the risk associated with a particular investment and come to a more accurate valuation. But as Moody's says, "...ratings are opinions, not recommendations to buy or sell, and their accuracy is not guaranteed. A rating should be weighed solely as one factor in an investment decision and you should make your own study and evaluation of any issuer whose securities or debt obligations you consider buying or selling." [11]

---

[10] Fred R. Bleakley, "S&P Rates Investors' Chances of Recovery If Bond Issues Fail." *The Wall Street Journal,* June 25, 1993.

[11] "Key to Moody's Corporate Ratings." *Moody's Bond Record*, October 1993, p.4.

THE RATING PROCESS

The *rating process* involves the analysis of a multitude of quantitative and qualitative factors over the past, present and future. The past and present are introductions to what the future may hold. Ratings should be prospective for it is future operations that should provide the wherewithal to repay the debt. The ratings apply to the particular issue, not the issuer. While bond analysts rely on numbers and calculate many ratios to get a picture of the company's debt servicing capacity, a rating is only an opinion or judgment of an issuer's ability to meet all of its obligations when due, whether during prosperity or during times of stress. The purpose of ratings is to rank issues in terms of the probability of default taking into account the special features of the issue, the relationship to other obligations of the issuer, and current and prospective financial condition and operating performance.

The Four C's

The rating of a security is assigned after a thorough analysis of the issuer's and, if applicable, the guarantor's, operations and need for funds. This isn't done in isolation but in conjunction with a review of the issuer's place within the industry and an overall analysis of where the industry fits within the national and, with increasing frequency, the global economies. In conducting this credit examination the analyst considers the four C's of credit — Character, Capacity, Collateral, and Covenants.

It is to the issuer's advantage to supply as much information to the rating agency so that it can come to a sound decision. The goal is for the analysts to thoroughly understand the nature of the business, its strong and weak points, so that the proper rating is assigned. Among the information usually required from a corporate issuer is a copy of the offering memorandum or registration statement; at least five years of audited financial statements, annual reports, and Forms 10-K along with other pertinent filings with the Securities and Exchange Commission and similar regulatory bodies. Of course, two or three years of quarterly or semi-annual statements should also be furnished if the issuer normally publishes these reports. Also, the proposed terms and indenture or note covenants should be supplied as well as any bank note agreements and indentures for debt that is expected to remain outstanding after the proposed transaction is consummated.

Other desirable information includes product descriptions and brochures, a summary of its business history, shareholder communications and press releases, and data and reports about the industries in which the company operates. A commercial paper issuer should also supply a summary of short-term borrowings over the past several years showing month end and peak outstandings. In addition, details of the bank back-up credit facilities and copies of these documents should be provided.

Projections are also of great importance to the forward-looking agency. Normally, three to five years is satisfactory, although in the case of cash-flow driven companies, such as those in the cable television industry, projections to the maturity of the subject debt are usually required. Management may be reluctant to give projections to outsiders, but it is this type of information that enables the rating agency to perform a thorough analysis. This confidential information remains in the hands of the rating agency for its own exclusive ratings use. According to an opinion from the Federal District Court in New York, rating agencies are covered by the same First Amendment constitutional protection as journalists and are not required to disclose notes and records of information obtained with meetings with companies.[12]

Finally, a due diligence meeting with senior management is a must. This may be at the rating agency's office, although on-site visits are preferable because analysts will get to meet more top level and operating personnel. A plant or other site visit is often an important aid to a better understanding of the company, its weaknesses and strengths. Analysts want to know about management's operating philosophy, long-term goals and short-term objectives, and acquisition and expansion policies. Of special importance is management's view of the capital structure and the desirable level of debt and equity.

The first of the C's stands for character of management, the foundation of sound credit. This includes the ethical reputation as well as the business qualifications and operating record of the board of directors, management and executives responsible for the use of the borrowed funds and the repayment thereof.[13] Character may sound old-fashioned and ob solete in these modern times but investors ignore it at their risk. If one cannot get a good sounding about the character of a debtor then the risk of debt repayment has to be increased resulting in a reduced rating.

The next C is capacity or the ability of an issuer to repay its obligations. The financial statements, past, present, and future, are studied for they are, to some extent, management's report card. Spreadsheets are made, ratios calculated, and footnotes to the financial statements studied. The ratios and projections are not the end of the rating process but the starting point for the analysis. From these figures a good analyst will delve behind the numbers, asking why, and how, and what do they mean. Projections must be carefully scrutinized, since few of us have good foresight. Analysts often will make their own projections, generally under a lower and worst case basis. What is important, however, are the assumptions behind the projections. Are they realistic or are they blue sky from some manager's daydream? Again, what is discovered through sound analysis leads to insightful questioning of management.

---

[12] See Wade Lambert, "S&P Is Backed In Court Ruling On Disclosing Data," *The Wall Street Journal*, December 9, 1993, and Michael Quint, "A Judge Upholds Confidentiality for S&P," *The New York Times*, December 9, 1993.

[13] In 1912 a subcommittee of the House Banking and Currency Committee investigated the "Money Trust." Known as the Pujo Inquiry after the name of its chairman, the committee's counsel was Samuel Untermeyer. The following is an exchange between Untermeyer (SU) and John Pierpont Morgan (JPM).

SU: Is not commercial credit based primarily upon money or property?
JPM: No, sir, the first thing is character.
SU: Before money or property?
JPM: Before money or anything else. Money cannot buy it... because a man I do not trust could not get money from me on all the bonds in Christendom.

The rating of cyclical companies can be quite perplexing, with agencies sometimes faulted for increasing ratings at the peak of a company's performance and lowering ratings at troughs. Rating agencies must take a longer-term but also a realistic view. Ratings are not based on the state of the economy at any particular point in time nor where the issuer is in its own business cycle, but rather on the fundamentals of the company and the issue. A corporation may have a poor year but this does not necessarily mean that a downgrading is imminent. If the raters feel, based on their experience and analysis, that the downturn is only temporary, that the poor results are due to special and nonrecurring factors, then the rating may remain unscathed. However, if the rating review reveals that the deterioration may be of a more permanent nature because debt servicing ability has been weakened to the extent that it is not expected to return to former favorable levels, then the rating can be lowered. It all boils down to an assessment of the degree of protection afforded the debtholder.

The third C, collateral, is looked at not only in the traditional sense of assets pledged to secure the debt, but also to the quality and value of those unpledged assets controlled by the issuer. In both senses the collateral is capable of supplying additional aid, comfort and support to the debt and the debtholder. Assets form the basis for the generation of cash flow which services the debt in good times as well as bad.

Additional security in the form of pledged assets may lead to a higher rating. For example, electric utility first mortgage bonds carry higher ratings than the unsecured debt of the same companies. At the end of 1993, Commonwealth Edison's first mortgage bonds were rated BBB/BBB/Baa2/BBB by Duff & Phelps, Fitch, Moody's, and Standard & Poor's, respectively. The company's debentures carried ratings of BBB-/BBB-/Baa3/BBB- a one rating notch difference from the mortgage bonds. Burlington Northern Railroad Company's consolidated mortgage bonds were rated A3 by Moody's and BBB+ by S&P. Due to the special considerations given to railroad equipment trust certificates under the bankruptcy code, the certificates carried ratings of Aa3 and A+, a full grade higher than the mortgage debt.

Security does not always result in a higher rating. While collateral can impact the ultimate recovery of principal, it has less bearing on timeliness of payment considerations. In the case of General American Transportation Company and other railroad car lessors, there is no special protection similar to that afforded to railroads under the bankruptcy laws. Thus, General American Transportation's debentures and equipment certificates have the same S&P ratings, namely A-. However, Moody's distinguishes between the two security types with the equipment certificates rated A3 and the debentures Baa1.

Another example where differences in security are not considered is New York Telephone Company. The company closed its refunding mortgage indenture a number of years ago. It pledged that as long as any previously issued mortgage bonds remain outstanding, it will not issue additional bonds under the mortgage; it can only issue unsecured debt. The outstanding mortgage bonds are secured by substantially all of the company's New York State property and certain investments. Fitch and Standard & Poor's rate the refunding mortgage bonds and the debentures the same, namely A+

for Fitch and A for S&P. Moody's, though, rates the mortgage debt A1 and the debentures A2, thus maintaining a one notch spread between secured and unsecured and recognizing the superior status of the bonds compared with the debentures in the event of bankruptcy.

The type of collateral and the status of the security under bankruptcy law are important rating elements. From a ratings viewpoint, the better quality assets are those that can maintain their value even though the business may falter. Receivables and other assets readily convertible into cash are preferred to highly specialized inventory. General purpose structures are looked at more favorably than specialty plants. Marketable securities are preferred to unmarketable ones. In the case of land, location is most important for that is a major determinant in its value. The analyst will get behind the book numbers trying to come up with real economic worth. In many cases, the book value of the assets may not truly reflect today's value. The value of assets may be understated since they might have been acquired many years ago at much lower prices. In other cases, they could be over valued having been purchased at the peak of the real estate market.

The final **C** is for covenants, the terms and conditions of the loan agreement. Covenants lay down restrictions on how management operates the company and conducts its financial affairs. Covenants can restrict management's discretion. A default or violation of any covenant may provide a meaningful early warning alarm enabling investors to take positive and corrective action before the situation deteriorates further. This is especially important in many debt private placements. It can mean that interest and principal payments may be satisfied in a timely manner instead of waiting until the issuer no longer has the ability to service its debt.

Nowadays, most public debt issues have little in the way of meaningful protective provisions. Some argue that covenants in publicly issued corporate bonds are not needed be cause the investor can sell the securities if the credit deteriorates while it is more difficult to do so with private issues of limited marketability. It is also true that it is more difficult to negotiate with widely dispersed public bondholders than with the fewer private holders. Without meaningful covenants, each public bond issue, all other things being equal, is fungible. There is one less thing to take into account when trading and swapping bonds.

All of the major rating agencies, to one degree or another, consider covenants in the rating process. For example, the introduction to Standard & Poor's Corporation's corporate debt rating definitions says that "... ratings are based, in varying degrees, on the... Nature and provisions of the obligation;..." The introduction to Duff & Phelps rating scale states that "the nature of covenant protection" is weighed in the rating process. It goes on, "Review of indenture restrictions is important to the analysis of a company's operating and financial constraints." Moody's also considers covenants when rating bonds.[14] The April 30, 1992 issue of *The Bond Buyer* comments on a Moody's rating assigned to an issue of revenue bonds saying, "The rating is based on bondholder protections included in the deal." These protections include "... covenants to maintain a specified leverage ratio and minimum fund balance, mandatory redemption if the [organization] voluntarily dissolves itself, and a pledge to limit the issuance of additional debt." And we have seen S&P's new private placement ratings with their increased emphasis on covenants.

Covenants providing security or higher ranking (such as senior debentures versus subordinated debentures) may result in a higher rating. Covenants are also used to put a fence or protective ring around a subsidiary borrower to protect it from being drained of cash and other assets to help support the parent company's debt service burden. For example, a meaningful restrictive payments provision limiting the upstreaming of cash through dividends and other disbursements may provide the necessary protection enabling an agency to rate the subsidiary entirely on its own merits. Of course, the parent should have sources other than the subject subsidiary for debt service needs since it must not be placed in a position of being unable to service its debt just because a subsidiary experiences difficulty.

Over the years rating agencies have been loathe to put investment grade ratings on smaller companies. Hickman says, "Market values generally reflect a preference for the power and financial strength of large corporations as distinguished from smaller ones of similar quality standards, and for the liquidity which is provided by larger issues of bonds. Default rates and loss rates were lower for larger issues than for smaller ones."[15] In the view of some rating agencies, a meaningful covenant package for the creditworthy but smaller company can offset the size issue to some degree, allowing a one notch higher rating than it would otherwise receive. This is important in the private placement market where insurance companies and other knowledgeable investors are the traditional lenders to middle market companies.

Covenants have value as they play an important part in minimizing risk to bond investors. They help prevent the unconscionable transfer of wealth from bondholders to shareholders. A study of public bonds involved in leveraged buyouts shows that bonds with strong covenant protection gained value, while those with no protection lost value.[16] A good covenant package cannot, however, turn a weak credit into a higher rated one.

Assigning the Rating

After the complete analysis of the bond issue is finished, the agency assigns a rating. Generally, the review is done by a committee consisting of the senior members of the department concerned with the issue. In most cases, the analyst responsible for the rat-

---

[14] The following articles provide additional insight into the views of the rating agencies regarding covenants. Richard S. Wilson and Thomas B. Harker, "Covenants Enhance Private Placements," Fitch Investors Service, Inc., October 28, 1991. M. Douglas Watson, Jr. and Harold H. Goldberg, "Indenture Protection for the 1990s," Moody's Investors Service, December 1991. Sanford B. Bragg and Kenneth C. Pfeil, "The Role of Covenants in Ratings," *Standard & Poor's CreditWeek*, Standard & Poor's Corporation, February 3, 1992.

[15] W. Braddock Hickman, *Corporate Bond Quality and Investor Experience*, (Princeton University Press, Princeton, New Jersey, 1958).

[16] Paul Asquith and Thierry A. Wizman, "Event risk, covenants, and bondholder returns in leveraged buyouts." *Journal of Financial Economics 27*, pp. 195-213.

ing presentation is a voting member of the committee. The analyst makes the presentation putting forth the strengths and weaknesses of the issuer and describing the particular transaction. The indenture terms are reviewed to see if they provide additional support to the credit. The analyst often undergoes detailed questioning by the other committee members searching for a thorough understanding of the deal. Finally, after the issue has been reviewed, the analyst makes a rating recommendation. It may not be the one he originally thought it would be when he entered the meeting since additional insight might have been obtained from the other committee members. In any case, a vote is taken and a rating is assigned. It isn't unusual for a vote to be delayed pending receipt of additional information demanded by other committee members.

Once the vote is taken, it is relayed to the issuer and, if applicable, the investment banker involved with the transaction. If the rating is accepted it is released to the public via a press release sent over the financial news wire services. The agency may also issue special reports and comments on the rating in their various publications. If the rating is for a private placement transaction, a rating letter is sent to the issuer and the investment banker giving the rating and the rationale for the decision. Ratings for private transactions are not usually published or publicly discussed without issuer approval.

If the rating decision is an unpleasant surprise to the requesting parties, they usually have a chance to make an appeal to the rating committee for a review of the decision. In such cases, additional new and important information must be brought forth which is of such a nature that it could lead to a higher rating. Appeals are not common if the analysts and the committees have done a proper job. Further, changes in the decision are even less common although they do occur. The rating agencies usually go out of their way to provide as fair of a hearing as possible to issuers and their representatives throughout the rating process so to keep appeals at a minimum.

The rating process requires that care must be taken by all parties to make sure that all pertinent information is brought up and analyzed. Every time a rating is assigned, the agency's name, integrity, and credibility are on the line and subject to inspection by the whole investment community. Ratings should not be assigned lightly.

The Cost

Prior to the 1970s, the agencies generally didn't charge for public ratings and fees for private placements were nominal. The income of the firms was derived from the sale of their various publications. However, the demand for rating services rose. New issue debt volume increased resulting in the need for outstanding ratings to be more frequently and seriously monitored. The agencies were accused of being asleep at the switch, failing to downgrade (or upgrade) issues in a timely fashion. Inflation was beginning to take its toll on the credit quality of America's corporations thus requiring more surveillance than previously.

Additional services to bond market participants could no longer be provided without charge. The agencies expanded their staffs and, and since it was necessary to compete with Wall Street for analytical talent, wages had to increase. It became necessary to charge for ratings to provide the wherewithal for the expanded services and products. At first, issuers and investment bankers did not take kindly to being charged for something they used to get free. But as time passed, they recognized the importance of good analysis in the rating process and went along with the fees.

No two financings are ever exactly alike, each having different problems and each requiring different expertise. Depending on the size and complexity of the issue being rated, rating charges may vary from as low as $1,000 to as much as $750,000. Other fees for legal services and special consultants as well as for travel expenses are often added to the basic rating fee. The charges for public issues covers the initial rating and surveillance for as long as the securities are outstanding, assuming that the company continues to provide adequate and timely information. Ratings can be withdrawn because of insufficient information or if the outstanding amount falls below a certain minimum. Whether a public or private issue, the issuer is the party usually paying the fees although there may occasions when the investment banker or another party pays.

An increasing number of issuers are establishing longer-term relationships with the rating agencies. These arrangements provide for the rating of a certain number or all of the issuer's senior securities, outstanding issues as well as new offerings, and continual monitoring for an annual relationship fee ranging from $10,000 to $1,500,000. Again, the fee schedule depends on the complexity and the size of the issues.

Ratings Without Request

Obviously, the above section on fees applies to ratings requested by the issuer or its agent. But there are situations when an agency will do a rating without a request from the issuer or investment banker. It is with these situations where there is the greatest ruckus, especially if the rating is lower than the other agencies' ratings and was done after the deal was priced and placed with investors. It may appear to some that a full-fledged analysis may not have been made since a proper rating ought to have the co-operation of the issuer and the provision of projections and other privileged information. A due diligence meeting with management is generally thought to be a necessary step in the rating process. Admittedly, there is often substantial information available on the largest public companies which may provide the analyst with much that is needed to reach a rating decision.

Unsolicited ratings are not taken lightly by the acting agencies as it is in their own best interests to make sure that all available information is reviewed and properly acted upon. However, bond market participants may still view with suspicion some of these ratings. At best, they may be only partially informed opinions since the full rating process may not have taken place despite the agency's best efforts. A rating agency may justify an unrequested rating by saying it is performing a service to investors. One agency official said: "Investor opinion is that something is better than nothing." An officer at a competing agency argues: "Ratings are about much more than financial statements. They're about what a company's strategy is, what its plans are, what its projections are." [17]

Rating agencies can use unsolicited ratings as a wedge to maintain market share. It sends a message to the issuer and the investment banker that it may be better do business with that particular agency or agencies even though investors and the issuer may find other ratings more than satisfactory. If the agencies really feel that they want to help the investor, then these unsolicited ratings should be differentiated from formal ratings. They ought to be called "credit opinions" or "assessments" so as to not confuse the investor community.

Rating Changes or Drift

Ratings have always been subject to changes (or drift, as some call it) since the economy is ever fluctuating. Only the naive believe that a corporate bond, once rated, will maintain that rating throughout its life. Corporations go through life cycles and are subject to many pressures, stresses and strains. There are depressions, recessions, recoveries, stagnation, competition, inflation and deflation, government regulation, changing climate, war and peace, greed and the other deadly sins, all influencing human action in great and small ways.

Graham and Dodd quote Horace's *Ars Poetica,* "Many shall be restored that now are fallen and many shall fall that are now in honor." [18] This most certainly applies to corporate bonds! Many of the high and mighty triple-A rated giants of the past have fallen from grace and are now of more lowly status. After all, AAA's can't go any higher: they can only decline. General Motors and International Business Machines are just two of the well-known and formerly revered fallen heroes from yesteryear.

Altman and Kao studied corporate bond rating drift using Standard & Poor's ratings for 1970 through 1979. [19] They found that the longer a bond is outstanding, the less likely it is to retain its original rating. For example, in the AAA category, 94.3 percent of the issues were so rated one year after issuance; 81 percent retained the AAA three years afterwards; 69.8 percent were still AAA after five years, and 52.1 percent hung in after ten years. For AA bonds, 92.6 percent were 'AA's after one year; 77.8 percent were unchanged after three years; 67.9 percent remained 'AA's five years out, and only 46.7 per cent maintained the AA rating ten years after issuance. In the A ranking, the one, three, five and ten-year percentages are 92.1 percent, 78.9 percent, 72.5 percent, and 61.5 per cent, respectively. Finally, the BBB rating drift figures are 90.1 percent one year after issuance; 73.4 percent three years out; 65.7 percent after five years, and 43.3 percent after ten years.

---

[17] Ann Monroe, "When Ratings are Unsolicited." *Global Finance,* May 1990, 74-75. See also Abby Schultz, "Divergent Ratings of Bonds Underscore How Guideposts Aren't Always Clear." *The Wall Street Journal,* November 9, 1993.

[18] Benjamin Graham, David L. Dodd and Charles Tatham, Jr., *Security Analysis, Principles and Technique.* (New York: McGraw-Hill Book Company, Inc., 1951). A variation of this from the third edition of *The Oxford Dictionary of Quotations* (New York: Oxford University Press, 1980) reads, "Many terms which have now dropped out of favor, will be revived, and those that are at present respectable will drop out, if usage so choose, with whom resides the decision and the judgment and the code of speech."

[19] Edward I. Altman and Duen Li. Kao, *"The Implications of Corporate Bond Rating Drift,"* New York University Salomon Center, Leonard N. Stern School of Business, Working Paper Series S-91-51, 1991.

Of course, with the exception of AAAs, ratings can go up or down. Looking at the issues ten years after issuance shows that 3.5 percent of those originally rated AA moved into the AAA class; 27.6 percent were now in the 'A' class; 19.2 percent were BBBs, and 2.9 percent noninvestment grade. For bonds originally rated A, ten years later 0.8% were AAA and 12.5 percent were AA, 20.2 percent were BBB and 5 percent noninvestment grade. None of the original BBB issues moved to the AAA rank. Only 2.8 percent made it to AA while 36.8 percent made it up a notch to the A grade. However, 17.1 percent could be found in the less-than-investment-grade category.

Standard & Poor's also published a rating transition study covering 1981 to 1991.[20] It had some similar findings saying that "...nearly 20% of issuers moved out of their original letter ratings each year." Further, the "study indicates that the average stability of higher ratings is greater than those lower ratings." These studies suggest that a buy-and-hold strategy for corporate bond portfolios may not be the best. Bond ratings change and so do their values. It is imperative for money managers to be alert to changes in their portfolios; complacency can be dangerous to one's financial health.

Exhibit 7 presents data on Moody's corporate rating changes for the years 1984 through 1993. In all but two years — 1984 and 1993 — downgrades exceeded upgrades. In that ten-year period there were 3,802 companies that had their bond ratings changed and only 34.9 percent or 1,326 were upgrades. The dollar volume of affected bonds was $3.41 trillion with downgrades posting a more than two-to-one lead over upgrades.

The main reason for rating downgrades is deterioration in the issuers' credit fundamentals with a concomitant increase in default risk. However, another cause often talked about is the increase in default risk due to what Moody's calls "decapitalizations" or "special events." These are "... those management actions which result in a leveraging of company financials following treasury stock purchases, leveraged buyouts, or acquisitions financed through borrowings." It does not include asset write-offs and operating losses. According to Moody's, in the 1984 to 1993 period there were about 444 special event downgrades covering some $290 billion of debt. This amounts to 17.9% of the total number of companies given lower ratings, or 12.8% of the total dollar volume of downgraded debt.

Rating downgrades due to special events peaked at 77 for $49.9 billion in 1989. Since then, the number of companies and the affected dollar volume has declined considerably. In 1993, special event downgrades numbered only about 29 companies with a total par value of $10.4 billion. The decline in this type of downgrade reflects a drop in debt financed takeovers, leveraged buyouts, mergers and acquisitions, a restoration of sounder thinking on the part of many corporate managements, and a less sanguine view of the role that debt plays in the corporate marketplace.

---

[20] Chao Y. Wang, "Corporate Default, Rating Transition Study Updated," *Standard & Poor's Credit Review*, Standard & Poor's Corporation, January 25, 1993.

Exhibit 7: Annual Corporate Rating Changes by Moody's Investors Service

	Number of Companies			Volume of Debt ($ Billions)		
Year	Up	Down	Total	Up	Down	Total
1993	163	154	317	$182.0	$160.0	$342.0
1992	136	227	363	$125.6	$377.0	$502.6
1991	119	350	469	131.8	372.7	504.5
1990	98	443	531	86.2	394.5	480.7
1989	138	339	477	86.0	207.9	293.9
1988	142	237	379	110.3	219.5	329.8
1987	102	189	291	96.9	156.1	253.0
1986	143	246	389	89.6	197.3	286.9
1985	124	153	277	127.8	107.5	236.2
1984	161	148	309	99.7	81.1	180.8

Source: *Moody's Bond Survey*, September 26, 1993, May 31, 1993, and January 18, 1988.

DO RATING CHANGES IMPACT BOND PRICES?

Since ratings address the default risk of a particular debt issue or issues, many in the investment world believe that changes in that debt risk assessment, i.e. rating changes, have a direct impact on the prices of the respective bonds. Academic studies have produced conflicting results concerning the impact on corporate bond prices. Some say rating upgrades and downgrades provide little or new information to market participants since the causes leading up to the changes have been discounted by the market prior to the action of the agencies. That is, bond investors and traders have factored into their transaction decisions the positive or negative information that has gradually passed into the investment information stream.

Professor L. Macdonald Wakeman of the University of Rochester writes, "A bond rating does not actively determine, but simply mirrors the market's assessment of a bond's risk. Hence, a rating change does not affect, but merely reflects, the market's altered estimation of a bond's value."[21] Market experience has shown that rating changes can have some price impact, but that is normally when the change is unexpected. It would usually not be due to the normal credit degeneration or improvement, but to the more abrupt notice of major information such as various events having a dramatic impact on an issuer's fortunes over a short period of time. These events have not been entered into the data banks of the bond market movers and shakers.

---

[21] L. Macdonald Wakeman, "The Real Function of Bond Rating Agencies," in Joel M. Stern and Donald H. Chew, Jr. (eds.), *The Revolution in Corporate Finance* (New York: Basil Blackwell Ltd., 1986), pp. 17-20.

Major investors and investment banking firms rely on their own analytical staffs to provide the traders, salesmen and portfolio managers with up-to-date opinions about the credit standing of the bonds in which they are interested. Bond analysts sit on the trading floors with the traders at many dealers so their thoughts can be obtained at a moment's notice. Obviously, they incorporate into their analyses information from a myriad of sources including that from the rating agencies, company reports, news services, and industry spokesmen. They monitor many of the liquid issues on a more or less consistent basis and review the less active ones when the traders are in a position to deal in the bonds. We know that there are a limited number of rating categories and only three levels or notches in most of them, but there are many more levels in the price structure allowing market participants to continually fine tune their analysts' opinions.

One study concludes that recent financial information is a more important consideration in bond evaluation than agency ratings, especially in cases where the rating hadn't been reviewed for a period of time. [22] The summary says, in part:

> Market participants base their evaluations of a bond issue's credit-worthiness on more than Moody's and Standard and Poor's rating. Specifically, it is clear that they consider recent financial statistics even on issues with new or recently revised ratings.
>
> The data suggest that market participants pay less attention to ratings and more to publicly available accounting information if the rating has not been reviewed in some time.

This latter point focuses in on a concern many have had with rating agencies. They have been under the gun for years because of the tardiness, real or perceived, in changing their ratings. Downgrades have come after a company performs poorly for a period and upgrades come after a period of good financial and operating performance. But investors fail to consider that ratings are not signals for the buy and sell orientation of short term portfolio managers and traders. Ratings properly reflect the longer term view. And while agencies must take the longer term into consideration, it should not be a backward look but a prospective one. However, rating changes should only be made after a careful and thorough analysis. This takes time and it is in the investors interest that rating changes are not "knee jerk" reactions to short-term and temporary events. Rating agencies do not have the luxury of "quick and dirty" reviews that often pass for solid research in other parts of the investment business. Increasing competition in the rating agency business will force the agencies to keep on top of developments more closely than in the past while maintaining their usual careful analysis.

A recent paper looked at rating changes that were not preceded by company-specific events. [23] The authors reported that significant excess returns were

---

[22] Louis H. Ederington, Jess B. Yawitz, and Brian E. Roberts, "The Informational Content of Bond Ratings," *Journal of Financial Research* (Fall 1987), pp. 211-226.

found only for issues that were upgraded from speculative grade to investment grade (BB/Ba and lower to BBB/Baa and higher). Other major upgrades and downgrades within the investment grade rankings had no bondholder wealth impact. It concludes:

> ...the major rating change announcements that follow these company-specific events have an insignificant impact on bond returns. As a result, we conclude that changes in default risk are reflected in bond prices when the company-specific events are announced and that bond investors fully anticipate the major rating changes that follow.
>
> The results of this study indicate that most major rating changes do not convey new information to the bond market and that the bond market is informationally efficient. The single exception to this result, significant abnormal returns for upgrade from speculative to investment grade, supports the conclusion that the constraints placed on institutional investors inhibit the price of speculative-grade bonds from rising to reflect decreases in default risk until the rating change actually occurs. As a result, investment constraints for institutional investors produce an inefficiency in the bond market.

WHY RATINGS ARE IMPORTANT TO MARKET PARTICIPANTS?

Well, if rating changes generally don't have a significant impact on bond prices over the short term, why then are they useful? They are useful because they convey to the bond market information about the level of default risk associated with a particular issue. There is a close correlation between the level of a rating and the default rate. The agencies have a good record of downgrading prior to default.

Standard & Poor's rating transition study mentioned above covered more than 3,600 corporate debt issuers of which 339 eventually defaulted. It found that only one defaulted while its debt was rated in the investment grade category (BBB), although three other defaulting issuers had debt rated in the BB category with an implied senior rating of BBB. The lower the rating, the more likely a default will occur. Ten issuers were rated BB at the time of default, 115 were rated B, 174 were CCC and lower, and 36 were not rated. The average length of time between the last rating prior to default was found to range between 1.4 and 1.9 years with the exception of the CCC and lower category: these issuers defaulted in less than six months on average!

---

[23] Delvin D. Hawley, and M. Mark Walker, "An Empirical Test of Investment Restriction and Efficiency in the High-Yield Debt Market," *The Financial Review*, (May 1992), pp. 273-287.

Investment grade bonds have defaulted but not while they were so rated with the one 'BBB' exception. Two issuers with original AAA ratings eventually defaulted, six original AAs, 18 in the A category, and 25 original BBBs. In the noninvestment grade category 114 original BB issuers defaulted, 151 of the B issuers, and 23 original CCC and lower rated issuers. And the lower the original rating, the shorter the time to default. It took 8.3 years for the two original AAAs to reach the time when they failed to meet their debt payments, 6.3 years for the BBB issuers, 3.5 years for the B companies, and only 2.6 years for the CCC and lower rated issuers.

Prudent investment management requires that definite standards be applied in the selection of securities. This is true for equities as well as bonds, and institutions as well as for individuals. As Charles D. Ellis writes:

> In investment management, the real opportunity to achieve superior results is not in scrambling to outperform the market, but in establishing and adhering to appropriate investment policies over the long term — policies that position the portfolio to benefit from riding with the main long-term forces in the market. Investment policy, wisely formulated by realistic and well-informed clients with a long-term perspective and clearly defined objectives, is the foundation upon which portfolios should be constructed and managed over time and through market cycles.[24]

Because ratings are important as indicators of the level of default risk, they are an important ingredient in bond valuation. A bond's value is determined by a number of factors. One is based on the Treasury yield curve, i.e., the maturity of the issue, its coupon and the level of interest rates, using U. S. Treasury issues as the benchmark. Treasury issues are regarded as free from default risk and the basis from which all other credit instruments are priced. The actual or perceived quality of the bond issue must be reflected in its valuation since increased default risk means that investors will want a greater return.[25] If analysis suggests that the issue may be upgraded, investors might be willing to pay a higher price and a lower yield premium compared to Treasury issues. If it appears vulnerable to down grading, investors will want the bonds at a cheaper price (higher yield).

Another factor bearing on a bond's price is the indenture features including protective covenants and redemption terms. Investors must also consider the outstanding size of the issue; if it is a sinking fund issue, how much is controlled by a few investors or sinking fund accumulators; whether it is a public or privately-placed issue; whether it is a foreign or domestic bond, and the technical condition of the market,

---

[24] Charles D. Ellis, *Investment Policy: How to Win the Loser's Game.* (Homewood, Illinois: Dow-Jones Irwin, 1985).

[25] Aberrations, however, do occur. *Barron's National Business and Financial Weekly* said in its Trading Points column on June 8, 1992: "J.P. Morgan is a fine bank, but is it a better risk than Uncle Sam? Some investors apparently think so, because they were willing to buy a one-year Morgan note last week at 4.35%, just *below* the yield on some Treasury securities of similar maturity."

among others. If a dealer is short the particular bonds, he might be willing to pay more for the issue in question than other dealers. If the dealer feels that interest rates are about to rise, he may be willing to sell his inventory at lower prices while his bids will be less aggressive. These factors affect liquidity and marketability of the bond and thus impact what investors and traders are willing to pay for an issue.

After the issue's quality and expected rating trend, its vulnerability to premature redemption, and its place on the yield curve have been determined, a value will be given to the bond. Depending on the issue, it might be given a valuation of, say, 85 basis points above the level of the Treasury yield curve at a similar maturity date. Another issue of similar but slightly different terms might be valued at 90 basis points above the yield curve. Thus, at that time, they should trade at a spread of five basis points from one another. If the actual spread is different, then a trade might be accomplished by selling the richer bond and buying the cheaper one. Investors constantly compare one bond with another since bond investment is, to a great extent, based on relative valuation.

It should now be obvious that a lower bond rating means that it will cost an issuer more to raise funds due to the increased risk of default than if its bonds were higher rated. It makes sense that investors want to get paid more for taking on additional risk, and ratings indicate that risk. Ratings are also important to issuers as a lower than expected rating may result cancellation, restructuring or repricing of a proposed new issue. In May 1970, Standard & Poor's Corporation gave a BB rating to the proposed $100 million debt offering of Pennsylvania Co., a real estate operation in the Penn Central System. This rating had tremendous information content and market clout, alerting investors that all was not rosy with the System's finances. The deal never made it to the market and was another event leading up to the subsequent bankruptcy filing of Penn Central a few months later.

And, what about split ratings that differ between the agencies. A majority of out standing public bonds carry equivalent ratings by at least two agencies (and sometimes more), but not always. Ratings, after all, are subjective and differences of opinion do occur. One study says:

> We find that in general split ratings represent random differences of opinion on issues whose creditworthiness is close to the borderline between ratings. The respective positions of the two agencies [Moody's and Standard & Poor's] could easily have been reversed; i.e., on another day or with a slightly different set of analysts, either agency might assign a different rating. In only a decided minority of cases do splits appear to represent a more fundamental difference of opinion, and in those cases the differences appear to be with respect to aspects of the issue other than public accounting information... therefore, split ratings evince the complexity and subjectivity of bond creditworthiness evaluations and it is this subjectivity that leads most users to demand a second rating.[26]

---

[26] Louis H. Ederington, "Why Split Ratings Occur," *Financial Management* (Spring 1986), p. 46.

Split ratings affect what investors are willing to pay for bonds. One study on split ratings and reoffering yields on new debt issues appeared in *Financial Management* in the summer of 1985. It concludes:

> The paper's empirical analysis reveals that the reoffering yields on split-rated bonds are not significantly different from the yields on the lower rating involved in the split while they are significantly different from the yields on the higher rating involved in that same split. It thus appears that investors' perceptions of the true default risk of a split-rated issue are more accurately represented by the lower of the two ratings.[27]

Changes in credit ratings can affect the interest rate paid on some corporate debt issues. For example, in 1989, Enron Corp. sold $100 million of noncallable 9½% Credit Sensitive Notes due June 15, 2001. At the time of the offering the securities carried ratings of BBB- and Baa3 from Standard & Poor's and Moody's. If, during the time the notes are outstanding, there is a change in the issue's debt rating by either of the services, the interest coupon would be correspondingly adjusted. The coupon remains at 9.50% as long as both agencies rate the issue within the BBB/Baa category. However, upon any drop to the speculative grade area, the higher coupon kicks in. For example, a BB+ or Ba1 will make the rate 12%, a BB or Ba2 means a 12.50% coupon, BB- or Ba3 moves the rate to 13%, and a rating decline to B+ or B1 or lower results in a 14% interest rate. Of course, it isn't a one-way street. Higher ratings (with the lower of the two still the ruling rating) will mean lower interest costs. If both ratings are in the single-A range, the rate drops to 9.40%, within the AA/Aa ranking the coupon is 9.30%, and a 9.20% applies at the triple-A level. The underwriters estimated that Enron saved about 35 basis points over what a fixed coupon 12-year bullet maturity would have cost.

Institutional And Regulatory Uses Of Ratings

For years investors and regulators have used ratings for establishing investment parameters and lists of legal investments. Many mutual funds prohibit investments in bonds rated less than investment grade, or may allow a modest portion to be in speculative grade bonds. This, of course, excludes funds which, by their very charter, invest in speculative grade debt. Some institutions look upon the bottom rung of the investment grade ladder, namely BBB/Baa, as semi-speculative in nature and thus prohibit investment in bonds with these ratings.

The restricted investments covenant found in many bond indentures usually limits investments in commercial paper to the highest rating category of a recognized rating agency. Other short-term type investments such as auction rate preferred stock and bank deposits are also similarly restricted to the top rating lev-

---

[27] Randall S. Billingsley, Robert E. Lamy, M. Wayne Marr, and G. Rodney Thompson, "Split Ratings and Bond Reoffering Yields," *Financial Management* (Spring 1985), p. 65.

els. The commercial paper rates published in the Board of Governors of the Federal Reserve System's Statistical Release H.15 (519) — Selected Interest Rates are those of companies whose bond rating is AA or the equivalent. These rates are used to set the dividend rates on auction market and remarketed preferred stock.

If a taxable money market mutual fund maintains its commercial paper investments to those rated in the top two rating categories of at least two recognized agencies, it will then be able to price the fund by adjusting the yield so as to maintain the $1.00 per share net asset value. The SEC's amendment to Rule 2a-7, the regulation governing money market fund investments, also establishes several other criteria for commercial paper investment. Paper rated in the highest category by at least two agencies (one NRSRO if only one rates the issue) must comprise at least 95% of the portfolio. If there are three ratings, then two of the three ratings must be in the highest rating classification. The remaining 5% can consist of paper in the second highest category. Limits are also placed on the investment concentration in any one issuer. Also, if the paper is downgraded so as to violate the criteria, the fund must divest it, subject to limitations.[28]

In the 1930s, the Comptroller of the Currency issued regulations governing bond investments of banks under its control. National banks and members of the Federal Reserve System can invest in debt securities rated in the top four categories, that is, investment grade. Thrift institutions chartered by the Office of Thrift Supervision can invest in corporate debt securities rated investment grade at the time of purchase and in commercial paper rated in the top two grades. States also use ratings in establishing criteria for investment by fiduciaries and other entities under their supervision.

Ratings are used in determining net capital requirements of securities dealers with the reserves based on the type and quality of the security. The more liquid and the higher rated the security, the less capital is required, with the least capital reserves required for top-rated, highly liquid issues. Again, investment grade is the key for bonds and preferred stock and the top three categories for publicly issued commercial paper. The latter point is somewhat moot when it comes to commercial paper rated in the third category since there are few buyers of such paper and few firms will carry it in their inventory. Until March 1992, privately-placed commercial paper required 100% reserves if held by broker-dealers. *The Wall Street Journal* reported that the Securities and Exchange Commission changed the rule allowing privately placed paper to be held "... without setting aside reserves if the paper is top-rated, an indication that it would find a ready market if the firms needed to sell the issue." Further, it stated that "the SEC decided that it would rely on the rating agencies to determine whether the paper was of high quality...." [29]

---

[28] A more complete review of the uses of ratings may be found in Neil D. Baron and Leah W. Murch, "Statutory and Regulatory Uses of Ratings in the United States and Other Jurisdictions," Fitch Investors Service, Inc., April 16, 1991.

[29] "SEC Waives Reserves On Some Top Private Commercial Paper," *The Wall Street Journal*, March 18, 1992.

Exhibit 8: National Association of Insurance Commissioners and the Rating Agency Equivalents

NAIC Meaning	NAIC Designation	Agency Rating	MSVR (%)
Highest quality	1	AAA/Aaa, AA/Aa,A, PPR1	1
High quality	2	BBB/Baa, PPR2	2
Medium quality	3	BB/Ba, PPR3	5
Low quality	4	B, PPR4	10
Lower quality	5	CCC/Caa, CC/Ca, PPR5	20
Bonds in or near de fault	6	C, D, PPR6	20

Source: *Purposes and Procedures of the Securities Valuation Office of the National Association of Insurance Commissioners Effective for 1993 Annual Statements*, January 1, 1994.

Finally, the National Association of Insurance Commissioners' Securities Valuation Office (NAIC and SVO, respectively) sets quality ratings on securities held by insurance companies for the purpose of establishing reserve requirements. The lower the ratings, the greater the mandatory securities valuation reserve requirement (ms-vr). The ratings or "NAIC Designations" are required to be used by insurers in the preparation of the annual statements filed with the state regulators and the NAIC. Agency ratings are "directly translated into an NAIC designation." [30] If an issue carries a rating from one or more of the agencies, the NAIC can use it as the basis for its designation. Thus an A-rated issue becomes an NAIC "1" and a BBB bond is the equivalent to an NAIC "2" rating (see Exhibit 8). The SVO has the authority to downgrade agency ratings but not to upgrade them. In the case of split ratings, they may often use the lower of the two ratings. However, they can use the higher if they feel it is more reflective of the true quality and risk of the issue.

In situations where the issue doesn't have an agency rating, the staff of the SVO conducts its own analysis to arrive at an NAIC designation. This involves a quantitative review using scores derived from financial models, a the financial history and projections, if any, and a look at the covenants, structure, collateral, third party support and other factors it deems relevant.

In the case of private placements, since they are usually rated by only one agency, that rating will normally be accepted by the SVO. However, because agency fees are higher than those charged by the SVO, investment bankers will generally use the SVO for most ratings. However, in the case of borderline credits (that is, where the issue straddles a rating grade category such as "2" and "3" or "1" and "2") and difficult and complex financings, private placement agents tend to use the rating agencies. Some agents feel that the agencies do a more thorough analysis than the SVO on these "story" credits. In addition, some of the agencies work closely with the investment bankers, keeping them informed of the progress of the analysis throughout the rating

---

[30] For a complete review of the NAIC's procedures for rating securities see *Purposes and Proce- dures of the Securities Valuation Office of the National Association of Insurance Commissioners Effective for 1993 Annual Statements* published in January 1994.

process. This allows for a quick review of the rating impact of any proposed changes in the structure and covenants of the transaction. Also, since the SVO has a relatively small staff, it sometimes gets large backlogs of rating requests and cannot promptly service the demands and timing needs of investment bankers and insurance companies. The rating agencies help by rating some of these proposed transactions and relieving some of the pressure from the SVO's shoulders.

The SVO isn't a rubber stamp for agency ratings although nonacceptance of an NRSRO rating is rare. But it does occasionally happen. Of the many hundreds of ratings issued by rating agencies in the years since the new NAIC designations became effective for the year-end 1990 financial reporting statements, only a handful were not accepted, according to some market observers.

CONCLUSION

Rating agencies perform an important function for the capital markets of America. They are independent, third party appraisers of the default risk associated with fixed income investments. Their functions and services are becoming increasingly recognized and used in other parts of the world as their capital markets evolve with the expansion of free market economies and the demise of socialism. Rating agencies require free markets and competition in order to be of the most value to market participants. Rating agencies will continue to play a major role in the market place as long as they remember that along with their power they have responsibility — the responsibility and duty to perform rating analyses with diligence and thoughtfulness.

A P P E N D I X

RATING DEFINITIONS

LONG-TERM DEBT RATING DEFINITIONS

Duff & Phelps Credit Rating	Fitch Investors Service, Inc.	Moody's Investors Service	Standard & Poor's
AAA Highest credit quality. The risk factors are negligible, being only slightly more than for risk-free U.S. Treasury debt.	**AAA** Bonds considered to be investment grade and of the highest credit quality. The obligor has an exceptionally strong ability to pay interest and repay principal, which is unlikely to be affected by reasonably foreseeable events.	**Aaa** Bonds which are rated **Aaa** are judged to be of the best quality. They carry the smallest degree of investment risk and are generally referred to as "gilt edged." Interest payments are protected by a large or by an exceptionally stable margin and principal is secure. While the various protective elements are likely to change, such changes as can be visualized are most unlikely to impair the fundamentally strong position of such issues.	**AAA** Debt rated **AAA** has the highest rating assigned by Standard & Poor's. Capacity to pay interest and repay principal is extremely strong.
AA High credit quality. Protection factors are strong. Risk is modest but may vary slightly from time to time because of economic conditions.	**AA** Bonds considered to be investment grade and of very high credit quality. The obligor's ability to pay interest and repay principal is very strong, although not quite as strong as bonds rated AAA. Because bonds rated in the AAA and AA categories are not significantly vulnerable to foreseeable future developments short-term debt of these issuers is generally rated **F-1+**.	**Aa** Bonds which are rated **Aa** are judged to be of high quality by all standards. Together with the **Aaa** group they comprise what are generally known as high grade bonds. They are rated lower than the best bonds because margins of protection may not be as large as in **Aaa** securities or fluctuation of protective elements may be of greater amplitude or there may be other elements present which make the long-term risk appear somewhat larger than the Aaa securities.	**AA** Debt rated **AA** has a very strong capacity to pay interest and repay principal and differs from the higher rated issues only in small degree.
A Protection factors are average but adequate. However, risk factors are more variable and greater in periods of economic stress.	**A** Bonds considered to be investment grade and of high credit quality. The obligor's ability to pay interest and repay principal is considered to be strong, but may be more vulnerable to adverse changes in economic conditions and circumstances than bonds with higher ratings.	**A** Bonds which are rated **A** possess many favorable investment attributes and are to be considered as upper-medium-grade obligations. Factors giving security to principal and interest are considered adequate, but elements may be present which suggest a susceptibility to impairment some time in the future.	**A** Debt rated **A** has a strong capacity to pay interest and repay principal although it is somewhat more susceptible to the adverse effects of changes in circumstances and economic conditions than debt in the higher rated categories.

Duff & Phelps Credit Rating	Fitch Investors Service, Inc.	Moody's Investors Service	Standard & Poor's
BBB Below average protection factors but still considered sufficient for prudent investment. Considerable variability in risk during economic cycles.	**BBB** Bonds considered to be investment grade and of satisfactory credit quality. The obligor's ability to pay interest and repay principal is considered to be adequate. Adverse changes in economic conditions and circumstances, however, are more likely to have adverse impact on these bonds, and therefore impair timely payment. The likelihood that the ratings of these bonds will fall below investment grade is higher than for bonds with higher ratings.	**Baa** Bonds which are rated **Baa** are considered as medium-grade obligations, (i.e., they are neither highly protected nor poorly secured). Interest payments and principal security appear adequate for the present but certain protective elements may be lacking or may be characteristically unreliable over any great length of time. Such bonds lack outstanding investment characteristics and in fact have speculative elements as well.	**BBB** Debt rated **BBB** is regarded as having an adequate capacity to pay interest and repay principal. Whereas it normally exhibits adequate protection parameters, adverse economic conditions or changing circumstances are more likely to lead to a weakened capacity to pay interest and repay principal for debt in this category than in higher rated categories.
BB Below investment grade but deemed likely to meet obligations when due. Present or prospective financial protection factors fluctuate according to industry conditions or company fortunes. Overall quality may move up or down frequently within this category.	**BB** Bonds are considered speculative. The obligor's ability to pay interest and repay principal may be affected over time by adverse economic changes. However, business and financial alternatives can be identified which could assist the obligor in satisfying its debt service requirements.	**Ba** Bonds which are rated **Ba** are judged to have speculative elements; their future cannot be considered as well-assured. Often the protection of interest and principal payments may be very moderate, and thereby not well safeguarded during both good and bad times over the future. Uncertainty of position characterizes bonds in this class.	**BB** Debt rated **BB** has less near-term vulnerability to default than other speculative issues. However, it faces major ongoing uncertainties or exposure to adverse business, financial, or economic conditions which could lead to inadequate capacity to meet timely interest and principal payments. The **BB** rating category is also used for debt subordinated to senior debt that is assigned an actual or implied **BBB-** rating.
B Below investment grade and possessing risk that obligations will not be met when due. Financial protection factors will fluctuate widely according to economic cycles, industry conditions and/or company fortunes. Potential exists for frequent changes in the rating within this category or into a higher or lower rating grade.	**B** Bonds are considered highly speculative. While bonds in this class are currently meeting debt service requirements, the probability of continued timely payment of principal and interest reflects the obligor's limited margin of safety and the need for reasonable business and economic activity throughout the life of the issue.	**B** Bonds which are rated **B** generally lack characteristics of the desirable investment. Assurance of interest and principal payments or of maintenance of other terms of the contract over any long period of time may be small.	**B** Debt rated **B** has a greater vulnerability to default but currently has the capacity to meet interest payments and principal repayments. Adverse business, financial, or economic conditions will likely impair capacity or willingness to pay interest and repay principal. The **B** rating category is also used for debt subordinated to senior debt that is assigned an actual or implied **BB** or **BB-** rating.

Duff & Phelps Credit Rating	Fitch Investors Service, Inc.	Moody's Investors Service	Standard & Poor's
CCC Well below investment grade securities. Considerable uncertainty exists as to timely payment of principal, interest or preferred dividends. Protection factors are narrow and risk can be substantial with unfavorable economic/industry conditions, and/or with unfavorable company developments.	**CCC** Bonds have certain identifiable characteristics which, if not remedied, may lead to default. The ability to meet obligations requires an advantageous business and economic environment.	**Caa** Bonds which are rated **Caa** are of poor standing. Such issues may be in default or there may be present elements of danger with respect to principal or interest.	**CCC** Debt rated **CCC** has a currently identifiable vulnerability to default, and is dependent upon favorable business, financial, and economic conditions to meet timely payment of interest and repayment of principal. In the event of adverse business, financial, or economic conditions, it is not likely to have the capacity to pay interest and repay principal. The **CCC** rating category is also used for debt subordinated to senior debt that is assigned an actual or implied **B** or **B-** rating.
	CC Bonds are minimally protected. Default in payment of interest and/or principal seems probable over time.	**Ca** Bonds which are rated **Ca** represent obligations which are speculative in a high degree. Such issues are often in default or have other marked shortcomings.	**CC** The rating **CC** is typically applied to debt subordinated to senior debt that is assigned an actual or implied **CCC** rating.
	C Bonds are in imminent default in payment of interest or principal.	**C** Bonds which are rated **C** are the lowest rated class of bonds, and issues so rated can be regarded as having extremely poor prospects of ever attaining any real investment standing.	**C** The rating **C** is typically applied to debt subordinated to senior debt which is assigned an actual or implied **CCC-** debt rating. The **C** rating may be used to cover a situation where a bankruptcy petition has been filed, but debt service payments are continued. **CI** The rating **CI** is reserved for income bonds on which no interest is being paid.
DD Defaulted debt obligations. Issuer failed to meet scheduled principal and/or interest payments.	**DDD, DD**, and **D** Bonds are in default on interest and/or principal payments. Such bonds are extremely speculative and should be valued on the basis of their ultimate recovery value in liquidation or reorganization of the obligor. **DDD** represents the highest potential for recovery on these bonds, and **D** represents the lowest potential for recovery.		**D** Debt rated **D** is in payment default. The **D** rating category is used when interest payments or principal payments are not made on the date due even if the applicable grace period has not expired, unless S&P believes that such payments will be made during such grace period. The **D** rating will also be used upon the filing of a bankruptcy petition if debt service payments are jeopardized.

Duff & Phelps Credit Rating	Fitch Investors Service, Inc.	Moody's Investors Service	Standard & Poor's
Plus (+) and Minus (-) modifiers are used in the **AA** to **B** rating categories to indicate the relative ranking of a particular issue within the rating category.	**Plus (+) Minus (-)** Plus and minus signs are used with a rating symbol to indicate the relative position of a credit within the rating category. Plus and minus signs, however, are not used in the **AAA** category.	Moody's applies numerical modifiers, **1, 2** and **3** in each generic rating classification from **Aa** to **B**. The modifier **1** indicates that the company ranks in the higher end of its generic rating category; the modifier **2** indicates a mid-range ranking; and the modifier **3** indicates that the company ranks in the lower end of its generic rating category.	**Plus (+) or Minus (-):** The ratings from **AA** to **CCC** may be modified by the addition of a plus or minus sign to show relative standing within the major categories.

SHORT-TERM RATINGS

Duff & Phelps Credit Rating	Fitch Investors Service, Inc.	Moody's Investors Service	Standard & Poor's
Duff 1+ Highest certainty of timely payment. Short-term liquidity, including internal operating factors and/or access to alternative sources of funds, is outstanding, and safety is just below risk-free U.S. Treasury short-term obligations.	**F-1+ Exceptionally Strong Credit Quality.** Issues assigned this rating are regarded as having the strongest degree of assurance for timely payment.		**A-1+** see below..
Duff 1 Very high certainty of timely payment. Liquidity factors are excellent and supported by good fundamental protection factors. Risk factors are minor.	**F-1 Very Strong Credit Quality.** Issues assigned this rating reflect an assurance of timely payment only slightly less in degree than issues rated **F-1+**.	**Prime-1** Issuers rated **Prime-1** (or supporting institutions) have a superior ability for repayment of short-term debt obligations. **Prime-1** repayment ability can often be evidenced by many of the following characteristics: Leading market positions in well-established industries. High rates of return on funds employed. Conservative capitalization structure with moderate reliance on debt and ample asset protection. Broad margins in earnings coverage of fixed financial charges and high internal cash generation. Well-established access to a range of financial markets and assured sources of alternate liquidity.	**A-1** This highest category indicates that the degree of safety regarding timely payment is strong. Those issues determined to possess extremely strong safety characteristics are denoted with a plus sign (+) designation.
Duff 1- High certainty of timely payment. Liquidity factors are strong and supported by good fundamental protection factors. Risk factors are very small.			

Duff & Phelps Credit Rating	Fitch Investors Service, Inc.	Moody's Investors Service	Standard & Poor's
Duff 2 Good Grade Good certainty of timely payment. Liquidity factors and company fundamentals are sound. Although ongoing funding needs may enlarge total financing requirements, access to capital markets is good. Risk factors are small.	**F-2 Good Credit Quality** Issues assigned this rating have a satisfactory degree of assurance for timely payment, but the margin of safety is not as great as for issues assigned **F-1+** and **F-1** ratings.	**Prime-2** Issuers rated **Prime-2** (or supporting institutions) have a strong ability for repayment of senior short-term debt obligations. This will be evidenced by many of the characteristics cited above, but to a lesser degree, earnings trends and coverage ratios, while sound, may be more subject to variation. Capitalization characteristics, while still appropriate, may be more affected by external conditions. Ample alternate liquidity is maintained.	**A-2** Capacity for timely payment on issues with this designation is satisfactory. However, the relative degree of safety is not as high as for issues designated **A-1**.
Duff 3 Satisfactory Grade Satisfactory liquidity and other protection factors qualify issue as to investment grade. Risk factors are larger and subject to more variation. Nevertheless, timely payment is expected.	**F-3 Fair Credit Quality.** Issues assigned this rating have characteristics suggesting that the degree of assurance for timely payment is adequate, however, near-term adverse changes could cause these securities to be rated below investment grade.	**Prime-3** Issuers rated **Prime-3** (or supporting institutions) have an acceptable ability for repayment of short-term obligations. The effect of industry characteristics and market compositions may be more pronounced. Variability in earnings and profitability may result in changes in the level of debt protection measurements and may require relatively high financial leverage. Adequate alternate liquidity is maintained.	**A-3** Issues carrying this designation have adequate capacity for timely payment. They are, however, more vulnerable to the adverse effects of changes in circumstances than obligations carrying the higher designations.
Duff 4 Non-Investment Grade Speculative investment characteristics. Liquidity is not sufficient to insure against disruption in debt service. Operating factors and market access may be subject to great variation.	**F-S Weak Credit Quality.** Issues assigned this rating have characteristics suggesting a minimal assurance for timely payment and are vulnerable to near-term adverse changes in financial and economic conditions.	**Not Prime** Issuers rated **Not Prime** do not fall within any of the Prime rating categories.	**B** Issues rated **B** are regarded as having only speculative capacity for timely payment.
			C This rating is assigned to short-term debt obligations with a doubtful capacity for payment.
Duff 5 Default Issuer failed to meet scheduled principal and/or interest payments.	**D Default.** Issues assigned this rating are in actual or imminent payment default.		**D** Debt rated **D** is in payment default. Used when interest payments or principal payments are not made on the date due, even if the applicable grace period has not expired, unless S&P believes that such payments will be made during this time.
Source: *The Duff & Phelps Rating Guide,* September 1994.	Source: *Fitch Ratings Book,* September 1994.	Source: *Moody's Bond Record,* November 1993.	Source: *Standard & Poor's Bond Guide,* November 1993

SECTION II

CHAPTER 9

Bond Pricing and Yield Measures

In Section I of this book, we described the different types of corporate bonds and their features. In the five chapters in Section II, we set forth the techniques for valuing corporate bonds and managing a corporate bond portfolio. This chapter and the next provide the fundamental principles of bond valuation. Chapter 11 sets forth a specific valuation model — the arbitrage-free binomial model. The valuation of some types of structured notes and convertible bonds is provided in Chapter 12. Techniques for managing a corporate bond portfolio are the subject of Chapter 13.

PRICING A BOND

The price of any financial instrument (common stock, bond, mortgage, real estate) is equal to the present (discounted) value of its *expected* cash flows. By discounting, allowance is made for the timing of the cash flows. Consequently, determining the price requires that an investor estimate the following:

- the expected cash flows, and
- the appropriate required yield.

The expected cash flows for some financial instruments are simple to compute; for others, the task is not as simple. The required yield reflects the yield for financial instruments with *comparable* risk and features.

Assuming that a corporate issuer does not default, it is simple to compute the cash flows for a fixed-rate, option-free bond (that is, a noncallable, nonputable or nonconvertible bond). The cash flows are (1) coupon interest payments to the maturity date and (2) the par (or maturity) value at maturity.

Exhibit 1: Calculation of the Price of a 7%, 5-Year Bond Selling to Yield 10%

Period (1)	Cash flow per $100 par (2)	Present Value of $1 at 5% (3)*	Present Value of Cash Flow (4) = (2) × (3)
1	3.5	0.952380	3.33333
2	3.5	0.907029	3.17460
3	3.5	0.863837	3.02343
4	3.5	0.822702	2.87945
5	3.5	0.783526	2.74234
6	3.5	0.746215	2.61175
7	3.5	0.710681	2.48738
8	3.5	0.676839	2.36893
9	3.5	0.644608	2.25613
10	103.5	0.613913	63.54002
		Price = Total present value =	88.41739

*Present value of $1 at 5% calculated as follows:

$$\frac{1}{1.05^{period}}$$

Two bonds will be used to illustrate how the price of a bond is calculated: a 7% coupon, 5-year bond and a 7% coupon, 20-year bond. Assuming that the next coupon payment for both bonds is six months from now, the second column of Exhibits 1 and 2 set forth the cash flow that the investor will realize every six months until the bond matures.

To calculate the price of each bond, the yield required by an investor must be determined. For purposes of our illustrations, we shall assume that the investor wants a 10% yield in order to invest in either of these bonds. The cash flows should be discounted at one-half the required yield, or 5% in our illustration. The third column of Exhibits 1 and 2 gives the present value of $1 for each period using an interest rate of 5%. The last column of the exhibits gives the present value of the cash flows, which is found by multiplying the cash flow in the second column by the present value of $1 at 5%. The sum of the present value of the cash flows is the price of the bond.

In practice, hand-held calculators and PC software are used to compute the price of a bond given the (1) coupon rate, (2) maturity date, and (3) required yield.

The required yield is determined by investigating the yields offered on comparable bonds in the market. By comparable, we mean issues of the same credit quality, features, and maturity. The required yield is typically expressed as an annual interest rate. Since the cash flows for corporate bonds are every six months, the market convention is to use one-half the annual interest rate as the periodic interest rate with which to discount the cash flows. This is the practice we followed in calculating the price in Exhibits 1 and 2.

Exhibit 2: Calculation of the Price of a 7%, 20-Year Bond Selling to Yield 10%

Period (1)	Cash flow per $100 par (2)	Present Value of $1 at 5% (3)*	Present Value of Cash Flow (4) = (2) × (3)
1	3.5	0.952380	3.33333
2	3.5	0.907029	3.17460
3	3.5	0.863837	3.02343
4	3.5	0.822702	2.87945
5	3.5	0.783526	2.74234
6	3.5	0.746215	2.61175
7	3.5	0.710681	2.48738
8	3.5	0.676839	2.36893
9	3.5	0.644608	2.25613
10	3.5	0.613913	2.14869
11	3.5	0.584679	2.04637
12	3.5	0.556837	1.94893
13	3.5	0.530321	1.85612
14	3.5	0.505067	1.76773
15	3.5	0.481017	1.68355
16	3.5	0.458111	1.60339
17	3.5	0.436296	1.52703
18	3.5	0.415520	1.45432
19	3.5	0.395733	1.38506
20	3.5	0.376889	1.31911
21	3.5	0.358942	1.25629
22	3.5	0.341849	1.19647
23	3.5	0.325571	1.13949
24	3.5	0.310067	1.08523
25	3.5	0.295302	1.03355
26	3.5	0.281240	0.98434
27	3.5	0.267848	0.93746
28	3.5	0.255093	0.89282
29	3.5	0.242946	0.85031
30	3.5	0.231377	0.80982
31	3.5	0.220359	0.77125
32	3.5	0.209866	0.73453
33	3.5	0.199872	0.69955
34	3.5	0.190354	0.66624
35	3.5	0.181290	0.63451
36	3.5	0.172657	0.60430
37	3.5	0.164435	0.57552
38	3.5	0.156605	0.54811
39	3.5	0.149147	0.52201
40	103.5	0.142045	14.70172
		Price = Total present value =	74.26137

*Present value of $1 at 5% calculated as follows:

$$\frac{1}{1.05^{period}}$$

Exhibit 3: Price/Yield Relationship for Six Bonds

Coupon/Term	7%	8%	9%	10%	11%	12%	13%
7%/5	100.00	95.94	92.09	88.42	84.92	81.60	78.43
7%/20	100.00	90.10	81.60	74.26	67.91	62.38	57.56
10%/5	112.47	108.11	103.96	100.00	96.23	92.64	89.22
10%/20	132.03	119.79	109.20	100.00	91.98	84.95	78.78
13%/5	124.95	120.28	115.83	111.58	107.54	103.68	100.00
13%/20	164.07	149.48	136.80	125.74	116.05	107.52	100.00

The price of a zero coupon bond is simply the present value of the maturity value. However, in the present value computation, the number of periods used for discounting is *double* the number of years to maturity of the bond, not the number of years.

Price/Yield Relationship of an Option-Free Bond

A fundamental property of a bond is that its price changes in the opposite direction of the change in the required yield. The reason is that the price of the bond is the present value of the cash flows. As the required yield increases, the present value of the cash flows decreases; hence, the price decreases. The opposite is true when the required yield decreases: the present value of the cash flows increases and, therefore, the price of the bond increases. This is illustrated in Exhibit 3 for the two 7% coupon bonds whose price we calculated in Exhibits 1 and 2 and for four other bonds.

If we graphed the price/yield relationship for any option-free bond, we would find that it has the "bowed" shape shown in Exhibit 4. This shape is referred to as *convex*. The convexity of the price/yield relationship has important implications for the investment properties of a bond, as we will see in Chapter 10.

The Relationship Between Coupon Rate, Required Yield, and Price

As yields in the marketplace change, the only variable that an investor can change to compensate for the new required yield in the market is the price of the bond. When the coupon rate is equal to the required yield, the price of the bond will be equal to its par value.

When yields in the marketplace rise above the coupon rate, the price of the bond adjusts so that any investor who wishes to purchase the bond can realize additional interest. To do so, the price of the bond must sell below its par value. The capital appreciation realized by holding the bond to maturity represents a form of interest to the investor to compensate for the lower coupon rate than the yield required in the market. A bond selling below its par value is said to be selling at a *discount*. In our earlier calculation of a bond's price, we saw that when the required yield is greater than the coupon rate, the price of the bond is less than the par value.

Exhibit 4: Price/Yield Relationship for an Option-Free Bond

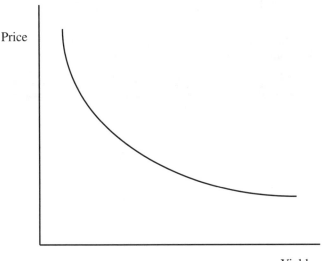

When the required yield in the market is below the coupon rate, the price of the bond must sell above its par value. This occurs because investors who would have the opportunity to purchase the bond at par would be getting a coupon rate in excess of what the market would require. As a result, investors would bid up the price of the bond because its yield is attractive. It will be bid up to a price at which it offers the required yield in the market. A bond whose price is above its par value is said to be selling at a *premium*.

The relationship between coupon rate, required yield, and price is summarized below:

coupon rate < required yield then price < par
coupon rate = required yield then price = par
coupon rate > required yield then price > par

These relationships can be verified for the six bonds whose price we show at various required yields in Exhibit 3.

Relationship Between Bond Price and Time If Interest Rates Are Unchanged

If the required yield is unchanged between the time the bond is purchased and the maturity date, what will happen to the price of the bond? For a bond selling at par value, the coupon rate is equal to the required yield. As the bond moves closer to maturity, the bond will continue to sell at par value. Thus, for a bond selling at par, its price will remain at par as the bond moves toward the maturity date.

Exhibit 5: Price of Discount and Premium Bond as Bond Approaches Maturity

Bonds

7% coupon, 20-year bond, selling at 74.26 to yield 10%

11.5% coupon, 20-year bond, selling at 112.87 to yield 10%

After	Years to maturity	Bond	
		7% coupon (discount)	11.5% coupon (premium)
1 yr.	19	74.70	112.65
2	18	75.18	112.41
3	17	75.71	112.14
4	16	76.30	111.85
5	15	76.94	111.53
6	14	77.65	111.17
7	13	78.44	110.78
8	12	79.30	110.35
9	11	80.26	109.87
10	10	81.31	109.35
11	9	82.47	108.77
12	8	83.74	108.13
13	7	85.15	107.42
14	6	86.71	106.65
15	5	88.42	105.79
16	4	90.31	104.85
17	3	92.39	103.81
18	2	94.68	102.66
19	1	97.21	101.39
20	0	100.00	100.00

The price of a bond will *not* remain constant for a bond selling at a premium or a discount. Exhibit 5 shows the price movement of two 20-year bonds not selling at par value as they approach maturity. Notice that the discount bond will increase in price as it approaches maturity assuming the required yield does not change. For a premium bond, the opposite occurs. For both bonds, the price will equal par value at the maturity date.

Reasons for the Change in the Price of a Corporate Bond

The price of a bond will change due to one or more of the following reasons:

1. *A change in the level of interest rate rates in the economy.* For example, if interest rates in the economy increase (fall) because of Fed policy, the price of a bond will decrease (increase).

2. *As it moves to maturity.* As we demonstrated, over time a discount bond's price rises in value if yields do not change; a premium bond's price declines over time if yields do not change.

3. *A change in the required yield due to changes in the spread between corporate and Treasuries.* If the Treasury rate does not change, but the spread to Treasuries for all corporate bonds changes (narrows or widens), corporate bond prices will change.

4. *A change in the perceived credit quality of the issuer.* Assuming interest rates in the economy and yield spreads between corporates and Treasuries do not change, the price of a corporate bond will increase (decrease) if its perceived credit quality has improved (deteriorated).

Accrued Interest

When an investor purchases a bond between coupon payments, if the issuer is not in default, the buyer must compensate the seller of the bond for the coupon interest earned from the time of the last coupon payment to the settlement date of the bond. This amount is called *accrued interest* and is computed as follows:

$$(\text{coupon rate}) \times \frac{\text{number of days from last coupon to settlement date}}{\text{number of days in coupon period}}$$

Market conventions determine the number of days in a coupon period and the number of days from the last coupon to settlement date. For corporate bonds, the day count convention is "30/360" which means a year is treated as having 360 days and each month as having 30 days. Therefore, the number of days in a coupon period is 180.

For example, suppose that a corporate bond in which the last coupon payment was made on March 1 is purchased with a settlement date of July 17. The number of days from settlement to the next coupon payment (September 1) is determined as follows:

	Days
Remainder of July	13
August	30
September 1	1
Total	44

Since there are 180 days in a coupon period, the number of days from the last coupon to the settlement date is 136 (180 minus 44). Accrued interest for this bond is then:

$$(\text{coupon rate}) \times \frac{136}{180}$$

There are financial calendars available that provide the day count. Most money managers use software programs that furnish this information.

The price of a bond excluding accrued interest is called the *clean price*. The total proceeds that the buyer of the bond pays the seller is equal to the price agreed upon by the buyer and the seller plus accrued interest. This amount is called the *dirty price*.

CONVENTIONAL YIELD MEASURES

An investor who purchases a corporate bond can expect to receive a dollar return from one or more of the following sources:

- the coupon interest payments made by the issuer,
- any capital gain (or capital loss — negative dollar return) when the bond matures, is called or is sold, and
- income from reinvestment of the coupon interest payments. This source of dollar return is referred to as *interest-on-interest*.

For corporate bonds, several yield measures are commonly cited by market participants — current yield, yield to maturity, yield to call, and yield to worst. These yield measures are expressed as a percent return rather than a dollar return. However, the yield measure should consider each of the three potential sources of return cited above.

Current Yield

The current yield relates the *annual* coupon interest to the market price. The formula for the current yield is:

$$\text{current yield} = \frac{\text{annual dollar coupon interest}}{\text{price}}$$

For example, the current yield for a 7%, 20-year bond whose price is 74.26 is 9.43% as shown below:

$$\text{annual dollar coupon interest} = 0.07 \times \$100 = \$7$$
$$\text{price} = \$74.26$$

$$\text{current yield} = \frac{\$7}{\$74.26} = 0.0943 = 9.43\%$$

The current yield will be greater than the coupon rate when the bond sells at a discount; the reverse is true for a bond selling at a premium. For a bond selling at par, the current yield will be equal to the coupon rate.

The drawback of the current yield is that it considers only the coupon interest and no other source of return that will impact an investor's return. No consideration is given to the capital gain that the investor will realize when a bond is purchased at a discount and held to maturity; nor is there any recognition of the capital loss that the investor will realize if a bond purchased at a premium is held to maturity.

Yield to Maturity

The most popular measure of yield in the bond market is the yield to maturity. The yield to maturity is the interest rate that will make the present value of the cash flows from a bond equal to its dirty price. Calculation of the yield to maturity of a bond is the reverse process of calculating the price of a bond. To find the price of a bond we determined the cash flows and the required yield, then we calculated the present value of the cash flows. To find the yield to maturity, we first determine the cash flows. Then we search by trial and error for the interest rate that will make the present value of the cash flows equal to the dirty price.[1]

To illustrate, consider a 7%, 20-year bond selling for 67.91. The cash flows for this bond are (1) 40 six-month payments of $3.50 and (2) $100 40 six-month periods from now. The present value using various discount (interest) rates is:

Interest rate	3.5%	4.0%	4.5%	5.0%	5.5%	6.0%	6.5%
Present value	100.00	90.10	81.60	74.26	67.91	62.38	57.56

When a 5.5% interest rate is used, the present value of the cash flows is equal to 67.91, which is the price of the bond. Hence, 5.5% is the semiannual yield to maturity.

The market convention adopted is to double the semiannual interest rate and call that interest rate the yield to maturity. Thus, the yield to maturity for the above bond is 11% (2 times 5.5%). The yield to maturity computed using this convention — doubling the semiannual yield — is called a *bond equivalent yield* or *coupon equivalent yield*.

The following relationship between the price of a bond, coupon rate, current yield, and yield to maturity holds:

Bond selling at a	Relationship
par	coupon rate = current yield = yield to maturity
discount	coupon rate < current yield < yield to maturity
premium	coupon rate > current yield > yield to maturity

The yield to maturity considers not only the coupon income but any capital gain or loss that the investor will realize by *holding the bond to matu*rity. The yield to maturity also considers the timing of the cash flows. It does consider interest on interest; *however, it assumes that the coupon payments can be reinvested at an interest rate equal to the yield to maturity.* So, if the yield to maturity for a bond is 10%, for example, to earn that yield the coupon payments must be reinvested at an interest rate equal to 10%. The following illustration clearly demonstrates this.

Suppose an investor has $74.26 and places the funds in a certificate of deposit that pays 5% every six months for 20 years or 10% per year (on a bond equivalent basis). At the end of 20 years, the $74.26 investment will grow to $522.79.

---

[1] In the illustrations presented in this chapter, we assume that the next coupon payment will be six months from now so that the relevant price is the clean price.

Instead, suppose an investor buys the following bond: a 7%, 20-year bond selling for $74.26. The yield to maturity for this bond is 10%. The investor would expect that at the end of 20 years, the total dollars from the investment will be $522.79.

Let's look at what the investor will receive. There will be 40 semiannual interest payments of $3.5 which will total $140. When the bond matures, the investor will receive $100. Thus, the total dollars that the investor will receive is $240 if he held the bond to maturity. But this is less than the $522.79 necessary to produce a yield of 10% on a bond equivalent basis by $282.79 ($522.79 minus $240). How is this deficiency supposed to made up? If the investor reinvests the coupon payments at a semiannual interest rate of 5% (or 10% annual rate on a bond equivalent basis), then the interest earned on the coupon payments will be $282.79. Consequently, of the $448.53 total dollar return ($522.79 minus $74.26) necessary to produce a yield of 10%, about 63% ($282.79 divided by $448.52) must be generated by reinvesting the coupon payments.

Clearly, the investor will only realize the yield to maturity that is stated at the time of purchase if (1) the coupon payments can be reinvested at the yield to maturity, and (2) if the bond is held to maturity. With respect to the first assumption, the risk that an investor faces is that future reinvestment rates will be less than the yield to maturity at the time the bond is purchased. This risk is referred to as *reinvestment risk*. If the bond is not held to maturity, the price of the bond may have to be sold for less than its purchase price, resulting in a return that is less than the yield to maturity. The risk that a bond will have to be sold at a loss is referred to as *interest rate risk* or *price risk*.

Reinvestment Risk: There are two characteristics of a corporate bond that determine the degree of reinvestment risk. First, for a given yield to maturity and a given coupon rate, the longer the maturity the more the bond's total dollar return is dependent on the interest-on-interest to realize the yield to maturity at the time of purchase. That is, the greater the reinvestment risk. The implication is that the yield to maturity measure for long-term coupon bonds tells little about the potential yield that an investor may realize if the bond is held to maturity. For long-term bonds, in high interest rate environments the interest on interest component may be as high as 70% of the bond's potential total dollar return.

The second characteristic that determines the degree of reinvestment risk is the coupon rate. For a given maturity and a given yield to maturity, the higher the coupon rate, the more dependent the bond's total dollar return will be on the reinvestment of the coupon payments in order to produce the yield to maturity at the time of purchase. This means that holding maturity and yield to maturity constant, premium bonds will be more dependent on interest on interest than bonds selling at par. In contrast, discount bonds will be less dependent on interest on interest than bonds selling at par. For zero coupons bonds, none of the bond's total dollar return is dependent on interest on interest. So, a zero coupon bond has no zero reinvestment risk if held to maturity.

Interest Rate Risk: As we explained earlier in this chapter, a bond's price moves in the opposite direction of the change in interest rates. As interest rates rise (fall), the price of a bond will fall (rise). For an investor who plans to hold a bond to maturity and does not have to mark a position to market, the change in the bond's price prior to maturity is of no concern; however, for an investor who may have to sell the bond prior to the maturity date, an increase in interest rates subsequent to the time the bond was purchased will mean the realization of a capital loss. Not all bonds have the same degree of interest rate risk. In Chapter 10 we shall explain the characteristics of a bond that determines its interest rate risk.

Given the assumptions underlying yield to maturity, we now can drive home with an illustration the key point that yield to maturity has limited value in assessing the relative value of corporate bonds. Suppose that an investor who has a five-year investment horizon is considering the following four corporate bonds:

Bond	Coupon	Maturity	Yield to Maturity
W	5%	3 years	9.0%
X	6%	20 years	8.6%
Y	11%	15 years	9.2%
Z	8%	5 years	8.0%

Assuming that all four corporate bonds are of the same credit quality, which one is the most attractive to this investor? An investor who selects Bond Y because it offers the highest yield to maturity is failing to recognize that the bond must be sold after five years, the price of the bond depending on the yield required in the market for 10-year, 11% coupon bonds at the time. That is, there is interest rate risk. Hence, there could be a capital gain or capital loss that will make the return higher or lower than the yield to maturity promised now. Moreover, the higher coupon on Bond Y relative to the other three bonds means that more of this bond's return will be dependent on the reinvestment of coupon interest payments.

Bond W offers the second highest yield to maturity. On the surface, it seems to be particularly attractive because it eliminates the interest rate risk faced by purchasing Bond Y. In addition, the reinvestment risk seems to be less than for the other three bonds because the coupon rate is the lowest. However, the investor would not be eliminating the reinvestment risk since after three years he must reinvest the proceeds received at maturity for two more years. The yield that the investor will realize will depend on interest rates three years from now when the investor must reinvest the proceeds.

Which is the best bond? The yield to maturity doesn't seem to be helping us identify the best bond. The answer depends on the expectations of the investor. Specifically, it depends on the interest rate at which the coupon interest payments can be reinvested until the end of the investor's investment horizon. Also, for bonds with a maturity longer than the investment horizon, it depends on the investor's expectations about interest rates at the end of the investment horizon.

Consequently, any of these bonds can be the best investment vehicle based on some reinvestment rate and some future interest rate at the end of the investment horizon. In Chapter 13 a framework for assessing the performance of a corporate bond over some investment horizon will be presented.

Yield to Call

When a corporate bond is callable, the practice has been to calculate a yield to call as well as a yield to maturity. The yield to call assumes that the issuer will call the bond at the first call date. The yield then calculated is called the *yield to first call.*

The procedure for calculating the yield to call is the same as for any yield calculation: determine the interest rate that will make the present value of the expected cash flows equal to the price. In the case of yield to call, the expected cash flows are the coupon payments to the first call date and the call price.

To illustrate the computation, consider an 18-year, 11% coupon bond with a maturity value of $100 selling for $116.90. Suppose that the first call date is 13 years from now and the call price is $105.50. The cash flows for this bond if it is called in 13 years are (1) 26 coupon payments of $5.50 every six months and (2) $105.50 in 26 six month periods from now.

The process for finding the yield to call is the same as for finding the yield to maturity. The present value for several periodic interest rates is shown below:

Annual interest rate	Semiannual rate	Present value of 26 payments of $5.5	Present value of $105.50 26 periods from now	Present value of cash flows
8.0	4.00	87.91	38.05	125.96
8.5	4.25	85.56	35.75	121.31
9.0	4.50	83.31	33.59	116.90
9.5	4.75	81.14	31.57	112.71
10.0	5.50	79.06	29.67	108.74

Since a periodic interest rate of 4.5% makes the present value of the cash flows equal to the price, 4.5% is the yield to call. Therefore, the yield to call on a bond equivalent basis is 9%.

The market convention is to calculate the yield to call and yield to maturity for a callable bond selling at a premium, selecting the lower of the two as a measure of potential yield.

Let's take a closer look at the yield to call as a measure of the potential return of a security. The yield to call does consider all three sources of potential return from owning a bond. However, as in the case of the yield to maturity, it assumes that all cash flows can be reinvested at the yield to call until the assumed call date. As we just demonstrated, this assumption may be inappropriate. Moreover, the yield to call assumes that (1) the investor will hold the bond to the assumed call date and (2) the issuer will call the bond on that date.

These assumption underlying the yield to call are often times unrealistic. They do not take into account how an investor will reinvest the proceeds if the issue is called. For example, consider two bonds, M and N. Suppose that the yield to maturity for Bond M, a five-year noncallable bond, is 10% while for Bond N the yield to call assuming the bond will be called in three years is 10.5%. Which bond is better for an investor with a five year investor horizon? It's not possible to tell for the yields cited. If the investor intends to hold the bond for five years and the issuer calls in the bond after three years, the total dollars that will be available at the end of five years will depend on the interest rate that can be earned from investing funds from the call date to the end of the investment horizon.

The framework described in Chapter 13 takes these factors into account.

Yield to Worst

The yield to first call is only the yield to the first call date. Since most bonds can be called at any time after the first call date, a yield to every coupon anniversary date following the first call date can be calculated. Then, all yield to calls calculated and the yield to maturity are compared. The lowest of these yields is called the *yield to worst*. For example, suppose that there are only four possible call dates for a callable bond and that a yield to call assuming each possible call date is 6%, 6.2%, 5.8% and 5.7%, and that the yield to maturity is 7.5%. Then the yield to worst is the minimum of these values, 5.7% in our example.

Yield Measure for Floating-Rate Securities

The coupon rate for a floating-rate security changes periodically according to some reference rate (such as LIBOR or a Treasury rate). Since the value for the benchmark in the future is not known, it is not possible to determine the cash flows. This means that a yield to maturity cannot be calculated.

A conventional measure used to estimate the potential return for a floating-rate security is the security's *effective margin*. This measure estimates the average spread or margin over the reference rate that the investor can expect to earn over the life of the security. The procedure for calculating the effective margin is as follows:

1. Determine the cash flows assuming that the reference rate does not change over the life of the security.
2. Select a margin (spread).
3. Discount the cash flows found in (1) by the current value for the reference rate plus the margin selected in (2).
4. Compare the present value of the cash flows as calculated in (3) to the price. If the present value is equal to the security's price, the effective margin is the margin assumed in (2). If the present value is not equal to the security's price, go back to (2) and try a different margin.

Exhibit 6: Calculation of the Effective Margin for a Floating-Rate Security

	Floating rate security:
	Maturity = 6 years
	Rate = LIBOR + 80 basis points
	Reset every six months

			Assumed margin (in bp)				
Period	LIBOR (%)	Cash flow*	40	42	44	48	50
1	10	5.4	5.1233	5.1224	5.1214	5.1195	5.1185
2	10	5.4	4.8609	4.8590	4.8572	4.8535	4.8516
3	10	5.4	4.6118	4.6092	4.6066	4.6013	4.5987
4	10	5.4	4.3755	4.3722	4.3689	4.3623	4.3590
5	10	5.4	4.1514	4.1474	4.1435	4.1356	4.1317
6	10	5.4	3.9387	3.9342	3.9297	3.9208	3.9163
7	10	5.4	3.7369	3.7319	3.7270	3.7171	3.7122
8	10	5.4	3.5454	3.5401	3.5347	3.5240	3.5186
9	10	5.4	3.3638	3.3580	3.3523	3.3409	3.3352
10	10	5.4	3.1914	3.1854	3.1794	3.1673	3.1613
11	10	5.4	3.0279	3.0216	3.0153	3.0028	2.9965
12	10	105.4	56.0729	55.9454	55.8182	55.5647	55.4385
		Present value	100.0000	99.8269	99.6541	99.3098	99.1381

* For periods 1-11:

   Cash flow = 100 (0.5LIBOR + Assumed margin)

For period 12:

   Cash flow = 100 (0.5LIBOR + Assumed margin) + 100

For a security selling at par, the effective margin is simply the stated spread over the reference rate.

To illustrate the calculation, suppose that a six-year floating-rate security selling for $99.3098 pays a rate based on LIBOR plus 80 basis points. The coupon rate is reset every six months. Assume that the current value for LIBOR is 10%. Exhibit 6 shows how to calculate the effective margin for this security. The second column shows the value for LIBOR. The third column sets forth the cash flows for the security. The cash flow for the first 11 periods is equal to one-half the value for LIBOR (5%) plus the semiannual spread of 40 basis points multiplied by 100. In the twelfth six-month period, the cash flow is 5.4 plus the maturity value of 100. The top row of the last five columns shows the assumed margin. The rows below the assumed margin show the present value of each cash flow. The last row gives the total present value of the cash flows.

For the five assumed margins, the present value is equal to the price of the floating-rate security (99.3098) when the assumed margin is 96 basis points. Therefore, the effective margin on a semiannual basis is 48 basis points and 96 basis points on an annual basis. (Notice that the effective margin is 80 basis points, the same as the spread to LIBOR, when the security is selling at par.)

There are two drawbacks of the effective margin as a measure of the potential return from investing in a floating-rate security. First, the measure assumes that the index will not change over the life of the security. Second, if the floating-rate security has a cap or floor, this is not taken into consideration. A methodology for valuing floaters is described in Chapter 12.

CHAPTER 10

Principles of Valuing Corporate Bonds

Valuation is the process of determining the fair value of a financial asset. The fundamental principle of valuation is that the value of any financial asset is the present value of the expected cash flow. In this chapter, the principles for valuing a bond with one or more embedded options are discussed. In the next chapter, a valuation model — the binomial method — is presented.

COMPLICATIONS IN ESTIMATING THE CASH FLOW OF A CORPORATE BOND

The cash flow for only a few types of fixed income securities are simple to project. Noncallable Treasury securities have a known cash flow. For a Treasury coupon security, the cash flow is the coupon interest payments every six months up to the maturity date and the principal payment at the maturity date. For any fixed income security in which neither the issuer nor the investor can alter the repayment of the principal before its contractual due date, the cash flow can easily be determined assuming that the issuer does not default.

Embedded Options
The difficulty in determining the cash flow is for corporate bonds under the following circumstances:

> 1. either the issuer or the investor has the option to change the contractual due date of the repayment of the principal;

2. the coupon payment is reset periodically based on some reference rate and there are restrictions on the new coupon rate (that is, there is a cap or a floor); or,
3. the investor has an option to convert the fixed income security to an equity issue.

In Chapter 5 we discussed provisions for altering principal repayment of a corporate bond. When the indenture grants the issuer or the security holder the right to change the scheduled date or dates when the principal repayment is due, the investor knows that the principal amount will be repaid, but does not know when that principal will be received. Because of this, the cash flow — which includes principal repayment and coupon interest payments — is not known with certainty.

The three most common provisions in fixed income securities that allow for the altering of the principal repayment are (1) call and refunding provisions, (2) accelerated sinking fund provisions, and (3) put provisions. In addition, as explained in Chapter 6, a conversion or an exchange provision entitles the security holder to change the cash flows. When either the issuer or security holder has the option to alter a bond's cash flows, the issue is said to have an *embedded option*. By an embedded option we mean an option that is part of the structure of a bond, as opposed to bare options, which trade separately from an underlying security.

Interest Rate Volatility

A key factor that determines whether either the issuer of the security or the investor would exercise an option is the level of interest rates in the future relative to the security's coupon rate. Specifically, for a callable bond, if the prevailing market rate at which the issuer can refund an issue is sufficiently below the issue's coupon rate to justify the costs associated with refunding the issue, the issuer is likely to call the issue. For a putable bond, if the rate on comparable securities rises such that the value of the putable bond falls below the value at which it must be repurchased by the issuer, then the investor will put the issue.

What this means is that to properly estimate the cash flow of a fixed income security it is necessary to incorporate into the analysis how interest rates can change in the future and how such changes affect the cash flow. As we will see in the next chapter, this is done in by introducing a parameter that reflects the volatility of interest rates.

SELECTING THE APPROPRIATE DISCOUNT RATE

Once the cash flow for a corporate bond is estimated, the next step is to determine the appropriate discount rate. To determine the appropriate rate, the investor must address the following three questions:

1. What is the minimum interest rate the investor should require?
2. How much more than the minimum interest rate should the investor require?
3. Should the investor use the same interest rate for each estimated cash flow or a unique interest rate for the estimated cash flow of each period?

The minimum interest rate that an investor should require is the yield available in the marketplace on a default-free cash flow. In the U.S., this is the yield on a U.S. Treasury security. The premium over the yield on a Treasury security that the investor should require should reflect the risks associated with realizing the estimated cash flow for the corporate bond. Below we address the third question.

Traditional versus Contemporary Approach

The traditional approach to valuing corporate bonds is to value all cash flows using one interest rates. The fundamental flaw with this approach is that it views each corporate bond as the same package of cash flows. For example, consider a 10-year bullet corporate bond with an 8% coupon rate. The cash flow per $100 of par value would be 19 payments of $4 every six months and $104 20 six-month periods from now. The traditional practice would discount the cash flow for all 20 periods using the same interest rate.

The proper way to view the 10-year 8% coupon bond is as a package of zero-coupon instruments. Each period's cash flow should be considered a zero-coupon instrument whose maturity value is the amount of the cash flow and whose maturity date is the date of the cash flow. Thus, the 10-year 8% coupon bond should be viewed as 20 zero-coupon instruments. The reason that this is the proper way is because it does not allow a market participant to realize an arbitrage profit by coupon stripping.

By viewing any financial asset in this way, a consistent valuation framework can be developed. For example, under the traditional approach to the valuation of fixed income securities, a 10-year zero-coupon bullet corporate bond would be viewed as the same financial asset as a 10-year 8% coupon bullet corporate bond. Viewing a bullet corporate bond as a package of zero-coupon instruments means that these two bonds would be viewed as different packages of zero-coupon corporate instruments and valued accordingly.

The difference between the traditional valuation approach and the contemporary approach is depicted in Exhibit 1 which shows how three corporate bonds should be valued. With the traditional approach, the minimum interest rate for all three securities is the yield on a 10-year U.S. Treasury security. With the contemporary approach the minimum yield for a cash flow is the theoretical rate that the U.S. Treasury would have to pay if it issued a zero-coupon bond with a maturity date equal to the maturity date of the cash flow.

Exhibit 1: Comparison of Traditional Approach and Contemporary Approach in Valuing a Corporate Bond
(Each period is six months)

Period	Discount (Interest) Rate		Corporate Bond		
	Traditional Approach (From Treasury yield curve)	Contemporary Approach (From Treasury spot rate curve)	12%	8%	0%
1	10-year	1-period	$60	$40	$0
2	10-year	2-period	60	40	0
3	10-year	3-period	60	40	0
4	10-year	4-period	60	40	0
5	10-year	5-period	60	40	0
6	10-year	6-period	60	40	0
7	10-year	7-period	60	40	0
8	10-year	8-period	60	40	0
9	10-year	9-period	60	40	0
10	10-year	10-period	60	40	0
11	10-year	11-period	60	40	0
12	10-year	12-period	60	40	0
13	10-year	13-period	60	40	0
14	10-year	14-period	60	40	0
15	10-year	15-period	60	40	0
16	10-year	16-period	60	40	0
17	10-year	17-period	60	40	0
18	10-year	18-period	60	40	0
19	10-year	19-period	60	40	0
20	10-year	20-period	1,060	1,040	1,000

Therefore, to implement the contemporary approach it is necessary to determine the theoretical rate that the U.S. Treasury would have to pay to issue a zero-coupon instrument for each maturity. Another name used for the zero-coupon rate is the *spot rate*. The spot rate can be estimated from the Treasury yield curve. The procedure for estimating the theoretical Treasury spot rates is beyond the scope of this chapter.[1] The relationship between the maturity of a Treasury zero-coupon bond and the spot rate is called the *term structure of interest rates*.

---

[1] See Chapter 2 in Frank J. Fabozzi, *The Valuation of Fixed Income Securities and Derivatives* (New Hope, PA: Frank J. Fabozzi Associates, 1995).

TRADITIONAL STATIC SPREAD ANALYSIS

Traditional analysis of the yield premium for a corporate bond involves calculating the difference between the yield to maturity (or yield to call) of the corporate issue in question and the yield to maturity of a comparable maturity Treasury coupon security. The latter is obtained from the Treasury yield curve. For example, consider the following 10-year bonds:

Issue	Coupon	Price	Yield to maturity
Treasury	6%	100.00	6.00%
Corporate	8%	104.19	7.40%

The yield spread for these two bonds as traditionally computed is 140 basis points (7.4% minus 6%). We refer to this traditional yield spread as the *nominal spread*.

Drawbacks of the Conventional Nominal Spread Measure

The drawbacks of the nominal spread are (1) for both bonds, the yield fails to take into consideration the term structure of the spot rates, and (2) in the case of callable and/or putable bonds, expected interest rate volatility may alter the cash flow of the corporate bond. Here, we focus only on the first problem: failure to consider the spot rate curve. We will deal with the second problem in the next chapter when we present the binomial model.

Determination of the Static Spread

The *static spread* is a measure of the spread that the investor would realize over the entire Treasury spot rate curve if (1) the bond is held to maturity and (2) the spot rates do not change. It is not a spread off one point on the Treasury yield curve, as is the nominal spread. The static spread is calculated as the spread that will make the present value of the cash flow from the non-Treasury bond, when discounted at the Treasury spot rate plus the spread, equal to the non-Treasury bond's price. A trial-and-error procedure is required to determine the static spread.

To illustrate how this is done, we will use the theoretical Treasury spot rates shown in the fourth column of Exhibit 2 and the 8%, 10-year corporate bond used in our earlier illustration. The third column in the exhibit is the cash flow for this corporate bond. The goal is to determine the spread that when added to all the Treasury spot rates that will produce a present value for the cash flow of the corporate bond equal to its market price, 104.19.

Exhibit 2: Determination of the Static Spread for the 8%, 10-Year Corporate Bond Selling at 104.19 to Yield 7.4%

Period	Years	Cash flow	Spot rate (%)	Present value:		
				Spread 100 bp	Spread 125 bp	Spread 146 bp
1	0.5	4.00	3.0000	3.9216	3.9168	3.9127
2	1.0	4.00	3.3000	3.8334	3.8240	3.8162
3	1.5	4.00	3.5053	3.7414	3.7277	3.7163
4	2.0	4.00	3.9164	3.6297	3.6121	3.5973
5	2.5	4.00	4.4376	3.4979	3.4767	3.4590
6	3.0	4.00	4.7520	3.3742	3.3497	3.3293
7	3.5	4.00	4.9622	3.2565	3.2290	3.2061
8	4.0	4.00	5.0650	3.1497	3.1193	3.0940
9	4.5	4.00	5.1701	3.0430	3.0100	2.9826
10	5.0	4.00	5.2772	2.9366	2.9013	2.8719
11	5.5	4.00	5.3864	2.8307	2.7933	2.7622
12	6.0	4.00	5.4976	2.7255	2.6862	2.6537
13	6.5	4.00	5.6108	2.6210	2.5801	2.5463
14	7.0	4.00	5.6643	2.5279	2.4855	2.4504
15	7.5	4.00	5.7193	2.4367	2.3929	2.3568
16	8.0	4.00	5.7755	2.3472	2.3023	2.2652
17	8.5	4.00	5.8331	2.2596	2.2137	2.1758
18	9.0	4.00	5.9584	2.1612	2.1148	2.0766
19	9.5	4.00	6.0863	2.0642	2.0174	1.9790
20	10.0	104.00	6.2169	51.1833	49.9638	48.9630
			Total:	107.5414	105.7165	104.2145*

* Closest spread to four decimals.

Suppose we select a spread of 100 basis points. To each Treasury spot rate shown in the fourth column 100 basis points is added. So, for example, the 5-year (period 10) spot rate is 6.2772% (5.2772% plus 1%). The spot rate plus 100 basis points is then used to calculate the present value of 107.5414. Because the present value is not equal to the corporate bond's price (104.19), the static spread is not 100 basis points. If a spread of 125 basis points is tried, it can be seen from the next-to-the-last column of Exhibit 2 that the present value is 105.7165; again, because this is not equal to the corporate bond's price, 125 basis points is not the static spread. The last column of Exhibit 2 shows the present value when a 146 basis point spread is tried. The present value is equal to the corporate bond's price. Therefore 146 basis points is the static spread, compared to the nominal spread of 140 basis points.

Typically, for standard coupon paying corporate bonds with a bullet maturity the static spread and the nominal spread will not differ significantly. In our example it is only six basis points. For short-term issues, there is little divergence. The main factor causing any difference is the shape of the yield curve. The steeper the yield curve, the greater the difference. The difference between the static spread and the nominal spread is greater for issue's in which the principal is repaid over time rather than only at maturity. Thus the difference between the nominal spread and the static spread can be large for sinking fund bonds in a steep yield curve environment.

TERM STRUCTURE OF CREDIT SPREADS

The term structure of U.S. Treasury securities reflects the spot rate on default-free securities. The Treasury spot rates can then be used to value any default-free security. For a corporate bond, the theoretical value is not as easy to determine. The value of a corporate bond must reflect not only the spot rate for default-free bonds but also a risk premium to reflect default risk and any options embedded in the issue. For now, we will skip the problems associated with options embedded in bonds.

In practice, the spot rate that has been used to discount the cash flow of a corporate bond is the Treasury spot rate plus a constant credit spread. For example, if the six-month Treasury spot rate is 3%, and the 10-year Treasury spot rate is 6%, and a suitable credit spread is deemed to be 100 basis points, then a 4% spot rate is used to discount a 6-month cash flow of a corporate bond and a 7% discount rate to discount a 10-year cash flow.

The drawback of this approach is that there is no reason to expect the credit spread to be the same, whenever the cash flow is expected to be received. Instead, it might be expected that the credit spread increases with the maturity of the corporate bond. That is, there is a term structure for credit spreads.

In practice, the difficulty in estimating a term structure for credit spreads is that unlike Treasury securities in which there is a wide range of maturities from which to construct a Treasury spot rate curve, there are no issuers that offer a sufficiently wide range of corporate zero-coupon securities to construct a zero-coupon spread curve. Robert Litterman and Thomas Iben of Goldman Sachs describe a procedure to construct a generic zero-coupon spread curve by credit rating and industry using data provided from a trading desk.[2]

---

[2] Robert Litterman and Thomas Iben, "Corporate Bond Valuation and the Term Structure of Credit Spreads," *Journal of Portfolio Management* (Spring1991), pp. 52-64. The original paper was published by Goldman Sachs in 1988.

Exhibit 3: Generic Zero Spread Curves for Industrial Corporations by Credit Quality (As of September 8, 1993)

Credit rating	Maturity (in years)								
	2	3	5	7	10	15	20	25	30
Aaa	22	25	28	31	33	37	41	45	48
Aa	28	32	36	38	41	49	57	65	71
A	38	47	52	58	63	71	79	88	94
Baa	55	71	77	83	89	98	107	116	123

Source: Goldman Sachs & Co.

Exhibit 3 shows in tabular form a generic zero-coupon spread term structure for industrial corporations for each investment grade credit rating as of September 8, 1993. Notice that the credit spread increases with maturity. This is a typical shape for the term structure of credit spreads.[3] In addition, the shape of the term structure is not the same for all credit ratings. The lower the credit rating, the steeper the term structure.

One implication of an upward-sloping term structure for credit spreads is that it is inappropriate to discount the cash flow from a corporate bond at a constant spread to the Treasury spot rate curve. The short-term cash flows will be undervalued, and the long-term cash flows will be overvalued.

Benchmark Spot Rate Curve

When the generic zero spreads for a given credit quality and in a given industry are added to the default-free spot rates, the resulting term structure is used to value bonds of issuers of the same credit quality in the industry sector. This term structure is referred to as the *benchmark spot rate curve* or *benchmark zero coupon rate curve*.

For example, Exhibit 4 reproduces the default-free spot rate curve in Exhibit 2. Also shown in the exhibit is a hypothetical generic zero spread for AAA industrial bonds. The resulting benchmark spot rate curve is in the next-to-the-last column. It is this spot rate curve that is used to value a AAA industrial bond. This is done in Exhibit 4 for a hypothetical 8% 10-year AAA industrial bond. The theoretical value is 108.4615.

Static Spread for any Benchmark

In the same way that a static spread relative to a default-free spot rate curve can be calculated, a static spread to any benchmark spot rate curve can be calculated. To illustrate, suppose that a hypothetical AAA industrial bond with a coupon rate of 8% and a 10-year maturity is trading at 105.5423. The static spread relative to the AAA industrial term structure is the spread that must be added to that term structure that will make the present value of the cash flow equal to the market price. In our illustration, the static spread relative to this benchmark is 40 basis points.

---

[3] Theoretical evidence for this relationship is given in Robert C. Merton, "On the Pricing of Corporate Debt: The Risk Structure of Interest Rates," *Journal of Finance* (May 1974), pp. 449-470. For empirical evidence, see O. Sarig and Arthur D. Warga, "Bond Price Data and Bond Market Liquidity," *Journal of Financial and Quantitative Analysis* (September 1989), pp. 1351-1360; and, Jerome S. Fons, "Using Default Rates to Model the Term Structure of Credit Risk," *Financial Analysts Journal* (September/October 1994), pp. 25-32.

Exhibit 4: Calculation of Value
of a Hypothetical AAA Industrial 8%, 10-Year Bond
Using Benchmark Credit Structure

Period	Years	Cash flow	Spot rate (%)	Credit spread (%)	Credit structure (%)	Present value
1	0.5	4.00	3.0000	0.20	3.2000	3.9370
2	1.0	4.00	3.3000	0.20	3.5000	3.8636
3	1.5	4.00	3.5053	0.25	3.7553	3.7829
4	2.0	4.00	3.9164	0.30	4.2164	3.6797
5	2.5	4.00	4.4376	0.35	4.7876	3.5538
6	3.0	4.00	4.7520	0.35	5.1020	3.4389
7	3.5	4.00	4.9622	0.40	5.3622	3.3237
8	4.0	4.00	5.0650	0.45	5.5150	3.2177
9	4.5	4.00	5.1701	0.45	5.6201	3.1170
10	5.0	4.00	5.2772	0.50	5.7772	3.0088
11	5.5	4.00	5.3864	0.55	5.9364	2.8995
12	6.0	4.00	5.4976	0.60	6.0976	2.7896
13	6.5	4.00	5.6108	0.65	6.2608	2.6794
14	7.0	4.00	5.6643	0.70	6.3643	2.5799
15	7.5	4.00	5.7193	0.75	6.4693	2.4813
16	8.0	4.00	5.7755	0.80	6.5755	2.3838
17	8.5	4.00	5.8331	0.85	6.6831	2.2876
18	9.0	4.00	5.9584	0.90	6.8584	2.1801
19	9.5	4.00	6.0863	0.95	7.0363	2.0737
20	10.0	104.00	6.2169	1.00	7.2169	51.1833
					Total	108.4615

Thus, when a static spread is cited, it must be cited relative to some benchmark spot rate curve. This is necessary because it indicates the credit and sector risks that are being considered when the static spread was calculated.

THE COMPONENTS OF A BOND
WITH AN EMBEDDED OPTION

To develop an analytical framework for valuing a bond with an embedded option, it is necessary to decompose a corporate bond into its component parts. A callable corporate bond is a bond in which the bondholder has sold the issuer an option (more specifically, a call option) that allows the issuer to repurchase the contractual cash flows of the bond from the bond's call date until the maturity date.

Consider the following two corporate bonds: (1) a callable bond with an 8% coupon, 20 years to maturity and callable in five years at 104 and (2) a 10-year 9% coupon bond callable immediately at par. For the first corporate bond, the bondholder owns a 5-year noncallable corporate bond and has sold a call option granting the issuer the right to call away from the bondholder 15 years of cash flows 5 years from now for a price of 104. The investor who owns the second corporate bond has a 10-year noncallable corporate bond and has sold a call option granting the issuer the right to immediately call the entire 10-year contractual cash flows, or any cash flows remaining at the time the issue is called, for 100.

Effectively, the owner of a callable corporate bond is entering into two separate transactions. First, he buys a noncallable corporate bond from the issuer for which he pays some price. Then, he sells the issuer a call option for which he receives the option price. Therefore, we can summarize the position of a callable bondholder as follows:

long a callable bond = long a noncallable bond + short a call option

In terms of value, the value of a callable bond is therefore equal to the value of the two components parts. That is,

value of a callable bond = value of a noncallable bond – value of a call option

The reason the call option value is subtracted from the value of the noncallable bond is that when the bondholder sells a call option, he receives the option value.

Actually, the position is more complicated than we just described. The issuer may be entitled to call the bond at the first call date and anytime thereafter, or at the first call date and any subsequent coupon anniversary. Thus the investor has effectively sold an American-type call option to the issuer but the call price may vary with the date the call option is exercised. This is because the call schedule for a bond may have a different call price depending on the call date. Moreover, the underlying bond for the call option is the remaining coupon payments that would have been made by the issuer had the bond not been called. For exposition purposes, it is easier to understand the principles associated with the investment characteristics of callable bonds by describing the investor's position as long a noncallable bond and short a call option.

The same logic applies to putable corporate bonds. In the case of a putable bond, the bondholder has the right to sell the bond to the issuer at a designated price and time. A putable bond can be broken into two separate transactions. First, the investor buys a nonputable bond. Second, the investor buys a put option from the issuer that allows the investor to sell the bond to the issuer. Therefore, the position of a putable bondholder can be described as:

long a putable bond = long a nonputable bond + long a put option

The value of a putable bond is then

value of a putable bond = value of a nonputable bond + value of a put option

We will use these decomposition principles in the next two chapters.

CHAPTER 11

Valuing Callable Corporate Bonds

The traditional approach to assessing the relative value of a callable corporate bond has been compare its yield to worst to the yield on a comparable maturity Treasury. There are several drawbacks of this approach. First, it assumes that the issue will be called on the date used in the yield to worst calculation. Second, it gives no recognition to the volatility of interest rates which would affect future interest rates and therefore whether the issue will be called in the future. Thus, the traditional approach can best be described as static valuation analysis since only a single interest rate scenario, usually assuming that the yield curve remains unchanged, is used.

Another pitfall of the traditional valuation approach is that in the valuation of bonds only one yield, the yield to worst, is used to discount all cash flows to the assumed call or maturity date. As we noted in the previous chapter, the appropriate discount rates are based on the theoretical spot rates. To resolve this pitfall, the static spread can be calculated. It is called a static spread since it assumes a static interest rate scenario; that is, it assumes no volatility of interest rates in the future.

In this chapter a model for valuing callable corporate bonds that overcomes the limitations of the traditional approach is described. This model is called the *binomial model*.[1] In the next chapter, we extend the model to valuing corporate bonds with other types of embedded options.

---

[1] The model described in this chapter was presented in Andrew J. Kalotay, George O. Williams, and Frank J. Fabozzi, "A Model for the Valuation of Bonds and Embedded Options," *Financial Analysts Journal* (May-June 1993), pp. 35-46.

VALUING OPTION-FREE BONDS: A REVIEW

We begin with a review of how to value an option-free corporate bond. We start with the on-the-run yield curve for the particular issuer whose bonds we want to value. The starting point is the Treasury's on-the-run yield curve. To obtain a particular issuer's on-the-run yield curve, an appropriate credit spread is added to each on-the-run Treasury issue. The credit spread need not be constant for all maturities. For example, the credit spread may increase with maturity.

In our illustration, we use the following hypothetical on-the-run issues for an issuer:

Maturity	Yield to maturity	Market Price
1 year	3.5%	100
2 years	4.2%	100
3 years	4.7%	100
4 years	5.2%	100

Each bond is trading at par value (100) so the coupon rate is equal to the yield to maturity. We will simplify the illustration by assuming annual-pay bonds.

It can be demonstrated that the spot rates would be as follows:

Year	Spot Rate
1	3.5000%
2	4.2147%
3	4.7345%
4	5.2707%

Now consider an option-free corporate bond with four years remaining to maturity and a coupon rate of 6.5%. The value of this bond is determined by discounting this issue's cash flows by the spot rates as shown below:

$$\frac{\$6.5}{(1.035)^1} + \frac{\$6.5}{(1.042147)^2} + \frac{\$6.5}{(1.047345)^3} + \frac{\$100 + \$6.5}{(1.052707)^4} = \$104.643$$

INTRODUCING INTEREST RATE VOLATILITY

Once we allow for embedded options, consideration must be given to interest rate volatility. This can be done by introducing a binomial interest rate tree. This tree is nothing more than a graphical depiction of the one-period or short rates over time based on some assumption about interest rate volatility. How this tree is constructed is illustrated next.

Exhibit 1: Four-Year Binomial Interest Rate Tree

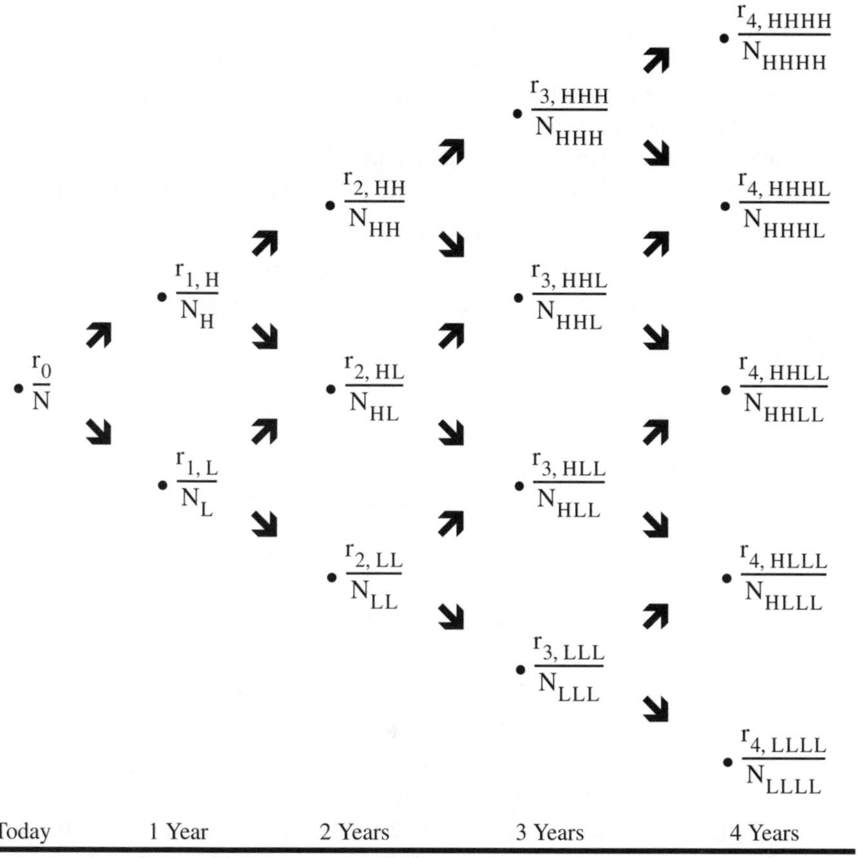

| Today | 1 Year | 2 Years | 3 Years | 4 Years |

BINOMIAL INTEREST RATE TREE

Exhibit 1 shows an example of a binomial interest rate tree. In this tree, each node (bold circle) represents a time period that is equal to one year from the node to its left. Each node is labeled with an N, representing node, and a subscript that indicates the path that the one-year rate took to get to that node. L represents the lower of the two one-year rates and H represents the higher of the two one-year rates. For example, node N_{HH} means to get to that node the following path for one-year rates occurred: the one-year rate realized is the higher of the two rates in the first year and then the higher of the one-year rates in the second year.[2]

---

[2] Note that N_{HL} is equivalent to N_{LH} in the second year and that in the third year N_{HHL} is equivalent to N_{HLH} and N_{LHH} and that N_{HLL} is equivalent to N_{LLH}. We have simply selected one label for a node rather than clutter up the figure with unnecessary information.

Look first at the point denoted by just N in Exhibit 1. This is the root of the tree and is nothing more than the current one-year spot rate, or equivalently the current one-year rate, which we denote by r_0. What we have assumed in creating this tree is that the one-year rate can take on two possible values the next period and the two rates have the same probability of occurring. One rate will be higher than the other. It is assumed that the one-year rate can evolve over time based on a random process called a lognormal random walk with a certain volatility.

We use the following notation to describe the tree in the first year. Let

$$\sigma = \text{assumed volatility of the one-year rate}$$
$$r_{1,L} = \text{the lower one-year rate one year from now}$$
$$r_{1,H} = \text{the higher one-year rate one year from now}$$

The relationship between $r_{1,L}$ and $r_{1,H}$ is as follows:

$$r_{1,H} = r_{1,L}(e^{2\sigma})$$

where e is the base of the natural logarithm 2.71828.

For example, suppose that $r_{1,L}$ is 4.4448% and σ is 10% per year, then:

$$r_{1,H} = 4.4448\% \, (e^{2 \times 0.10}) = 5.4289\%$$

In the second year, there are three possible values for the one-year rate, which we will denote as follows:

$$r_{2,LL} = \text{one-year rate in second year assuming the lower rate in the}$$
first year and the lower rate in the second year
$$r_{2,HH} = \text{one-year rate in second year assuming the higher rate in the}$$
first year and the higher rate in the second year
$$r_{2,HL} = \text{one-year rate in second year assuming the higher rate in the}$$
first year and the lower rate in the second year or equivalently the lower rate in the first year and the higher rate in the second year

The relationship between $r_{2,LL}$ and the other two one-year rates is as follows:

$$r_{2,HH} = r_{2,LL}(e^{4\sigma}) \quad \text{and} \quad r_{2,HL} = r_{2,LL}(e^{2\sigma})$$

So, for example, if $r_{2,LL}$ is 4.6958%, then assuming once again that σ is 10%, then

$$r_{2,HH} = 4.6958\% \, (e^{4 \times 0.10}) = 7.0053\%$$

and

$$r_{2,HL} = 4.6958\% \, (e^{2 \times 0.10}) = 5.7354\%$$

Exhibit 2: Four-Year Binomial Interest Rate Tree with One-Year Rates*

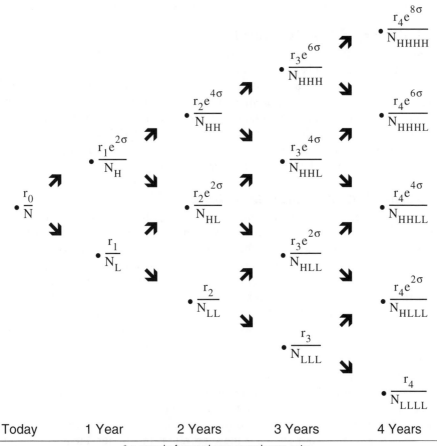

Today	1 Year	2 Years	3 Years	4 Years

* r_t equals forward one-year lower rate.

In the third year there are four possible values for the one-year rate, which are denoted as follows: $r_{3,HHH}$, $r_{3,HHL}$, $r_{3,HLL}$, and $r_{3,LLL}$, and whose first three values are related to the last as follows:

$$r_{3,HHH} = (e^{6\sigma})\, r_{3,LLL}$$
$$r_{3,HHL} = (e^{4\sigma})\, r_{3,LLL}$$
$$r_{3,HLL} = (e^{2\sigma})\, r_{3,LLL}$$

Exhibit 1 shows the notation for a 4-year binomial interest rate tree. We can simplify the notation by letting r_t be the one-year rate t years from now for the lower rate since all the other short rates t years from now depend on that rate. Exhibit 2 shows the interest rate tree using this simplified notation.

Before we go on to show how to use this binomial interest rate tree to value bonds, let's focus on two issues here. First, what does the volatility parameter σ represent? Second, how do we find the value of the bond at each node?

Volatility and the Standard Deviation

It can be shown that the standard deviation of the one-year rate is equal to $r_0\sigma$.[3] The standard deviation is a statistical measure of volatility. It is important to see that the process that we assumed generates the binomial interest rate tree (or equivalently the short rates), implies that volatility is measured relative to the current level of rates. For example, if σ is 10% and the one-year rate (r_0) is 4%, then the standard deviation of the one-year rate is 4% × 10% = 0.4% or 40 basis points. However, if the current one-year rate is 12%, the standard deviation of the one-year rate would be 12% × 10% or 120 basis points.

Determining the Value at a Node

To find the value of the bond at a node, we first calculate the bond's value at the two nodes to the right of the node we are interested in. For example, in Exhibit 2, suppose we want to determine the bond's value at node N_H. The bond's value at node N_{HH} and N_{HL} must be determined. Hold aside for now how we get these two values because as we will see the process involves starting from the last year in the tree and working backwards to get the final solution we want, so these two values will be known.

Effectively what we are saying is that if we are at some node, then the value at that node will depend on the future cash flows. In turn, the future cash flows depend on (1) the bond's value one year from now and (2) the coupon payment one year from now. The latter is known. The former depends on whether the one-year rate is the higher or lower rate. The bond's value depending on whether the rate is the higher or lower rate is reported at the two nodes to the right of the node that is the focus of our attention. So, the cash flow at a node will be either (1) the bond's value if the short rate is the higher rate plus the coupon payment, or (2) the bond's value if the short rate is the lower rate plus the coupon payment. For example, suppose that we are interested in the bond's value at N_H. The cash flow will be either the bond's value at N_{HH} plus the coupon payment, or the bond's value at N_{HL} plus the coupon payment.

---

[3] This can be seen by noting that

$$e^{2\sigma} \approx 1 + 2\sigma.$$

Then the standard deviation of the one-period rate is

$$\frac{re^{2\sigma} - r}{2} \approx \frac{r + 2\sigma r - r}{2} = \sigma r.$$

Exhibit 3: Calculating a Value at a Node

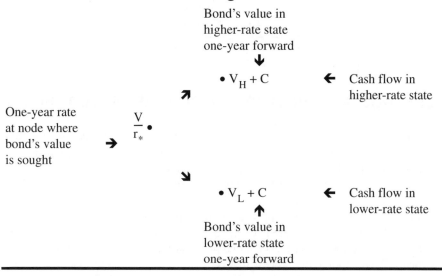

Bond's value in
higher-rate state
one-year forward

$\bullet\, V_H + C$ ⟵ Cash flow in
higher-rate state

One-year rate
at node where
bond's value
is sought

$\dfrac{V}{r_*} \bullet$

$\bullet\, V_L + C$ ⟵ Cash flow in
lower-rate state

Bond's value in
lower-rate state
one-year forward

To get the bond's value at a node we follow the fundamental rule for valuation: the value is the present value of the expected cash flows. The appropriate discount rate to use is the one-year rate at the node. Now there are two present values in this case: the present value if the one-year rate is the higher rate and one if it is the lower rate. Since it is assumed that the probability of both outcomes is equal, an average of the two present values is computed. This is illustrated in Exhibit 3 for any node assuming that the one-year rate is r_* at the node where the valuation is sought and letting:

$$V_H = \text{the bond's value for the higher one-year rate}$$
$$V_L = \text{the bond's value for the lower one-year rate}$$
$$C = \text{coupon payment}$$

Using our notation, the cash flow at a node is either:

$$V_H + C \text{ for the higher one-year rate}$$
$$V_L + C \text{ for the lower one-year rate}$$

The present value of these two cash flows using the one-year rate at the node, r_*, is:

$$\frac{V_H + C}{(1 + r_*)} = \text{present value for the higher one-year rate}$$

$$\frac{V_L + C}{(1 + r_*)} = \text{present value for the lower one-year rate}$$

Then, the value of the bond at the node is found as follows:

$$\text{Value at a node} = \frac{1}{2}\left[\frac{V_H + C}{(1 + r_*)} + \frac{V_L + C}{(1 + r_*)}\right]$$

CONSTRUCTING THE BINOMIAL INTEREST RATE TREE

To see how to construct the binomial interest rate tree, let's use the assumed on-the-run yields we used earlier. We will assume that volatility, σ, is 10% and construct a two-year tree using the two-year bond with a coupon rate of 4.2%.

Exhibit 4 shows a more detailed binomial interest rate tree with the cash flow shown at each node. We'll see how all the values reported in the exhibit are obtained. The root rate for the tree, r_0, is simply the current one-year rate, 3.5%.

In the first year there are two possible one-year rates, the higher rate and the lower rate. What we want to find is the two one-year rates that will be consistent with the volatility assumption, the process that is assumed to generate the short rates, and the observed market value of the bond. There is no simple formula for this. It must be found by an iterative process (i.e., trial-and-error). The steps are described and illustrated below.

Step 1: Select a value for r_1. Recall that r_1 is the lower one-year rate. In this first trial, we *arbitrarily* selected a value of 4.75%.

Step 2: Determine the corresponding value for the higher one-year rate. As explained earlier, this rate is related to the lower one-year rate as follows: $r_1 e^{2\sigma}$. Since r_1 is 4.75%, the higher one-year rate is 5.8017% (= 4.75% $e^{2 \times .10}$). This value is reported in Exhibit 4 at node N_H.

Step 3: Compute the bond value's one year from now. This value is determined as follows:

> *3a.* Determine the bond's value two years from now. In our example, this is simple. Since we are using a two-year bond, the bond's value is its maturity value ($100) plus its final coupon payment ($4.2). Thus, it is $104.2.

> *3b.* Calculate the present value of the bond's value found in 3a for the higher rate in the second year. The appropriate discount rate is the higher one-year rate, 5.8017% in our example. The present value is $98.486 (= $104.2/1.058017). This is the value of V_H that we referred to earlier.

Exhibit 4: The One-Year Rates for Year 1
Using the Two-Year 4.2% On-the-Run Issue: First Trial

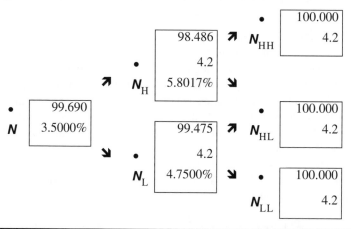

3c. Calculate the present value of the bond's value assumed in 3a for the lower rate. The discount rate assumed for the lower one-year rate is 4.75%. The present value is \$99.475 (= \$104.2/1.0475) and is the value of V_L.

3d. Add the coupon to both V_H and V_L to get the cash flow at N_H and N_L, respectively. In our example we have \$102.686 for the higher rate and \$103.675 for the lower rate.

3e. Calculate the present value of the two values using the one-year rate r_*. At this point in the valuation, r_* is the root rate, 3.50%. Therefore,

$$\frac{V_H + C}{1 + r_*} = \frac{\$102.686}{1.035} = \$99.213$$

and

$$\frac{V_L + C}{1 + r_*} = \frac{\$103.675}{1.035} = \$100.169$$

Step 4: Calculate the average present value of the two cash flows in Step 3. This is the value we referred to earlier as

$$\text{Value at a node} = \frac{1}{2}\left[\frac{V_H + C}{(1 + r_*)} + \frac{V_L + C}{(1 + r_*)}\right]$$

In our example, we have

$$\text{Value at a node} = \frac{1}{2}[\$99.213 + \$100.169] = \$99.691$$

Step 5: Compare the value in Step 4 to the bond's market value. If the two values are the same, then the r_1 used in this trial is the one we seek. This is the one-year rate that would then be used in the binomial interest rate tree for the lower rate and used to calculate the corresponding higher rate. If, instead, the value found in Step 4 is not equal to the market value of the bond, this means that the value r_1 in this trial is not the one-year rate that is consistent with (1) the volatility assumption, (2) the process assumed to generate the one-year rate, and (3) the observed market value of the bond. In this case, the five steps are repeated with a different value for r_1.

When r_1 is 4.75%, a value of $99.691 results in Step 4 which is less than the observed market price of $100. Therefore, 4.75% is too large and the five steps must be repeated trying a lower rate for r_1.

Let's jump right to the correct rate for r_1 in this example and rework steps 1 through 5. This occurs when r_1 is 4.4448%. The corresponding binomial interest rate tree is shown in Exhibit 5.

Step 1: In this trial we select a value of 4.4448% for r_1, the lower one-year rate.

Step 2: The corresponding value for the higher one-year rate is 5.4289% (= 4.4448% $e^{2x.10}$).

Step 3: The bond's value one year from now is determined as follows:

3a. The bond's value two years from now is $104.2, just as in the first trial.

3b. The present value of the bond's value found in 3a for the higher one-year rate, V_H, is $98.834 (= $104.2/1.054289).

3c. The present value of the bond's value found in 3a for the lower one-year rate, V_L, is $99.766 (= $104.2/1.044448).

3d. Adding the coupon to V_H and V_L, we get $103.034 as the cash flow for the higher rate and $103.966 as the cash flow for the lower rate.

3e. The present value of the two cash flows using the one-year rate at the node to the left, 3.5%, gives

$$\frac{V_H + C}{1 + r_*} = \frac{\$103.034}{1.035} = \$99.550$$

and,

$$\frac{V_L + C}{1 + r_*} = \frac{\$103.966}{1.035} = \$100.450$$

Exhibit 5: The One-Year Rates for Year 1 Using the Two-Year 4.2% On-the-Run Issue

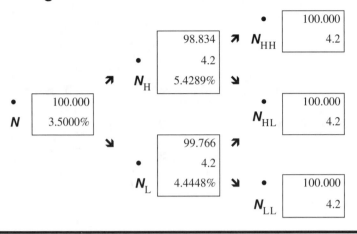

Step 4: The average present value is $100, which is the value at the node.

Step 5: Since the average present value is equal to the observed market price of $100, r_1 or $r_{1,L}$ is 4.4448% and $r_{1,H}$ is 5.4289%.

We can "grow" this tree for one more year by determining r_2. Now we will use the three-year on-the-run issue, the 4.7% coupon bond, to get r_2. The same five steps are used in an iterative process to find the one-year rates in the tree two years from now. Our objective is now to find the value of r_2 that will produce a bond value of $100 (since the three-year on-the-run issue has a market price of $100) and is consistent with (1) a volatility assumption of 10%, (2) a current one-year rate of 3.5%, and (3) the two rates one year from now of 4.4448% (the lower rate) and 5.4289% (the higher rate).

We explain how this is done using Exhibit 6. Let's look at how we get the information in the exhibit. The maturity value and coupon payment are shown in the boxes at the four nodes three years from now. Since the three-year on-the-run issue has a maturity value of $100 and a coupon payment of $4.7, these values are the same in the box shown at each node. For the three nodes two years from now the coupon payment of $4.7 is shown. Unknown at these three nodes are (1) the three rates two years from now and (2) the value of the bond two years from now. For the two nodes one year from now, the coupon payment is known, as are the one-year rates one year from now. These are the rates found earlier. The value of the bond, which depends on the bond values at the nodes to the right, are unknown at these two nodes. All of the unknown values are indicated by a question mark.

Exhibit 6: Information for Deriving the One-Year Rates for Year 3 Using the Three-Year 4.7% On-the-Run Issue

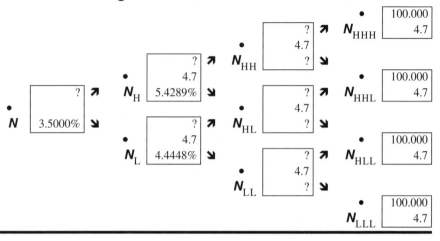

Exhibit 7 is the same as Exhibit 6 complete with the values previously unknown. As can be seen from Exhibit 7, the value of r_2, or equivalently $r_{2,LL}$, which will produce the desired result is 4.6958%. We showed earlier that the corresponding rates $r_{2,HL}$ and $r_{2,HH}$ would be 5.7354% and 7.0053%, respectively. To verify that these are the one-year rates two years from now, work backwards from the four nodes at the right of the tree in Exhibit 7. For example, the value in the box at N_{HH} is found by taking the value of $104.7 at the two nodes to its right and discounting at 7.0053%. The value is $97.846. (Since it is the same value for both nodes to the right, it is also the average value.) Similarly, the value in the box at N_{HL} is found by discounting $104.70 by 5.7354% and at N_{LL} by discounting at 4.6958%. The same procedure used in Exhibits 4 and 5 is used to get the values at the other nodes.

VALUING AN OPTION-FREE BOND WITH THE TREE

Exhibit 8 shows the one-year rates or binomial interest rate tree that can then be used to value any bond for this issuer with a maturity up to four years. To illustrate how to use the binomial interest rate tree, consider a 6.5% option-free corporate bond with four years remaining to maturity. Also assume that the issuer's on-the-run yield curve is the one given earlier and hence the appropriate binomial interest rate tree is the one in Exhibit 8. Exhibit 9 shows the various values in the discounting process, and produces a bond value of $104.643.

It is important to note that this value is identical to the bond value found earlier when we discounted at either the spot rates or the one-year forward rates. We should expect to find this result since our bond is option free. This clearly demonstrates that the valuation model is consistent with the standard valuation model for an option-free bond.

Exhibit 7: The One-Year Rates for Year 2 Using the Three-Year 4.7% On-the-Run Issue

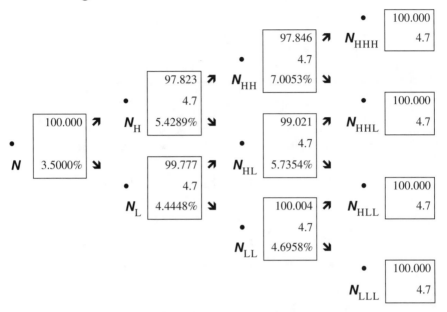

Exhibit 8: Binomial Interest Rate Tree for Valuing Up to a Four-Year Bond for Issuer (10% Volatility Assumed)

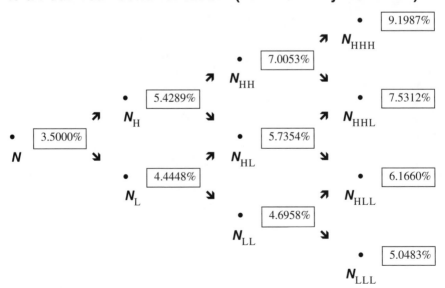

Exhibit 9: Valuing an Option-Free Corporate Bond with Four Years to Maturity and a Coupon Rate of 6.5% (10% Volatility Assumed)

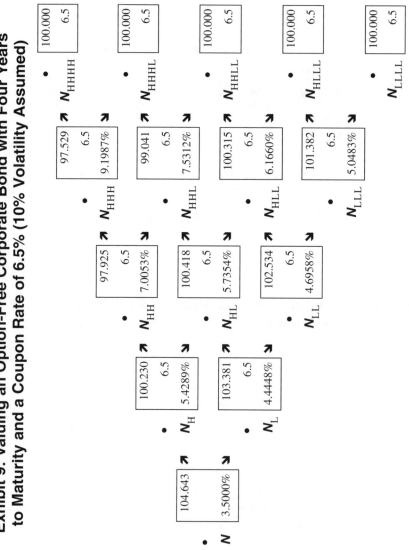

VALUING A CALLABLE CORPORATE BOND

Now we will demonstrate how the binomial interest rate tree can be applied to value a callable corporate bond. The valuation process proceeds in the same fashion as in the case of an option-free bond, but with one exception: when the call option may be exercised by the issuer, the bond value at a node must be changed to reflect the lesser of its values if it is not called (i.e., the value obtained by applying the recursive valuation formula described above) and the call price.

For example, consider a 6.5% corporate bond with four years remaining to maturity that is callable in one year at $100. Exhibit 10 shows two values at each node of the binomial interest rate tree. The discounting process explained above is used to calculate the first of the two values at each node. The second value is the value based on whether the issue will be called. For simplicity, let's assume that this issuer calls the issue if it exceeds the call price. Then, in Exhibit 10 at nodes N_L, N_H, N_{LL}, N_{HL}, N_{LLL}, and N_{HLL}, the values from the recursive valuation formula are $101.968, $100.032, $101.723, $100.270, $101.382, and $100.315. These values exceed the assumed call price ($100) and therefore the second value is $100 rather the calculated value. It is the second value that is used in subsequent calculations. The root of the tree indicates that the value for this callable bond is $102.899.

The question that we have not addressed in our illustration, which is nonetheless important, is the circumstances under which the issuer will call the bond. A detailed explanation of the call rule is beyond the scope of this chapter. Basically, it involves determining when it would be economic for the issuer on an after-tax basis to call the issue.

Suppose instead that the call price schedule is 102 in year 1, 101 in year 2, and 100 in year 3. Also assume that the bond will not be called unless it exceeds the call price for that year. Exhibit 11 shows the value at each node and the value of the callable bond. The call price schedule results in a greater value for the callable bond, $103.942 compared to $102.899 when the call price is 100 in each year.

Determining the Call Option Value

As explained in Chapter 5, the value of a callable bond is equal to the value of an option-free bond minus the value of the call option. This means that:

> Value of a call option =
> Value of an option-free bond – Value of a callable bond

We have just seen how the value of an option-free bond and the value of a callable bond can be determined. The difference between the two values is therefore the value of the call option.

In our illustration, the value of the option-free bond is $104.643. If the call price is $100 in each year and the value of the callable bond is $102.899, the value of the call option is $1.744 (= $104.634 – $102.899).

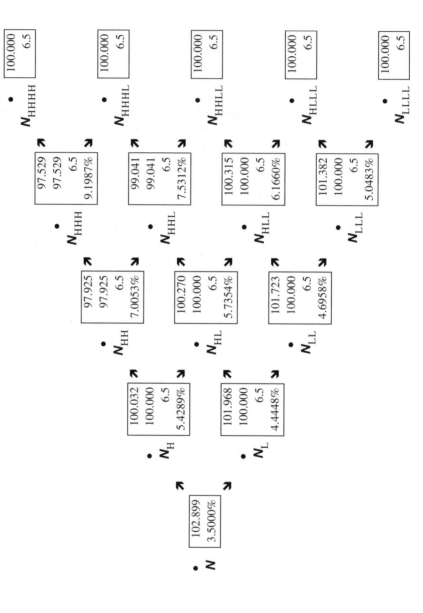

Exhibit 10: Valuing a Callable Corporate Bond with Four Years to Maturity, a Coupon Rate of 6.5%, and Callable in One Year at 100 (10% Volatility Assumed)

N
102.899
3.5000%

N_H
100.032
100.000
6.5
5.4289%

N_L
101.968
100.000
6.5
4.4448%

N_{HH}
97.925
97.925
6.5
7.0053%

N_{HL}
100.270
100.000
6.5
5.7354%

N_{LL}
101.723
100.000
6.5
4.6958%

N_{HHH}
97.529
97.529
6.5
9.1987%

N_{HHL}
99.041
99.041
6.5
7.5312%

N_{HLL}
100.315
100.000
6.5
6.1660%

N_{LLL}
101.382
100.000
6.5
5.0483%

N_{HHHH}
100.000
6.5

N_{HHHL}
100.000
6.5

N_{HHLL}
100.000
6.5

N_{HLLL}
100.000
6.5

N_{LLLL}
100.000
6.5

Exhibit 11: Valuing a Callable Corporate Bond with Four Years to Maturity, a Coupon Rate of 6.5%, and with a Call Price Schedule (10% Volatility Assumed)

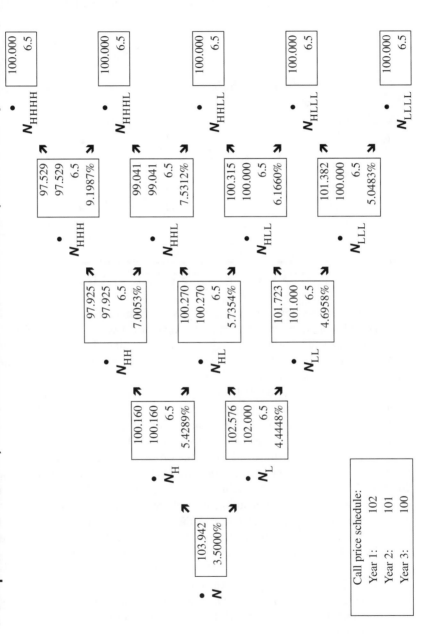

Call price schedule:
Year 1:   102
Year 2:   101
Year 3:   100

Exhibit 12: Binomial Interest Rate Tree for Valuing Up to a Four-Year Bond for Issuer (20% Volatility Assumed)

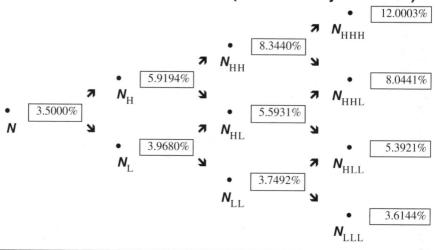

VOLATILITY AND THE THEORETICAL VALUE

In our illustration, interest rate volatility was assumed to be 10%. The volatility assumption has an important impact on the theoretical value. More specifically, the higher the expected volatility, the higher the value of an option. The same is true for an option embedded in a bond. Correspondingly, this affects the value of the bond with an embedded option.

For example, for a callable bond, a higher interest rate volatility assumption means that the value of the call option increases and, since the value of the option-free bond is not affected, the value of the callable bond must be lower. For a putable bond, higher interest rate volatility means that its value will be higher.

We will demonstrate this using the on-the-run yield curve in our previous illustrations. In the previous illustrations, we assumed interest rate volatility of 10%. To show the effect of higher volatility, we will assume volatility of 20%. Exhibit 12 gives the corresponding binomial interest rate tree. Exhibit 13 verifies that the binomial interest rate tree provides the same value for the option-free bond, $104.643.

Exhibits 14 shows the calculation for the callable bond assuming interest rate volatility of 20%. It is assumed that the issue is callable at par beginning in year 1. The value of the callable bond is $102.108 if volatility is assumed to be 20% compared to $102.899 if volatility is assumed to be 10%.

In the construction of the binomial interest rate, it was assumed that volatility is the same for each year. The methodology can be extended to incorporate a term structure of volatility.

Exhibit 13: Valuing an Option-Free Corporate Bond with Four Years to Maturity and a Coupon Rate of 6.5% (20% Volatility Assumed)

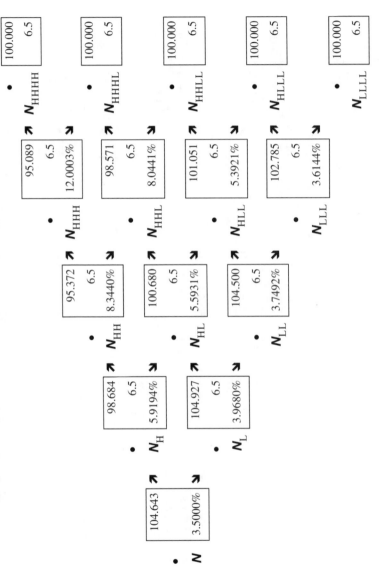

Exhibit 14: Valuing a Callable Corporate Bond with Four Years to Maturity, a Coupon Rate of 6.5%, and Callable in One Year at 100 (20% Volatility Assumed)

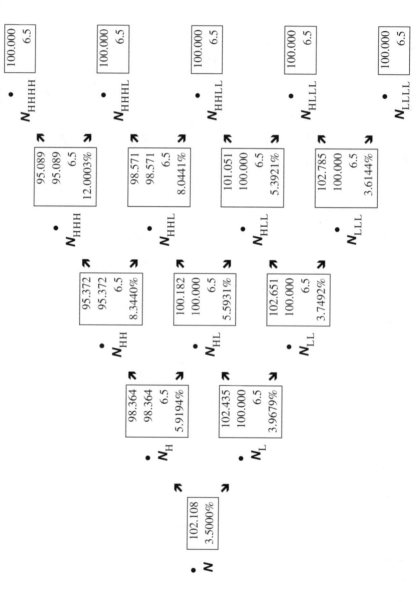

OPTION-ADJUSTED SPREAD

What an investor seeks to do is to buy corporate bonds whose value is greater than their market price. A valuation model such as the binomial model allows an investor to estimate the value of a corporate bond, which at this point would be sufficient to determine the fairness of the price of the security. That is, the investor can say that this bond is 1 point cheap or 2 points cheap, and so on.

A valuation model need not stop here, however. Instead, it can convert the divergence between the price observed in the market for the corporate bond and the value derived from the model into a yield spread measure. This step is necessary since most market participants find it more convenient to think about yield spread than about price differences.

The *option-adjusted spread* (OAS) was developed as a measure of the yield spread that can be used to convert dollar differences between value and price. The option-adjusted spread is the constant spread that when added to all the rates on the binomial interest rate tree will make the theoretical value equal to the market price.

To illustrate how to calculate the OAS for a corporate bond, suppose the market price of the four-year, 6.5% callable bond is $102.218 and the theoretical value assuming 10% volatility is $102.899. This means that this bond is cheap by $0.681 according to the valuation model. if the market price is $102.218, the OAS would be the constant spread added to every rate in Exhibit 8 that will make the theoretical value equal to $102.218. The solution in this case would be 35 basis points. This can be verified in Exhibit 15 which shows the value of this issue by adding 35 basis points to each rate.

The reason that the resulting spread is referred to as "option-adjusted" is because the cash flows of the security whose value we seek are adjusted to reflect any embedded options. In contrast, the static spread does not consider how the cash flows will change when interest rates change in the future. That is, the static spread assumes that interest rate volatility is zero. Consequently, the static spread is also referred to as the *zero volatility OAS*.

While the product of a valuation model is the OAS, the process can be worked in reverse. For a specified OAS, the valuation model can determine the theoretical value of the security that is consistent with that OAS.

As with the value of a bond with an embedded option, the OAS will depend on the volatility assumption. For a given bond price, the higher the interest rate volatility assumed, the lower the OAS for a callable bond and the higher the OAS for a putable bond. For example, if volatility is 20% rather than 10%, the OAS would be -11 basis points. This illustration clearly demonstrates the importance of the volatility assumption. Assuming volatility of 10%, the OAS is 35 basis points. At 20% volatility, the OAS declines and, in this case is negative and therefore overvalued.

Exhibit 15: Demonstration that the Option-Adjusted Spread is 35 Basis Points For a 6.5% Callable Bond Selling at 102.218 (Assuming 10% Volatility)

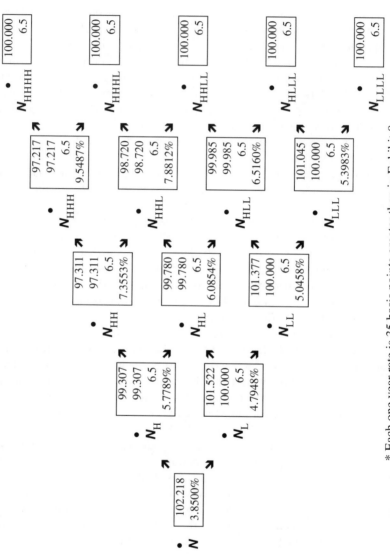

				N_{HHHH}	100.000	6.5
			N_{HHH}	97.217	97.217	6.5	9.5487%
		N_{HH}	97.311	97.311	6.5	7.3553%		N_{HHHL}	100.000	6.5
	N_H	99.307	99.307	6.5	5.7789%		N_{HHL}	98.720	98.720	6.5	7.8812%
N	102.218	3.8500%		N_{HL}	99.780	99.780	6.5	6.0854%		N_{HHLL}	100.000	6.5
	N_L	101.522	100.000	6.5	4.7948%		N_{HLL}	99.985	99.985	6.5	6.5160%
		N_{LL}	101.377	100.000	6.5	5.0458%		N_{HLLL}	100.000	6.5
			N_{LLL}	101.045	100.000	6.5	5.3983%
				N_{LLLL}	100.000	6.5

* Each one year rate is 35 basis points greater than in Exhibit 8

CHAPTER 12

Valuing Other Corporate Bond Structures

The bond valuation framework presented in the previous chapter can be used to analyze other embedded options such as put options, floating-rate notes, the optional accelerated redemption granted to an issuer in fulfilling its sinking fund requirement, stepped-up callable notes, and range notes. The model can also be used to value a bond with multiple or interrelated embedded options. The procedure is to adjust the bond value at each node of the tree based on whether the embedded option is granted. In this chapter, we demonstrate how this is done for several corporate bond structures.[1] We also look at how to value inverse floaters and present an option-based approach to the valuation of convertible bonds.

PUTABLE BOND

A putable bond is one in which the bondholder has the right to force the issuer to pay off the bond prior to the maturity date. To illustrate how the binomial method can be used to value a putable bond, suppose that a 6.5% corporate bond with four years remaining to maturity is putable in one year at par ($100). Also assume that the appropriate binomial interest rate tree for this issuer is the one in Exhibit 8 of Chapter 11.

---

[1] For an explanation how the binomial model can be used to value the accelerated sinking fund provision, see Andrew J. Kalotay and George O. Williams, "The Valuation and Management of Bonds with Sinking Fund Provisions," *Financial Analysts Journal* (March-April 1992), pp. 59-67.

Exhibit 1 shows the binomial interest rate tree with the bond value altered at three nodes (N_{HH}, N_{HHH}, and N_{HHL}) because the bond value at these nodes is less than $100, the assumed value at which the bond can be put. The value of this putable bond is $105.327.

Since the value of an option-free bond can be expressed as the value of a putable bond minus the value of a put option on that bond, this means that:

Value of a put option = Value of an option-free bond − Value of a putable bond

In our example, since the value of the putable bond is $105.327 and the value of the corresponding option-free bond is $104.643, the value of the put option is − $0.684. The negative sign indicates the issuer has sold the option, or equivalently, the investor has purchased the option.

Suppose that a bond is both putable and callable. The procedure for valuing such a structure is to adjust the value at each node to reflect whether the issue would be put or call. To illustrate this, consider the 4-year callable bond analyzed in the previous chapter that had a call schedule. The valuation of this issue is shown in Exhibit 11 of the previous chapter. Suppose the issue is putable in year 3 at par value. Exhibit 2 shows how to value this callable/putable issue. In year 3, the put value is shown as the second value in the two boxes where the value at the top of the box is less than par. The value of this callable/putable issue is 104.413, which is greater than the callable issue whose value is 103.942.

STEP-UP CALLABLE NOTES

Step-up callable notes are callable fixed income instruments whose coupon rate is increased (i.e., "stepped up") at designated times. When the coupon rate is increased only once over the security's life, it is said to be a *single step-up callable note*. A *multiple step-up callable note* is a step-up callable note whose coupon is increased more than one time over the life of the security.

To illustrate how the binomial method can be used to value step-up callable notes, let's begin with a single step-up callable note. Suppose that a four-year step-up callable note pays 4.25% for two years and then 7.5% for two more years. Assume that this note is callable at par at the end of years two and three. We will use the binomial interest rate tree given in Exhibit 8 of Chapter 11 to value this note.

Exhibit 3 shows the value of a corresponding single step-up *noncallable* note. The valuation procedure is identical to that performed in Exhibit 9 of Chapter 11 except that the coupon in the box at each node reflects the step-up terms. The value is 102.082. Exhibit 4 shows that the value of the single step-up callable note is 100.031. The value of the embedded call option is equal to the difference in the step-up noncallable note value and the step-up callable note value, 2.051.

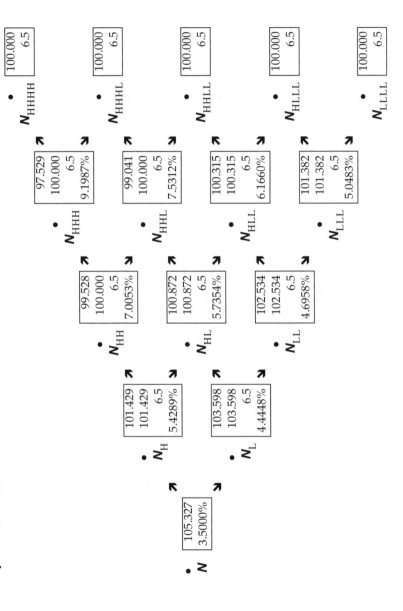

Exhibit 1: Valuing a Putable Corporate Bond with Four Years to Maturity, a Coupon Rate of 6.5%, and Putable in One Year at 100 (10% Volatility Assumed)

Exhibit 2: Valuing a Putable/Callable Issue (10% Volatility Assumed)

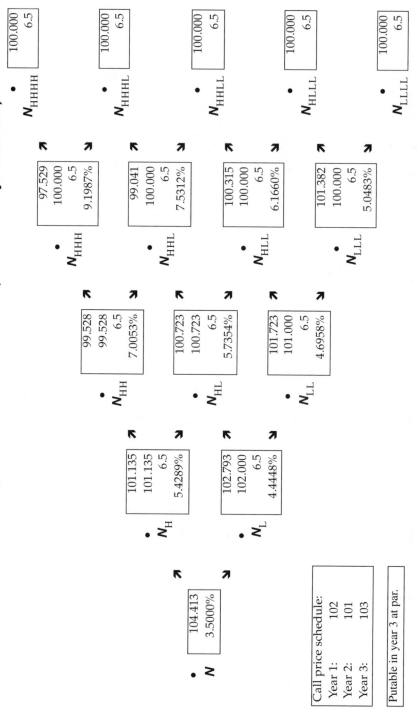

N	104.413
	3.5000%

*N*_H	101.135
	101.135
	6.5
	5.4289%

*N*_L	102.793
	102.000
	6.5
	4.4448%

*N*_HH	99.528
	99.528
	6.5
	7.0053%

*N*_HL	100.723
	100.723
	6.5
	5.7354%

*N*_LL	101.723
	101.000
	6.5
	4.6958%

*N*_HHH	97.529
	100.000
	6.5
	9.1987%

*N*_HHL	99.041
	100.000
	6.5
	7.5312%

*N*_HLL	100.315
	100.000
	6.5
	6.1660%

*N*_LLL	101.382
	100.000
	6.5
	5.0483%

*N*_HHHH	100.000
	6.5

*N*_HHHL	100.000
	6.5

*N*_HHLL	100.000
	6.5

*N*_HLLL	100.000
	6.5

*N*_LLLL	100.000
	6.5

Call price schedule:
Year 1: 102
Year 2: 101
Year 3: 103

Putable in year 3 at par.

Exhibit 3: Valuing a Single Step-Up Noncallable Note with Four Years to Maturity (10% Volatility Assumed)

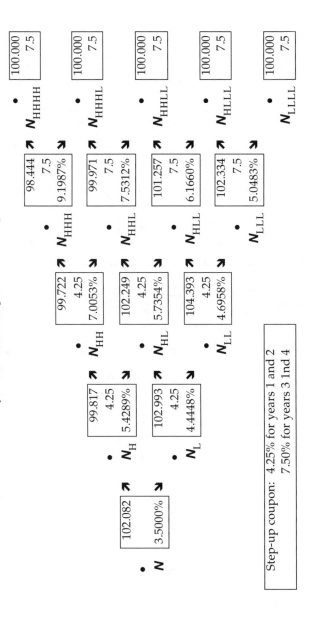

									100.000
									7.5
								N_{HHHH}	
							98.444		100.000
							7.5		7.5
							9.1987%		
						N_{HHH}		N_{HHHL}	
					99.722		99.971		100.000
					4.25		7.5		7.5
					7.0053%		7.5312%		
				N_{HH}		N_{HHL}		N_{HHLL}	
			99.817		102.249		101.257		100.000
			4.25		4.25		7.5		7.5
			5.4289%		5.7354%		6.1660%		
		N_H		N_{HL}		N_{HLL}		N_{HLLL}	
	102.082		102.993		104.393		102.334		100.000
	3.5000%		4.25		4.25		7.5		7.5
N		N_L		4.4448%		4.6958%		5.0483%	
				N_{LL}		N_{LLL}		N_{LLLL}	

Step-up coupon: 4.25% for years 1 and 2
7.50% for years 3 1nd 4

Exhibit 4: Valuing a Single Step-Up Callable Note with Four Years to Maturity, Callable in Two Years at 100 (10% Volatility Assumed)

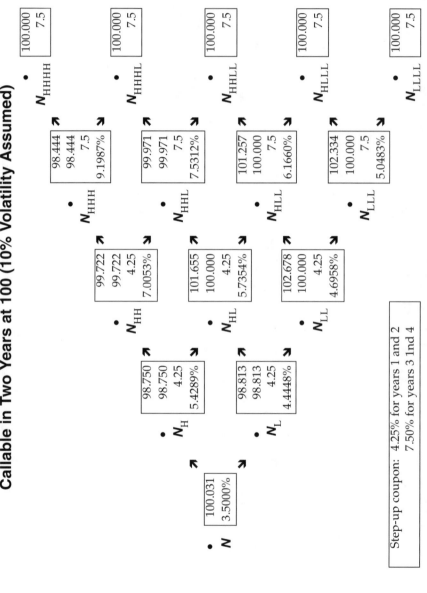

	N_{HHHH}	100.000	7.5
	N_{HHHL}	100.000	7.5
	N_{HHLL}	100.000	7.5
	N_{HLLL}	100.000	7.5
	N_{LLLL}	100.000	7.5

N_{HHH} — 98.444 / 98.444 / 7.5 / 9.1987%

N_{HHL} — 99.971 / 99.971 / 7.5 / 7.5312%

N_{HLL} — 101.257 / 100.000 / 7.5 / 6.1660%

N_{LLL} — 102.334 / 100.000 / 7.5 / 5.0483%

N_{HH} — 99.722 / 99.722 / 4.25 / 7.0053%

N_{HL} — 101.655 / 100.000 / 4.25 / 5.7354%

N_{LL} — 102.678 / 100.000 / 4.25 / 4.6958%

N_H — 98.750 / 98.750 / 4.25 / 5.4289%

N_L — 98.813 / 98.813 / 4.25 / 4.4448%

N — 100.031 / 3.5000%

Step-up coupon: 4.25% for years 1 and 2
7.50% for years 3 1nd 4

The procedure is the same for a multiple step-up callable note. Suppose that a multiple step-up callable note has the following coupon rates: 4.2% in year 1, 5% in year 2, 6% in year 3, and 7% in year 4. Also assume that the note is callable at the end of one year at par. Exhibit 5 shows that the value of this note if it noncallable is 101.012. The value of the multiple step-up callable note is 99.996 as shown in Exhibit 6. The value of the embedded call option is 1.016.

RANGE NOTES

A range note is a security that pays the reference rate with no spread if the reference rate is within a band. If the reference rate falls outside of the band (lower or upper), the coupon rate is zero. The band increases over time.

To illustrate, suppose that the reference rate is the short-term rate we have been using in our illustrations. Suppose further that the bands are as shown below:

	Year 1	Year 2	Year 3
Lower limit of range	4.50%	5.25%	6.00%
Upper limit of range	5.50%	6.75%	6.75%

Using the binomial interest rate tree in Exhibit 8 of Chapter 11, Exhibit 7 shows how to value a three-year range note. The coupon rate at each node is the forward rate if the rate is within the band and zero otherwise. The value of this range note is 96.773. Exhibit 8 shows the value of the range note if the coupon rate is the short rate plus a spread of 200 basis points. This means that at each node, the coupon rate is increased by 200 basis points. In this case, the value of the range note is 99.965.

Range notes can also be putable. The procedure for valuing a putable range note is the same as illustrated in Exhibit 1.

FLOATING RATE NOTES

The valuation of floating rate notes using the binomial model requires that the coupon rate be adjusted based on the short rate (which is assumed to be the reference rate). Exhibit 9 shows the binomial tree and the relevant values at each node for a floater whose coupon rate is the short rate flat and in which there are no restrictions on the coupon rate.

Exhibit 5: Valuing a Multiple Step-Up Noncallable Note with Four Years to Maturity (10% Volatility Assumed)

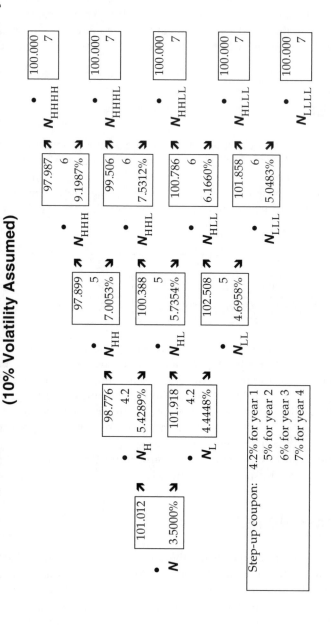

Step-up coupon:	4.2% for year 1
	5% for year 2
	6% for year 3
	7% for year 4

Exhibit 6: Valuing a Multiple Step-Up Noncallable Note with Four Years to Maturity, and Callable in One Year at 100 (10% Volatility Assumed)

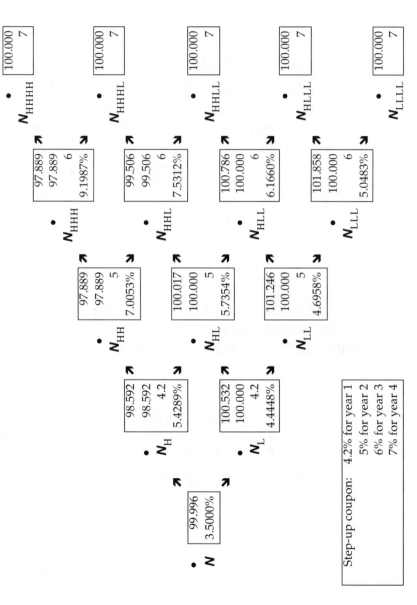

Step-up coupon:	4.2% for year 1
	5% for year 2
	6% for year 3
	7% for year 4

Exhibit 7: Valuing a Range Note with Three Years to Maturity (10% Volatility Assumed)

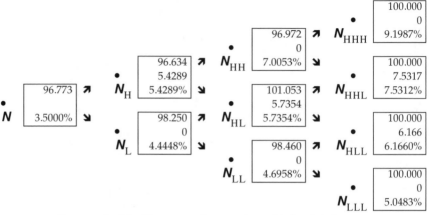

Coupon schedule: Short rate unless rate is outside bands below.

	Year 1	Year 2	Year 3
Lower limit of range	4.50%	5.25%	6.00%
Upper limit of range	5.50%	6.75%	8.00%

Exhibit 8: Valuing a Range Note with Three Years to Maturity with the Coupon Rate Equal to the Short Rate Plus 200 Basis Points (10% Volatility Assumed)

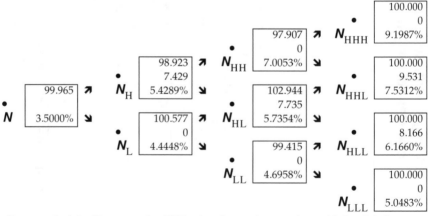

Coupon schedule: Short rate plus 200 basis points, unless rate is outside bands below.

	Year 1	Year 2	Year 3
Lower limit of range	4.50%	5.25%	6.00%
Upper limit of range	5.50%	6.75%	8.00%

Exhibit 9: Valuing A Floating Rate Note With No Cap
(10% Volatility Assumed)

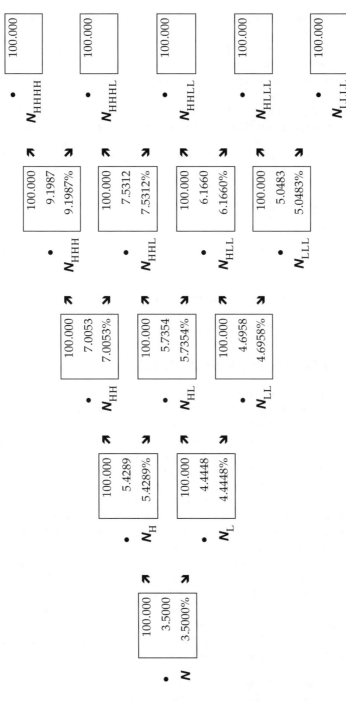

Note: The coupon rate shown at a node is the coupon rate to be received in the next year.

The valuation procedure is identical to that for the other structures described with one exception. While the coupon rate is set at the beginning of the period, it is paid in arrears. In the valuation procedure, the coupon rate set for the next period is shown in the box at which the rate is determined. For example, in Exhibit 9, the coupon rate shown in the top box in year 2 is 7.0053 as determined by the short rate at that node. Since the payment will not be made to the next year, the value of 100 shown in the same box is determined by using the standard procedure but discounting the coupon rate in the same box. For example, let's see how we get the value of 100 in the top box in year 2. The procedure is to calculate the average of the two present values of the bond value and coupon. Since the bond values and coupons are the same, the present value is simply:

$$\frac{100 + 7.0053}{1.070053} = 100$$

Suppose that the floater has a cap of 7.25%. Exhibit 10 shows how this floater would be valued. At each node where the short rate exceeds 7.25%, a coupon of \$7.25 is substituted. The value of this capped floater is 99.724. Thus, the cost of the cap is the difference between par and 99.725. If the cap for this floater was 7.75% rather than 7.25%, it can be shown that the value of this floater would be 99.958. That is, the higher the cap, the closer the capped floater will trade to par.

VALUATION OF INVERSE FLOATERS

In recent years, inverse floating-rate securities have been introduced to the corporate bond market. The coupon rate on an inverse floating-rate security, or simply, inverse floater, changes in the direction opposite to that of some reference rate or market rate.

An inverse floater can be created from a fixed-rate security. The security from which the inverse floater is created is called the collateral. From the collateral two bonds, or tranches, are created: a floater and an inverse floater. This is depicted in Exhibit 11.

The two tranches are created such that (1) the total coupon interest paid to the two tranches in each period is less than or equal to the collateral's coupon interest in each period, and (2) the total principal paid in each period to the two tranches is less than or equal to the collateral's total principal in each period. Equivalently, the floater and inverse floaters are structured so that the cash flow from the collateral in each period will be sufficient to satisfy the obligation of the two tranches.

For example, consider a 10-year 7.5% coupon semiannual-pay bond. Suppose \$100 million of the bond is used as collateral to create a floater with a principal of \$50 million and an inverse floater with a principal of \$50 million. Suppose that the reference rate is six-month LIBOR and that the coupon rate for the floater and the inverse floater are reset every six months based on the following formula:

Floater coupon: LIBOR + 1%
Inverse floater coupon: 14% – LIBOR

Exhibit 10: Valuing A Floating Rate Note With a 7.25% Cap (10% Volatility Assumed)

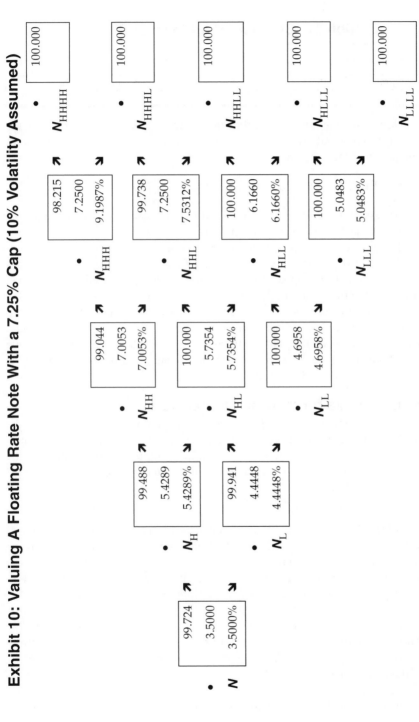

Note: The coupon rate shown at a node is the coupon rate to be received in the next year.

Exhibit 11: Creation of an Inverse Floater

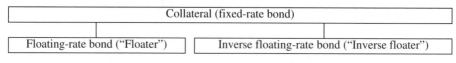

Notice that the total principal of the floater and inverse floater equals the principal of the collateral, $100 million. The weighted average of the coupon rate of the combination of the two tranches is:

$$0.5\,(\text{LIBOR} + 1\%) + 0.5\,(14\% - \text{LIBOR}) = 7.5\%$$

Thus, regardless of the level of six-month LIBOR, the combined coupon rate for the two tranches is equal to the coupon rate of the collateral, 7.5%.

There is one problem with the coupon formula for the inverse floater. Suppose that LIBOR exceeds 14%. Then the formula for the inverse floater will be negative. To prevent this from happening a restriction, or floor, is placed on the coupon rate for the inverse floater. Typically, the floor is set at zero. Because of the floor, the coupon rate on the floater must be restricted so that the coupon interest paid to the two tranches does not exceed the collateral's coupon interest. In our hypothetical structure, the maximum coupon rate that must be imposed on the floater is 15%. Thus, when a floater and an inverse floater are created from the collateral, a floor is imposed on the inverse and a cap is imposed on the floater.

General Formula for Inverse Floater Coupon

In our simple structure, we assumed an equal allocation of the par value between the two tranches. This need not happen. In general, a wide range of allocations of the collateral's principal are possible, permitting an infinite number of possibilities for the formula for the inverse floater. The general formula for the inverse floater is:

$$K - L \times R$$

where R is the reference rate, and K and L are values that can be selected by the creator of the floater and the inverse floater. Let's interpret the two parameters. K is the maximum coupon rate that the inverse floater can realize; that is, it is the cap of the inverse floater. This occurs when the reference rate is zero. L is the coupon leverage, or simply, leverage. It indicates the multiple by which the coupon rate will change for a 100 basis point change in the reference rate. For example, if L is 4, this means that the coupon rate on the inverse floater will change 400 basis points for each 100 basis point change in the reference rate (subject to any restrictions imposed on the coupon rate). Thus, the general formula for the coupon rate of an inverse floater can be expressed as:

$$\text{Inverse cap} - \text{Leverage} \times (\text{Reference rate})$$

Any cap or floor imposed on the coupon rate for the floater and the inverse floater must be selected so as to maintain the integrity of the combined coupon rate. That is, the combined coupon rate must be less than or equal to the collateral's coupon rate.

Fundamental Valuation Principle

We can express the relationships among the collateral, the corresponding floater, and an inverse floater as follows:

$$\text{Collateral} = \text{Floater} + \text{Inverse floater}$$

This relationship applies as well to valuation. That is, the sum of the value of the floater and the value of the inverse floater must be equal to the value of the collateral from which they are created. If this relationship is violated, arbitrage profits are possible.

An alternative way to express the relationship is:

$$\text{Value of inverse floater} = \text{Value of collateral} - \text{Value of floater}$$

This expression states that the value of an inverse floater can be found by valuing the collateral and valuing the floater, then calculating the difference between these two values. In this case, the value of an inverse floater is not found directly, but is instead inferred from the value of the collateral and the floater. Since the floater has a cap, the inverse floater's value is the difference between the value of the collateral and the value of the capped floater.

AN OPTION-BASED APPROACH
TO THE VALUATION OF CONVERTIBLE BONDS

In Chapter 6, we discussed convertible bonds and explained the traditional approach for analyzing these bonds. In our discussion of convertible securities, we did not address the following questions:

1. What is a fair value for the conversion premium per share?
2. How do we handle convertible securities with call and/or put options?
3. How does a change in interest rates affect the stock price?

Consider first a noncallable/nonputable convertible security. The investor who purchases this security would be entering into two separate transactions: (1) buying a noncallable/nonputable straight security and (2) buying a call option (or warrant) on the stock, where the number of shares that can be purchased with the call option is equal to the conversion ratio.

The question is: What is the fair value for the call option? The fair value depends on the factors that affect the price of a call option. A key factor is the expected price volatility of the stock: the more the expected price volatility, the greater the value of the call option. The theoretical value of a call option can be valued using the Black-Scholes option pricing model.[2] As a first approximation to the value of a convertible security, the formula would be:

Convertible security value = Straight value + Value of the call option on the stock

The value of the call option is added to the straight value because the investor has purchased a call option on the stock.

Now let's add in a common feature of a convertible security: the issuer's right to call the security. The issuer can force conversion by calling the security. For example, suppose that the call price is 103 and the conversion value is 107. If the issuer calls the security, the optimal strategy for the investor is to convert the security and receive shares worth \$107.[3] The investor, however, loses any premium over the conversion value that is reflected in the market price. Therefore, the analysis of convertible securities must take into account the value of the issuer's right to call. This depends, in turn, on (1) future interest rate volatility, and (2) economic factors that determine whether it is optimal for the issuer to call the security. The Black-Scholes option pricing model cannot handle this situation.

To link interest rates and stock prices together (the third question we raise above), statistical analysis of historical movements of these two variables must be estimated and incorporated into the model.

Valuation models based on an option pricing approach have been suggested by several researchers.[4] These models can generally be classified as one-factor or multi-factor models. By factor we mean the stochastic (random) variables that are assumed to drive the value of a convertible security. The obvious candidates for factors are the price movement of the underlying common stock and the movement of interest rates. According to Mihir Bhattacharya and Yu Zhu, two experts in convertible bond valuation, the most widely used convertible valuation model has been the one-factor model and the factor is the price movement of the underlying common stock.[5]

---

[2] Fischer Black and Myron Scholes, "The Pricing of Corporate Liabilities," *Journal of Political Economy* (May-June 1973), pp. 637-659.

[3] Actually, the conversion value would be less than \$107 because the per share value after conversion would decline.

[4] See, for example: Michael Brennan and Eduardo Schwartz, "Convertible Bonds: Valuation and Optimal Strategies for Call and Conversion," *Journal of Finance* (December 1977), pp. 1699-1715; Jonathan Ingersoll, "A Contingent-Claims Valuation of Convertible Securities," *Journal of Financial Economics* (May 1977), pp. 289-322; Michael Brennan and Eduardo Schwartz, "Analyzing Convertible Bonds," *Journal of Financial and Quantitative Analysis* (November 1980), pp. 907-929; and, George Constantinides, "Warrant Exercise and Bond Conversion in Competitive Markets," *Journal of Financial Economics* (September 1984), pp. 371-398.

Specifically, the valuation model is based on the solution to a partial differential equation. The no arbitrage conditions that the convertible bond price must satisfy is:[6]

$$\frac{\delta V}{\delta t} + \frac{1}{2}\sigma^2 S^2 \frac{\delta^2 V}{\delta S^2} + rS\frac{\delta V}{\delta S} = rV$$

where

V = Value of convertible bond = V(S,t)

S = Price of the underlying stock

t = time

r = short rate

σ^2 = instantaneous variance of the stock price return

The characteristics of the issue such as the maturity, coupon rate, conversion ratio, call and put provisions, and changing conversion ratios and provisional call features are incorporated into the boundary conditions to solve the partial differential equation.

To illustrate the valuation process, we will use the General Signal Corporation (ticker symbol "GSX") 5¾% convertible issue due June 1, 2002. Information about the issue and the stock of this issuer is provided in Exhibit 12.

The conversion value for this issue as of 10/7/93 per $1,000 of par value was equal to:

Conversion value = $33 × 25.32 = $835.56

Therefore, the conversion value per $100 of par value was 83.556.

To simplify the analysis of the straight value of the bond, we will discount the cash flows to maturity by the yield on the 10-year on-the-run Treasury at the time, 5.32%, plus a credit spread of 70 basis points that appeared to appropriate at that time. The straight value using a discount rate of 6.02% and assuming same day settlement for theoretical purposes only is 98.19. Actually, the straight value would be less than this because no recognition was given to the call feature.

Since the minimum value of the GSX convertible issue is the greater of the conversion value and the straight value, the minimum value was 98.19.

The price that an investor effectively pays for the common stock if the convertible security is purchased and then converted into the common stock is the market conversion price, found as follows:

---

[5] Mihir Bhattacharya and Yu Zhu, "Valuation and Analysis of Convertible Securities," Chapter 36 in Frank J. Fabozzi and T. Dessa Fabozzi (eds.), *The Handbook of Fixed Income Securities* (Burr Ridge, IL: Business One-Irwin, 1994).

[6] Bhattacharya and Zhu.

Exhibit 12: Information About General Signal Corporation Convertible Bond 5¾% Due June 1, 2002 and Common Stock

Convertible bond
Market price (as of 10/7/93): $106.50
Issue proceeds: $100 million
Issue date: 6/1/92
Maturity date: 6/1/02
Non-call until 6/1/95

Call price schedule

6/1/95	103.59
6/1/96	102.88
6/1/97	102.16
6/1/98	101.44
6/1/99	100.72
6/1/00	100.00
6/1/01	100.00

Coupon rate: 5¾%
Conversion ratio: 25.320 shares of GSX shares per $1,000 par value
Rating: A3/A-

GSX common stock
Expected volatility: 17%
Dividend per share: $0.90 per year
Dividend yield (as of 10/7/93): 2.727%
Stock price: $33

$$\text{Market conversion price} = \frac{\text{Market price of convertible security}}{\text{Conversion ratio}}$$

An investor who purchases a convertible security rather than the underlying stock, pays a premium over the current market price of the stock. This premium per share is equal to the difference between the market conversion price and the current market price of the common stock. That is,

Market conversion premium per share =

Market conversion price – Current market price

The market conversion premium per share is usually expressed as a percentage of the current market price as follows:

$$\text{Market conversion premium ratio} = \frac{\text{Market conversion premium per share}}{\text{Market price of common stock}}$$

Since the minimum price of a convertible security is the greater of its conversion value or its straight value, as the common stock price declines, the price of the convertible security will not fall below its straight value. The straight value therefore acts as a floor for the convertible security's price.

Viewed in this context, the market conversion premium per share can be seen as the price of a call option. However, the buyer of a call option limits the downside risk to the option price. In the case of a convertible security, for a premium, the securityholder limits the downside risk to the straight value of the security. The difference between the buyer of a call option and the buyer of a convertible security is that the former knows precisely the dollar amount of the downside risk, while the latter knows only that the most that can be lost is the difference between the convertible security's price and the straight value. The straight value at some future date, however, is unknown; the value will change as interest rates in the economy change.

The calculation of the market conversion price, market conversion premium per share, and market conversion premium ratio for the GSX convertible issue based on market data as of 10/7/93 is shown below:

$$\text{Market conversion price} = \frac{\$1,065}{25.32} = \$42.06$$

$$\text{Market conversion premium per share} = \$42.06 - \$33 = \$9.06$$

$$\text{Market conversion premium ratio} = \frac{\$9.06}{\$33} = 0.275 \text{ or } 27.5\%$$

For the GSX convertible issue, the solution to the partial differential equation given above as of 10/7/93, assuming that the standard deviation of the stock price return is 17%, is 106.53. This value was equal to the actual market price at the time of 106.5 which suggests that the issue was fairly priced.

The difference between the value of the convertible bond as determined from the valuation model and the straight value (properly adjusted for the call option granted to the issuer and any put option) is the value of the embedded call option for the stock. That is,

Value of the embedded call option for underlying stock =
Theoretical value of convertible bond – Straight value

For the GSX convertible issue, since the theoretical value for the issue is 106.53 and the straight value is 98.19 (recall that this was not adjusted for the issuer's call option), the approximate value of the embedded call option for the underlying stock is 8.34.

Exhibit 13: Motorola LYONs: Market Price vs. Theoretical Value (9/7/89 — 3/26/93)

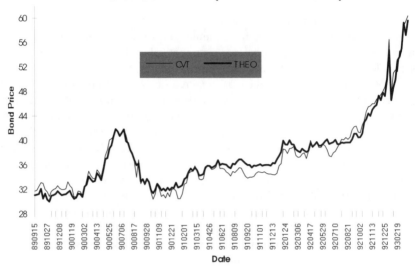

Source: Mihir Bhattacharya and Yu Zhu.

The valuation model as applied to the GSX issue indicated that the issue was fairly priced. Exhibit 13 compares the theoretical value of Motorola's Liquid Yield Option Notes (LYONs)[7] to the actual market price of the convertible issue from the issue date (9/7/89) to 3/26/93. During this period, the price of Motorola's stock increased from $28 1/16 to $65 1/4. In January 1991, the market conversion premium ratio reached a high of 44%. The exhibit indicates that the valuation appears to track the market price well.

Because the inputs into the valuation model are not known with certainty, it is important to test the sensitivity of the model. As an example, the Merrill Lynch theoretical valuation model was used to value as of November 20, 1992 the Whirlpool Corporation zero-coupon bond due 5/14/11 (a LYON) assuming the following as a base case: a common stock price of $43 5/8, volatility for the stock price of 25.21%, a constant dividend yield, a yield to maturity of 8.10%, and a yield to put of 6.98%. The theoretical value for the Whirlpool issue for this base case was $33.16.[8] The market price for this issue at the time was $33, so the issue appeared to be cheap relative to its theoretical value.

---

[7] LYON is a Merrill Lynch trademark name for zero-coupon convertible bonds that are both callable and putable.

[8] Preston M. Harrington II, Bernie Moriarty, and Hareesh Paranjape, *LYONs Review*, November/December 1992 Quarterly Update, Merrill Lynch, Pierce, Fenner & Smith, Inc., p. 104.

Tests of the sensitivity of the model to the base case inputs indicated the following for the theoretical value as of November 20, 1992 and also one year later by changing each input:

	Theoretical value (% change)			
	11/20/92		11/20/93	
Base case	$33.16		$33.33	
Stock volatility = 20%	32.67	(-1.0%)	33.07	(0.2%)
Stock price up 25%	39.52	(19.8%)	39.46	(19.6%)
Stock price down 25%	29.59	(-10.3%)	30.93	(-6.3%)
Interest rate down 100 bp	33.47	(1.44%)	33.66	(1.9%)
Interest rate up 100 bp	32.89	(-0.3%)	33.05	(0.15%)

The results for the stock volatility analysis indicate that if stock price volatility is 20% rather than the 25.21% assumed in the base case, the theoretical value as of November 20, 1992 would be less. This is expected since the value of a call option on a stock is lower the lower the expected stock price volatility. Thus, while the Whirlpool issue would be cheap relative to its market price of $33 if stock price volatility is 25.21%, it is expensive if stock price volatility is 20%.

CHAPTER 13

Managing a Corporate Bond Portfolio

In this chapter we discuss how to manage a corporate bond portfolio and the various strategies that can be employed. Since yield measures offer little insight into the potential performance of a corporate bond or corporate bond portfolio over some investment horizon, a framework that allows us to assess the potential performance is needed. The framework is the total return which we describe first in this chapter. We then show how the interest rate risk of a corporate bond or corporate bond portfolio can be measured. After describing the various corporate bond indexes, we discuss active and passive strategies.

TOTAL RETURN FRAMEWORK

As explained in Chapter 9, an investor who purchases a corporate bond can expect to receive a *dollar* return from one or more of the following sources: (1) the coupon interest payments, (2) any capital gain (or capital loss — negative dollar return) when the bond matures, is called, is put, is refunded, or is sold, and (3) income from reinvestment of the coupon interest payments (i.e., interest-on-interest).

If yields to maturity, call and put offer little insight into the relative value of a corporate bond, what measure of return can be used? The proper measure is one that considers all three sources of potential dollar return over the investment horizon. It is the return (interest rate) that will make the proceeds invested

313

(full price) grow to the projected total dollar return at the end of the investment horizon and is referred to as the *total return*.[1]

The total return requires that the investor specify:

- an investment horizon
- a reinvestment rate
- a selling price of the bond at the end of the investment horizon (which depends on the assumed yield to maturity for the bond at the end of the investment horizon).

More formally, the steps for computing a total return over some investment horizon are as follows:

Step 1: Compute the total coupon payments plus the interest-on-interest based on an assumed reinvestment rate. The reinvestment rate is one-half the annual interest rate that the investor assumes can be earned on the reinvestment of coupon interest payments.[2]

Step 2: Determine the projected sale price at the end of the planned investment horizon. We refer to this as the *horizon price*. The projected sale price will depend on the projected yield on comparable bonds at the end of the planned investment horizon. We refer to the yield at the end of the investment horizon as the *horizon yield*.

Step 3: Add the values computed in Steps 1 and 2. The sum is the total future dollars that will be received from the investment given the assumed reinvestment rate and projected horizon yield.

Step 4: To obtain the semiannual total return, use the following formula:[3]

$$\left(\frac{\text{total future dollars}}{\text{full purchase price of bond}} \right)^{1/\text{length of horizon}} - 1$$

Step 5: Since coupon interest is assumed to be paid semiannually, double the interest rate found in Step 4. The resulting interest rate is the total return expressed on a bond equivalent basis. Instead, the total return can be expressed on an effective interest rate basis by using the following formula:

$$(1 + \text{semiannual total return})^2 - 1$$

---

[1] The total return is also referred to as the *horizon return*.

[2] An investor can choose multiple reinvestment rates for cash flows from the bond over the investment horizon.

[3] Note that this calculation is the same as the yield calculation for a zero-coupon bond.

Exhibit 1: Illustration of Calculation of Total Return

Assumptions
• Corporate bond: 8%, 20-year bond selling for $82.84 (yield to maturity is 10%)
• Reinvestment rate: 6%
• Investment horizon: 3 years
• Horizon yield: 7%

Calculation

Step 1: Compute the total coupon payments plus the interest-on-interest assuming an annual reinvestment rate of 6%, or 3% every six months. The coupon payments are $4 per $100 of par value every six months for 3 years or 6 periods (the length of the investment horizon). The total coupon interest plus interest-on-interest is $25.874.

Step 2: The projected sale price at the end of 3 years (i.e., the horizon price) assuming that the required yield to maturity for 17-year bonds is 7% is $109.851.

Step 3: Adding the amount in Steps 1 and 2 gives total future dollars of $1,357.25.

Step 4: Compute the following:

$$\left(\frac{\$1,357.25}{\$828.40}\right)^{1/6} - 1 = (1.63840)^{0.16667} - 1 = 1.0858 - 1 = 0.0858 \text{ or } 8.58\%$$

Step 5: Doubling 8.58% gives a horizon return of 17.16% on a bond equivalent basis. On an effective interest rate basis, the horizon return is

$$(1.0858)^2 - 1 = 1.1790 - 1 = 0.1790 = 17.90\%$$

To illustrate the computation of the total return, suppose that an investor with a 3-year investment horizon is considering purchasing a 20-year, 8% coupon corporate bond for $82.84 (par is $100). The next coupon payment is six months from now. The yield to maturity for this bond is 10%. The investor expects that he can reinvest the coupon interest payments at an annual interest rate of 6% and that at the end of the planned investment horizon the 17-year bond will be selling to offer a yield to maturity of 7% (i.e., the horizon yield is 7%). The total return for this bond is computed in Exhibit 1.

An often-cited objection to the total return is that it requires the portfolio manager to make assumptions about reinvestment rates and horizon yields, as well as to think in terms of an investment horizon. Unfortunately, some portfolio managers are reluctant to do so, finding comfort in meaningless measures such as the yield to maturity because they do not require them to incorporate their expectations into the calculations. Total return, however, enables the portfolio manager to analyze the performance of a corporate bond based on different interest rate scenarios for reinvestment rates and horizon yields. This type of analysis, referred to as *scenario analysis*, allows a portfolio manager to see how sensitive the corporate bond's performance is to each assumption. There is no need to assume that the reinvestment rate will be constant for the entire investment horizon, which is not realistic for longer investment horizons. We believe that portfolio managers should be more comfortable looking at a corporate bond's total return profile using different interest rate assumptions rather than blindly relying upon the implicit assumptions incorporated into conventional yield measures.

Using Total Return to Compare Corporate and Municipal Bonds

The conventional method for comparing the relative value of a tax-exempt municipal bond and a taxable corporate bond is to compute the *taxable equivalent yield*. The taxable equivalent yield is the yield that must be earned on a taxable bond in order to produce the same return as a tax-exempt municipal bond. The formula is:

$$\text{taxable equivalent yield} = \frac{\text{tax-exempt yield}}{1 - \text{marginal tax rate}}$$

For example, suppose an investor in the 39.6% marginal tax bracket is considering a 10-year municipal bond with a yield to maturity of 6.04%. The taxable equivalent yield is:

$$\frac{6.04\%}{1 - 0.396} = 10\%$$

If the investor can earn more than 10% on a comparable quality corporate bond with 10 years to maturity, those who use this approach would recommend that the corporate bond be purchased. If, instead, less than 10% can be earned on a comparable corporate bond, the investor should invest in the municipal bond.

What's wrong with this approach? The tax-exempt yield of the municipal bond and the taxable equivalent yield suffer from the same limitations that we discussed earlier about yield to maturity. Consider the difference in reinvestment opportunities for a corporate bond and municipal bond. For the former, coupon payments will be taxed; therefore, the amount to be reinvested is not the entire coupon payment but an amount net of taxes. In contrast, since the coupon payments are free from taxes for a municipal bond, the entire coupon can be reinvested. However, taxes might have to be paid on any capital gain realized at the time the security is sold or matures. The total return framework can accommodate this situation by allowing us to compare the reinvestment opportunities.

There is another advantage to the total return framework compared to the conventional taxable equivalent yield approach. Changes in tax rates (either because the investor expects his or her tax rate to change or the tax structure to change) can be incorporated into the analysis.

Portfolio Total Return

A more appropriate measure for assessing the potential performance of a portfolio is its total return. This is determined by first calculating the total future dollars of each bond in the portfolio under a given scenario considering horizon yields, reinvestment rates, and spreads. The sum of all the total future dollars for each bond in the portfolio is then calculated. The portfolio total return is then found as explained earlier for a given bond: It is the interest rate that will make the market value of the portfolio today grow to the sum of all the total future dollars.

By using scenario analysis, a portfolio manager, an investment (or asset/ liability) committee, or a board can assess the potential performance of the portfolio or the potential performance of a financial institution. Corrective action can be taken to rebalance a portfolio if a scenario that is expected to occur will be detrimental to the performance of the portfolio or financial institution. The other portfolio yield measures discussed in Chapter 6 provide no such warning.

CONTROLLING INTEREST RATE RISK

Portfolio managers are concerned with how the value of a corporate bond will change when interest rates change. The responsiveness of a bond's price to interest rate changes is popularly referred to as *duration*.

Price Volatility Characteristics of Option-Free Bonds

As explained in Chapter 9, a fundamental principle of an option-free bond (that is, a bond that does not have any embedded options) is that the price of the bond changes in the opposite direction from a change in the bond's yield. Exhibit 2 illustrates this property for four hypothetical bonds, where the bond prices are shown assuming a par value of $100. When the price/yield relationship for any option-free bond is graphed, the shape is convex as shown in Exhibit 4 of Chapter 9.

Properties of Option-Free Bonds: Exhibit 3 uses the four hypothetical bonds in Exhibit 2 to show the percentage change in each bond's price for various changes in the yield, assuming that the initial yield for all four bonds is 6%. An examination of Exhibit 3 reveals several properties concerning the price volatility of an option-free bond.

- *Property 1*: Although the prices of all option-free bonds move in the opposite direction from the change in yield, the percentage price change is not the same for all bonds.

Exhibit 2: Price/Yield Relationship
for Four Hypothetical Bonds

New Yield (%)	Price			
	6%/5-year	6%/20-year	9%/5-year	9%/20-year
4.00	108.9826	127.3555	122.4565	168.3887
5.00	104.3760	112.5514	117.5041	150.2056
5.50	102.1600	106.0195	115.1201	142.1367
5.90	100.4276	101.1651	113.2556	136.1193
5.99	100.0427	100.1157	112.8412	134.8159
6.00	100.0000	100.0000	112.7953	134.6722
6.01	99.9574	99.8845	112.7494	134.5287
6.10	99.5746	98.8535	112.3373	133.2472
6.50	97.8944	94.4479	110.5280	127.7605
7.00	95.8417	89.3225	108.3166	121.3551
8.00	91.8891	80.2072	104.0554	109.8964

Exhibit 3: Instantaneous Percentage Price Change
for Four Hypothetical Bonds
(Initial yield for all four bonds is 6%)

New Yield (%)	Percent Price Change			
	6%/5-year	6%/20-year	9%/5-year	9%/20-year
4.00	8.98	27.36	8.57	25.04
5.00	4.38	12.55	4.17	11.53
5.50	2.16	6.02	2.06	5.54
5.90	0.43	1.17	0.41	1.07
5.99	0.04	0.12	0.04	0.11
6.01	-0.04	-0.12	-0.04	-0.11
6.10	-0.43	-1.15	-0.41	-1.06
6.50	-2.11	-5.55	-2.01	-5.13
7.00	-4.16	-10.68	-3.97	-9.89
8.00	-8.11	-19.79	-7.75	-18.40

- *Property 2*: For small changes in yield, the percentage price change for a given bond is roughly the same, whether the yield increases or decreases.

- *Property 3*: For large changes in yield, the percentage price change is not the same for an increase in yield as it is for a decrease in yield.

- *Property 4*: For a given large change in basis points, the percentage price increase is greater than the percentage price decrease.

The implication of Property 4 is that if an investor is long a bond, the price appreciation that will be realized if the yield decreases is greater than the capital loss that will be realized if the yield rises by the same number of basis points. For an investor who is short a bond, the reverse is true: the potential capital loss is greater than the potential capital gain if the yield changes by a given number of basis points.

An explanation for these four properties of bond price volatility lies in the convex shape of the price/yield relationship.

Characteristics of a Bond that Affect its Price Volatility: There are two characteristics of an option-free bond that determine its price volatility: coupon and term to maturity.

- *Characteristic 1*: For a given term to maturity and initial yield, the lower the coupon rate the greater the price volatility of a bond.

- *Characteristic 2*: For a given coupon rate and initial yield, the longer the term to maturity, the greater the price volatility.

These properties can be verified by examining Exhibit 3.

An implication of the second characteristic is that investors who want to increase a portfolio's price volatility because they expect interest rates to fall, all other factors being constant, should hold bonds with long maturities in the portfolio. To reduce a portfolio's price volatility in anticipation of a rise in interest rates, bonds with shorter-term maturities should be held in the portfolio.

The Effects of Yield to Maturity: We cannot ignore the fact that credit considerations cause different corporate bonds to trade at different yields, even if they have the same coupon and maturity. How, then, holding other factors constant, does the yield to maturity affect a bond's price volatility? As it turns out, the higher the yield to maturity that a bond trades at, the lower the price volatility.

Exhibit 4: Price/Yield Relationship
for an Option-Free Bond and a Callable Bond

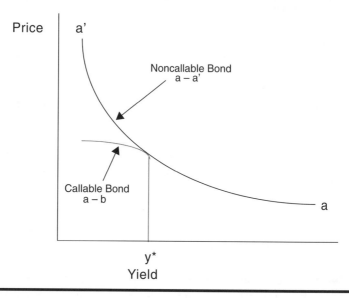

To see this, we can compare a 6% 20-year bond initially selling at a yield of 6%, and a 6% 20-year bond initially selling at a yield of 10%. The former is initially at a price of 100, and the latter carries a price of 65.68. Now, if the yields on both bonds increase by 100 basis points, the first bond trades down by 10.68 points (10.68%). After the assumed increase in yield, the second bond will trade at a price of 59.88, for a price decline of only 5.80 (or 8.83%). Thus, we see that the bond that trades at a lower yield is more volatile in both percentage price change and absolute price change, as long as the other bond characteristics are the same.

An implication of this is that, for a given change in yields, price volatility is lower when yield levels in the market are high, and price volatility is higher when yield levels are low.

Price Volatility Characteristics of Callable Corporate Bonds

The price appreciation potential for a callable corporate bond in a declining interest rate environment is limited. The price of the callable corporate bond will not rise as much as an otherwise comparable noncallable corporate bond. This can be seen in Exhibit 4. The price/yield relationship for an option-free (i.e., noncallable/nonputable) corporate bond is convex. The convex curve a-a' shows the price/yield relationship. The exhibit also shows the price/yield relationship for an otherwise equivalent callable corporate bond as depicted by the unusual shape of the curve denoted by a-b.

The reason for the shape of the price/yield relationship for the callable corporate bond is as follows. When the prevailing market yield for comparable corporate bonds is higher than the coupon rate on the bond, it is unlikely that the issuer will call the bond. For example, if the coupon rate on a corporate bond is 7% and the prevailing yield on comparable corporate bonds is 13%, it is highly improbable that the issuer will call the outstanding issue. Since the bond is unlikely to be called, the callable corporate bond will have the same price/yield relationship as a noncallable corporate bond. However, even when the coupon rate is just below the market yield, investors may not pay the same price for the callable corporate bond had it been noncallable because there is still the chance that the market yield may drop further making it beneficial for the issuer to call the bond.

The exact yield level at which investors begin to view the issue likely to be called may not be known, but we do know that there is some level. In Exhibit 4, at yield levels below y*, the price/yield relationship for the callable bond departs from the price/yield relationship for the noncallable bond. If, for example, the market yield is such that a noncallable bond would be selling for 109, but as the callable bond would be called at 104, investors would not pay 109. If they did and the bond is called, investors would receive 104 (the call price) for a bond they purchased for 109. Notice that for a range of yields below y*, there is price compression — that is, there is limited price appreciation as yields decline. The portion of the callable bond price/yield relationship below y* is said to be *negatively convex*.

Negative convexity means that the price appreciation will be less than the price depreciation for a large change in yield of a given number of basis points. For a bond that is option-free and exhibits positive convexity, the price appreciation will be greater than the price depreciation for a large change in yield of a given number of basis points. The price changes resulting from bonds exhibiting positive convexity and negative convexity can be expressed as follows:

	Absolute value of percentage price change for:	
Change in interest rates	Positive convexity	Negative convexity
−100 basis points	X%	less than Y%
+100 basis points	less than X%	Y%

Measuring Interest Rate Risk

Now we know that coupon and maturity affect a corporate bond's price volatility when yield changes, and that the yield level affects price volatility. What is needed is a measure that encompasses these three factors that affect a corporate bond's price volatility when yields change. The most obvious way to measure the price sensitivity of a corporate bond to changes in interest rates is to change rates by a small number of basis points and calculate how the price or value of the bond will change.

To do this, we introduce the following notation. Let

Δy = change in the yield of a bond (in decimal)
V_+ = the estimated value of the bond if yield is increased by Δy
V_- = the estimated value of the bond if yield is decreased by Δy
V_0 = initial price of the bond (per $100 of par value)

There are two key points to keep in mind in the foregoing discussion. First, the change in yield referred to above is the same change in yield for all maturities. This assumption is commonly referred to as a *parallel yield curve shift assumption*. Thus, the foregoing discussion about the price sensitivity of a security to interest rate changes is limited to parallel shifts in the yield curve. Later in this chapter we will address the case where the yield curve shifts in a nonparallel manner.

Second, the notation refers to the estimated value of the security. This value is obtained from a valuation model such as the binomial model described in Chapter 11. Consequently, the resulting measure of the price sensitivity of a security to interest rates changes is only as good as the valuation model employed to obtain the estimated value of the bond.

Now let's focus on the measure of interest. We are interested in the percentage change in the price of a security when interest rates change. The percentage change in price per basis point is found by dividing the percentage price change by the number of basis points (Δy) times 100. That is,

$$\frac{V_- - V_0}{V_0 (\Delta y) 100}$$

Similarly, the percentage change in price per basis point change for an increase in yield of Δy times 100 is:

$$\frac{V_0 - V_+}{V_0 (\Delta y) 100}$$

As explained earlier, the percentage price change for an increase and decrease in interest rates will not be the same. Consequently, the average percentage price change per basis point change in yield can be calculated. This is done as follows:

$$\frac{1}{2} \left[\frac{V_- - V_0}{V_0 (\Delta y) 100} + \frac{V_0 - V_+}{V_0 (\Delta y) 100} \right]$$

or equivalently,

$$\frac{V_- - V_+}{2 V_0 (\Delta y) 100}$$

The approximate percentage price change for a 100 basis point change in yield is found by multiplying the previous formula by 100. The name popularly used to refer to the approximate percentage price change is *duration*. Thus,

$$\text{Duration} = \frac{V_- - V_+}{2V_0\,(\Delta y)} \tag{1}$$

To illustrate this formula, consider the following option-free bond: a 9% coupon 20-year bond trading to yield 6%. The initial price or value (V_0) is 134.6722. Suppose the yield is changed by 20 basis points. If the yield is decreased to 5.8%, the value of this bond (V_-) would be 137.5888. If the yield is increased to 6.2%, the value of this bond (V_+) would be 131.8439. Thus,

$$\Delta y \;=\; 0.0020$$
$$V_+ \;=\; 131.8439$$
$$V_- \;=\; 137.5888$$
$$V_0 \;=\; 134.6722$$

Substituting these values into the duration formula,

$$\text{Duration} = \frac{137.5888 - 131.8439}{2\,(134.6722)\,(0.002)} = 10.66$$

The duration of a security can be interpreted as the approximate percentage change in the price for a 100 basis point parallel shift in the yield curve. Thus a bond with a duration of 4.8 will change by approximately 4.8% for a 100 basis point parallel shift in the yield curve. For a 50 basis point parallel shift in the yield curve, the bond's price will change by approximately 2.4%; for a 25 basis point parallel shift in the yield curve, 1.2%, etc.

Modified Duration versus Effective Duration

A popular form of duration that is used by practitioners is *modified duration*. Modified duration is the approximate percentage change in a bond's price for a 100 basis point parallel shift in the yield curve assuming that the bond's cash flow does *not* change when the yield curve shifts. What this means is that in calculating the values of V_- and V_+ in equation (1), the cash flow used to calculate V_0 is used. Therefore, the change in the bond's price when the yield curve is shifted by a small number of basis points is due solely to discounting at the new yield level.

The assumption that the cash flow will not change when the yield curve shifts in a parallel fashion makes sense for option-free bonds such as noncallable Treasury securities. This is because the payments made by the U.S. Department of the Treasury to a holder of its obligations does not change when the yield curve changes. However, the same can not be said for corporate bonds with embedded options. For such bonds, a change in yield will alter the expected cash flow.

Exhibit 5: Modified Duration Versus Effective Duration

Duration
Interpretation: Generic description of the sensitivity of a bond's price (as a percentage of initial price) to a parallel shift in the yield curve

Modified Duration	*Effective Duration*
Duration measure in which it is assumed that yield changes do not change the expected cash flow	Duration in which recognition is given to the fact that yield changes may change the expected cash flow

The binomial model takes into account how shifts in the yield curve will affect cash flow. Thus, when V_- and V_+ are the values produced from the binomial model, the resulting duration takes into account both the discounting at different interest rates and how the cash flow can change. When duration is calculated in this manner, it is referred to as *effective duration* or *option-adjusted duration*. Exhibit 5 summarizes the distinction between modified duration and effective duration.

The difference between modified duration and effective duration for fixed-income securities with an embedded option can be quite dramatic. For example, a callable corporate bond could have a modified duration of 6 but an effective duration of only 4.5. Thus, using modified duration as a measure of the price sensitivity of a security to a parallel shift in the yield curve would be misleading. The more appropriate measure for a corporate bond with an embedded option is effective duration.

Modified Duration and Macaulay Duration

Before leaving this topic, it is worth comparing the modified duration formula presented above to that commonly found in the literature. It is common in the literature to find the following formula for modified duration:[4]

$$\frac{1}{(1 + \text{yield}/k)} \left[\frac{1\,(\text{PVCF}_1) + 2\,(\text{PVCF}_2) + 3\,(\text{PVCF}_3) + \ldots + n\,(\text{PVCF}_n)}{k\,(\text{Price})} \right] \quad (2)$$

where

k = number of periods, or payments, per year (e.g., $k = 2$ for semiannual pay bonds and $k = 12$ for monthly pay bonds)

n = number of periods until maturity (i.e., number of years to maturity times k)

yield = yield to maturity of the bond

PVCF_t = present value of the cash flow in period t discounted at the yield to maturity

---

[4] More specifically, this is the formula for modified duration for a bond on a coupon anniversary date.

The expression in the bracket for the modified duration formula in equation (2) is a measure formulated in 1938 by Frederick Macaulay.[5] This measure is popularly referred to as *Macaulay duration*. Thus, modified duration is commonly expressed as:

$$\text{Modified duration} = \frac{\text{Macaulay duration}}{(1 + \text{yield}/k)}$$

The general formulation for duration as given by equation (1) provides a short-cut procedure for determining a bond's modified duration. Because it is easier to calculate the modified duration using the short-cut procedure, many vendors of analytical software will use equation (1) rather than equation (2) to reduce computation time. But, once again, it must be emphasized that modified duration is a flawed measure of a bond's price sensitivity to interest rate changes for a bond with an embedded option.

Calculating the Effective Duration Using the Binomial Model

The procedure for calculating the values to be substituted into the duration formula [equation (1)] using the binomial model is described below. First, V_+ is determined as follows:

Step 1: Calculate the option-adjusted spread (OAS) for the issue.

Step 2: Shift the on-the-run yield curve up by a small number of basis points.

Step 3: Construct a binomial interest rate tree based on the new yield curve in Step 2.

Step 4: To each of the short rates in the binomial interest rate tree, add the OAS to obtain an "adjusted tree."

Step 5: Use the adjusted tree found in Step 4 to determine the value of the security, which is V_+.

To determine the value of V_-, the same five steps are followed except that in Step 2, the on-the-run yield curve is shifted down by a small number of basis points.

To illustrate how V_+ and V_- are determined in order to calculate effective duration, we will use the same on-the-run yield curve that we used in Chapter 11 assuming a volatility of 10%. The four-year callable bond with a coupon rate of 6.5% and callable at par selling at 102.218 will be used in this illustration. The OAS for this issue is 35 basis points.

---

[5] Frederick Macaulay, *Some Theoretical Problems Suggested by the Movement of Interest Rates, Bond Yields, and Stock Prices in the U.S. Since 1856* (New York: National Bureau of Economic Research, 1938).

Exhibit 6 shows the adjusted tree by shifting the yield curve up by an arbitrarily small number of basis points, 25 basis points, and then adding 35 basis points (the OAS) to each one-year rate. The adjusted tree is then used to value the bond. The resulting value, V_+, is 102.765. Exhibit 7 shows the adjusted tree by shifting the yield curve down by 25 basis points and then adding 35 basis points to each one-year rate. The resulting value, V_-, is 101.676.

The results are summarized below:

$$\Delta y = 0.0025$$
$$V_+ = 101.6760$$
$$V_- = 102.7650$$
$$V_0 = 102.2180$$

Therefore,

$$\text{Effective duration} = \frac{102.765 - 101.676}{2\,(102.218)\,(0.0025)} = 2.1$$

Duration for Noncallable Corporate Bonds

In recent years, the issuance of noncallable corporate bonds has increased. The yield on a noncallable corporate bond is composed of the Treasury base rate plus a credit spread. Duration measures the sensitivity of the price of a security to the general level of interest rates. Thus the duration of a noncallable corporate bond depends on the change in the level of Treasury rates and the change in credit spreads. If the change in Treasury rates and credit spreads is highly correlated, a duration measure for a noncallable corporate bond will do an effective job of estimating its price sensitivity to rate changes. However, if the correlation is low, duration will not be an effective measure of price sensitivity.

Ilmanen, McGuire, and Warga empirically examined this issue.[6] For the period covering 1985 to December 1991, they analyzed the relative monthly performance of investment grade noncallable corporate bonds due to general market-wide parallel yield shifts (duration and convexity) and a change in credit spreads. They found that for portfolios of Aaa-rated bonds, duration is able to explain almost 90% of portfolio returns. For portfolios comprising Aaa- and Aa-rated bonds, duration explains about 80% of portfolio returns. However, for portfolios comprised of all investment grade noncallable corporate bonds, only 35% of portfolio returns are explained by duration. By incorporating credit spread as a variable to explain portfolio returns, no major improvement is made in the explanatory power. The conclusion of Ilmanen, McGuire, and Warga is that while duration does a good job of explaining returns for portfolios of Aaa- and Aa-rated noncallable, it does not do so for portfolios that include A- and Baa-rated issues.

---

[6] Antti Ilmanen, Donald McGuire, and Arthur Warga, "The Value of Duration as a Risk Measure for Corporate Debt," *Journal of Fixed Income* (June 1994), pp. 70-79.

Exhibit 6: Determination of V₊ for Calculating Effective Duration and Convexity*

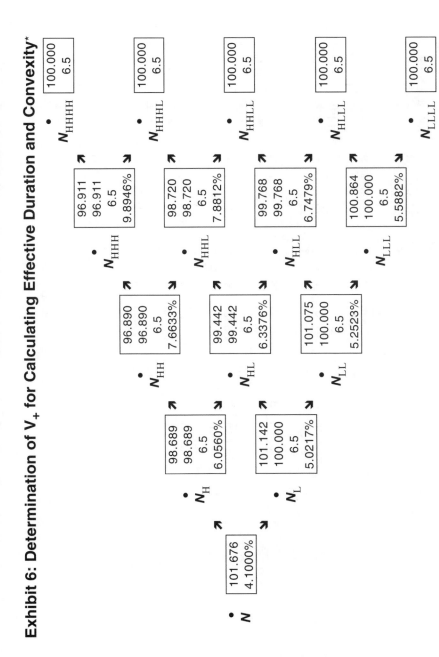

* +25 basis point shift in on-the-run yield curve.

Exhibit 7: Determination of V_ for Calculating Effective Duration and Convexity*

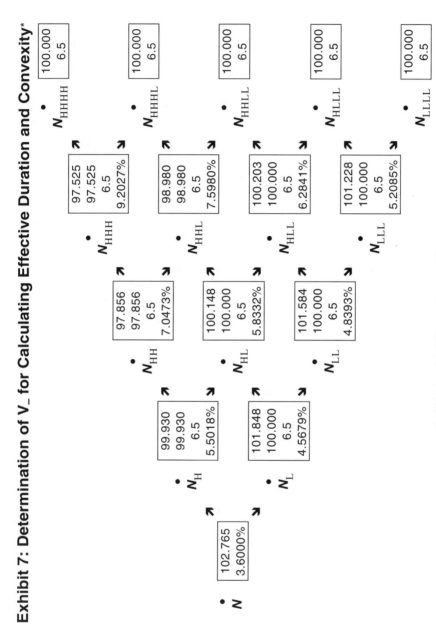

* −25 basis point shift in on-the-run yield curve.

Price Sensitivity to Non-Parallel Yield Curve Shifts

Both modified duration and effective duration assume that any change in interest rates is the result of a parallel shift in the yield curve. For some fixed-income securities, the price sensitivity to most nonparallel shifts will be very close to the estimated price sensitivity for a parallel shift in the yield curve. This is generally true for option-free bonds with a bullet maturity. However, for sinking-fund corporate bonds and corporate bonds with embedded options, the price sensitivity to a nonparallel shift in the yield curve can be quite different from that estimated for a parallel shift.

Several measures have been proposed in the literature to estimate the price sensitivity of a bond to nonparallel yield curve shifts.[7] A discussion of these measures is beyond the scope of this chapter. However, the binomial model can be used to determine the price sensitivity to specific nonparallel yield curve shifts assumed by an investor.

Convexity Correction

Notice that the duration measure indicates that regardless of whether the yield curve is shifted up or down, the approximate percentage price change is the same. However, this does not agree with the properties of a bond's price volatility described earlier in this chapter. Specifically, Property 2 states that for small changes in yield the percentage price change will be the same for an increase or decrease in yield. Property 3 states that for large changes in yield this is not true. This suggests that duration is only a good approximation of the percentage price change for a small change in yield.

To see this, consider once again the 9%, 20-year bond selling to yield 6% with a duration of 10.66. If yields increase instantaneously by 10 basis points (from 6% to 6.1%), then using duration the approximate percentage price change would be -1.066% (-10.66% divided by 10, remembering that duration is the percentage price change for a 100 basis point change in yield). Notice from Exhibit 3 that the actual percentage price change is -1.06%. Similarly, if the yield decreases instantaneously by 10 basis points (from 6.00% to 5.90%), then the percentage change in price would be +1.066%. From Exhibit 3, the actual percentage price change would be +1.07%. This example illustrates that for small changes in yield, duration does an excellent job of approximating the percentage price change.

---

[7] See, for example, Thomas E. Klaffky, Y.Y. Ma, and Ardavan Nozari, "Managing Yield Curve Exposure: Introducing Reshaping Durations," *Journal of Fixed Income* (December 1992), pp. 5-15; Robert R. Reitano, "Non-Parallel Yield Curve Shifts and Durational Leverage," *Journal of Portfolio Management* (Summer 1990), pp. 62-67; Thomas Y. Ho, "Key Rate Durations: Measures of Interest Rate Risks," *Journal of Fixed Income* (September 1992), pp. 29-44; Brian D. Johnson and Kenneth R. Meyer, "Managing Yield Curve Risk in an Index Environment," *Financial Analysts Journal* (November/December 1989), pp. 51-59; Ravi E. Dattatreya and Frank J. Fabozzi, "The Risk Point Method for Measuring and Controlling Yield Curve Risk," *Financial Analysts Journal* (July/August 1995); and, Chapter 3 in Frank J. Fabozzi and H. Gifford Fong, *Advanced Fixed Income Portfolio Management* (Chicago: Probus Publishing, 1994).

Instead of a small change in yield, let's assume that yields increase by 200 basis points, from 6% to 8%. The approximate percentage change is -21.32% (-10.66% times 2). As can be seen from Exhibit 3, the actual percentage change in price is only -18.40%. Moreover, if the yield decreased by 200 basis points from 6% to 4%, the approximate percentage price change based on duration would be +21.32%, compared to an actual percentage price change of +25.04%. Thus, the approximation is not as good for a 200 basis point change in yield.

Duration is in fact a first approximation for a small parallel shift in the yield curve. The approximation can be improved by using a second approximation. This approximation is referred to as a bond's *convexity*.[8] The use of this term in the industry is unfortunate since the term convexity is also used to describe the shape or curvature of the price/yield relationship. The convexity measure of a security is the approximate change in price that is not explained by duration.

The convexity of any bond can be approximated using the following formula:

$$\text{Convexity} = \frac{V_+ + V_- - 2V_0}{2V_0 (\Delta y)^2} \tag{3}$$

For our hypothetical 9%, 20-year bond selling to yield 6%, we know that

Δy = 0.0020
V_+ = 131.8439
V_- = 137.5888
V_0 = 134.6722

Substituting these values into the convexity formula,

$$\text{Convexity} = \frac{137.5888 + 131.8439 - 2\,(134.6722)}{2\,(134.6722)\,(0.002)^2} = 81.96$$

Given the convexity measure, the approximate percentage change in price due to the bond's convexity that is not explained by duration is:

$$\text{Convexity} \times (\Delta y)^2$$

For example, for the 9% coupon bond maturing in 20 years, the approximate percentage price change due to convexity if the yield increases from 6% to 8% is

$$81.96 \times (0.02)^2 = 0.0328 = 3.28\%$$

---

[8] Mathematically, any function can be estimated by a series of approximations referred to as a Taylor series. Each approximation or term of the Taylor series is based on the corresponding derivative. For a bond, duration is the first approximation to price change and is related to the first derivative of the bond's price. The convexity measure is the second approximation and is related to the second derivative of the bond's price. It turns out that in general the first two approximations do a good job of estimating the bond's price so no additional derivatives are needed. The derivation is provided in Chapter 4 of Frank J. Fabozzi, *Bond Markets, Analysis and Strategies* (Englewood Cliffs, N.J.: Prentice Hall, 1993).

If the yield decreases from 6% to 4%, the approximate percentage price change due to convexity would also be 3.28%.

The approximate percentage price change based on both duration and convexity is found by simply adding the two estimates. So, for example, if yields change from 6% to 8%, the estimated percentage price change would be:

Duration	=	– 21.32%
Convexity	=	+ 3.28%
Total	=	– 18.04%

The actual percentage price change is -18.40%. For a decrease of 200 basis points, from 6% to 4% the approximate percentage price change would be as follows:

Duration	=	+ 21.32%
Convexity	=	+ 3.28%
Total	=	+ 24.60%

The actual percentage price change is +25.04%. Thus, both duration and convexity together do a good job of estimating the sensitivity of a bond's price change to large changes in yield.

While it is easy to interpret what duration means, it is more difficult to interpret the convexity measure because it is multiplied by the square of the change in yield. Basically, convexity is the rate of change of duration when yields change.[9]

Modified Convexity and Effective Convexity

The prices used in equation (3) to calculate convexity can be obtained by either assuming that when the yield curve shifts in a parallel way the expected cash flow does not change or it does change. In the former case, the resulting convexity is referred to as *modified convexity*.[10] Actually, in the industry, convexity is not qualified by the adjective modified. Thus, in practice the term convexity typically means the cash flow is assumed not to change when yields change. *Effective convexity*, in contrast, assumes that the cash flow does change when yields change. This is the same distinction made for duration.

As with duration, for bonds with embedded options there could be quite a difference between the calculated modified convexity and effective convexity. In fact, for all option-free bonds, either convexity measure will have a positive value. For callable bonds, the calculated effective convexity can be negative when the calculated modified convexity gives a positive value.

---

[9] More specifically, convexity is the rate of change a bond's *dollar* price change (or *dollar duration*).

[10] The formula for modified convexity is

$$\frac{1\,(2)\,\text{PVCF}_1 + 2\,(3)\,\text{PVCF}_2 + 3\,(4)\,\text{PVCF}_3 + \ldots + n\,(n+1)\,\text{PVCF}_n}{(1 + \text{yield}/k)^2\, k^2\, \text{Price}}$$

Using this formula, the modified convexity for the 9%, 20-year bond selling to yield 6% is 82.04. While this number is slightly different from that obtained using equation (3), when we use this measure to obtain the approximate percentage price change due to convexity, the result will be the same.

Exhibit 8: Actual versus Required
Corporate Bond Yield Premium: 1985-1994

	Actual Yield Spread over U.S. Treasury (bp)	Actual Yield Required to Offset Credit Losses (bp)
AAA	41	4
AA	56	6
A	77	27
BBB	114	37
BB	313	176
B	534	338

Note: Data obtained from Salomon Brothers, Moody's Investors Service, and
Miller Anderson & Sherrerd
Source: Thomas L. Bennett, Stephen F. Esser, and Christian G. Roth, *Corporate Credit Risk and Reward*, Miller Anderson & Sherrerd, 1993. (Update furnished by Stephen Esser.)

RISK AND RETURN IN THE CORPORATE BOND MARKET

Because of the credit risk associated with corporate bonds, it is expected that the performance of this sector of the market would outperform Treasury securities. Moreover, within the corporate bond market, because of the greater credit risk associated with high-yield bonds compared to investment grade bonds, it is expected that the former would outperform the latter. Below we discuss several empirical studies that address these questions.

Performance of Investment Grade Corporate Bonds

A study by Thomas Bennett, Stephen Esser, and Christian Roth reported the risk and reward relationship in the corporate bond market.[11] Exhibit 8 shows for the four investment grade ratings and the first two non-investment grading ratings the actual yield spread over U.S. Treasuries for the 10-years ending 1994. Also shown in the exhibit is the yield spread required to offset credit losses for each quality rating. As indicated in Exhibit 8, investors have been rewarded for accepting corporate credit risk.

Exhibit 9 shows the annualized total returns and return spreads versus U.S. Treasuries for investment grade corporates and the Standard & Poor's 500 for various periods ending 1994. The two key findings as reported in Exhibit 9 are (1) corporate bonds outperformed Treasuries and (2) the lower the credit rating the better the performance relative to Treasuries. Thus, the ratings appear to do a good job of differentiating the credit risk associated with investing in corporate bonds.

---

[11] Thomas L. Bennett, Stephen F. Esser, and Christian G. Roth, *Corporate Credit Risk and Reward*, Miller Anderson & Sherrerd, 1993.

Exhibit 9: Annualized Total Returns and Return Spreads for U.S. Treasuries, Investment-Grade Corporates, and S&P 500 for Periods Ending December 1994

	20 Years	10 Years	5 Years
Treasuries	9.22%	10.38%	7.40%
Corporates[a]	10.30%	10.66%	8.27%
Spread vs. Treasuries	+108 bp	+28 bp	+87 bp
AAA	9.60%	10.40%	8.12%
Spread vs. Treasuries	+38 bp	+2 bp	+72 bp
AA	9.90%	10.50%	8.15%
Spread vs. Treasuries	+68 bp	+12 bp	+75 bp
A	10.47%	10.67%	8.46%
Spread vs. Treasuries	+125 bp	+29 bp	+106 bp
BBB	11.86%	11.33%	8.66%
Spread vs. Treasuries	+264 bp	+95 bp	+126 bp
S&P 500	14.58%	14.40%	8.70%

[a] The returns are duration matched to the Lehman Corporate Index.

Note: Data obtained from Lehman Brothers and Miller Anderson & Sherrerd
Source: Thomas L. Bennett, Stephen F. Esser, and Christian G. Roth, *Corporate Credit Risk and Reward*, Miller Anderson & Sherrerd, 1993. (Update furnished by Stephen Esser.)

Performance of High-Yield Bonds

There have been several studies of the risk and return in the high-yield bond market. Historically, the promised yields offered on high-yield bonds have been substantial. For example, the yield spread over Treasury bonds between 1980 and 1989 ranged from 300 to 650 basis points, at least according to the Drexel Burnham Lambert 100 Bond Index. In late 1989 and 1990, a turbulent time for the high-yield sector, the yield spread increased to 700 to 800 basis points. Is this spread justified by a higher potential default rate? This intriguing question has been extensively investigated.

Most of the research on the high-yield bond sector focuses on default rates.[12] From an investment perspective, default rates by themselves are not of paramount significance: it is perfectly possible for a portfolio of high-yield bonds to suffer defaults and to outperform Treasuries at the same time, provided the yield spread of the portfolio is sufficiently high to offset the losses from default. Furthermore, because holders of defaulted bonds typically recover at least 30% of the face amount of their investment, the default loss rate is substantially lower than the default rate.[13] Therefore, focusing exclusively on default rates merely highlights the worst possible outcome that a diversified portfolio of high-yield bonds would suffer, assuming all defaulted bonds would be totally worthless. Assessing the potential rewards from investing in this market sector requires understanding not only default and default loss rates, but also total returns offered over various investment horizons.

First, let's look at what research has found for the default rate experience of low-quality corporate bonds. In their 1987 study, Altman and Nammacher found that the annual default rate for low-rated corporate debt was 2.15%, a figure that Altman has updated since to 2.40%. Drexel Burnham Lambert's (DBL) estimates have also shown default rates of about 2.40% per year. Asquith, Mullins, and Wolff, however, found that nearly one out of every three junk bonds defaults. The large discrepancy arises because the researchers use three different definitions of "default rate"; even if applied to the same universe of bonds (which they are not), all three results could be valid simultaneously.[14]

Altman and Nammacher define the default rate as the par value of all high-yield bonds that defaulted in a given calendar year, divided by the total par value outstanding during the year. Their estimates (2.15% and 2.40%) are simple averages of the annual default rates over a number of years. DBL takes the cumulative dollar value of all defaulted high-yield bonds, divides by the cumulative dollar value of all high-yield issuance, and further divides by the weighted average number of years outstanding to obtain an average annual default rate. Asquith, Mullins, and Wolff use a cumulative default statistic. For all bonds issued in a given year, the default rate is the total par value of defaulted issues as of the date of their study, divided by the total par amount originally issued to obtain a cumulative default rate. Their result (that about one in three high-yield bonds default) is not normalized by the number of years outstanding.

---

[12] See, for example, Edward I. Altman, "Measuring Corporate Bond Mortality and Performance," *Journal of Finance* (September 1989), pp. 909-922; Edward I. Altman, "Research Update: Mortality Rates and Losses, Bond Rating Drift," unpublished study prepared for a workshop sponsored by Merrill Lynch Merchant Banking Group, High Yield Sales and Trading, 1989; Edward I. Altman and Scott A. Nammacher, *Investing in Junk Bonds* (New York: John Wiley, 1987); Paul Asquith, David W. Mullins, Jr., and Eric D. Wolff, "Original Issue High Yield Bonds: Aging Analysis of Defaults, Exchanges, and Calls," *Journal of Finance* (September 1989), pp. 923-952; Marshall Blume and Donald Keim, "Risk and Return Characteristics of Lower-Grade Bonds 1977-1987," Working Paper (8-89), Rodney L. White Center for Financial Research, Wharton School, University of Pennsylvania, 1989; Marshall Blume and Donald Keim, "Realized Returns and Defaults on Lower-Grade Bonds," Rodney L. White Center for Financial Research, Wharton School, University of Pennsylvania, 1989; Bond Investors Association, "Bond Investors Association Issues Definitive Corporate Default Statistics," press release dated August 15, 1989; Gregory T. Hradsky and Robert D. Long, "High Yield Default Losses and the Return Performance of Bankrupt Debt," *Financial Analysts Journal* (July-August 1989), pp. 38-49; "Historical Default Rates of Corporate Bond Issuers 1970-1988," *Moody's Special Report, July 1989* (New York: Moody's Investors Service); "High-Yield Bond Default Rates," *Standard & Poor's Creditweek*, August 7, 1989, pp. 21-23; David Wyss, Christopher Probyn, and Robert de Angelis, "The Impact of Recession on High-Yield Bonds," *DRI-McGraw-Hill* (Washington, D.C.: Alliance for Capital Access, 1989); and the 1984-1989 issues of *High Yield Market Report: Financing America's Futures* (New York and Beverly Hills: Drexel Burnham Lambert, Incorporated).

[13] For instance, a default rate of 5% and an average recovery rate of 30% imply a default loss rate of only 3.5% (70% of 5%).

[14] As a parallel, we know that the mortality rate in the United States is currently less than 1% per year, but we also know that 100% of all humans (eventually) die.

While all three measures are useful indicators of bond default propensity, they are not directly comparable. Even when restated on an annualized basis, they do not all measure the same quantity. The default statistics from all studies, however, are surprisingly similar once cumulative rates have been annualized. A majority of studies place the annual default rates for all original issue high-yield bonds between 3% and 4%.[15]

But, as we indicated earlier, default rates do not tell us how the securities in this market sector have performed. While there have been a number of studies on total returns, the findings have not been uniform, as the periods and the bonds studied differ substantially among researchers. Furthermore, each study employs different assumptions about a broad range of important factors, including reinvestment rates, treatment of defaults, and accrued interest. Studies by Cheung, Bencivenga, and Fabozzi,[16] Blume, Keim, and Patel,[17] and Cornell and Green[18] provide empirical evidence on the performance of the high-yield bond market. The first two studies examine original-issue high-yield bonds. Both find that from 1977 (the start of the modern high-yield bond market) to December 31, 1989, the actual return on original-issue high yield bonds was greater than that on Treasuries and high-grade corporate bonds, but less than that on common stock. As a result, both studies conclude that there is no evidence that this sector of the bond market is systematically mispriced.

Cornell and Green do not look at individual bonds. Instead, for the period 1977 to 1989, they investigated the performance of mutual funds specializing in high-yield bonds. There are several drawbacks to this approach. First, there is an implicit assumption that the high-yield market is efficient so that fund managers cannot systematically find undervalued bonds. Second, fund managers are given the discretion to not fully allocate their funds to the high-yield market. To the extent that mutual fund managers pursue an active asset allocation strategy between the money market and long-term debt markets, performance will be misleading because it encompasses the timing ability of managers. The third disadvantage is that mutual fund managers are not restricted to original issue high-yield bonds (i.e., they can invest in fallen angels). Finally, there are management fees, administrative fees, and custodial fees that reduce returns. Despite these drawbacks, the Cornell and Green approach provides useful information about this sector of the bond market. They conclude that high-yield bonds are fairly priced relative to high-grade bonds after adjusting for risk.

---

[15] The Altman and Nammacher and Hradsky and Long studies cite significantly lower default rates, but they employ a definition of default rate that ignores the effect of aging on the propensity to default.

[16] Rayner Cheung, Joseph C. Bencivenga, and Frank J. Fabozzi, "Original Issue High-Yield Bonds: Historical Return and Default Experiences 1977-1989," *Journal of Fixed Income* (September 1992), pp. 58-76

[17] Marshall E. Blume, Donald B. Keim, and Sandeep A. Patel, "Returns and Volatility of Low-Grade Bonds 1977-1989," *Journal of Finance* (March 1991), pp. 49-74.

[18] Bradford Cornell and K. Green, "The Investment Performance of Low-Grade Bond Funds," *Journal of Finance* (March 1991), pp. 29-48.

Exhibit 10: Components of the Broad-Based Indexes as of December 31, 1994

Sector	Lehman Aggregate (%)	Merrill Domestic Master (%)	Salomon BIG (%)
Treasury	47	50	46
Agency	7	7	6
Corporate	17[a]	17	18
Mortgages	29	26	30
Total	100%	100%	100%
No. of issues	4,854	5,456	4,211
Par value ($ millions)	4,094	4,121	4,018
Market value ($ millions)	3,954	4,019	3,940
Average price	96.59	97.53	—
Average coupon	7.54%	7.55%	7.39%
Average maturity (years)	8.83	12.86	9.03
Average yield	8.21%	8.23%	8.24%
Duration	5.08	5.04	5.00

[a] The composition of the corporate sector in the Lehman Brothers index is as follows: Industrial, 6%; Utility, 3%; Financial, 4%; Yankee, 3%; and, Asset-backed, 1%.

Source: Data compiled by authors from information provided by Ryan Labs, Inc.

Consequently, none of the studies seem to suggest that investing in the high-yield market offers exceptional value. Rather, long-run returns are in line with what capital market theory would suggest: in the long-run, high-yield bonds have outperformed both high grade corporate bonds and Treasuries but have been outperformed by common stock. Therefore, any claim of superior performance by advocates of high-yield bonds must be taken with the greatest caution.

CORPORATE BOND INDEXES

The performance of a money manger is evaluated relative to some benchmark. The benchmark could be a set of liabilities or a bond index. In the case of the manager of a corporate bond portfolio, there are several corporate bond indexes by which a manager can be evaluated. In this section we review the more popular corporate bond indexes.

The wide range of bond market indexes available can be classified as broad-based market indexes and specialized market indexes. The three broad-based market indexes most commonly used by institutional investors are the Lehman Brothers Aggregate Index, the Salomon Brothers Broad Investment-Grade Bond Index (BIG), and the Merrill Lynch Domestic Market Index. The bond market sectors covered by these three indexes are the Treasury, agency, investment-grade corporate, mortgage-backed, and Yankee sectors. Exhibit 10 shows the corporate bond components of the three broad-based indexes and a detailed breakdown of the sectors within the corporate bond market as of the end of 1994.

All three broad-based indexes and their component sectors are market-value weighted indexes and they are priced daily by the traders of the firm. The corporate bonds included in each index are those rated at least BBB. That is, only investment grade bonds are included. Excluded from all three indexes are convertible bonds. Floating rate bonds are excluded from the Lehman Brothers and Salomon Brothers indexes.

It is important to keep in mind that the values reported for price, coupon, and yield are average values. Basically, they are meaningless for any analytical purposes. As we know from Chapter 9, price/yield relationships are convex, not linear. This means parameters such as price and yield cannot be averaged. In some instances, the average yield reported for an index may exceed the average coupon while the average price is reported as being greater than par. This strange result is due to the inappropriate procedure of calculating averages.

Based on the corporate bond sector of the three broad-based indexes, Exhibit 11 reports the annual returns for the years 1981 to 1994. Exhibit 12 shows the standard deviation of returns for various periods ending in 1994. Exhibit 13 shows how one index tracks the other each year from 1981 to 1994. The measure used is the mean absolute tracking deviations and is used so that positive and negative deviations in return do not offset each other.

ACTIVE PORTFOLIO STRATEGIES WITH CORPORATE BONDS

A portfolio must select a corporate bond portfolio strategy that is consistent with the objectives and policy guidelines of the client or institution. Corporate bond portfolio strategies can be classified as either active strategies or passive strategies. Essential to all active strategies is specification of expectations about the factors that influence the performance of corporate bonds. This section describes several popular corporate bond active portfolio strategies within the context of the total return framework discussed above. In the next section we discuss the most popular form of passive strategy, indexing.

The starting point in our discussion of active strategies is an investigation of the various sources of return from a corporate bond portfolio. As we explain in Chapter 9, the three sources of return are coupon income, any capital gain (or loss), and reinvestment income. Here we explore the factors that affect one or more of these sources. In general, the following factors affect a corporate bond portfolio's return:

1. Changes in the level of Treasury rates
2. Changes in the shape of the Treasury yield curve
3. Changes in credit spreads between corporates and Treasuries
4. Changes in the yield spread for a particular corporate issue

Exhibit 11: Annual Returns for Corporate Bond Components of the Three Broad-Based Indexes (1981 to 1994)

Index	1981	1982	1983	1984	1985	1986	1987	1988	1989	1990	1991	1992	1993	1994
ML Corporate	2.30	35.53	9.32	16.21	25.36	16.30	1.84	9.76	14.12	7.37	18.24	9.12	12.43	-3.34
SB Corporate	2.75	37.12	8.95	16.04	24.93	17.03	2.06	9.47	13.97	7.28	18.05	8.87	12.11	-4.17
LB Corporate	2.95	39.20	9.27	16.62	24.06	16.53	2.56	9.22	14.09	7.05	18.51	8.69	12.16	-3.93

Source: Ryan Labs, Inc.

Exhibit 12: Standard Deviation for Corporate Bond Components of the Three Broad-Based Indexes (Period Ending 1994)

Index	Last 10 Yrs	Last 7 Yrs	Last 5 Yrs	Last 3 Yrs	Last 12 Mos
ML Corporate	5.51	4.68	4.52	4.58	4.68
SB Corporate	5.50	4.77	4.53	4.72	5.02
LB Corporate	5.50	4.82	4.79	5.02	5.41

Source: Ryan Labs, Inc.

Exhibit 13: Mean Absolute Monthly Tracking Deviations for Corporate Bond Components of the Three Broad-Based Indexes by Year (1981-1994)

Index	1981	1982	1983	1984	1985	1986	1987	1988	1989	1990	1991	1992	1993	1994
LB C vs. ML C	35	37	18	29	19	34	29	21	17	19	12	15	12	19
LB C vs. SB C	34	39	19	34	23	13	16	21	13	10	14	15	8	17
ML C vs. SB C	30	43	15	20	26	22	31	29	11	19	13	14	12	18

Source: Ryan Labs, Inc.

A money manager who pursues an active strategy will position a portfolio, subject to client and/or regulatory constraints, to capitalize on expectations about the above factors. Other active strategies are based not on the traditional yield spread but on the option-adjusted spread discussed in Chapter 11.

The total return framework should be employed to analyze the effect of an expected outcome or outcomes on a corporate bond portfolio's return. Recall from our discussion in Chapter 9 that yield measures are inadequate for assessing the potential performance of an individual bond. For a corporate bond portfolio, the meaning of a "portfolio yield" is questionable and certainly provides no insight into the return for a portfolio over some investment horizon.

What is critical in assessing strategies that are not based on expected changes in the level of interest rates is to compare corporate bond positions that have the same dollar duration. To understand why, consider two corporate bonds, X and Y. Suppose that the price of X is 80 and has a modified duration of 5 while Y has a price of 90 and has a modified duration of 4. Since modified duration is the approximate change per 100 basis point change in yield, a 100 basis points change in yield for bond X would change its price by about 5%. Based on a price of 80, its price will change by about $4 per $80 of market value. Thus, its dollar duration for a 100 basis point change in yield is $4 per $80 of market value. Similarly, for Y, its dollar duration for a 100 basis point change in yield per $90 of market value can be determined. In this case it is $3.6. So, if bonds X and Y are being considered as alternative investments in some strategy other than one based on anticipating interest rate movements, the amount of each bond in the strategy should be such that they will both have the same dollar duration.

To illustrate this, suppose that a portfolio manager owns $10 million of par value of X which has a market value of $8 million. The dollar duration of X per 100 basis point change in yield for the $8 million market value is $400,000. Suppose further that this portfolio manager is considering exchanging X that it owns in its portfolio for Y. If the portfolio manager wants to have the same interest rate exposure (i.e., dollar duration) for Y that he currently has for X, he will buy a market value amount of Y with the same dollar duration. If the portfolio manager purchased $10 million of *par value* of Y and therefore $9 million of *market value* of Y, the per 100 basis change in yield would be only $360,000. If, instead, the portfolio manager purchased $10 million of *market value* of Y, the dollar duration per 100 basis point change in yield would be $400,000. Since Y is trading at 90, $11.11 million of par value of Y must be purchased to keep the dollar duration of the position from Y the same as for X.

Mathematically, this problem can be expressed as follows:

Let:

$\$D_X$ = dollar duration per 100 basis point change in yield for bond X for the market value of bond X held

MD_Y = modified duration for bond Y

MV_Y = market value of bond Y needed to obtain the same dollar duration as bond X

Then, the following equation sets the dollar duration for bond X equal to the dollar duration for bond Y:

$$\$D_X = (MD_Y/100)\,MV_Y$$

Solving for MV_Y,

$$MV_Y = \$D_X/(MD_Y/100)$$

Dividing by the price per \$1 of par value of Y gives the par value of Y that has an approximately equivalent dollar duration as bond X.

In our illustration, $\$D_X$ is \$400,000 and MD_Y is 4, then

$$MV_Y = \$400,000/(4/100) = \$10,000,000$$

Since the market value of Y is 90 per \$100 of par value, the price per \$1 of par value is 0.9. Dividing \$10 million by 0.9 indicates that the par value of Y that should be purchased is \$11.11 million.

Interest Rate Expectations Strategies

A money manager who believes that he or she can accurately forecast the future level of interest rates will alter the portfolio's sensitivity to interest rate changes. As duration is a measure of interest rate sensitivity, this involves increasing a portfolio's duration if interest rates are expected to fall and reducing it if interest rates are expected to rise. For those money managers whose benchmark is a bond index, this means increasing the portfolio duration relative to the benchmark index if interest rates are expected to fall and reducing it if interest rates are expected to rise. The degree to which the duration of the managed portfolio is permitted to diverge from that of the benchmark index may be limited by the client.

A portfolio's duration may be altered by swapping bonds in the portfolio for new bonds that will achieve the target portfolio duration. Such swaps are commonly referred to as *rate anticipation swaps*. A more efficient means for altering the duration of a bond portfolio is to use interest rate futures contracts. Buying futures increases a portfolio's duration, while selling futures decreases it.

The key to this active strategy is, of course, an ability to forecast the direction of future interest rates. The academic literature, however, does not support the view that interest rates can be forecasted so that risk-adjusted excess returns can be consistently realized. It is doubtful whether betting on future interest rates will provide a consistently superior return.

While a money manager may not pursue an active strategy based strictly on future interest rate movements, there can be a tendency to make an interest rate bet to cover inferior performance relative to a benchmark index. For example, suppose a money manager holds himself or herself out to a client as pursuing one of the active strategies discussed later in this chapter. Suppose further that the money manager is evaluated over a one-year investment horizon, and that three months before the end of the investment horizon, the money manager is performing below the client-specified benchmark index. If the money manager believes the account will be lost because of underperformance, there is an incentive to bet on interest rate movements. If the manager is correct, the account will be saved, although an incorrect bet will result in underperforming the benchmark index by a greater amount. In this case, the account might probably be lost regardless of the level of underperformance. A client can prevent this type of gaming by a money manager by imposing constraints on the degree that the portfolio's duration can vary from that of the benchmark index. Also, in evaluating the performance of a money manager, decomposing the portfolio's return into the factors that generated the return will highlight the extent to which a portfolio's return is attributable to changes in the level of interest rates.

There are other active strategies that rely on forecasts of future interest rate levels. Future interest rates, for instance, affect the value of options embedded in callable corporate bonds. Callable corporate bonds with coupon rates above the expected future interest rate will underperform relative to noncallable bonds or low-coupon bonds. This is because of the negative convexity feature of callable bonds.

Yield Curve Strategies

As we explain in Chapter 10, the yield curve is the relationship between maturity and yield on issues of the same credit quality. The shape of the Treasury yield curve changes over time. Because a portfolio consists of corporate with different maturities, changes in the shape of the Treasury yield curve will have varying price effects on each bond.

Two portfolios with the same duration will perform differently if the yield curve does not shift in a parallel fashion. To see this point, consider the three bonds and two portfolios shown in Exhibit 14.[19] Portfolio I consists of only bond C, the ten-year bond, and is referred to as the "bullet portfolio." Portfolio II consists of 50.2% of bond A and 49.8% of bond B, and we call this portfolio the "barbell portfolio." The dollar duration of the bullet portfolio per 100 basis point change in yield is 6.43409.

Note in Exhibit 14 that the dollar duration of the barbell — which is just the weighted average of the dollar duration of the two bonds — is the same as that of the bullet portfolio. In fact, the barbell portfolio was designed to produce this result. Duration is just a first approximation of the change in price resulting from a change in interest rates. Convexity provides a second approximation. The dollar convexity of the two portfolios, shown in Exhibit 14, is not equal. The dollar convexity of the bullet portfolio is less than that of the barbell portfolio.

The "yield" for the two portfolios likewise is not the same. The yield (yield to maturity) for the bullet is simply the yield to maturity of bond C, 9.25%. The traditional yield calculation for the barbell portfolio, which is found by taking a weighted average of the yield to maturity of the two bonds included in the portfolio, is 8.998%. This approach suggests that the "yield" of the bullet portfolio is 25.2 basis points greater than the barbell portfolio. Although both portfolios have the same dollar duration, the yield of the bullet portfolio is greater than the yield of the barbell portfolio. However, the dollar convexity of the barbell portfolio is greater than that of the bullet portfolio. The difference in the two yields is sometimes referred to as the "cost of convexity."

---

[19] This illustration is adapted from Ravi E. Dattatreya and Frank J. Fabozzi, *Active Total Return Management of Fixed Income Portfolios* (Burr Ridge, IL: Irwin, 1989).

Exhibit 14: Three Hypothetical Securities
for Bullet-Barbell Analysis

Bond	Coupon	Maturity (years)	Price plus accrued	Yield (%)	Dollar Duration	Dollar Convexity
A	8.50	5	100	8.50	4.00544	19.8164
B	9.50	20	100	9.50	8.88151	124.1702
C	9.25	10	100	9.25	6.43409	55.4506

Bullet: Bond C
Barbell: Bonds A and B
Composition of barbell: 50.2% of Bond A; 49.8% of Bond B
Dollar duration of barbell = 0.502 × 4.00544 + 0.498 × 8.88151 = 6.434
Dollar convexity of barbell = 0.502 × 19.8164 + 0.498 × 124.1702 = 71.7846

$$\text{Cash-flow yield of barbell}^* = \frac{(8.5 \times 0.502 \times 4.00544) + (9.5 \times 0.498 \times 8.88151)}{6.434} = 9.187$$

Yield pickup = Yield on bullet – Dollar-duration weighted yield
         = 9.25 – 9.187 = 0.063 or 6.3 basis points
Convexity give-up = Convexity of barbell – Convexity of bullet
         = 71.7846 – 55.4506 = 16.334
* The calculation shown is actually a dollar-duration-weighted yield, a very close approximation to cash-flow yield.

The column labeled "Parallel Shift" in Exhibit 15 shows the difference in the total return over a six-month investment horizon for the two portfolios assuming that the yield curve shifts in a "parallel" fashion.[20] By parallel it is meant that the yields for the short-term bond (A), the intermediate-term bond (C), and the long-term bond (B) change by the same number of basis points, shown in the "Yield Change" column of the exhibit. The total return reported is:

Bullet portfolio's total return – Barbell portfolio's total return

Thus a positive value in the total return column means that the bullet portfolio outperformed the barbell portfolio, while a negative sign means that the barbell portfolio outperformed the bullet portfolio.

Which portfolio is the better investment alternative if the yield curve shifts in a parallel fashion and the investment horizon is six months? The answer depends on the amount by which yields change. Notice that when yields change by less than 100 basis points, the bullet portfolio outperforms the barbell portfolio. The reverse is true if yields change by more than 100 basis points.

---

[20] Note that no assumption is needed for the reinvestment rate because the three bonds shown in the exhibit are assumed to be trading right after a coupon payment has been made and therefore there is no accrued interest.

Exhibit 15: Relative Performance of Bullet Portfolio and Barbell Portfolio Over a Six-Month Investment Horizon[*]

Yield Change	Parallel Shift (%)	Flattening(%)[a]	Steepening (%)[b]
-3.500	-2.82	-5.44	-0.35
-3.250	-2.32	-4.82	0.03
-3.000	-1.88	-4.26	0.36
-2.750	-1.49	-3.75	0.65
-2.500	-1.15	-3.30	0.89
-2.250	-0.85	-2.90	1.09
-2.000	-0.59	-2.55	1.25
-1.750	-0.38	-2.24	1.37
-1.500	-0.20	-1.97	1.47
-1.250	-0.05	-1.74	1.53
-1.000	0.06	-1.54	1.57
-0.750	0.15	-1.38	1.58
-0.500	0.21	-1.24	1.57
-0.250	0.24	-1.14	1.53
0.000	0.25	-1.06	1.48
0.250	0.24	- 1.01	1.41
0.500	0.21	-0.98	1.32
0.750	0.16	-0.97	1.21
1.000	0.09	-0.98	1.09
1.250	0.01	- 1.00	0.96
1.500	-0.08	- 1.05	0.81
1.750	-0.19	- 1.10	0.66
2.000	-0.31	-1.18	0.49
2.250	-0.44	-1.26	0.32
2.500	-0.58	- 1.36	0.14
2.750	-0.73	-1.46	-0.05
3.000	-0.88	-1.58	-0.24
3.250	-1.05	-1.70	-0.44
3.500	-1.21	-1.84	-0.64

[*] Performance is based on the difference in total return over a six-month investment horizon. Specifically:

Bullet portfolio's total return – Barbell portfolio's total return

Therefore a negative value means that the barbell outperformed the bullet portfolio.

[a] Change in yield for bond C. Non-parallel shift as follows (flattening of yield curve):

Yield change bond A = yield change bond C + 25 basis points
Yield change bond B = yield change bond C – 25 basis points

[b] Change in yield for bond C. Non-parallel shifts as follows (steepening of yield curve):

Yield change bond A = yield change bond C – 25 basis points
Yield change bond B = yield change bond C + 25 basis points

Now let's look at what happens if the yield curve does not shift in a parallel fashion. The last two columns of Exhibit 15 show the relative performance of the two portfolios for a nonparallel shift of the yield curve. Specifically, the first nonparallel shift column assumes that if the yield on bond C (the intermediate-term bond) changes by the amount shown in the first column, bond A (the short-term bond) will change by the same amount plus 25 basis points, whereas bond B (the long-term bond) will change by the same amount shown in the first column less 25 basis points. That is, the nonparallel shift assumed is a flattening of the yield curve. For this yield curve shift, the barbell always outperforms the bullet. In the last column, the nonparallel shift assumes that for a change in bond C's yield, the yield on bond A will change by the same amount less 25 basis points, whereas that on bond B will change by the same amount plus 25 points. That is, it assumes that the yield curve will steepen. In this case, the bullet portfolio outperforms the barbell portfolio so long as the yield on bond C does not rise by more than 250 basis points or fall by more than 325 basis points.

The key point here is that looking at measures such as yield (yield to maturity or some type of portfolio yield measure), duration or convexity tells us little about performance over some investment horizon, because performance depends on the magnitude of the change in yields and how the yield curve shifts.

Yield Spread Strategies

Yield spread strategies involve positioning a portfolio to capitalize on expected changes in yield spreads between sectors of the bond market. Bond swaps or exchanges undertaken when the money manager believes that the prevailing yield spread between two bonds in the market is out of line with their historical yield spread, and that the yield spread will realign by the end of the investment horizon, are called *intermarket spread swaps*.

Yield spreads between maturity sectors involve changes in the yield curve as we have discussed in the previous section. Credit or quality spreads change because of expected changes in economic prospects. Credit spreads between triple-A corporate issues and lower rated issues widen in a declining or contracting economy and narrow during economic expansion. The economic rationale is that in a declining or contracting economy, corporations experience a decline in revenue and reduced cash flow, making it difficult for issuers to service their contractual debt obligations. Investors will attempt a flight to quality, increasing the demand for higher credit quality issues. To induce investors to hold securities of lower quality corporate issuers, the yield spread relative to triple-A rated issues must widen. The converse is that during economic expansion and brisk economic activity, revenue and cash flow pick up, increasing the likelihood that corporate issuers will have the capacity to service their contractual debt obligations.

Exhibit 16: Relative Yield

Period	Average 10-Year treasury Yield (%)	Average BBB Utility Yield (%)	Average Spread (%)	Relative Yield (%)	Yield Ratio
1955-1959	3.46	4.21	75	22	1.217
1960-1964	4.03	4.79	76	29	1.189
1965-1969	5.32	6.22	95	17	1.169
1970-1974	6.82	8.75	197	28	1.283
1975-1979	8.17	10.04	191	23	1.229
1980-1984	12.30	15.18	276	23	1.234
1985-1989	8.81	10.92	209	24	1.240

Source: Chris P. Dialynas and David H. Edington, "Bond Yield Spreads — A Postmodern View,"
Journal of Portfolio Management (Fall 1992), Exhibit 6.
This copyrighted material is reprinted with permission from Institutional Investor, Inc.
Journal of Portfolio Management, 488 Madison Avenue, New York, NY 10022.

Yield spreads are also related to the level of interest rates. For example, in 1957, when the yield on Treasuries was 3%, the yield spread between a triple-B rated utility bond and Treasuries was 40 basis points. This represented a relative yield spread of 13% (.4% divided by 3%). When the yield on Treasuries exceeded 10% in 1985, however, a yield spread of 40 basis points would have meant only a relative yield spread of 4%.[21] Consequently, the yield spread measured in basis points had to be greater than 40 basis points to produce a similar relative yield. Exhibit 16 suggests that the relative yield spread — as measured by the ratio of the yield spread to the level of Treasury yields — and the yield ratio — the ratio of non-Treasury and Treasury yields — tends to be relatively stable over time.

Spreads attributable to differences in callable and noncallable corporate bonds and differences in coupons of callable corporate bonds will change as a result of expected changes in (1) the direction of the change in interest rates, and (2) interest rate volatility. An expected drop in the level of interest rates will widen the yield spread between callable bonds and noncallable corporate bonds as the prospects that the issuer will exercise the call option increase. The reverse is true: the yield spread narrows if interest rates are expected to rise. An increase in interest rate volatility increases the value of the embedded call option, and thereby increases the yield spread between callable corporate bonds and noncallable corporate bonds.

Individual Security Selection Strategies

There are several active strategies that managers of corporate bond portfolios pursue to identify mispriced issues. The most common strategy identifies an issue as undervalued because either (1) its yield is higher than that of comparably rated issues, or (2) its yield is expected to decline (and price therefore rise) because credit analysis indicates that its rating will improve.

---

[21] Chris P. Dialynas and David H. Edington, "Bond Yield Spreads — A Postmodern View," *Journal of Portfolio Management* (Fall 1992).

A swap in which a money manager exchanges one bond for another bond that is similar in terms of coupon, maturity, and credit quality, but offers a higher yield, is called a *substitution swap*. This swap depends on a capital market imperfection. Such situations sometimes exist in the bond market owing to temporary market imbalances and the fragmented nature of certain sectors within the corporate bond market. The risk the money manager faces in making a substitution swap is that the corporate issue purchased may not be truly identical to the corporate issue for which it is exchanged. Moreover, typically corporate issues will have similar but not identical maturities and coupon. This could lead to differences in the convexity of the two bonds, and any yield spread may reflect this.

We emphasized that nominal yield spreads are not a measure of relative value or potential return performance. The same is true for the option-adjusted spread (OAS) measure described in Chapter 11. A strategy that is too often suggested is that a manager should seek to maximize OAS. However, there is no reason to suspect *a priori* that a relative ranking of securities on the basis of OAS will correlate with actual total return rankings.

The Bond Strategy Group of Lehman Brothers investigated this issue.[22] Structurally homogeneous utility bonds were ranked based on OAS at the end of 1987. Actual returns for the subsequent five years were then calculated. Exhibit 17 shows the correlation between the computed OAS in 1987 and the actual cumulative total return for each year for the next five years. The OAS rankings did not correlate well with actual performance. In fact, the preponderance of negative correlations suggests that a strategy of OAS minimization would have resulted in better performance. Also shown in Exhibit 17 are the correlations based on one-year annual total return rankings.

An interesting strategy for dealing with individual issues that have switched classification from investment grade to noninvestment grade and vice versa has been suggested by the Bond Strategy Group of Lehman Brothers.[23] This group investigated the performance of downgraded issues from triple-B rating (lowest investment grade rating) to double-B rating (highest noninvestment grade rating), and upgraded issues from double B-rating to triple-B rating.

For the period investigated, November 1, 1989 through December 31, 1994, the study found that downgraded issues underperformed the triple-B and double-B Lehman Brothers indices the most during the month prior to the downgrade (probably due to the fact that the market anticipated the downgrades due to watchlistings) and the actual month of downgrading. There was also underperformance in the first month after downgrading. However, in subsequent months, downgraded issues tended to outperform triple-B issues. For issues that were upgraded from double B to triple B, superior performance was realized two months prior, a month prior, and the month of the upgrade. However, the relative performance of the new triple B issues was poor relative to other triple Bs in subsequent months.

---

[22] Jack Malvey, Steve Mandl, and Arang Varadhachary, *Corporate Bond Strategy Playbook: Part II*, Fixed Income Research, Lehman Brothers, January 31, 1995, Appendix, pp. C-D.

[23] Malvey, Mandl, and Varadhachary, *Corporate Bond Strategy Playbook: Part II*, Appendix, p. C.

Exhibit 17: Correlations Between
Ex Ante OAS and Total Returns

Correlations between Cumulative Total Return Rankings and OAS

		1-Year	2-Year	3-Year	4-Year	5-Year
Electrics	Aa	0.32	0.36	-0.86	-0.39	-0.63
	A	-0.75	-0.69	-0.39	-0.89	-0.88
	BBB	-0.12	-0.60	-0.79	-0.62	-0.85
Telephones		-0.30	-0.32	0.07	-0.66	-0.25

Correlations between Annual Total Return Rankings and OAS

		1988	1989	1990	1991	1992
Electrics	Aa	0.32	0.29	-0.79	-0.71	-0.50
	A	-0.75	-0.12	0.09	-0.51	0.02
	BBB	-0.12	-0.52	-0.57	-0.62	0.70
Telephones		-0.30	0.16	0.25	-0.60	0.39

Source: Jack Malvey, Steve Mandl, and Arang Varadhachary, *Corporate Bond Strategy Playbook: Part II*, Fixed Income Research, Lehman Brothers, January 31, 1995, Appendix, p. 13.

There are two implications of this study. First, downgrades from triple-B should be considered for purchase in months following the downgrade ("buy the downgrade"). Second, upgrades to triple B should be considered for sale in months subsequent to the upgrade ("sell the upgrade").

FRAMEWORK FOR CORPORATE BOND SECTOR SELECTION

Leland Crabbe of Merrill Lynch has demonstrated that incremental corporate bond returns over Treasuries can be attributed to three factors: (1) the initial yield spread between corporates and Treasuries; (2) the change in yield spreads over the investment horizon; and, (3) the change in the credit quality.[24] Even if there is no change in the second factor over the investment horizon, changes in credit quality are critical.

Downgraded bonds will decline in price while upgrades bonds will appreciate in price. The net effect on the portfolio's return will depend on the mix of upgraded and downgraded bonds, and the slope of the credit quality curves. Crabbe sets forth a useful framework that takes into account the factors that affect incremental returns over Treasuries for corporate bonds by ranking credit quality sectors according to their expected incremental returns. What Crabbe emphasizes, and what we have emphasized throughout Section II, is that the richness or cheapness of a sector of the corporate bond market cannot be assessed merely based on the yield spread.

---

[24] Leland E. Crabbe, "A Framework for Corporate Bond Strategy," *Journal of Fixed Income* (June 1995), pp. 15-25.

Exhibit 18: One Year Rating Transition Probabilities (%)

	Rating at End of Year							
Rating at Start of Year	Aaa	Aa	A	Baa	Ba	B	C or D	Total
Aaa	91.90	7.38	0.72	0.00	0.00	0.00	0.00	100.00
Aa	1.13	91.26	7.09	0.31	0.21	0.00	0.00	100.00
A	0.10	2.56	91.20	5.33	0.61	0.20	0.00	100.00
Baa	0.00	0.21	5.36	87.94	5.46	0.82	0.21	100.00

Source: Exhibit 1 of Leland E. Crabbe, "A Framework for Corporate Bond Strategy," *Journal of Fixed Income* (June 1995), p. 16.

The framework proposed by Crabbe begins with an analysis of the historical experience of credit quality changes. This is done in the form of a *rating transition matrix*. Exhibit 18 shows a one-year rating transition matrix (table) based on a Moody's study for the period 1970-1993. Here is how to interpret the table. The rows indicate the rating at the beginning of a year. The columns show the rating at the end of the year. For example, look at the second row. This row shows the transition for double-A rated bonds at the beginning of a year. The number 91.26 in the second row means that on average 91.26% of double-A rated bonds at the beginning of the year remained double-A rated at year end. The value of 1.13 means that on average 1.13% of double-A rated bonds at the beginning of the year were upgraded to triple A. The value of 0.31 means that on average 0.31% of double-A rated bonds at the beginning of the year were downgraded to a triple B rating.

From Exhibit 18 it should be clear that the probability of a downgrade is much higher than for an upgrade for investment grade bonds. While the historical rating transition matrix is a useful starting point since it represents an average over the 1970-1993 period, a manager must modify the matrix based on expectations of upgrades and downgrades given current and anticipated economic conditions.

Given the rating transition matrix that the manager expects, an expected incremental return can be calculated for each credit quality sector. This involves four steps. First, estimate what the spread over Treasuries will be for all ratings at the end of the investment horizon. Second, estimate the price change for upgraded and downgraded bonds based on the new spreads. Third, compute the return for upgraded and downgraded bonds based on the price change calculated in the first step and the coupon interest. Finally, calculate the expected incremental return for the credit quality sector by weighting the returns by the probabilities as given in the manager's rating transition matrix.

To illustrate this, suppose that the manager's rating transition matrix is the one shown in Exhibit 18. Suppose also that the manager expects that the spreads will not change over the one year investment horizon. Consider the double-A rated sector. Exhibit 19 shows the expected incremental return estimates for a portfolio consisting of only three-year double-A rated bonds. The first column shows the initial spread. The second column is the rating at the end of the investment horizon. The horizon spread is the spread over Treasuries at the end of the investment horizon for each of the credit quality sectors for the three-year maturity sector shown in the second column. For example, if there is no change in the rating, the horizon spread is the same as the initial spread of 30 basis points. An upgrade reduces the spread, a downgrade increases it. The assumption in our illustration is that the horizon spread is the same as currently observed. The fourth column shows the horizon return over Treasuries based on price change and coupon interest. The next to the last column gives the probabilities from the rating transition matrix (i.e., the second row of Exhibit 18). The sum of the product of the fourth and fifth columns gives the expected incremental return over Treasuries of 28.9 basis points.

There are two reasons why the expected incremental return over Treasuries of 28.9 basis points is less than the initial spread of 30 basis points. First, the probability of an upgrade is significantly less than for a downgrade. Second, the steepness of the credit spread curve at the end of the investment horizon penalizes downgrades.

From this illustration it can be seen that the incremental return over Treasuries depends on the initial spread, the change in the spread, and the probability of a rating change.

The framework can be extended to any maturity sector. Exhibit 20 shows expected incremental returns over Treasuries assuming the rating transition matrix given in Exhibit 18 and assuming that the horizon spreads are the same as the initial spreads. For example, the first box in Exhibit 20 shows that the expected incremental return in the three-year maturity sector of the corporate bond market is 28.9 basis points for double-A rated bonds and 46.3 basis points for triple-B rated bonds.

The exhibit provides a guide for assessing relative value within each maturity sector. Notice that for all rating sectors and maturity sectors, expected incremental returns are less than the initial spread. For the three-year and five-year maturity sectors, the ranking by expected incremental return is the same as for the ranking by initial spread. However, this is not true for the ten-year and 30-year maturity sectors. This is because of the significant influence of the duration of the bonds in these sectors and the steepness of the credit quality spread. Exhibit 20 can also be used to assess relative value among maturity sectors for a given rating sector.

While the illustrations assumed the rating transmission matrix in Exhibit 18 and that the spread over Treasuries at the end of the investment horizon would be unchanged from the initial spread, this will not be the case in practice. The manager will modify both assumptions based on prevailing and expected market conditions. For example, Exhibit 21 shows the expected incremental returns by maturity sector assuming that the transition matrix is the same as in Exhibit 18 but that the credit curve steepens at the end of the one year investment horizon.

Exhibit 19: Expected Incremental Return Estimates for Three-Year AA-Rated Bonds Over a One-Year Horizon

Initial Spread	Horizon Rating	Horizon Spread	Return over Treasuries (bp)	×	Transition Probability (%)	=	Contribution to Incremental Return (bp)
30	Aaa	25	38		1.13		0.43
30	Aa	30	30		91.26		27.38
30	A	35	21		7.09		1.49
30	Baa	60	-24		0.31		-0.07
30	Ba	130	-147		0.21		-0.31
			Portfolio Incremental Return over Treasuries		=		28.90

Source: Exhibit 2 of Leland E. Crabbe, "A Framework for Corporate Bond Strategy,"
Journal of Fixed Income (June 1995), p. 17.
This copyrighted material is reprinted with permission from Institutional Investor, Inc.
Journal of Fixed Income, 488 Madison Avenue, New York, NY 10022.

Exhibit 20: Expected Incremental Returns Over Treasuries When Rating Transitions Match Historical Experience (One-year Horizon; bp)

Rating at Start of Year	3-Year		5-Year		10-Year		30-Year	
	Initial Spread	Incremental Return	Initial Spread	Incremental Return	Initial Spread	Incremental Return	Initial Spread	Incremental Return
Aaa	25	24.2	30	28.4	35	31.7	45	34.6
Aa	30	28.9	35	31.4	40	30.3	55	34.8
A	35	31.1	45	37.3	55	37.9	75	42.7
Baa	60	46.3	70	39.9	85	21.9	115	27.4

Source: Exhibit 3 of Leland E. Crabbe, "A Framework for Corporate Bond Strategy,"
Journal of Fixed Income (June 1995), p. 18.
This copyrighted material is reprinted with permission from Institutional Investor, Inc.
Journal of Fixed Income, 488 Madison Avenue, New York, NY 10022.

Exhibit 21: Expected Incremental Returns Over Treasuries When the Spread Curve Steepens and Rating Transitions Match Historical Experience (One-year Horizon, bp)

Rating at Start of Year	3-Year			5-Year		
	Initial Spread	Horizon Spread	Incremental Return	Initial Spread	Horizon Spread	Incremental Return
Aaa	25	25	23.9	30	30	27.8
Aa	30	32	25.0	35	37	24.1
A	35	39	23.6	45	49	23.4
Baa	60	66	35.3	70	76	19.6

Rating at Start of Year	10-Year			30-Year		
	Initial Spread	Horizon Spread	Incremental Return	Initial Spread	Horizon Spread	Incremental Return
Aaa	35	35	30.6	45	45	32.7
Aa	40	42	16.7	55	57	11.5
A	55	59	12.1	75	79	-0.8
Baa	85	91	-15.4	115	121	-33.6

Source: Exhibit 13 of Leland E. Crabbe, "A Framework for Corporate Bond Strategy,"
Journal of Fixed Income (June 1995), p. 24.
This copyrighted material is reprinted with permission from Institutional Investor, Inc.
Journal of Fixed Income, 488 Madison Avenue, New York, NY 10022.

TECHNICAL TIMING STRATEGIES

In the stock market, there have been numerous studies of whether during particular times during the year, month, or day there are opportunities to implement a strategy that will add incremental returns. These market anomalies are sometimes referred to as the *calendar* or *seasonality effect*.

In the corporate bond market, it has been observed that there is a seasonality effect. Specifically, finance theory proffers that there is an inverse relationship between credit quality and expected total return. That is, lower credit quality issues should have higher expected total returns. Earlier we cited the empirical evidence to support that historical returns have actually followed that pattern. However, the Bond Strategy Group at Lehman Brothers has documented a direct relationship between credit quality and fourth quarter total returns since the inception of the Lehman Brothers investment grade index in 1973 through December 31, 1994.[25] That is, total returns in the fourth quarter are higher the higher the credit rating. The pattern reverts to that expected in the first quarter.

For the period studied, the fourth quarter and first quarter average returns reported by Lehman Brothers are shown below:

Rating	Total Return	
	1994 Fourth Quarter	1995 First Quarter
Aaa	3.62%	0.87%
Aa	3.57%	1.14%
A	3.30%	1.43%
Baa	3.10%	2.16%

This market anomaly is dubbed the *fourth-quarter and first-quarter effects*. The Lehman Brothers study found that the fourth-quarter effect was evident in 13 of the 22 years studied (the exceptions being 1974, 1977, 1980, 1981, 1982, 1984, 1988, 1993, and 1994). The first-quarter effect was found for 18 of the 22 years investigated. Upgrading the portfolio by trading out of triple Bs at the start of the fourth quarter and downgrading to triple Bs at the end of the fourth quarter produced an average incremental return of 93 basis points before transaction costs.

In the opinion of Lehman's Bond Strategy Group, the fourth-quarter and first-quarter effects appear to have been "the best technical technique to add incremental value to corporate portfolios during the past two decades..."[26] This would suggest upgrading a portfolio going into the fourth quarter ("upgrade trade") and downgrading at the end of the fourth quarter ("spread-maximization trade"). While the discussion has concentrated on investment grade bonds, there appears to be evidence that this seasonality effect may also hold in the high yield market.

---

[25] Malvey, Mandl, and Varadhachary, *Corporate Bond Strategy Playbook: Part II*, Appendix, pp. A-C.

[26] Malvey, Mandl, and Varadhachary, *Corporate Bond Strategy Playbook: Part II*, Appendix, p. A.

INDEXING A CORPORATE BOND PORTFOLIO

Now let's look at passive strategies. The most popular form of passive strategy is indexing. This strategy involves designing a portfolio so that its performance will match the performance of some bond index. In indexing, performance is measured in terms of total rate of return achieved (or simply, total return) over some investment horizon.

Indexing an equity portfolio is commonplace. On the bond side, index-ing is a relatively recent phenomenon. A manager who is seeking to match the corporate bond sector of the index but actively manage the MBS or Treasury/ agency sector can pursue an indexing strategy for just the corporate sector.

Indexing Methodologies

In this section, we discuss the issues involved in creating a portfolio to track the per-formance of the corporate bond sector of an index. Any discrepancy between the per-formance of the indexed portfolio and the index (whether positive or negative) is referred to as *tracking error.* Tracking error has three sources: (1) transaction costs in constructing the indexed portfolio; (2) differences in the composition of the indexed portfolio and the index itself; and (3) discrepancies between prices used by the organi-zation constructing the index and transaction prices paid by the indexer.

One approach in constructing the indexed portfolio is for the money man-ager to purchase all the issues in the corporate index according to their weight in the index. However, substantial tracking error will result from the transaction costs (and other fees) associated with purchasing all the issues and reinvesting cash flow (maturing principal and coupon interest). The corporate sector of a broad-based market index has more than 4,000 issues (see Exhibit 10), so large transactions costs may make this approach impractical. In addition, some issues in the index may not be available at the prices used in constructing the index.

Instead of purchasing all issues in the index, the money manager may purchase just a sample of issues. While this approach reduces tracking error re-sulting from high transaction costs, it increases tracking error resulting from the mismatch of the indexed portfolio and the index.

Generally speaking, the fewer the number of issues used to replicate the index, the smaller the tracking error due to transaction costs but the greater the tracking error risk due to the mismatch of the characteristics of the indexed port-folio and the index. In contrast, the more issues purchased to replicate the index, the greater the tracking error due to transaction costs, but the smaller the tracking error risk due to the mismatch of the indexed portfolio and the index. Obviously, then, there is a trade-off between tracking error and the number of issues used to construct the indexed portfolio.

There are three methodologies for designing a portfolio to replicate an in-dex: (1) stratified sampling or cell approach; (2) the optimization approach; and (3) the variance minimization approach. For each of these approaches, the initial question that the indexer must ask is: What are the factors that affect a corporate bond index's performance? Each approach assumes that the performance of an individual corporate bond depends on a number of systematic factors that affect the performance of all corporate bonds and on a factor unique to the individual issue. This last risk is diversifiable risk. The objective of the three approaches is to construct an indexed portfolio that eliminates this diversifiable risk.

Stratified Sampling or Cell Approach: Under the *stratified sampling approach to indexing,* the corporate sector of the index is divided into cells, each cell representing a different characteristic of the index. The characteristics that can be used to break down the corporate index are: (1) duration; (2) coupon; (3) maturity; (4) corporate sector (industrials, utilities, financials); (5) credit rating; (6) call factors; and (7) sinking fund features. The last two factors are particularly important because the call and sinking fund features of an issue will impact its performance.

The objective is then to select from all of the issues in the index one or more issues in each cell that can be used to represent that entire cell. The total dollar amount purchased of the issues from each cell will be based on the percentage of the index's total market value that the cell represents. For example, if x% of the market value of all the issues in the index is made up of utilities, then x% of the market value of the indexed portfolio should be composed of utility issues.

The number of cells that the money manager uses will depend on the dollar amount of the portfolio to be indexed. In indexing a portfolio of less than $50 million, for example, using a large number of cells would require purchasing odd lots of issues. This increases the cost of buying the issues to represent a cell, and thus would increase the tracking error. Reducing the number of cells to overcome this problem increases tracking error risk of index mismatch because the characteristics of the indexed portfolio may differ materially from those of the index.

Optimization Approach: In the *optimization approach to indexing* the money manager seeks to design an indexed portfolio that will match the cell breakdown just as described, and satisfy other constraints, but also optimize some objective. An objective might be to maximize the portfolio yield, to maximize convexity, or to maximize expected total returns.[27] Constraints other than matching the cell breakdown might include not purchasing more than a specified amount of one issuer or group of issuers.

The computational technique used to derive the optimal solution to the indexing problem in this approach is mathematical programming. When the objective function that the indexer seeks to optimize is a linear function, linear pro-

---

[27] For a mathematical presentation of this approach as well as the variance minimization approach, see Christina Seix and Ravi Akoury, "Bond Indexation: The Optimal Quantitative Approach," *Journal of Portfolio Management* (Spring 1986), pp. 50-53. For an illustration, see Philip Galdi, "Indexing Fixed Income Portfolios," in Frank J. Fabozzi and T. Dessa Garlicki (eds.), *Advances in Bond Analysis and Portfolio Strategies* (Chicago, IL: Probus Publishing, 1987).

gramming (a specific form of mathematical programming) is used. If the objective function is quadratic, then the particular mathematical programming technique used is quadratic programming.

How well do indexed portfolios constructed using an optimization approach track the corporate bond sector of an index? Salomon Brothers looked at the tracking error for the Salomon Brothers BIG using an optimal indexed portfolio methodology devised by Salomon Brothers. The tracking error was computed each month between January 1985 and November 1986 as the difference between the monthly return on the indexed portfolio and the monthly return on the benchmark index. After considering transaction costs, the average *monthly* tracking error was 9 basis points with a standard deviation of 17 basis points. The monthly tracking error ranged from -26 basis points to 40 basis points. Of the three sectors in the broad-based index, the corporate sector had the greatest tracking error. The annualized tracking error over the January 1985 to November 1986 was 156 basis points.[28]

Variance Minimization Approach: The *variance minimization approach to indexing* is by far the most complex. This approach requires using historical data to estimate the variance of the tracking error. This is done by estimating a price function for every corporate bond issue in the index. The price function is estimated on the basis of two sets of factors: (1) the cash flows from the issue discounted at the theoretical spot rates, and (2) other factors such as the duration or sector characteristics discussed earlier. Using a large universe of corporate issues and statistical techniques, the price function is estimated from historical data. Once the price function for each issue is obtained, a variance equation for the tracking error can be constructed. The objective then is to minimize the variance of the tracking error in constructing the indexed portfolio. As the variance is a quadratic function (the difference between the benchmark return and the indexed portfolio return, squared), quadratic programming is used to find the optimal indexed portfolio in terms of minimized tracking error. The biggest problem with this approach is that estimating the price function from historical data is very difficult in the corporate market or the new issue market. Also, the price function may not be stable.

Logistical Problems in Implementing an Indexing Strategy[29]

An indexer faces several logistical problems in constructing an indexed portfolio. First of all, the prices for each issue used by the organization that publishes

---

[28] The results of the study cited were reported in Sharmin Mossavar-Rahmani, "Understanding and Evaluating Index Fund Management," in *Advances in Bond Analysis and Portfolio Strategies.*

[29] For a more detailed discussion, see Mossavar-Rahmani, "Understanding and Evaluating Index Fund Management," pp. 438-440.

the index may not be execution prices available to the indexer. In fact, they may be materially different from the prices offered by some dealers.

In addition, the prices used by organizations reporting the value of indexes are based on bid prices. Dealer ask prices, however, are the ones that the money manager would have to transact at when constructing or rebalancing the indexed portfolio. Thus there will be a bias between the performance of the index and the indexed portfolio that is equal to the bid-ask spread.

Furthermore, because of the illiquidity of some of the corporate issues in the index, not only may the prices used by the organization that publishes the index be unreliable, but also many of the issues may not even be available.

Finally, recall that the total return depends on the reinvestment rate available on coupon interest. The index providers make certain assumptions as to how intramonth cash flows will be reinvested. Lehman Brothers does not assume that intramonth cash flows are reinvested. Merrill Lynch assumes that intramonth cash flows are reinvested back in the specific bond. Salomon Brothers assumes that the intramonth cash flows are reinvested at the one-month Treasury bill rate. To the extent that the actual reinvestment income by the manager deviates from that assumed by the index provider, there will be tracking error.

Index

A

357

FRANK J. FABOZZI
858 Tower View Circle, New Hope, PA 18938
Phone: (215) 598-8928 Fax: (215) 598-8932

Book Order Form

Name: _____

Company: _____

Address: _____

City: _____ State: _____ Zip: _____

Phone: _____ FAX: _____

E-Mail: _____

Books published by Frank J. Fabozzi	Price	Quantity	Sub-Total
The Handbook of Equity Style Management Coggin and Fabozzi (Eds.), (FJF, 1995)	$50.00		
Valuation of Fixed Income Securities and Derivatives Fabozzi, (FJF, 1995)	$50.00		
Corporate Bonds: Structures & Analysis Wilson and Fabozzi, (FJF, 1996)	$65.00		
Collateralized Mortgage Obligations: Structures & Analysis (2nd Ed.) Fabozzi, Ramsey, and Ramirez, (FJF, 1994)	$50.00		
CMO Portfolio Management Fabozzi (Ed.), (FJF, 1994)	$50.00		
Bond Portfolio Management Fabozzi, (FJF, 1996)	$65.00		
Whole-Loan CMOs Fabozzi, Ramsey, and Ramirez (Eds.), (FJF, 1995)	$55.00		
Other Books Distributed by Frank J. Fabozzi			
Fixed Income Mathematics (Revised Edition) Fabozzi, (Probus, 1993)	$49.95		
The Handbook of Mortgage-Backed Securities (4th Ed.) Fabozzi (Ed.), (Probus, 1995)	$85.00		
The Handbook of Fixed Income Securities (4th Ed.) Fabozzi and Fabozzi (Eds.), (Irwin, 1994)	$90.00		
Advanced Fixed Income Portfolio Management Fabozzi and Fong, (Probus, 1994)	$65.00		
Active Total Return Management of Fixed Income Portfolios Dattatreya and Fabozzi, (Irwin, 1995)	$65.00		
Municipal Bond Portfolio Management Fabozzi, Fabozzi, and Feldstein, (Irwin, 1994)	$80.00		
The Trading and Securitization of Senior Bank Loans Carlson and Fabozzi (Eds.), (Probus, 1992)	$75.00		
Pension Fund Investment Management Fabozzi (Ed.), (Probus, 1990)	$70.00		
Active Asset Allocation (Revised Edition) Arnott and Fabozzi (Eds.), (Probus, 1992)	$70.00		
Handbook of Fixed Income Options (Revised Edition) Fabozzi, (Probus, 1996)	$65.00		
Handbook of Asset/Liability Management (Revised Edition) Fabozzi and Konishi (Eds.), (Irwin, 1995)	$75.00		

Shipping ($3.00 for first book; $1.00 for each additional book):

TOTAL (Make checks drawn on U.S. funds payable to Frank J. Fabozzi. No credit card sales.): _____

Call for Special Prices for Course Adoption!

$$G \wedge T > \sum_{t=1987}^{\infty} \text{Analytics}_t + \text{Consulting}_t + \text{Research}_t$$

The Whole is Greater than the Sum of its Parts

Analytics, consulting, and research aren't three areas of our business. At GAT, we don't specialize in fixed-income software only. Our practice is not limited to consulting. And our think tank is not in an ivory tower. Because we know that the only way to make sense of increasingly volatile financial markets, and constantly changing regulatory requirements is with a structured integration of these key elements. Based on a foundation of research established by Dr. Thomas S.Y. Ho—author of the "Ho-Lee Model"—GAT's sophisticated fixed-income analytics are an implementation of our research. As head of the consulting team, Dr. Ho has constant exposure to the real-life concerns of investors. So whether you need analytics that are backed by innovative research, developed with the latest technological advances (including object-oriented programming, cross-platform support, and ODBC-compliance) or high-level consulting that is supported by the most advanced software, your only solution is the answer that's greater than the sum of its parts.

Analytics · Consulting · Research

For more information about GAT's triangle of services and products, please call Rhoda Woo at (212) 785-9630.

ANDREW KALOTAY

ASSOCIATES, INC.

PRECISION YOU CAN TRADE ON
TECHNOLOGY

BONDVAL

> Option-adjusted arbitrage-free bond valuation

SWAPVAL

> Valuation for interest-rate swaps, forward swaps
> and options on swaps

DERIVVAL

> Arbitrage-free valuation for complex variable-rate
> instruments, caps, floor, and collars

ARMVAL

> Valuation and prepayment sensitivity analysis for
> adjustable-rate mortgages

BONDPORT

> Fair value and OAS analysis for fixed income portfolios

RETVAL

> Scenario-dependent cashflows and total return analysis

BONDREF

> Refunding efficiency for calls, tenders and
> open-market purchases

NEWBOND

> New issue structuring and comparative analysis

Appropriate expertise.

Specialists in locating and placing the best
candidates with expertise in:

- ` Asset/Liability Management
- ` Treasury Management
- ` Asset Securitization
- ` Funds Management
- ` Investment Portfolio Management
- ` Credit Management
- ` Capital Markets

Our clients, domestically and internationally,
are:

- ` Banks
- ` Thrifts
- ` Credit Unions
- ` Finance Companies
- ` Investment Banks
- ` Corporations
- ` Consultancy Firms
- ` Credit Card and
  Mortgage Specialty Firms

Many claim it.

Few have it.

Contact us for more information on our :

- `Success guaranteed searches
- `Unique candidate screening and testing process
- `Comprehensive and in-depth candidate evaluation

Please contact:

Deedee Myers, President
2303 N. 44th Street #14-280
Phoenix, AZ 85008
800.574.8877 telephone
602.840.9595 telephone
602.840.6486 fax

John Myers, Vice President
40 W. Newton Street
Fourth Floor
Boston, MA 02118
617.267.2141 telephone
617.267.4829 fax

Boston   *Phoenix*   *New York*

leadership

influence

experience

access

reliability

FITCH
ESTABLISHED 1913
A FULL SERVICE RATING AGENCY

insight

FITCH INVESTORS SERVICE, L.P.
One State Street Plaza
New York, NY 10004
(212) 908-0500
(800) 75-FITCH

InformationManagementNetwork

Leading-Edge FINANCIAL CONFERENCES, SEMINARS & TUTORIALS

25 West 45th Street, Suite 1505, New York, NY 10036

Our Comprehensive Annual Events Include:

Asset Allocation
Asset Securitization
Asset/Liability Management
Collateralized Mortgage Obligations
Commercial Mortgage Securitization
Derivatives in Investment Management
Equity Style Management
Fixed Income Accounting
Fixed Income Analytics
Fixed Income Portfolio Management
Fixed Income Pricing & Valuation
Foreign Currency Risk Management
Foundations & Endowments
Health Care Finance
Hedge Fund Investment Management
International Securities Lending
Mortgage-Backed Securities
Municipal Bond Portfolio Management
Public Fund Boards
Private Placements
Real Estate Investment Trusts
Repurchase Agreements
Telecommunications Finance
Whole Loan CMOs

*To be added to the IMN mailing list or to discuss customized
programs, please call us at **(212) 293-7300***

CORPORATE BOND COVERAGE...

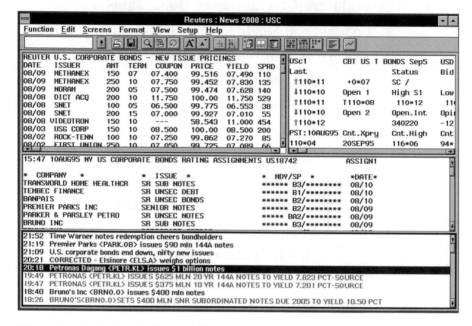

Minute by minute, hour by hour, day by day, Reuters brings you the global news, historical market data and real-time financial information you need to make the most of your investment opportunities.

To help you track the U.S. corporate bond market, Reuters offers you instant access to new corporate issues, earnings announcements, ratings changes, live prices for both stocks and bonds, the latest news and much more.

A BROADER VIEW...

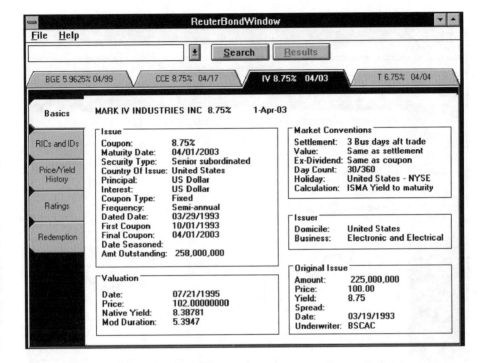

To provide a broader view of the market, a new application from Reuters enables you to search, display and export terms, conditions and historical prices and yields. With an intuitive Windows® interface you will quickly master searches - by name, yield, and other criteria.

Making the best information work harder

For further information please contact International Marketing in the US at (1-203) 425-2650.
®Windows is a registered trademark of Microsoft Corporation

OPEN ACCESS...

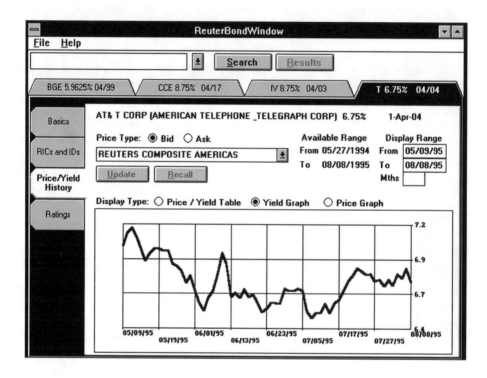

The Reuter global Fixed Income database contains terms and conditions for more than 180,000 bonds from over 80 countries, and price and yield histories for more than 40,000 bonds, many of which have multiple contributors. For custom analysis you can easily export the bond data into your own applications.

HOT NEWS

Reuters delivers unparalleled coverage of U.S. corporate bonds – investment-grade and junk, from shelf registration through issuance – to give you up-to-the-minute pricing information, detailed analysis of deals, market trends and M&A activity. We also provide details on the last 150 priced deals enabling you to accurately gauge market levels.

Three times each day we offer a snapshot of market activity, informing you of secondary trading activity, bid levels, new issues, spreads and the days' biggest winners and losers.

Our credit ratings coverage provides you with up-to-the-second details from Standard & Poor's and other major ratings agencies. We also follow high-yield trends, and publish a daily forward calendar of high-yield deals, to keep you informed about forthcoming supply.

To round out the hot news our coverage includes extensive municipals, emerging markets, equities, U.S. Treasury securities, the Federal Reserve system, and the foreign exchange market.

REUTERS

Making the best information work harder

For further information please contact International Marketing in the US at (1-203) 425-2650.

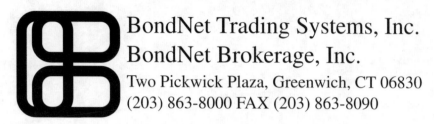

CAMRA™

COMPLETE ASSET MANAGEMENT, REPORTING AND ACCOUNTING

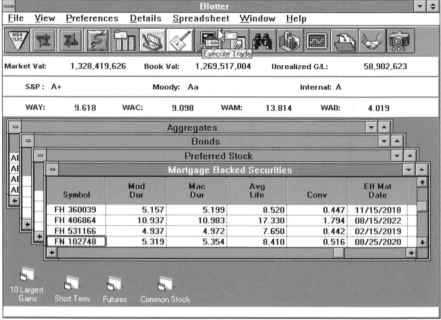

CAMRA gives you on-line, real-time access to all information you need to effectively manage your investment process.

CAMRA for Windows™, the Complete Asset Management, Reporting and Accounting system, allows you to capture and maneuver information about your investment portfolio. CAMRA is a fully integrated relational database operating on a client/server platform. CAMRA was developed by professionals with a wide range of expertise in the investment industry. We understand your complex process, so we've designed CAMRA to adapt to your rapidly changing needs.

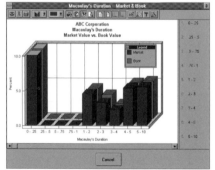

CAMRA's in-depth analytics include duration, convexity, average life, yield, WAC, WAL, WAM, what-if analysis, and a book value calculator.

CAMRA has the power and flexibility to support your entire investment process, from portfolio analysis, management, and trading, to back office accounting and operations.

CAMRA allows you to manage an unlimited number of accounts and portfolios. CAMRA handles all of the intricate securities accounting requirements for your investment holdings. Futures, options, equities, and fixed income, including mortgage-backed securities, CMOs, I/Os, and P/Os are supported. Most important, CAMRA gives you the flexibility to adapt to change instantly, adding new securities as they enter the marketplace.

CAMRA features include:

- ❑ Investment Portfolio Management
- ❑ Custodian, Pricing, Factor, F/X, and G/L Interfaces
- ❑ Market Analytics Database
- ❑ AIMR-Compliant Performance Measurement
- ❑ Multicurrency Processing
- ❑ Mutual Fund Accounting
- ❑ Four Accounting Bases: GAAP, STAT, Management, and Tax
- ❑ Regulatory Reporting
- ❑ Securities Settlement
- ❑ Integrated SQL Report Writer with ODBC

Call SS&C at 800-234-0556 for more information, or for a demonstration of CAMRA or other SS&C products. Email: CAMRA@sscinc.com